The Qur'an and Its Interpreters

The Qur'an and Its Interpreters

Volume I

Dr. Mahmoud Ayoub
Centre for Religious Studies
University of Toronto
and
Muhammadi Islamic Centre, Toronto

State University of New York Press • Albany

Published by
State University of New York Press, Albany

© 1984 State University of New York

All rights reserved

For information, address State University of New York Press, State University Plaza, Albany, N.Y., 12246

Library of Congress Cataloging in Publication Data

Ayoub, Mahmoud.
  The Qur'an and its interpreters.

  Bibliography: v.l, p.
  1. Koran—Commentaries. I. Title.
BP130.4.A835 1983   297'.1226   82–21713
ISBN 0-87395-727-X (v. 1)

10 9 8 7 6 5 4 3 2 1

Contents

Preface

This volume is the first of a series that will cover the entire Qur'an. I have long dreamed of a work in English that would present the Qur'an to Western readers and non-Arabic-speaking Muslims as Muslims have understood it throughout their long history. Although such a task may be undertaken in many ways, a historical interpretation seems to be in some respects the easiest and most accessible. To ensure that the primary aim of this work is fulfilled, I have carefully chosen my sources so as to represent all the major trends in Islamic thought from the classical period to the present.

I have embarked on this task fully aware of its vastness and of my own limitations. The need, however, to approach the Qur'an as more than a piece of ancient literature, a historical document, or simply a sacred book outweighed all other considerations. This undertaking is prompted by the conviction that for almost fourteen centuries the Qur'an has been a source of inspiration and solace and, above all, a guide along the weary way of life into eternity for countless millions of people. It has shaped Muslim society, nourished its hope in times of despair, and expressed its joy and gratitude in times of happiness and prosperity. The Qur'an has lived in the hearts of pious Muslims and has been nourished by their devotion to it. Its importance is nowhere more forcefully expressed than in the sciences of the Qur'an, most important among which has been that of *tafsir* (interpretation). *Tafsir* is the unveiling of the meaning of the Divine Word; the aim of this work is to unveil the meaning and significance of the Qur'an for Muslims to the interested Western reader, the student of Islam, and non-Arabic-speaking Muslims.

The Qur'an is a beautiful and noble companion. I am grateful to the Muhammadi Islamic Centre in Toronto for giving me the opportunity to live close to the Qur'an for the past several years. I am also grateful to the Centre for Religious Studies of the University of Toronto for providing me with a rich library and a congenial atmosphere. I wish to thank my assistants in this work, Muhammad M. Abdelfattah, Salma Mirshak, and Todd Lawson, for their patience and dedication. I also wish to thank the Institute of Islamic Studies of McGill University and the Hartford Seminary Foundation for the great privilege, while the work was in progress, of teaching the Qur'an to eager students, who have been a source of help and encouragement. Finally, my greatest debt is to my wife, Lynda. She not only stood by me throughout the long hours spent on this work but also typed, proofread, and edited. For any inadequacies, I alone am responsible.

Notes on Style

It has not been possible in the printing of this work to supply all diacritical marks in transliteration; only ʿ*ayn* (ʿ) and *hamzah* (') are indicated. Otherwise the romanization of Arabic follows the Library of Congress system, with the exception that conjunctions are not linked with the word following (although inseparable prepositions continue to follow the L.C. rule and are linked). I have, after some trial and error, found it best to place verses of the Qur'an in logical groups in order to preserve the continuity of the text as well as of the *tafsir* discussions. As well, some *tafsir* masters treat verses in groups rather than dividing their dicussions by verse. The numbers in parentheses at the start of paragraphs, then, refer to the verse(s) commented on. The Egyptian official numbering is used throughout.

The translations of *tafsir* texts lean toward literalness; this approach has been guided by the nature of the texts at hand, which, I believe, in their own way, aim at exactitude. The translation of the Qur'anic texts also favors literalness (subordinate or apparently detached phrases, for example, are often left in their places, as they appeared in the Arabic); the job of *tafsir* in this way is done by the *mufassirun*— the authors of the translated texts—and not by myself.

This work appears with a somewhat limited index. However, in order to make the series more useful as a reference work the final volume will contain, besides a table of contents to all the volumes of the finished work, a comprehensive index to Qur'anic themes as well as Arabic terms, legal subjects, and so on. This detailed index will greatly increase the usefulness of the work when it is completed, if God wills.

Key to Sources

Ibn 'Arabi.

Muhyi al-Din ibn 'Arabi. *Tafsir al-Qur'an al-Karim.* Vol. I. Edited by Mustafa Ghalib. Beirut: Dar al-Andalus, 1399/1978.

Ibn Kathir.

al-Qurayshi al-Dimashqi 'Imad al-Din Abi al-Fida' Isma'il ibn Kathir. *Tafsir al-Qur'an al-'Azim.* Vol. I. Beirut: Dar al-Fikr, 1385/1966.

Nisaburi.

Nizam al-Din al-Hasan ibn Muhammad ibn al-Husayn al-Qummi al-Nisaburi. *Ghara'ib al-Qur'an wa Ragha'ib al-Furqan.* Vols. I–III. Edited by Ibrahim 'Atwah 'Awad. Cairo: Mustafa al-Babi al-Halabi, 1381–1962.

Qummi.

Abu al-Hasan 'Ali ibn Ibrahim al-Qummi. *Tafsir al-Qummi.* Vol. I. Edited by al-Sayyid Tayyib al-Musawi al-Jaza'iri. Najaf: Matba'at al-Najaf, 1386/1967.

Qurtubi.

Abu 'Abdallah Muhammad ibn Ahmad al-Ansari al-Qurtubi. *al-Jami' li-Ahkam al-Qur'an.* Vols. I–III. Cairo: Dar al-Katib al-'Arabi, 1387/1967.

Qutb.

Sayyid Qutb. *Fi Zilal al-Qur'an.* Vol. I. Beirut: Dar Ihya' al-Turath al-'Arabi, 1391/1971.

Razi.

Fakhr al-Din al-razi. *al-tafsir al-Kabir.* Vols. I–VII. Cairo: al-Matba'ah al-Bahiyah, N.D.

Shawkani.

Muhammad ibn 'Ali ibn Muhammad al-Shawkani. *Fath al-Qadir al-Jami' bayn Fannay al-Riwayah wa al-Dirayah fi 'Ilm al-Tafsir.* Vol. I. Beirut: Dar al-Fikr, 1393/1974.

Tabari.	Abu Ja'far Muhammad ibn Jarir al-Tabari. *Jami' al-Bayan 'an Ta'wil Ay al-Qur'an.* Vols. I–VI. Edited by Mahmud Muhammad and Ahmad Muhammad Shakir. Cairo: Dar al-Ma'arif, 1332/1954.
Tabarsi.	Abu 'Ali al-Fadl ibn al-Hasan al-Tabarsi. *Majma' al-Bayan fi Tafsir al-Qur'an.* Vols. I–II. Beirut: Dar Maktabat al-Hayat, 1380/1961.
Tabataba'i.	Sayyid Muhammad Husayn al-Tabataba'i. *al-Mizan fi Tafsir al-Qur'an.* Vols. I–III. Beirut: Mu'assasat al-A'lami lil-Matbu'at, 1393/1973.
Wahidi.	Abu al-Hasan al-Wahidi. *Asbab Nuzul al-Qur'an.* Cairo: Dar al-Kitab al-Jadid, 1389/1969.
Zamakhshari.	Abu al-Qasim Jar Allah Mahmud ibn 'Umar al-Zamakhshari. *al-Kashshaf 'an Haqa'iq al-Tanzil wa 'Uyun al-Aqawil fi Wujuh al-Ta'wil.* Vol. I. Cairo: Mustafa al-Babi al-Halabi, 1385/1966.

Introduction

Scope, Method, and Sources

THE PURPOSE OF THIS WORK is to introduce the English reader to the Qur'an as Muslims have understood it. The Qur'an has been regarded by Muslims as the word of God, which He revealed (literally "sent down" *nazzala*) to His prophet Muhammad. This earthly Qur'an, however, is only the concrete revelation whose original archetype is with God in the Well-Guarded Tablet (*al-lawh al-mahfuz*) (See Q. 85:22.) This fact is of crucial importance for any consideration of the Qur'an within the context of Muslim history. As the divine word addressed to humankind, the Qur'an participates in our history but at the same time transcends it. Hence its true inner meaning is with God, for "no one knows its true exegesis [*ta'wil*] except God" (Q. 3:7).

The Qur'an has its own history. It was revealed to the Prophet Muhammad, interiorized by the community, then shaped by it into an earthly book "contained between two covers." My concern in this work is not with the history of the Qur'an, but rather with the Qur'an as used in the community in its present order and form. Within less than two decades of the Prophet's death, when those who heard it directly from his mouth and had written it down were still alive, the Qur'an was collected and fixed into an official codex. It is this official collection which the community has accepted and which has come down to us with only minor adjustments, not in the text itself, but in the way it came to be written down. This recension has voiced the community's prayers and devotions, set its legal norms and moral standards, and occupied its best minds for more than thirteen hundred years.

The science of *tafsir* is primarily concerned with the interpretation and elucidation of the text of the Qur'an as a given entity. Thus the famous commentator Ibn Kathir placed the section dealing with the history of the Qur'an at the end of his commentary, because he regarded *tafsir* proper to be more important than history. In this ordering, he followed the example of the well-known *hadith* compiler al-Bukhari. Therefore, I feel justified in concentrating my effort on the *tafsir* of the Qur'an.

This introduction presents the main principles and development of the science of *tafsir*. Following these methodological remarks, the sources used in this work are discussed. The Qur'an as cherished and interiorized by the community is then discussed. This latter section deals with that aspect of Qur'anic studies known technically as the "excellences" (*fada'il*) of the Qur'an and its reciters. Finally, the principles and development of *tafsir*—its different branches, early masters, and various schools—are discussed.

Aspects of *tafsir* dealing with the actual history of the Qur'an and its miraculous character and inimitable style are not included in this study. Before the Qur'an was fixed into its present form, it seems fairly certain that Qur'an reciters and scholars differed substantially in their readings of certain words, phrases, and even verses. To justify these differences, a number of prophetic *hadiths* were adduced in support of the idea that the Qur'an was sent down in seven different modes or dialects (*ahruf*). The official collection compiled during the caliphate of 'Uthman (23/644–35/656) eventually superseded all other recensions. Different readings that continue to be observed and that affect the meaning of the verse in any significant way are noted in my discussions.

The other major aspect which will not be discussed is that of the *i'jaz* or inimitability of the Qur'an. The Qur'an in many places challenges the Arabs of the Prophet's time to produce the like of it. Based on this challenge, which was never seriously taken up then or later, the community constructed an elaborate theory of the miraculous character of the Qur'an. This theory is for the most part argued on the basis of the linguistic qualities of the sacred Book: its eloquence and rhetorical beauty, and the precision, economy, and subtlety of its style. Such technical points of language usage can be meaningfully discussed only in Arabic, the language of the Qur'an. Other aspects of *i'jaz al-Qur'an* such as the foretelling of future events, or revealing knowledge of the unknown, are discussed in their proper contexts.

Since the present work will consist of several volumes, a measure of consistency in approach and presentation of materials will be maintained. Three criteria were used in the selection of verses for commentary.The first is the need to establish the historical context of a verse or passage in order to elucidate both its literal meaning and practical application. The second is to present when necessary the theological questions or controversies which a verse or passage has raised for commentators. The final criterion is the relationship of the Qur'an and its community of faith with other religious communities and their scriptures, which may be discerned in a verse or passage. My aim, however, is not to engage in polemics or apologetics, nor is it to argue for any position or interpretation in favor of another. It is, rather, to present different views and interpretations coherently and candidly. This work is to be a guide to the Qur'an as Muslims have understood it. The realization of this goal is the primary aim of this endeavor, as well as the guiding principle in the choice and presentation of the primary sources used.

I have carefully chosen my sources so as to represent the long and complex history of Qur'anic interpretation. Early *tafsir* began as an oral tradition of *hadith* transmission from the Prophet and subsequently the views and interpretations of his Companions, their Successors, and the Successors' disciples. Written commentaries on the Qur'an began to appear during the period of the successors and especially of their disciples. These early commentaries were, for the most part, straightforward *hadith* transmissions. In time, however, *tafsir* works began to reflect the training, religious affiliation, and interest of their writers. Grammarians, jurists, mystics, philosophers, and theologians wrote commentaries representing their points of view. The sources chosen represent these different stages, schools of thought, and approaches in Muslim history. The approach adopted in this work begins with *tafsir* by means of tradition and moves on to examples of juristic, Mu'tazili, philosophical, and mystical *tafsir*. Shi'i *tafsir* is treated fairly extensively. Finally, modern *tafsir* is represented from both the Sunni and Shi'i points of view. Although it is not possible to follow a strict historical chronology, a chronological framework is preserved as far as possible. Sources are used in the order in which they are discussed below.

The *tafsir* of Muhammad ibn, Jarir al-Tabari (d. 310/923), *Jami' al-Bayan 'an Ta'wil Ay al-Qur'an*, is the first major work in the development of traditional Qur'anic sciences. It presents the entire tradition of *tafsir* critically and with admirable skill and fidelity. As well as being an important source of tradition, Tabari presents his own views, criticisms, evaluations, and analyses of the various traditions. His commentary is a valuable landmark in the history of this discipline. All those who came after Tabari have relied heavily on his work and acknowledged their debt to him. Tabari not only transmits and analyzes traditions but also discusses, whenever necessary, variant readings and grammatical points so as to elucidate the meaning and purport of a verse. Tabari describes his own work as follows: "It is a book containing all that people need [that is, concerning the interpretation of the Qur'an]. It is so comprehensive that with it there is no need to have recourse to other books. We shall relate in it arguments wherein agreement was achieved and where disagreement persisted. We shall present the reasons for every school of thought or opinion and elucidate what we consider to be the right view with utmost brevity" (Tabari, I, pp. 6–7).

My commentary on a verse or passage begins with the occasion of its revelation, where such information is important for a better understanding of it. In such instances, Wahidi will be used before Tabari.

Abu al-Hasan 'Ali ibn Ahmad al-Wahidi (d. 468/1076) was a famous commentator, grammarian, and man of letters. He wrote three short commentaries on the Qur'an besides the book used here. He was the student of the famous popular commentator and traditionist Abu Ishaq Ahmad ibn Muhammad ibn Ibrahim al-Tha'labi. Like his teacher, Wahidi was accused of having been a careless transmitter of tradition. Nonetheless, his book, *Asbab Nuzul al-Qur'an* , is one of the earliest extant works dealing with this subject.

Isma'il 'Imad al-Din Abu al-Fida' ibn Kathir (d. 774/1373) was a famous Shafi'i jurist, traditionist, and historian. He was a student and staunch defender of Ibn Taymiyah and thus of the "conservative" trend in *tafsir*. Ibn Kathir presents traditions that rely in a critical manner on a variety of sources. In many ways, Ibn Kathir was a man of his time, aware of the vicissitudes of Muslim history, mildly polemical, but always fair and informative. Ibn Kathir appended to his commentary, *Tafsir al-Qur'an al-'Azim*, a short treatise entitled *Fada'il al-Qur'an*, which is also used in this introduction. Although this author lived later than Zamakhshari, Qurtubi, or Razi, I have referred to his work immediately after Tabari's because his thought was based more on tradition than was that of the three exegetes named above.

Muhammad ibn Ahmad Abu 'Abdallah al-Qurtubi (d. 671/1273), although belonging to the Maliki school of jurisprudence, presents different opinions without polemic and even at times disagrees with the Maliki school. His *tafsir, al-Jami' li-Ahkam al-Qur'an*, is an encyclopedic work combining *hadith* with popular piety, jurisprudence, and linguistic considerations. It is well organized and extremely usable.

Abu al-Qasim Jar Allah Mahmud ibn 'Umar al-Zamakhshari (d. 538/1144) was a man of great learning, both in the religious and linguistic sciences. He was a subtle thinker whose *tafsir, al-Kashshaf 'an Haqa'iq al-Tanzil wa 'Uyun al-Aqawil fi Wujuh al-Ta'wil*, in spite of its evidence of his Mu'tazili persuasion, is regarded by Sunni *'ulama'* as one of the most important works of *tafsir.* Zamakhshari uses *hadith* tradition analytically but often with little regard to either the chain of transmitters or fidelity to the actual transmitted text. He lays great stress on linguistic explanations, having been a great authority on the Arabic language. His Mu'tazili ideas are so subtle that a number of commentaries have been written to determine where and how his theological bias has influenced his work. The edition used here has two such commentaries in the margin. Zamakhshari lived in Mecca for so long that he was given the epithet Jar Allah (God's neighbor).

Among the philosophically oriented *tafsirs*, the most well known is that of Fakhr al-Din al-Razi (d. 606/1209). Razi was one of the most learned and brilliant men in Muslim history. He was said to have been "one of those sent at the beginning of the seventh century to renew religion," thus making him a *mujaddid* (Dawudi, II, p. 214). It is generally believed that Razi died before completing his massive *tafsir*, sometimes known as *al-Tafsir al-Kabir*, but more commonly as *Mafatih al-Ghayb.* The work was finished by one of his disciples who followed his master's methodology and idiom so faithfully that it is virtually impossible to distinguish between the two styles. Hence scholars have differed as to where the master left off and the student began, or even whether it was one or two students who finally completed the work. Razi's *tafsir* is somewhat difficult for two reasons. Razi was a philosopher of high caliber and not primarily an exegete. He sets forth his opinions on verses in a complex and involved style with layer upon layer of arguments and counterarguments, although often without reaching any conclusion. He also digresses so far from his subject that one becomes lost in philosophical and theological arguments that are at best distantly related to *tafsir.* It is said of Razi's *Mafatih al-Ghayb* that "it has everything except *tafsir*" (Suyuti, II, p. 191). Nonetheless it is a unique and highly erudite work representing an important type of Qur'anic exegesis.

Two sources have been chosen to represent the Sufi understanding of the Qur'an. The first is *Ghara'ib al-Qur'an wa Ragha'ib al-Furqan* by Nizam al-Din al-Hasan ibn Muhammad ibn al-Husayn al-Qummi al-Nisaburi (d. 728/1327). This *tafsir* is a popular work. It combines the philosophical approach of Razi, whose *tafsir* it partially summarizes, with Sufi exegesis presented in the framework of popular piety. Although Nisaburi's work cannot be said to be original, since it relies heavily on both Razi and Zamakhshari, it nonetheless contains a great deal of popular Sufi material which is worth considering. It has been chosen to represent not technical Sufism but popular Sufi piety.

The second source that represents Sufi thought at its highest level of esoteric exegesis is *Tafsir al-Qur'an al-Karim* of Muhyi al-Din ibn 'Arabi (d. 638/1240). The editor of the work, Mustafa Ghalib, says in his introduction that Ibn 'Arabi wrote three *tafsirs:* one ordinary *tafsir* in twenty-four volumes, a shorter but more popular Sufi commentary, and the two-volume work used here. It is more commonly believed, however, that this work, the only extant one, was written by one of Ibn 'Arabi's disciples, the well-known 'Abd al-Razzaq al-Qashani. Whoever the author may be, the work clearly represents the thought and style of Ibn 'Arabi. In justification of his method of exegesis, the author says: "It is said that whoever interprets [the Qur'an] according to his own opinion commits an act of blasphemy [*kufr*]. But as for *ta'wil* [esoteric exegesis], it neither preserves nor spares anything." (Ibn 'Arabi likens *ta'wil* here to the fire that consumes everything [Q. 74:28]). "It varies with the state of the listener, his moments in the stations of his mystical journey [*suluk*] and his different degrees [of attainment]. As he reaches higher stations, new doors are open to him through which he looks upon new and subtle meanings" (Ibn 'Arabi, I, p. 5).

'Ali ibn Ibrahim al-Qummi (d. 328/939) was one of the important architects of Shi'i *hadith* tradition. He represents the formative and consequently isolated and somewhat extremist stage of Imami Shi'i *hadith* development. His *tafsir* is Shi'i in the fullest sense of the word. Qummi was a *hadith* transmitter who neither analyzed nor evaluated his materials. Thus his work, compared with later Shi'i comprehensive commentaries, is brief. It is, however, the most complete extant commentary of its time.

In contrast, *Majma' al-Bayan fi Tafsir al-Qur'an*, by Abu 'Ali al-Fadl ibn al-Hasan al-Tabarsi, is a comprehensive classical *tafsir*. Tabarsi (d. 548/1153) was a moderate scholar, and he presented the views of all major commentators fairly and comprehensively. He gives special prominence to Shi'i *tafsir*, but his work is not, strictly speaking, a Shi'i commentary. Tabarsi was a man of great erudition. He was a master of Arabic and a noted theologian and jurist. Since Shi'i thought has much in common with Mu'tazili rational theology, Tabarsi gives a special place to Mu'tazili commentators. His is one of the most comprehensive *tafsirs*. The author begins his commentary on every verse with explanations of key or uncommon words, both their meaning and grammatical problems. He then presents the different views of commentators, traditionists, and theologians, fairly and accurately.

As will be observed, modern *tafsirs* have a great deal in common in spite of their peculiar point of view or the religious affiliations of their authors. *Al-Mizan fi Tafsir al-Qur'an* by Sayyid Muhammad Husayn al-Tabataba'i is meant to speak to the young intellectuals of the Shi'i Muslim community and often approaches the verses of the Qur'an from philosophical, sociological, and traditional viewpoints. It reflects the wide and profound learning of one of the most respected recent religious scholars of the Shi'i community. (The great jurist doctor died in November 1981.) Tabataba'i's *tafsir* is also firmly rooted in tradition. The author adds a large section to each verse or passage commented on, citing both Shi'i and Sunni *hadiths*.

The work of the Egyptian thinker and head of the Muslim Brotherhood, Sayyid Qutb (d. 1386/1966), is the *tafsir* for today's Muslim youth, both Shi'i and Sunni. As the title, *Fi Zilal al-Qur'an* (In the Shadow of the Qur'an), indicates, the author is careful not to depart from the Qur'an in interpreting it. Three elements distinguish the work. The first is, as has already been mentioned, a conscious effort to remain within the purview of the Qur'an. The second is the sparing use of tradition; all but the most widely accepted *hadiths* are rejected. The third and perhaps most important is Sayyid Qutb's own view of Islam as a religious system and its relationship to other systems and ideologies. Coupled with the author's amazing command of the Arabic language, the presentation is indeed powerful.

The Qur'an and Its Bearers

The Qur'an has played two distinct but continuous roles in the lives of Muslims. It has been a guide along the weary way of this life and into the next, a source of blessing and honor for its bearers here on earth and their intercessor with God on the day of judgment. It is related that the Prophet said, "The Qur'an is right guidance from error and a light against blindness. It is a support against stumbling . . . a source of illumination against sorrow and a protection against perdition. It is the criterion of truth against sedition and the best way leading from this world to the next. No one turns away from the Qur'an but that he turns toward the Fire" ('Ayyashi, I, p. 5). The Qur'an as a book of guidance will be considered in the following section of the introduction dealing with *tafsir*. I feel that it is not possible to fully appreciate the care, determination, and seriousness with which commentators have treated the Qur'an as an object of study without some appreciation of the place which the Qur'an and its bearers have occupied in Muslim piety.

The Qur'an in itself is a source of sanctity and blessing not only for those who occupy themselves in reciting and studying it, but also for the world and its history. Ibn Kathir observes, "The Qur'an began to be sent down in a noble place, the sacred city of Mecca, and also in a noble time, the month of Ramadan. Thus it combined the nobility of space and time" (Ibn Kathir, VII, p. 430). Yet the Qur'an possesses a numinous quality which renders its power beyond the capacity of hard mountains to bear. This idea is clearly stated in the Qur'an: "Were We to cause this Qur'an to descend upon a mountain, you would see it humbled, torn asunder in awe of God" (Q. 59:21). This numinous power, however, is not only a negative force of destruction; it is also a positive source of healing and tranquility.

A number of traditions tell how one of the companions of the Prophet, Usayd ibn Hudayr, witnessed unusual portents when he recited the Qur'an in the night. It is reported that he came to the Prophet one day saying, "As I was reciting a *surah* of the Qur'an last night, I heard when I came to its end a noise behind me, so that I thought that my horse was being spurred on in fright. . . . I then looked back and saw something like lamps between heaven and earth. . . . I could not go on [reciting]." The Prophet then said, "These were angels, descended to hear the recitation of the Qur'an. Had you gone on, you would have seen wonders" (Ibn Kathir, VII, p. 474). The *sakinah* (divine tranquility) is said to have descended upon a man, as he was reciting the *surah* of the Cave (Q. 18), as a white cloud (Ibn Kathir, VII, p. 474). A well-known tradition tells that the Prophet said, "There are no people assembled in one of the houses of God to recite the Book of God and study it together but that the *sakinah* descends upon them. Mercy covers them, angels draw near to them and God remembers them in the company of those who are with Him" (Ibn Kathir, VII, p. 475).

In one of the earliest *surahs* of the Qur'an the Prophet is addressed with the words, "We shall surely lay upon you weighty speech" (Q. 73:5). The Qur'an has therefore been regarded as a great burden, and those who recite, study, and teach it are known as the bearers (*hamalah*) of the Qur'an. This charge is, however, equal to the honor and the reward of its bearers. Qurtubi describes them as follows: "They are the bearers of the hidden mysteries of God and keepers of His treasured knowledge. They are the successors [*khulafa'*] of His prophets and His trustees. They are His people and the elect of His creatures." Qurtubi then cites a tradition in which the Prophet declares the people of the Qur'an to be the people of God and His elect (Qurtubi, I, p. 1). Their occupation is considered to be more excellent in the eyes of God than any other form of devotion. Thus in a *hadith qudsi* (divine utterance) related from the Prophet on the authority of Abu Sa'id al-Khudri, God is said to have declared: "He who is occupied with the Qur'an and with remembrance of me from prayers to me for his needs, to him will I give the best of that which I grant to those who pray" (Qurtubi, I, p. 4; see also Ibn Kathir, VII, p. 510).

The Prophet's life, sayings, and actions (*sunnah*) have served as a model of moral conduct and devotion for Muslims of all times because the Prophet's moral and spiritual character was formed by the Qur'an. This prophetic character remains the ideal goal for the pious, but it is one in which the "people of the Qur'an" (that is, those who occupy themselves in reciting and studying it), have a special share. It is related on the authority of Abu Umamah that the Prophet said, "He who is given one-third of the Qur'an is given one-third of prophethood. He who is given two-thirds of the Qur'an is given two-thirds of prophethood, and he who can recite [from memory] the entire Qur'an is given complete prophethood, except that no revelation is sent down to him." The tradition then describes the status of such a person with God on the day of resurrection. "It shall be said to him . . . 'Recite and rise up!' He shall thus recite one verse and rise up one station until he recites all that he knows of the Qur'an. It shall then be said to him, 'Come forth! . . . Do you know what is in your hands?' He shall have in his right hand everlasting life and in his left the bliss [*na'im*] of Paradise" (Qurtubi, I, p. 8).

Muslim piety has endued the Qur'an with a living and dynamic personality. The Qur'an is a power against the arrogant tyrants of this world, a guide and protection for the pious, and their intercessor on the day of judgment. Perhaps in no other area of Muslim piety are such ideas and the traditions supporting them shared by Sunni and Shi'i Muslims alike. In a widely accepted tradition related by both Shi'i and Sunni traditionists on the authority of 'Ali, we are told that the Prophet said, "There shall be a great sedition after me." 'Ali asked how such calamity could be averted. The Prophet answered, "By means of the Book of God! In it is the report concerning those who were before you, the narrative of what is to come after you, and the criterion of judgment among you. . . . Whoever seeks guidance in anything other than it, God shall cause him to go astray. It is the rope of God; it is the 'wise remembrance' [Q. 3:58] and 'the straight way.' With it, hearts shall not swerve nor tongues utter confusion. The learned shall never be sated of it. It shall not wear out from constant use, nor will its marvels ever be exhausted. . . . Whoever utters it speaks truth, and whoever abides by it shall have his rich reward. Whoever judges by it shall judge justly, and whoever calls others to it shall be guided to the straight way" (Ibn Kathir, VII, p. 434; see also Majlisi, XCII, p. 24). Shi'i piety has been especially dramatic, unhampered in its portrayal of rich and fantastic imageries. In a long colloquy between the Prophet and Salman the Persian, who has been regarded as the father of Shi'i piety, the Prophet enjoins Salman to "recite the Qur'an, for its recitation is an expiation of sins . . . and security against punishment." He continues, "He who recites it shall have the reward of a thousand martyrs, and for every *surah* the reward of a prophet. Mercy shall descend upon the bearer of the Qur'an. Angels shall beg God's forgiveness for him; Paradise longs for him and the Lord shall be pleased with him." The tradition asserts further that any person of faith reciting the Qur'an will, at its conclusion, be granted the reward of 313 apostles. This is the number of apostles who are said, according to popular tradition, to have been sent to humankind. Such a person shall, moreover, receive the reward of having recited every book which God revealed to his prophets. Even before such a person rises from his seat, God will forgive all his sins and the sins of his parents. The tradition then describes in fantastic terms the riches of palaces and cities which are in store for him in Paradise. The Prophet finally concludes by saying, "Blessed is the seeker of knowledge and the bearer of the Qur'an" (Majlisi, XCII, pp. 17–19).

The Qur'an is for Muslims what Christ the Logos is for Christians. This analogy is carried even further in another tradition in which the Prophet is reported to have said, "The Qur'an is most excellent after God. Thus he who reverences the Qur'an reverences God, and he who does not reverence the Qur'an has taken lightly the sanctity [*hurmah*] of God. This is because the sanctity of the Qur'an with God is like the sanctity of a son in the eyes of his father" (Majlisi, XCII, p. 19).

I have already cited several traditions proclaiming the salvific role of the Qur'an. This role may be seen in two different ways. The first is through the interiorization of the Qur'an by the pious, and the second is through the direct intercession of the Qur'an with God on the day of resurrection on behalf of those who in this world had memorized it and lived by its precepts. Thus it is related that the Prophet said, "God shall never torment a heart which contains the Qur'an" (Majlisi, XCII, p. 178). The second way the salvific role of the Qur'an may be discerned is best illustrated in a dramatic dialogue between God and the Qur'an, related on the authority of Ja'far al-Sadiq, the sixth Shi'i imam. The tradition is meant to extol the reciters of the Qur'an and especially one who dedicates his life to this vocation from a young age. The Qur'an, we are told, shall intercede on behalf of such a person, saying, "O Lord, every laborer has received the wages of his labors except my laborer! Bestow therefore upon him of your generous bounties." God will then clothe him with two of the garments of Paradise, and the crown of honor shall be placed upon his head. Then the Qur'an shall be asked, "Are you pleased with this for him?" The Qur'an will answer, "My Lord, I had wished for him something more excellent still!" Then the man shall be given security in his right hand and eternal life in his left; he will be made to enter Paradise. There, he shall be told, "Recite one verse and attain a higher station." It shall then be said to the Qur'an, "Thus have we bestowed upon him such favors that you may be pleased with him." The Qur'an will affirm its pleasure, saying, "Yes, Lord, I am pleased" (Majlisi, XCII, p. 188).

We have already observed that the reciter of the Qur'an shares in the status of prophets, those who have been favored with the reception of the divine word. The reciter does not receive the Qur'an as revelation, yet he assimilates it into his entire being so that he lives in the Qur'an. Again the parallel with the idea of the person of faith living in Christ, who becomes infused into the person's body through communion, is striking. The tradition just cited begins with the assertion that "a person of faith who recites the Qur'an when yet a youth, the Qur'an shall be mingled with his flesh and blood" (Majlisi, XCII, p. 188).

Muslim piety has constructed a strict code of conduct for the bearers of the Qur'an. Those among them who possess purity of faith, moral integrity, and true piety are a blessing for the world. Their very existence is necessary for the well-being of the rest of humanity and the maintenance of order in nature. The fifth imam Muhammad al-Baqir distinguishes three varieties of reciters. The first uses the Qur'an as though it were a commodity of trade, seeking by his profession the rewards of kings and other men of wealth and power. The second learns the words of the Qur'an but neglects its precepts and admonitions. The third "recites the Qur'an employing its healing power as a cure for his ailments. He spends his nights with it and with it he thirsts during his days [that is, in fasting]. He spends his time with it in his places of worship and because of it abandons his bed." For the sake of such men, the imam went on, "God wards off calamities. For their sake, he protects men from their enemies. For the sake of such men, God sends down rain from heaven" (Majlisi, XCII, p. 178). In yet another tradition related on the authority of 'Ali, we see that the reciters of the Qur'an play a direct intercessory role on behalf of humankind. "God shall resolve to punish all the inhabitants of the earth for their acts of disobedience, not sparing a single one of them . . . but when he shall look upon gray-haired people moving their feet in prayers and youths learning the Qur'an, he shall show mercy toward them and mitigate their punishment" (Majlisi, XCII, p. 185).

Because of their high status with God, the bearers of the Qur'an deserve the love and respect of other men. As the Prophet shares with God and the Qur'an a special place in the hearts of Muslims, so, too, the bearers of the Qur'an share in this privilege because of their special relationship to the Qur'an. Thus the Prophet is said to have declared, as related on the authority of 'Ali, "The bearers of the Qur'an are they who are favored with the mercy of God. They are clothed with the light of God, instructed with the speech of God, and brought near to God. He who befriends them, befriends God and he who shows enmity toward them, shows enmity toward God" (Majlisi, XCII, p. 182). The bearers of the Qur'an must earn this great privilege. Before God their lives must be spent in prayer and thanksgiving. If misfortune befalls them they must turn to God in sincere repentance. As their reward shall be greater than that of other men, so also shall be their responsibility. In short, they must be true bearers of the Qur'an in word and deed. Ibn Mas'ud, one of the first bearers of the Qur'an, said: "The bearer of the Qur'an must be distinguished by night when people sleep and by day when they are awake. He must be distinguished by his weeping when people laugh and by his silence when they clamor. He must be distinguished by his meekness when people are haughty and by his sorrow when people rejoice" (Qurtubi, I, p. 21). Still other characteristics distinguishing the bearer of the Qur'an are given in the following prophetic *hadith*: "It is not proper for the bearer of the Qur'an to be foolish like those who are foolish, to be angry like those who are angry, or to lose his temper. Rather he should forgive and pardon by means of the virtue of the Qur'an" (Ibn Kathir, VII, p. 516).

One of the most controversial points in the relationship of the Qur'an to its reciters has been the way in which the Qur'an must be recited. The principle behind this long controversy is to guard against the recitation of the Qur'an becoming a show of vocal excellence or musical virtuosity. Qur'an scholars have been divided on this issue. Some have adduced *hadiths* extolling musical chanting (*taghanni*) of the Qur'an, and others have cited equally accepted traditions enjoining a simple chant (*tartil*). Two modes of Qur'anic recitations came to be accepted: *tajwid* (making good, that is, musically beautiful) and *tartil* (a slow ·and deliberate, simple chant). Scholars, however, are unanimous in forbidding the use of musical techniques and rhythms commonly used in profane singing. Dignity of demeanor, softness of voice, and a sorrowful tone are among the qualities required of a good Qur'an reciter. It is related that the Prophet was asked, "Who would have the best voice for chanting the Qur'an?" He answered, "It is he who, when you hear him, you see that he fears God" (Ibn Kathir, VII, p. 482).

In a widely quoted *hadith*, the Prophet is said to have enjoined the Muslims, saying, "Adorn the Qur'an with your voices!" (Ibn Kathir, VII, p. 481). Those, however, who preferred a simple mode of recitation have turned this injunction around to read, "Adorn your voices with the Qur'an" (Qurtubi, I, pp. 11–12). In this case the emphasis is on the beauty of the sacred word rather than the voice of the reciter. Nevertheless, the human voice as a vehicle of transmitting the divine word could not be underestimated. Therefore *taghanni*, or musical chanting of the Qur'an, has become both a great virtue, highly praised by tradition, and a technical skill of the reciter, greatly valued by his audience. Yet the emotion to be evoked is not one of joyful ecstasy (tarab) but rather of subdued sadness. The Prophet is reported to have said, "This Qur'an was sent down in sorrow. Weep, therefore, when you recite it. If you cannot weep, then pretend to weep. Chant it, for whoever does not chant it is not one of us" (Ibn Kathir, VII, p. 481). The relationship of chanting the Qur'an and profane singing (ghina') could not be totally extirpated. A well-known prophetic hadith relates, "God listens more attentively to a man with a beautiful voice chanting the Qur'an than would a man to his singing girl" (Ibn Kathir, VII, p. 479).

The Qur'an is divided into 114 surahs, varying in length from 3 to 286 verses. But because one of the most meritorious acts of a Muslim is to recite the Qur'an in its entirety over a specified period of time, the Qur'an has been conveniently divided into thirty equal parts (ajza') for that purpose. Tradition asserts that the Prophet recited the Qur'an in the presence of Gabriel every year during the month of Ramadan. The thirty-part division, therefore, is meant for the thirty days of that month. Other subdivisions of the thirty-part structure have also been constructed for the purpose of recitation over a longer or shorter period of time. In fact, a portion of the Qur'an is usually recited for every important occasion in the life of the Muslim individual and his immediate family as well as that of society at large.

The Qur'an has been regarded by Muslims not simply as a book in the usual sense but as a living and dynamic personality. It is the faithful companion of the Muslim throughout his journey from this world to the hereafter. Indeed, a Muslim journeys through this life in the Qur'an. The bearer of the Qur'an who completes a recitation and begins anew is therefore called the sojourning traveler (al-hall al-murtahil). Many traditions from the Prophet and the Shi'i imams declare such a person to be the best of men (see Majlisi, XCII, pp. 204–205; Qurtubi, I, p. 30 and many other places; and Ibn Kathir, VII, pp. 517ff.). Completing a recitation (khatm) of the Qur'an has been for Muslims a time of celebration and rejoicing. This event is best observed in traditional societies when a child completes the Qur'an under the tutelage of a Qur'an reciter. Abu 'Abd al-Rahman al-Sulami, a famous reciter and scholar who lived during the rule of 'Ali, would lay his hand on the head of a student after completing a Qur'an recitation, bless him, and say, "Fear God, for I know no one better than you if you abide by what you know" (Qurtubi, I, p. 6).

Scholars have differed as to whether it is more meritorious to recite the Qur'an from memory or from a written text (*mushaf*). To learn the entire Qur'an by heart has been the goal of many Muslims. Hence tradition has laid great stress on the merit of teaching and learning the Qur'an. Likewise one of the greatest sins is to neglect the Qur'an so as to forget it (see Ibn Kathir, VII, pp. 488–489). Nonetheless, the majority of scholars have recommended that a reciter should look at a written text so that he may have the reward of recitation and sight or the blessing of the voice and vision (see Ibn Kathir, VII, p. 488–491). It is related on the authority of the sixth imam that "he who recites the Qur'an looking at a *mushaf* shall be granted good sight to enjoy for a long time . . . for there is nothing of greater hurt to Satan than the recitation of the Qur'an from a written text" (Majlisi, XCII, p. 204).

Reciting the Qur'an has been for Muslims a total experience, an act in which the entire person and even his environment share. Thus while it is regarded as a great blessing for a home to contain a copy of the Qur'an, it is an equally great sin to let the Book lie neglected. The fifth imam is said to have told his followers, "It is pleasing to me that a *mushaf* be kept in the house, for by means of it God drives away satans." His son Ja'far al-Sadiq, on whose authority this tradition was related, warned, "Three shall complain to God on the day of resurrection: a mosque in ruins whose people did not use it for prayers, a learned man among fools, and a *mushaf* left hanging in the house on which dust accumulated because no one took it up for recitation" (Majlisi, XCII, pp. 195–196). As for the blessing (*barakah*) of a Qur'an in a house, Anas ibn Malik, a close companion of the Prophet, related that the Prophet said, "The provisions of a house in which the Qur'an is recited shall be increased, and the provisions of a house in which the Qur'an is not recited shall diminish" (Ibn Kathir, VII, p. 511; and Majlisi, XCII, p. 200).

Popular Muslim piety has regarded the Qur'an as a mediator between man and God. It is the vehicle through which prayers are offered to God with the hope that they will be answered. We are told that a man complained to the Prophet of a sharp pain in his breast and was advised to "seek healing in the Qur'an, for God the Exalted says, 'It is healing of what is in the breast'" (Q. 10:57; Majlisi, XCII, p. 176). Shi'i piety in particular has emphasized this point because for Shi'is the imams and the Qur'an occupy a similar position of intercession and favor with God. Hence in many traditions the faithful are advised to perform prayers during which specific verses of the Qur'an should be recited. Afterward, they should invoke God in the name of the Qur'an, the Prophet, and his descendants, the twelve imams (see Majlisi, XCII, pp. 113–114). I shall conclude this section with a prayer which the Prophet is said to have taught 'Ali and commanded him to recite after completing a full recitation of the Qur'an: "O God, I beg you for the modesty of those who are modest and the sincerity of those who are certain in their faith; for the companionship of the righteous and the worthiness of the truths of faith; for the riches of righteousness and safety from transgression; for worthiness of your mercy and the powers of your pardon; for the attainment of Paradise and salvation from the Fire" (Majlisi, XCII, p. 206).

The Principles and Development of Tafsir

It has already been observed that the Qur'an has occupied some of the best minds of the Muslim community since the beginning of Islamic history. This profound interest in the Qur'an resulted in the science of *tafsir* broadly understood, whose various branches and development will be the subject of our present discussion. The place of the Qur'an in the community has received scant attention from Western scholars. The science of *tafsir* has, in contrast, been the object of much concern and study by Western Islamicists. A selected bibliography of Western sources on this subject appears at the end of this volume. In accordance with the primary aim of this work, we shall let Muslims speak about *tafsir* as they did about their devotion to the Qur'an.

Before discussing the nature of the Qur'an and the need that it be interpreted and understood, it may be wise to consider briefly some of the names and epithets by which it is known. This description will shed some light on the nature of the Qur'an and its function in the life of the Muslim community.

The most widely used name for the Qur'an is, of course, simply "Qur'an," which may best be translated as "the recital." (For the Qur'anic use of this word, see Q. 12:3; 27:76; and 75:17–18. For a discussion, see Tabari, I, pp. 94ff.) The word Qur'an is an intensive form of the verbal root *qara'a* meaning to read or recite and may be used to designate the entire book or a single verse or passage. Another general designation is *kitab*, meaning book, or, more specifically, recited collection of revelations. The word *kitab* is also used to designate previous scriptures such as the Torah and Gospel.(For the Qur'anic use of this word see Q. 18:1 and for a discussion Tabari, I, p. 95.)

The Qur'an is also called *al-dhikr* (the remembrance) (see Q. 15:9 and 3:58). Tabari notes two meanings of the word *dhikr*. The first is "reminder," that is, from God "with which He reminded His servants, giving them knowledge of his *hudud* [bounds or limits], *fara'id* [obligations of prayers, fasting, and the like] and *ahkam* [moral and legal precepts]." The second meaning of *dhikr* is remembrance or honor for those who accept faith in it and in what it contains (see Q. 43:44; and Tabari, I, p. 99). The Qur'an has also been called *al-furqan* (the criterion distinguishing truth from falsehood or error; see Q. 3:3). This term has other meanings and uses which will be discussed in their proper contexts (see below, Q. 2:53).

These names and epithets are designations of the Qur'an as a whole. Its various parts have also been given particular designations. Thus the longest *surahs* (2, 3, 4, 5, 6, 7, and 10) are known as the seven long ones (*al-sab' al-tuwal*). The *surahs* that consist of one hundred or more verses are known as *al-mi'un* (the one hundreds). The seven longest *surahs* are also called *al-sab' al-mathani* (the seven *surahs* in which the number hundred is doubled). The word *mathani* has been interpreted as well to refer specifically to the opening *surah* (*al-Fatihah*), which consists of seven verses, as will be seen later. Some commentators, such as Ibn 'Abbas, interpreted the word *mathani* to mean repetition, hence designating those *surahs* in which parables or precepts are repeated more than once. Based on this view, some have regarded the entire Qur'an as *mathani* (see Q. 39:23; and Tabari, I, p. 103). Finally, the shorter *surahs* in which the dividing invocation, "In the name of God, the All-Merciful, the Compassionate," is frequently used, are known as *al-mufassal* (that which is elaborately divided). It is related that the Prophet said, "I was given instead of the Torah the Seven Long Ones, instead of the Psalms the One Hundreds and instead of the Gospel *al-mathani*. I was specially favored with the *mufassal*" (Tabari, I, p. 100).

Western scholars have generally considered such words as Qur'an, *furqan, surah*, and so on as loan words (see, for instance, Arthur Jeffery, *Foreign Vocabulary of the Qur'an*). Muslim scholars have generally, however, insisted that the Qur'an is all Arabic and that any foreign words in it are either words on which Arabs and non-Arabs agree or which were fully Arabicized before they came into the Qur'an. This assertion is based largely on the Qur'anic verses declaring the Qur'an to have been sent down in Arabic (see, for example, Q. 12:2 and 39:28; see also Tabari, I, pp. 13–21). Tabari derived the word *surah*, for example, from the word *sur* meaning high enclosure or wall such as the wall of an ancient city. Tabari observes further that some have read the word *surah* as *su'rah* (with a *hamzah*), which means the better portion of a thing or separate sections, that is, a chapter. Thus the word signifies a distinct section of the Qur'an separated from what is before and after it (see Tabari, I, pp. 104–105).

The first prayer with which the Qur'an opens is a prayer for guidance, "Guide us on the straight way" (Q. 1:6). It is perhaps not an accident that this prayer is immediately followed in the second *surah* with the declaration: "This is the book in which there is no doubt, a guidance to the God-fearing" (Q. 2:2). The primary function of the Qur'an is therefore to guide the faithful to God. Hence it must be understood, pondered, and lived by. Yet the Qur'an is more than a moral or legal code; it is the transcendent Divine Word which became human speech. It thus entered into human history, sharing in its mundane ephemerality but also linking it to the transcendent.

The Qur'an has two dimensions, a human dimension as a source of moral guidance, which is termed *zahir* (exoteric or outer dimension), and an inner dimension (*batin*), which is free from the limitations of time and history. The Qur'an must therefore be understood on two levels, a concrete or exoteric level, which I shall call interpretation, and an abstract or esoteric level, which I shall call exegesis. These terms are somewhat arbitrarily used to denote *tafsir* and *ta'wil* respectively, as these came to be distinguished by Muslim commentators.

The Qur'an, broadly speaking, consists of moral and legal precepts, commands and prohibitions with regard to lawful (*halal*) and unlawful (*haram*) actions, promise (*wa'd*) of Paradise for the pious and threat (*wa'id*) of punishment in Hell for the wicked. It also contains reports of bygone prophets and their peoples, parables, similes and metaphors, and admonitions. Finally, it sets forth for the pious obligations (*fara'id*) of prayer, fasting, almsgiving, the rites of pilgrimage, and struggle (*jihad*) in the way of God. It is therefore deeply involved with the daily life of Muslim society. For this reason, in some way it had to reflect the problems of society directly and concretely. This it does in its very structure and history.

According to tradition, many of the verses of the Qur'an were revealed in answer to a specific personal or social problem. Hence there are in the Qur'an verses which are clear in meaning, specific in reference, and thus liable to only one literal sense or interpretation. These constitute the *muhkam* (unambiguous) verses. There are, on the other hand, verses which are liable to more than one interpretation and so closely resemble one another in idiom and expression that they could lead those who are not firm in faith and knowledge to confusion and error. These are the *mutashabih* (ambiguous) verses, which constitute a major portion of the Qur'an.

The Qur'an describes itself variously as all *muhkam*, as all *mutashabih*, and as consisting of both *muhkam* and *mutashabih* verses. The Qur'an explains the first designation by declaring that it is "a book whose verses are precisely, clearly, or unambiguously set forth" (*uhkimat*). (See Q. 11:1.) Here the purpose of the *muhkam* is to provide clear guidance. With regard to the second designation the Qur'an says, "God has sent down the best speech, a *mutashabih* book," that is, one whose various parts resemble one another (see Q. 39:23). The word *mutashabih* here means resembling one another in verbal expression, not in meaning. The reference is thus to the linguistic excellence of the Qur'an and not to its precepts, commands, and prohibitions.

The third and most controversial statement is that asserting that the Qur'an is both *muhkam* and *mutashabih* (Q. 3:7). The *muhkam* verses here refer to those which are clear and precise in their meaning and must therefore be followed, whereas the *mutashabih* verses cannot be readily understood and must therefore be accepted in faith but not followed. This verse will be discussed at some length in its proper place. To conclude, it may be said that *muhkam* refers to verses whose meaning is apparent and are therefore in need of no interpretation. *Mutashabih*, on the other hand, is, in the view of the famous scholar of *tafsir* Badr al-Din Muhammad ibn 'Abdallah al-Zarkashi, "*mushkil* [problematic] because it . . . enters into the form [*shakl*] of something else whose form it assumes" (Zarkashi, II, p. 69). *Mutashabih* verses include references to the unknown of future events such as the day of resurrection, to the hand, face, and side of God, which are referred to in the Qur'an, and to precepts that have been suppressed or abrogated by other verses (see Zarkashi, II, pp. 69ff.)

An even closer expression of the Qur'an's involvement in the daily life and problems of human society is the principle of *naskh* (abrogation or suppression) of one verse by another. Abrogation may take one of several forms. The most common occurs when a legal precept is superseded by a later one. In this case, the verse remains and is recited, but its command or prohibition is suppressed.

Another form occurs when a verse is suppressed altogether in both its precepts and recitation. This is a rare and controversial form. Finally, there are a few cases where the text of a verse is superseded or abrogated but its precept remains operative. We can clearly see from all this that the Qur'an has had to meet the exigencies of the daily life of the community even in its formation and final structure. Yet, among Muslim scholars there is no general agreement as to what verses are abrogated and by what verses. We shall have many occasions to return to this problem in this and subsequent volumes (see in this volume *surah* 2, verse 106). Some scholars have identified the abrogating verses with the *muhkam* verses and the abrogated verses with the *mutashabih* ones.

A final example of the Qur'an's involvement in human history, which also illustrates its timeless and transcendent dimension, is that of *zahr* and *batn* (outer and inner dimensions). This principle will be discussed more fully later in consideration of the principles of *tafsir* and *ta'wil* (interpretation and exegesis). Suffice it to say that the outer dimension of the Qur'an is that apparent or public meaning suggested by the literal sense of a verse. Its inner dimension is the level or levels of meaning known partially to the elect few but ultimately to God alone. These two dimensions have also been identified with the *muhkam* and *mutashabih* of the Qur'an. Having so far examined the nature and structure of the Qur'an, we shall now turn to the principles and development of its interpretation.

Early commentators such as Tabari used the terms *tafsir* and *ta'wil* interchangeably. In time, however, the two terms came to designate two distinct branches of the general science (*'ilm*) of the Qur'an. *Tafsir* means uncovering or unveiling, as when a woman unveils her face or when dawn unveils the sky of the darkness of night. *Tafsir* is therefore the illumination of the various meanings or designations of a Qur'anic verse or passage. It includes the elucidation of the occasion or reason for the revelation of a verse, its place in the *surah* to which it belongs, and its story or historical reference. *Tafsir* must also determine whether a verse or passage belongs to the Meccan or Medinan period of revelation, whether it is *muhkam* or *mutashabih*, abrogating or abrogated, and whether it has a general or specific reference or purport (see Zarkashi, II, pp. 146–148).

Ta'wil means the final end (*'aqibah*) of a matter, as the Qur'an says: "On a day when its [the Qur'an's] *ta'wil* [that is, fulfillment] shall come" (Q. 7:53; see also 10:39). It is the final purpose, meaning, or end of a thing. Zarkashi defines *ta'wil* as the act of "referring a verse back to whatever meanings it can bear" (Zarkashi, II, p. 148). Still another view holds *ta'wil* to be the *iyalah* (shaping or arranging) of a thing so as to place its various significations in their proper perspectives (see Zarkashi, II, p. 148).

Tafsir may be characterized as the general elucidation of a verse with the view to discovering its exoteric meaning and application. One branch of *tafsir* is specifically concerned with the understanding of a verse, interpreting its obscure words or phrases, and elucidating its general linguistic problems. This branch is known as the science of meanings (*ma'ani*) of the Qur'an. A number of commentators have devoted their efforts to this branch.

Ta'wil is the science of elucidating the general as well as particular meanings of the words of the Qur'an. The difference between *tafsir* and *ta'wil*, according to some commentators, is that *tafsir* is concerned primarily with the transmission (*riwayah*) of tradition, whereas *ta'wil* is concerned with the deeper comprehension (*dirayah*) of the inner meaning of the sacred text (see Zarkashi, II, p. 150). *Ta'wil* must not, however, do violence to the literal sense or meaning of a verse or passage of the Qur'an or to the prophetic tradition (*sunnah*) because the *sunnah* is the first interpreter of the Qur'an. Scholars have therefore objected to farfetched exegeses of certain verses by Shi'i, Sufi, or popular Sunni commentators (see Zarkashi, II, p. 162, and Ibn Taymiyah, pp. 87–89).

Tabari relates on the authority of Ibn 'Abbas, "There are four aspects of *tafsir*: one which the Arabs know through their speech, another for the ignorance of which no one may be excused, another aspect which only the learned know, and finally an aspect which only God knows" (Tabari, I, p. 75). In another tradition related on the authority of Ibn 'Abbas, the Prophet declared, "The Qur'an was sent down in four modes" (corresponding to the four aspects of *tafsir* just cited). The first, he said, concerns lawful and unlawful actions, which everyone must know. The aspect about which the Arabs are best qualified to speak is that relating to their tradition of poetry, their history, and their customs. The mode that is known to God alone consists of the obscure (*mutashabih*) verses such as those dealing with the end of the world, the blowing of the trumpet on the day of resurrection (see Q. 18:99), and the like. "Anyone claiming knowledge of this aspect is a liar" (Tabari, I, p. 76). Thus we see that the true and final inner meaning of the Qur'an is known only by God. The Qur'an, however, was sent down as a book of guidance and must be understood if it is to be followed.

Muslim commentators have attempted to arrive at this understanding through several different approaches. The first and most important source for the interpretation of the Qur'an is the Qur'an itself. Thus whenever a verse, phrase, or word of the Qur'an may be elucidated by another, no recourse to any other source is necessary. The most important source outside the Qur'an is the Prophet, whose life, words, and actions (*sunnah*) are regarded as living commentary on the Qur'an and provide the framework within which *tafsir* is to be exercised. This mode is known as *tafsir bi-al-ma'thur, tafsir* through transmitted prophetic tradition (*hadith*), and refers primarily to precepts (*ahkam*) of the Qur'an, of which Tabari says, "Knowledge of [these] cannot be reached except through elucidation by the Apostle of God for his community. No one is allowed to speak concerning this aspect except through the elucidation of the Apostle of God of its interpretation to him, either by means of an actual text [*hadith*] or a proof which he [the Prophet] had established for his community concerning it" (Tabari, I, p. 74). Thus it is related on the authority of Sa'id ibn Jubayr, who related it on the authority of Ibn 'Abbas, that the Prophet said, "Whoever speaks concerning the Qur'an according to his own opinion, let him expect his seat in the Fire" (Tabari, I, p. 77). Because of this stern warning, relatively few traditions on *tafsir* have come down to us on the authority of the Prophet's close companions.

Nevertheless, a rich variety of works on *tafsir* according to individual opinion have been produced through the centuries. A tension may be observed between the use of unfettered imagination in interpreting the Qur'an and a strong reluctance to say anything at all concerning it. It is related that Abu Bakr was once asked about the interpretation of a verse of the Qur'an. He said, "What earth shall carry me, what heaven shall shelter me if I say concerning the Book of God things of which I have no knowledge!" (Tabari, I, p. 78). In contrast to Abu Bakr, both 'Ali and Ibn Mas'ud are said to have challenged people to ask them about anything concerning the Qur'an, because they claimed they knew all there was to know about it. 'Ali in one of his sermons is said to have addressed his audience thus: "Ask me! For by God, you shall not ask me about anything but that I shall tell you about it. Ask me about the Book of God! For by God, there is no verse but that I know whether it was sent down during the day or night, on a plain or mountaintop" (Suyuti,

II, p. 187). A similar challenge is attributed to Ibn Mas'ud. He said, "Were I to know of anyone who could be reached on horseback with greater knowledge of the Book of God than I, I would go to him" (Suyuti, II, p. 187). Shams al-Din al-Dhahabi, a famous biographer of *hadith* transmitters, says of Ibn Mas'ud, with approval, that he was reluctant to relate traditions from the Prophet without qualification. Thus Ibn Mas'ud always adds when relating a tradition, "something like that," or "the Apostle of God approximately said that" (Dhahabi, I, p. 15).

The need for interpreting the Qur'an, as well as the resulting tension in *tafsir* tradition, stems from the basic attitude of the Muslim community toward the Qur'an. From the beginning, *tafsir* has been both a matter of theory and practice. The Companions, we are told, used to learn ten verses at a time and then study their meaning and application, so that one of those who learned the Qur'an from the Companions said, "We were told by those who used to teach us the recitation of the Qur'an that when they were taught ten verses by the Prophet, they did not go beyond them until they had fulfilled their injunctions. Thus we learned the Qur'an and its applications simultaneously" (Tabari, I, p. 80). This emphasis is in accordance with the Quranic injunctions to the faithful to learn and live by the Qur'an (see, for example, Q. 2:2 and 38:29).

The Qur'an has many levels of meaning. Hence *tafsir* according to the individual opinion (*ra'i*) of the commentator was an inevitable development. We observe a growing acceptance of individual interpretation as Islam spread among many different cultures. Another reason was the realization that much of the *tafsir* based on prophetic tradition is actually based on doubtful, weak, and often spurious *hadiths*. Zarkashi comments on the prophetic warning against interpreting the Qur'an according to one's own opinion: "If this *hadith* is sound, then its true exegesis is that whoever speaks about the Qur'an merely according to his own opinion without recourse to anything but his own words, even if he arrives at the truth, would miss the right path . . . this is because this would be an opinion without any supporting evidence." Zarkashi then quotes a *hadith* of the Prophet in support of individual interpretation: "The Qur'an is malleable, capable of many types of interpretation. Interpret it, therefore, according to the best possible type" (Zarkashi, II, p. 163).

This *hadith*, Zarkashi argues, gives clear support for the need of personal reasoning (*ijtihad*) in *tafsir*. He then quotes a famous traditionist, Abu al-Layth, who argued, "Prohibition here refers only to the *mutashabih* of the Qur'an and not to all of it . . . because the Qur'an was sent down as a proof [*hujjah*] against humankind. If *tafsir* is not allowed, then the proof would not be decisive" (Zarkashi, II, p. 163).

Another reason for the acceptance of individual interpretation was the need to make the Qur'an relevant to every time and situation. It has been through *ta'wil* that Muslim scholars and mystics were able to bring the Qur'an into the hearts, imagination, and total life experience of the masses. A *mufassir* (exoteric commentator) is primarily a transmitter, but a *mu'awwil* (esoteric exegete) is a discoverer or deducer (see Zarkashi, II, p. 166). The latter enjoys an infinite scope for his imagination, though he is also subject to error and is generally suspect; the former is narrowly restricted by the paucity of his subject matter. Ibn Hanbal, the great traditionist and founder of the Hanbali rite (*madhhab*) argued, "Three subjects have no *isnad* [that is, proper transmission]: *tafsir*, *malahim* [apocalyptic *hadiths*], and *maghazi* [accounts of the early battles of Islam]" (Ibn Taymiyah, p. 60). But Qur'an scholars have always insisted that *tafsir* must ultimately rest on the *sunnah* of the Prophet and the views of his companions and their successors. Before we turn to the early generations of Muslims and their place in the development of *tafsir*, a word must be said about the qualifications of the *mufassir* and his responsibilities.

Knowledge of the religious sciences is the first necessary qualification of a good *mufassir*. Yet knowledge alone is not enough. Sincere piety and depth of intuition are requisite qualities if the *mufassir* is to be able to discover the many levels of inner meaning of the Qur'an. The Qur'an addresses every person at the level of his understanding and intuitional gifts. Zarkashi writes, "Outward expressions or explanations [*'ibarat*] are for the generality of men; they are for the ear. Subtle allusions [*isharat*] are for the elect; they are for the mind. Subtleties of meaning [*lata'if*] are for the friends [*awliya'*] of God; they are glimpses [*mashahid*] of divine presence. Truths or realities [*haqa'iq*] belong to the prophets; they are their submission [*istislam*] to God" (Zarkashi, II, pp. 153–154). The author argues further that there are those who, when they hear the Qur'an recited, hear it only from the lips of the reciter and only as the exoteric Qur'an. These listeners benefit from its precepts, commands, and prohibitions. Others hear the Qur'an as though it is being recited by the Prophet to his community, and he is elucidating its admonitions. Such people achieve greater benefits as their hearts become stirred by the gracious subtleties of the Prophet's words. Some listen to the Qur'an as though it is being recited by Gabriel to the Prophet; they see glimpses of hidden mysteries which the angel of revelation brought to Muhammad. "But those who hear in it the words of the Truth [God], they become annihilated before Him and their attributes effaced. They take on the attributes of truthfulness [*tahqiq*] by witnessing the knowledge of certainty [*'ilm al-yaqin*], the truth of certainty [*haqq al-yaqin*], and the reality of certainty [*'ayn al-yaqin*]" (Zarkashi, II, p. 154).

It is not possible to hear God's voice in the Qur'an, however, before one hears first the recited Qur'an warning and admonishing, promising bliss to the pious and condemnation to the wicked. Hence it is important for the *mufassir* to have a thorough knowledge of the transmitted tradition of *tafsir* from the Prophet and his companions. Zarkashi argues, "Whoever claims to have understanding of the mysteries of the Qur'an without attaining proper knowledge of its exoteric dimension is like one claiming to reach the inner part of a house without passing through the door" (Zarkashi, II, p. 155).

Suyuti gives three essential qualifications of the *mufassir*. First, the *mufassir* must have sound faith and must strictly observe the precepts of Islam. He must avoid erroneous views and spurious traditions and must take seriously his trust, which is the Book of God. Second, he must have a good purpose, that is, his aim should be only to serve God and not to acquire wealth or prestige. A good *mufassir* must therefore be totally detached from the world. Third, a *mufassir* must be an authority on the sciences of the Arabic language [see Suyuti, II, p. 175].

I have stressed in this discussion that Muslims believe the Qur'an was sent down as a Book of guidance. The Prophet was therefore the first interpreter of the Qur'an. He was charged by the Qur'an to be both its transmitter and interpreter. Thus we read, "We have sent down to you the remembrance [Qur'an] that you may elucidate for people what was sent down to them so that they may ponder" (Q. 16:44). Any discussion of the development of *tafsir* therefore must begin with the Prophet and the first two generations of the Muslim community. Having examined in some detail the principles of *tafsir*, I shall now present its early masters and their place in its development.

As has been observed, little has been transmitted from the first four caliphs, with the exception of 'Ali, who has been regarded by both Shi'i and Sunni traditionists as one of the great masters of early *tafsir*. Among the Companions, the three most important authorities were 'Abdallah ibn Mas'ud, Ubayy ibn Ka'b, and Zayd ibn Thabit.

'Abdallah ibn Mas'ud, also known as Ibn Umm 'Abd, was among the earliest Companions to accept Islam. He took part in all the battles of the Prophet and learned directly from him seventy or seventy-two *surahs* of the Qur'an. He was among the first to compile a collection (*mushaf*) of the Qur'an, which, even though no longer extant, has occupied an important place in the history of *tafsir*. His reading (*qira'ah*) was among the first to be recognized as an authentic reading of the Qur'an. The Prophet is said to have declared, "Whoever wishes to recite the Qur'an fresh, as it was sent down, let him recite it according to the reading of Ibn Umm 'Abd" (Dhahabi, I, p. 14; see also Ibn Sa'd, II, p. 342).

Ibn 'Abbas related that Gabriel reviewed the Qur'an with the apostle of God once a year, during Ramadan. In the year the Prophet died, it was reviewed twice. Ibn Mas'ud was present at all these occasions. He therefore knew "what was abrogated of the Qur'an and what was substituted" (Ibn Sa'd, II, p. 342). Tradition tells us that Ibn Mas'ud was a close companion of the Prophet. He helped in his personal affairs, kept his secrets, and behaved as though he was a member of his family. Ibn Mas'ud died in Medina in 32/652 (see Ibn Sa'd, III, pp. 150–160).

Ubayy ibn Ka'b ibn Qays, known as Abu al-Mundhir, was of the Khazraj tribe of Medina. He was regarded as a man of great knowledge, having learned to read and write before Islam. It is related that God Himself commanded the Prophet to recite the Qur'an before Ubayy. It is also said that when *Surat al-'Alaq* (Q. 96) was sent down, the Prophet came to Ubayy and said, "Gabriel commanded me to come to you so that you might take it [the *surah*] and memorize it." Ubayy asked tearfully, "O Apostle of God, did God mention me to you by name?" "Yes," he answered (Ibn Sa'd, II, p. 341). Ubayy was one of the scribes of revelation, and his reading has been especially important in the history of *tafsir*. Anas ibn Malik related that the Apostle of God said, "The best reciter of my community is Ubayy ibn Ka'b" (Ibn Sa'd, III, p. 499). Ubayy is reported to have died in 22/641 during the caliphate of 'Umar, but he may have died in 30/651 during the caliphate of 'Uthman, as it is related that he was one of those delegated by 'Uthman to collect the official recension of the Qur'an (see Ibn Sa'd, III, p. 502).

Zayd ibn Thabit was also of the tribe of Khazraj and grew up an orphan. It is related that shortly after the Prophet came to Medina he asked Zayd to learn the Hebrew or Syriac script because, he said, "I receive letters from people which I do not like just anyone to read to me" (Ibn Sa'd, II, p. 358). Zayd was recognized to have been the man of his time most knowledgeable in religious legal matters and especially in Qur'anic recitation. He was one of the earliest scribes of the Qur'an in Medina and later headed the committee entrusted by 'Uthman with the collection of the Qur'an. Many of the well-known traditionists among his successors, including Ibn 'Abbas, were his disciples. His traditions and opinions concerning *tafsir* were transmitted mainly by his son Kharijah, who is usually referred to as Ibn Zayd. Zayd died in Medina in 45/666 (Ibn Sa'd, II, p. 360; and Dhahabi, I, p. 32).

As Islam spread with the expansion of the Muslim domain into all parts of the Near East, distinct schools of *tafsir* arose in several centers of learning. Most important among these were Mecca, Medina, and Kufah. Each of these schools traced its origin to one of the companions of the Prophet or their immediate successors. It will not be possible to give an account of all the important authorities in each school; a few examples must suffice.

The most important early school of *tafsir* was that of Mecca, because most of its prominent figures were disciples of Ibn 'Abbas, who was the foremost authority on Qur'anic exegesis. 'Abdallah ibn 'Abbas ibn 'Abd al-Muttalib was born in Mecca before the *hijrah*; when the Prophet died he was a youth of about thirteen. It is related on the authority of 'Ikrimah that the Prophet prayed concerning Ibn 'Abbas, "O God! Grant Ibn 'Abbas wisdom and instruct him in exegesis [*ta'wil*]" (Ibn Sa'd, II, p. 365). His prominence in *tafsir* was attested to by the assertion of Ibn Mas'ud (some authorities even attribute this statement to the Prophet) that "the best interpreter [*tarjuman*] of the Qur'an is Ibn 'Abbas" (Dhahabi, I, p. 40; see also Suyuti, II, pp. 187–188). Ibn 'Abbas learned *hadith* from the Prophet's companions and especially Ubayy ibn Ka'b. He was particularly interested in Qur'anic exegesis and traditions concerning the Prophet's battles. He was called "al-Bahr" (the Ocean) because of his great learning (see Ibn Sa'd, II, p. 366).

Tradition asserts that Ibn 'Abbas was an independent thinker, as illustrated by the following passage: "When Ibn 'Abbas was asked about a matter, if the answer was to be found in the Qur'an, he related what the Qur'an had to say about it. If, however, there was nothing in the Qur'an, while the Apostle of God said something concerning it, he related what the Apostle of God said. If there was nothing in either the Qur'an or what the Apostle said, while Abu Bakr or 'Umar said something, Ibn 'Abbas related what they said. If, on the other hand, there was nothing on the authority of any of these, he gave his own opinion" (Ibn Sa'd, II, p. 367). This statement illustrates the important role Ibn 'Abbas played in the formation and growth of the exegetical tradition. As will be seen below, much is related on his authority that cannot realistically be attributed to him. Rather, such material reflects the lively interaction of the early Muslim community with the People of the Book, that is, Jews and Christians.

Several chains of transmission (*isnad*) go back to Ibn 'Abbas. Perhaps the earliest written source on *tafsir* was a *sahifah* (scroll), the contents of which were related from Ibn 'Abbas on the authority of 'Ali ibn Talhah al-Hashimi through Mu'awiyah ibn Salih. Bukhari, we are told, possessed a copy of this scroll which he used extensively in his *hadith* collection. A chain of transmission from Ibn 'Abbas by way of Mujahid is also generally well regarded. Still other traditions, related on the authority of al-Suddi from Ibn Mas'ud and others, are highly regarded (see Suyuti, II, pp. 188–189). Sa'id ibn Jubayr transmitted yet another chain from Ibn 'Abbas, which is also considered to be reliable.

'Ikrimah, the client (*mawla*) of Ibn 'Abbas, related many traditions from his master. When he and Sa'id ibn Jubayr agree, their transmission is of unquestionable authenticity in the view of most commentators. Some of the chains going back to Ibn 'Abbas are considered unreliable. That of al-Kalbi, especially when it includes Muhammad ibn Marwan al-Suddi al-Saghir ('the younger', not to be confused with Isma'il ibn 'Abd al-Rahman al-Suddi, who died in Kufah in 128/745), has been rejected by commentators (see Dawudi, I, p. 109; and Suyuti, II, pp. 188–189). Finally, the chain of transmitters from Ibn 'Abbas by way of al-Dahhak ibn Muzahim al-Hilali is considered weak because al-Dahhak, it is believed, did not meet Ibn 'Abbas but rather transmitted *hadith* from Sa'id ibn Jubayr. Al-Dahhak died in Khurasan in 105/723 (see Ibn Sa'd, VI, pp. 301–302). Perhaps because of this profusion of *hadith* related on the authority of Ibn 'Abbas, al-Shafi'i, who was a great champion of *hadith*, declared, "No more than a hundred of those *hadith* on *tafsir* attributed to Ibn 'Abbas may be regarded as sound (Suyuti, II, p. 189). Be that as it may, the significance of Ibn 'Abbas as an authority on *tafsir* cannot be overestimated. Ibn 'Abbas died in al-Ta'if, near Mecca, in 68/687 (see Ibn Sa'd, I, pp. 365–368). Of the many disciples of Ibn 'Abbas, 'Ikrimah, Mujahid, and Sa'id ibn Jubayr are especially important. 'Ikrimah Abu 'Abdallah al-Barbari was a *mawla* of Ibn 'Abbas and a very highly respected man of learning and piety. After the death of his master, 'Ali the son of Ibn 'Abbas sold 'Ikrimah to Khalid ibn Yazid ibn Mu'awiyah for four thousand dinars. 'Ikrimah is said to have reproached him, saying, "So you have sold the learning of your father for four thousand dinars!" Thus 'Ali bought him back and set him free (Ibn Sa'd, V, p. 287). 'Ikrimah died in 105/723 at a very advanced age.

Mujahid ibn Jabr was also a client. He was attached to the Makhzum tribe, hence his surname al-Makhzumi. Mujahid was widely acclaimed in his time as an authority on *tafsir* and as a reciter of the Qur'an. It is related that he declared with satisfaction, "I read the Qur'an three times with Ibn 'Abbas, each time stopping at every verse and asking about its meaning" (Suyuti, II, p. 190; see also Ibn Sa'd, V, p. 466). Thus the famous exegete and traditionist Sufyan al-Thawri declared, "If *tafsir* comes to you from Mujahid, it is enough for you" (Dhahabi, I, p. 92). Mujahid had a special interest in supernatural phenomena and is said to have gone to Hadramawt to see the well of Barhut, where the souls of the wicked dead were supposed to have been imprisoned. He also went to Babel to see the two fallen angels Harut and Marut (see Q. 2:102). This tradition may explain the mythological character of much that is related on his authority. Mujahid died in Mecca in 104/722 (Dhahabi, I, pp. 92–93).

In contrast to Ibn 'Abbas, many of the *tafsir* traditions related from Ubayy ibn Ka'b are generally accepted. A large number of these were related by Abu Ja'far al-Razi on the authority of al-Rabi' ibn Anas. Because I have omitted in this work all but the last link in chains of transmission, it is important to note that most of the traditions related on the authority of Rabi' ibn Anas were transmitted by Abu Ja'far al-Razi. Rabi' also related traditions from Abu al-'Aliyah al-Riyahi, who, like many early masters of *tafsir*, was a client. Abu al-'Aliyah transmitted *hadith* from 'Umar ibn al-Khattab, Ubayy ibn Ka'b, and others of the Companions. He died in 93/711 (see Ibn Sa'd, VI, p. 112; and Dhahabi, I, pp. 61–62). Qatadah ibn Di'amah al-Sadusi, the great jurist of Basrah, was among those who related tradition on his authority. Qatadah was blind from birth. He declared of himself, "There is not a verse of the Qur'an but that I have heard something [that is, an exegetical *hadith*] about it." (Dhahabi, I, pp. 123–124). Qatadah died during a plague in Wasit in 118/736.

'Ata' ibn Abi Rabah, Sa'id ibn al-Musayyab, and 'Amir al-Sha'bi were among the most important authorities on *tafsir* during the second generation of the Muslim community. 'Ata' was a black man, a client of a man of the tribe of Quraysh. He was known as the jurist of Mecca. He heard *hadith* traditions from several well-known Companions, as well as from 'A'ishah and Umm Salamah, two of the Prophet's wives. Many of the important authorities on *hadith* and Qur'anic exegesis were among his disciples. 'Ata' died in Mecca in 114/732 (Dhahabi, I, p. 98).

Sa'id ibn al-Musayyab was a great traditionist and one of the most respected of the Successors. His authorities for *hadith* included Ibn 'Abbas, Zayd ibn Thabit, 'Abdallah ibn 'Umar, and Abu Hurayrah, who was his father-in-law. Ibn al-Musayyab was also a well-known exegete. Nevertheless, he often replied when asked about a verse of the Qur'an, "I will say nothing concerning the Book of God" (Ibn Sa'd, V, p. 137). Sa'id ibn al-Musayyab died in Medina in 94/713 (see Ibn Sa'd, V, pp. 119–143, and II, pp. 379–384; see also Dhahabi, I, pp. 54–56). 'Amir Abu 'Amr al-Sha'bi, who died in 103/721, was considered one of the three men most learned in *hadith* and *tafsir*, the other two being Ibn 'Abbas and Sufyan al-Thawri. His authorities include 'Ali, Ibn 'Abbas, and Ibn 'Umar (see Dhahabi, I, pp. 79–88).

From a very early period, the People of the Book played an important and controversial role in the development of *hadith* and *tafsir* tradition. A need was felt from the beginning to know more about the prophets of old and their generations than the meager information which the Qur'an provided. Yet at the same time the exegetes were anxious that the integrity and status of the Qur'an not be undermined by excessive reliance on traditions of the People of the Book. Thus Dawudi relates, "A man asked al-A'mash [an important traditionist of the second century], 'Why do men avoid the *tafsir* of Mujahid?' He answered, 'Because they think that he used to ask the People of the Book'" (Dawudi, II, p. 307). The two most important traditionists credited with introducing Jewish and Christian hagiographical tales and interpretations into Qur'anic exegesis were Ka'b al-Ahbar and Wahb ibn Munabbih.

Ka'b al-Ahbar was a Yemenite Jewish rabbi who embraced Islam either toward the end of the caliphate of Abu Bakr or early in the caliphate of 'Umar. Ka'b al-Ahbar was highly regarded by early traditionists, who considered him the most learned of the People of the Book. Later scholars, however, have questioned his authority. Most recently he has been regarded as a negative influence on the development of *hadith* tradition. Even his conversion to Islam is surrounded with mystery. It is related that al-'Abbas ibn 'Abd al-Muttalib, the Prophet's uncle, asked Ka'b al-Ahbar, "What prevented you from embracing Islam during the life of the Apostle of God and the caliphate of Abu Bakr, while you now embrace it during the caliphate of 'Umar?" He answered, "My father inscribed for me a book of the Torah, which he gave to me saying, 'Live in accordance with it!' He, however, sealed all his other books and took an oath from me . . . that I would not open the seals. When I saw Islam spread and saw that there was no harm in it, I said to myself that perhaps my father wished to hide some knowledge from me. . . . Thus I opened the seals and read a book in which I found the description of Muhammad and his community. I accepted Islam" (Ibn Sa'd, VII, pp. 445–446). Ka'b al-Ahbar died in 32/652 or 34/654 (see Dhahabi, I, p. 52).

Wahb ibn Munabbih was a Yemenite Jewish convert born in San'a' ca. 34/654. He related *hadith* from several of the Companions but was especially famous for his knowledge of the traditions of the People of the Book, to which he directed all his energies (see Dhahabi, II, p. 101). It will be clearly seen that the traditions attributed to him present not only biblical and talmudic but even popular hagiographic materials. All these are woven together in interesting although often apparently confused narratives (see, for instance, his commentary at Q. 2:259 below). Islamic tradition recognizes very few ancient revelations apart from the Torah and the Gospel. Yet it is related that Wahb said, "I read ninety-two books and all of them were sent down from heaven. Seventy-two were in churches and synagogues and in the hands of men, and twenty only few men knew" (Ibn Sa'd, V, p. 543). Ibn Munabbih died in San'a' in 110/728 or 114/732 (see Ibn Sa'd, V, p. 543; and Dhahabi, I, pp. 100–101).

Ibn Taymiyah observes that the Companions and Successors did not sharply disagree in their interpretations of the Qur'an. Such disagreement as existed was largely one of variety rather than difference. They disagreed on the name of a thing, not the thing named. For example, some understood the *sirat* (way) in the first *surah* to mean Islam, others took it to mean the Qur'an, and still others the sacred law. All of these are possible, and perhaps all are intended. There was no disagreement, he says, on the fact that the *sirat* is the straight way leading to God, whether through the Qur'an, Islam, or its precepts. Another area of disagreement among early commentators, Ibn Taymiyah observes, was whether a verse should be interpreted in a general or specific way. This problem generally relates to occasions (*asbab*) of the revelation of some verses. But because the precepts enshrined in such verses are binding for all time (see, for instance, below Q. 2:196), the specific reason or occasion for the revelation is simply its story, which may differ in form and content (see Ibn Taymiyah, pp. 38–56).

Disagreement increased as people became interested in detail and in questions that could not be answered with certainty. Here traditions introduced by Jewish converts into *tafsir*, known as Isra'iliyat, played a major role. People wanted to know, for instance, the color of the dog of the people of the cave, the length of the staff of Moses and the size of the ark of Noah and of what wood it was made. These and similar questions were asked out of curiosity, and the answers to them would make no difference to the primary aim of the Qur'an. Yet such interest in details contributed greatly to the growth of *tafsir* into a vast literary corpus. The role of the People of the Book, Jews and Christians, in this development cannot be overestimated. It is related that the Prophet counseled Muslims, saying, "If the People of the Book tell you something, do not either accept it as true or reject it as false, for they may tell you something true and you may reject it as false or tell you something which is false but you may accept it as true" (Ibn Taymiyah, p. 57).

Another factor that contributed to difference and variety in *tafsir* was the rise of different schools of thought, sects, and legal schools in the Muslim community. In this introduction only the major trends and schools of *tafsir* represented in this work are considered. The early development of *tafsir* in the different centers of Islamic learning such as Mecca, Medina, and Kufah has been noted. Other such centers developed in Syria, Egypt, and other areas of the Muslim world. After the age of the Successors people began to write *tafsir*, whereas formerly it had been transmitted, for the most part, orally. It is even possible that some of the Successors themselves wrote brief commentaries in the form of *hadith* compilations. Bukhari used such a collection related from Ibn 'Abbas in the *tafsir* section of his *hadith* compendium.

The majority of Sunni religious scholars have been highly critical of *tafsirs* representing a specific school of thought, legal rite, or mystical point of view. One of the earliest and in some ways most influential schools of thought in Muslim theology and philosophy was the Mu'tazili school. Mu'tazilis insisted on strict rationality in human thought as well as divine action. God cannot but act rationally and in the best interest of His creatures. If God is good, He cannot do evil. Thus God is bound by His own goodness to absolute justice. Hence men are themselves responsible for their own acts.

Mu'tazili rationalism demanded a strict insistence on God's oneness [*tawhid*]. Everything except God, including even the Qur'an, His own word, is created in time. God alone is the One and eternal Being; Mu'tazilis therefore called themselves "The people of justice and divine oneness" (*ahl al-'adl wa al-tawhid*). These ideas are reflected in Mu'tazili *tafsir* and will be noted in their proper contexts. Even though I have chosen Zamakhshari to represent the Mu'tazili school, reference will be made to other thinkers who were used by Tabarsi in Shi'i *tafsir* and by Razi in his philosophical commentary.

Ibn Taymiyah observes in his sharp critique of such ideologically oriented *tafsirs* that this approach belongs to a people "who believed in some particular meanings and sought to identify them with those of the Qur'an. These people concern themselves with the meaning they held without due regard to the elucidation which the words of the Qur'an require" (Ibn Taymiyah, p. 81). This explanation is to some extent true of the Mu'tazili school but especially of Sufi and early Shi'i *tafsir*. Philosophical *tafsir* is in some ways guilty of the opposite tendency. It often reads more into the Qur'an than the literal sense seems to bear. Sufi and early Shi'i *tafsir*, on the other hand, resort to *ta'wil*, so that they find in the Qur'anic text levels of meaning which often bear no direct relationship to the literal sense of the text.

Razi, for instance, wrote an entire volume of his massive work on *Surat al-Fatihah* alone. In this volume he deduced every possible sense or interpretation of the text. His approach was at once theological, metaphysical, mystical, and even popular. His analytical approach, which is also circular and argumentative, earned his work the designation "philosophical" in the broad sense of the word. Razi differs from other philosophical commentators such as the Ikhwan al-Safa and other Isma'ili thinkers in that he was a strict Shafi'i Sunni Muslim in belief and theological preference.

Sufi *tafsir* was an early phenomenon in Islamic thought and piety. It is *ta'wil* at its highest level. Sufi masters such as Qushayri (d. 465/1074) sought in the Qur'an 'subtle allusions' (which is the title of his commentary, *Lata'if al-Isharat*) to spiritual realities which are thought to be beyond the ability of the generality of Muslims to discern. The words of Zarkashi (quoted above) characterizing those who hear in the Qur'an the voice of God and achieve absolute certainty describe well Sufi exegetes. Other Sufi masters such as Muhyi al-Din ibn 'Arabi used *ta'wil* to present ideas that go far beyond the pietistic spirituality evoked by the Qur'an. Zarkashi characterizes Sufi *tafsir* as inner meanings which the Sufis sense in their moments of ecstasy (*wajd*). He then quotes al-Wahidi, who said concerning the commentary of the famous Sufi master Abu 'Abd al-Rahman al-Sulami, *Haqa'iq al-Tafsir*, that anyone calling it *tafsir* must be considered a rejecter of faith (Zarkashi, II, p. 171). Suyuti comments further, "If he [its author] himself believed it to be *tafsir*, he would have committed an act of *kufr* [rejection of faith]." In spirit and to some extent in approach and purpose this commentary is very similar to that of Ibn 'Arabi (Suyuti, II, p. 184).

The objection to Sufi *tafsir* appears to be that it does not follow the accepted method of exoteric *tafsir*. Suyuti, who seems to have had Sufi sympathies, wished that the Sufis had been more rigorous in exegesis because of the misunderstanding their method could provoke (Suyuti, II, p. 184). Taftazani, the commentator on the famous Creed of Nasafi, defends Sufi *tafsir* against the sharp criticism of esoteric exegesis which Nasafi levels at the Sufis, calling their *tafsir* a denial of God (*ilhad*): "As for the view of some scholars, namely that the texts of the Qur'an must be taken in their literal sense, [it must be admitted] that they contain subtle allusions which become manifest to the masters of the *tariqah* [path of Sufism], but these can be harmonized with the literal sense of the Qur'an. This is because of the perfection of their faith and pure gnosis ['*irfan*]" (Suyuti, II, p. 184).

At least in its popular pietistic form, Sufi *tafsir* has been well regarded by all but the most fundamentalist Muslim scholars. It is, no doubt, this form of *tafsir* which men like Zarkashi, Suyuti, Taftazani and many others have defended. It is a warm and personal expression of Muslim Qur'anic piety, which I feel must be included in any representative treatment of the Qur'an as a vital force in the lives of Muslims throughout their long history. Nisaburi is a good representative of this aspect of *tafsir*, which, as we shall see, is also reflected in other commentaries.

The development of Shi'i *tafsir* has paralleled that of general Sunni *tafsir*. The principles presented above are true of Shi'i *tafsir* as well. It remains for me to point out the main features of Shi'i interpretation and emphasis which give this branch of *tafsir* its unique character, as well as some distinguishing characteristics in its development. A comprehensive discussion of this subject, however, requires an independent study, which is beyond the scope and aim of this work.

One of the most important principles of Shi'i *tafsir* is that the Qur'an must always be shown to have relevance or applicability to some persons and situations. All other principles implying a multiplicity of meanings such as *muhkam* and *mutashabih, nasikh* and *mansukh, zahir* and *batin,* and *ta'wil* and *tanzil* are explained on the basis of this assertion. True knowledge of the Qur'an encompasses all aspects of its exegesis. When such knowledge is achieved, the Qur'an becomes all *muhkam,* that is, unambiguous in both its meaning and application. The sixth imam is said to have declared, "The *muhkam* [of the Qur'an] is that which must be followed and the *mutashabih* is that which is obscure to the one ignorant of it" (Tabataba'i, *al-Qur'an,* p. 39). After quoting this *hadith,* Tabataba'i insists that the meaning of all verses of the Qur'an can be known in one way or another. It may therefore be said that the obscure or ambiguous verses are not so in themselves; rather, they appear to be so to those who have no real knowledge of the Qur'an.

Both Shi'i and Sunni traditionists relate that the Prophet received both the Qur'an and its exegesis through the angel Gabriel. For Sunni tradition, this simply meant that the Prophet was the only true interpreter of the Qur'an and therefore that any trustworthy interpretation ultimately had to go back to him. Shi'is have agreed but have further asserted that the Qur'an has two distinct levels of meaning: one that could be known by every person who knows the Arabic language and the other safeguarded or treasured by God (*maknun*). The latter is known only to those whom God has chosen for this favor. The first level is *tanzil,* or the Qur'an as the text sent down to the Prophet. The second is *ta'wil,* or that level of knowledge which only the pure can touch: "In a book safeguarded, none shall touch it save those who are purified" (Q. 56:78–79). Tabataba'i then declares, "Those who are purified are the People of the House [*ahl al-bayt*] of the Prophet, as may be inferred from the Qur'anic verse: 'Surely God wills to remove all abomination from you, O People of the House, and purify you with a great purification'" (Q. 33:33). Tabataba'i concludes, "They are the People of the House who have the knowledge of the exegesis of the Qur'an" (Tabataba'i, *al-Qur'an,* p. 49). These people are the *imams*—'Ali and his eleven descendants—who, according to Shi'i thought, have inherited the knowledge of the prophet Muhammad, who inherited the knowledge of all previous prophets.

The principles of continued relevance (*jari*) and application (*intibaq*) may be considered as the complete knowledge of the Qur'an which the imams possess. This knowledge of all aspects of the interpretation and exegesis of the Qur'an includes that of its continued relevance and application. The Qur'an pertains first to the imams and then, by extension, to the rest of humanity. In support of this idea we are told that the fifth imam said to one of his followers: "The Qur'an was sent down in thirds: a third concerning us and those we love, another concerning our enemies and the enemies of those [prophets and their vicegerents] who were before us, and another is *sunan* [laws and precepts] and parables. Were a verse to die with the people concerning whom it was sent down, nothing would remain of the Qur'an. Rather the beginning of the Qur'an continues, as does its end, so long as the heavens and earth shall endure. To every people belongs a verse which they follow and in accordance with which they continue to live in prosperity or misfortune" ('Ayyashi, I, p. 10).

Shi'is have generally agreed with the Sunni interpretation of the principle of the *zahr* (outer) and *batn* (inner) dimensions of the Qur'an. They have, however, added yet another level of interpretation. Since the Qur'an is primarily addressed to the imams, its first historical reference is to them and their followers (Shi'ah) and only by extension to those who came after them. Thus the fifth imam is said to have defined both the *zahr* and *batn* of the Qur'an as its exegesis (*ta'wil*). *Ta'wil* in this sense means not interpretation but fulfillment (see Q. 7:53 and Tabataba'i, *al-Qur'an*, pp. 40ff.). The fifth imam continues, "There is that of it [*ta'wil*] which has already been fulfilled and that which has not yet come to pass. It proceeds as do the sun and moon. Whenever the time of any of it comes, it is fulfilled" ('Ayyashi, I, p. 11). This view further implies that to know the Qur'an truly is to discern in it the special rights of the imams over the rest of the community and their special favor with God. The sixth imam Ja'far al-Sadiq is said to have claimed, "Had the Qur'an been read as it was sent down, you would have found us in it, mentioned by name." His father, the fifth imam Muhammad al-Baqir, was even more forthright in his accusation. He said, "Had it not been that things were added to the Book of God and others deleted, our rights would not have been obscured to anyone with discernment" ('Ayyashi, I, p. 13). The accusation of addition and omission (*tahrif*) in the Qur'an has been variously interpreted by Shi'i traditionists and commentators. Some have accepted it literally and thus claimed that the Qur'an has been altered. The majority, however, have understood it to refer only to the *ta'wil* of the Qur'an and not to the *tanzil* (revelation of the text of the Qur'an which is in our hands).

The imams are regarded by the Shi'i community as the only legitimate authorities on the Qur'an after the Prophet. They not only possess the knowledge of the Qur'an, but they are associated with it. In a well-known tradition related in many versions by both Shi'i and Sunni traditionists, the People of the House of the Prophet are declared to be the lesser weight (*al-thaqal al-asghar*) and the Qur'an the greater weight (*al-thaqal al-akbar*). Shi'i traditionists report that the Prophet warned the community shortly before his death, saying, "I am leaving behind with you the two weights, the greater and the lesser. As for the greater, it is the Book of my Lord and as for the lesser, it is my progeny, the people of my House. Guard well my memory through the two weights! You shall not go astray so long as you hold fast to them" ('Ayyashi, I, p. 5; see also p. 4).

Before discussing the development of Shi'i *tafsir*, a word must be said about the Shi'i attitude toward the *hadiths* transmitted from the imams, which constitute the major part of Shi'i *hadith* tradition. The six canonical *hadith* collections (*sihah*) in Sunni Muslim tradition have held a place second only to the Qur'an. Some jurists have even argued that the *sunnah* of the Prophet as recorded in these collections may in some cases supersede the Qur'an. Shi'is have, in contrast, taken an open and somewhat ambivalent attitude to their four canonical *hadith* collections. The authenticity of any *hadith*, whether Shi'i or Sunni, must in the end rest on the piety and trustworthiness of its transmitters. Hence it is significant that the fifth imam, who played a major role in the development of Shi'i tradition in all its aspects, warned one of his chief disciples, Muhammad ibn Muslim, not to accept any *hadith* if it did not agree with the Qur'an, whether its transmitter were a righteous or dissolute man. In yet another tradition he is said to have firmly declared, "Any *hadith* that may come to you from us, if the Book of God does not confirm it, it shall be false" ('Ayyashi, I, p. 8). Since early Shi'i *tafsir* consists mainly of *hadiths* from the imams, this attitude gave later scholars great freedom and scope in developing an ever-growing and open *tafsir* tradition.

The first authorities on Shi'i *tafsir* were the imams, whose *hadiths* are given equal weight with those of the Prophet because it is assumed that whatever the imams knew and taught, they inherited from the Prophet. The first generation of commentators were therefore disciples of the imams. They were simply *hadith* transmitters. The period of the living imams, including that of the four representatives of the twelfth imam during his lesser occultation, extended over nearly three centuries, so this formative period overlapped with what may be called the classical stage of Shi'i *tafsir*. The second stage witnessed the beginnings of written *hadith* and *tafsir* tradition. It includes such names as al-Furat ibn Ibrahim al-Kufi (d. late third/ninth or early fourth/tenth century), 'Ali ibn Ibrahim al-Qummi, whose *tafsir* has already been discussed, Muhammad ibn Mas'ud ibn 'Ayyash al-Samarqandi (known as al-'Ayyashi), and others. These commentators recorded the tradition as they received it without much comment of their own. Because they all lived at the time when Shi'i theology, jurisprudence, and *hadith* tradition were struggling to find a place within the wider spectrum of Islamic tradition, their tone is largely polemical and defensive.

The third or classical stage of Shi'i *tafsir* reflected a higher degree of erudition and openness to the wider scope of Islamic learning, theology, philosophy, literature, and other linguistic sciences. Tabarsi is a good representative of this period. I have called this the classical period because it forms an integral part of the general classical tradition of *tafsir*. Moreover, it was during this period that Shi'i thought reached its permanent level of crystallization through the appearance of two of the four books of *hadith*, compiled by Abu Ja'far al-Tusi (d. 460/1067). He is known as Shaykh al-Ta'ifah (jurist doctor of the Shi'i community). His commentary *al-Tibyan fi Tafsir al-Qur'an* is still regarded as one of the standard works of Shi'i *tafsir*. Tabarsi was a disciple of the great Shaykh and relied heavily on his commentary.

A fourth stage in the development of Shi'i *tafsir* may be termed as the period of consolidation. It was the period of the rise and consolidation of Shi'i power in Iran with the appearance of the Safavi dynasty at the beginning of the sixteenth century. The *tafsir* of this period resembles in some ways that of the formative stage discussed above. It again relies heavily on polemical *hadith* tradition buttressed by the accumulated wealth of hagiography and the euphoria of power after a long history of frustration. One of the best representatives of this period is Mulla Muhsin Fayd Kashani, author of two substantial *hadith* collections and a Qur'anic commentary entitled *al-Safi fi Tafsir Kalam Allah al-Wafi*. It was during this period as well that Mulla Muhammad Baqir Majlisi, the most famous of Shi'i scholars of that time, compiled his encyclopedic work *Bihar al-Anwar*, which preserves every branch of Shi'i religious tradition.

The modern period of this long development is still in progress. Tabataba'i represents the growth of the tradition in all its aspects. His commentary *al-Mizan fi Tafsir al-Qur'an* is at once juristic and theological, philosophical and mystical, social and scientific, and even moderate and polemical. It is also deeply rooted in classical Shi'i tradition. Others, however, have not been so expansive and erudite in their approach. They have concentrated more on contemporary issues facing the Muslim world such as the political, economical, intellectual, and social challenges posed by the West. This new emphasis is best exemplified by the new *tafsir* materials coming out of postrevolutionary Iran.

Modern Shi'i *tafsir* is not very different in its concerns from modern Sunni *tafsir*. The latter began in the nineteenth century as a reaction to the challenges of Western technology, science and education. It was rational and apologetic; its primary aim was to present Islam to Muslims and defend it against the Western secular and missionary onslaughts. Shaykh Muhammad 'Abduh (d. 1905) and his disciple Sayyid Muhammad Rashid Rida (d. 1935) are the best-known representatives of the early phases of this period. Sayyid Qutb represents a more confident return to the Qur'an without the need to apologize for it. Nonetheless, he remains an integral part of this new development. His *tafsir* has a wide appeal to the youth of both Shi'i and Sunni communities. There are other trends in modern *tafsir*, but they would require a separate study.

The purpose of this work, as I have stated several times, is to present the Qur'an to Western readers as Muslims have understood it. To this end, I have let Muslim commentators speak for themselves. I cannot, however, nor do I wish to, claim total objectivity. I undertook my task not merely to satisfy academic curiosity but as an expression of the concern of an involved Muslim in the faith of Islam and its sacred Book. This involvement, or subjectivity, if you will, may be seen to some extent in my choice of commentators as well as the verses for commentary. It may also be seen to an extent in my translation of the Qur'anic text and occasionally the conscious use of some uncommon, even cumbersome phrases to express what I take to be the meaning of a Qur'anic word or concept. Most of these phrases require no explanation because the context will, I trust, clarify the reason for my departure from accepted norms. Two key Qur'anic concepts that have, I think, been in the past badly rendered into English require explanation. The word *iman* and its derivative forms do not imply *belief* as an indifferent act of acquiescence, but rather denote an act of personal dynamic commitment to truth; a commitment that may require the person of faith to make the ultimate sacrifice of life itself. Hence the phrase "to have faith" is used instead of the phrase "to believe," except where doubt is clearly implied or the challenge of faith is absent. Here I am indebted to my teacher Wilfred Cantwell Smith, who has admirably illuminated the distinction both in his writing and teaching. Likewise, the word *kufr* and its derivative forms are rendered as "rejection of faith." *Kufr*, too, is an act of conscious and willful rejection of the truth after it has been known.

Finally, I consider the use of the Arabic name for God, "Allah," when writing about Islam in a European language, to be both erroneous and misleading. Allah is the name which Arabic-speaking religious communities—Muslims as well as Jews and Christians—have used. I wish to uphold the principle that one should employ whatever name for God is appropriate in the language one is using.

Sa'id ibn Jubayr is said to have declared, "Whoever recites the Qur'an and does not interpret it is like a blind man" (Tabari, I, p. 80). It is hoped that this contribution will shed some light on the Qur'an for readers who are separated from the rich literature of its *tafsir* by the thick veil of a difficult foreign language.

Surat al-Fatihah (The Opening)

Occasion of Revelation and Titles of *Surat al-Fatihah*

COMMENTATORS ARE NOT UNANIMOUS with regard to the occasion and place of revelation of this *surah*. The majority, however, have asserted that it was revealed in Mecca very early in the Prophet's career. Wahidi relates on the authority of Abu Maysarah and 'Ali that "whenever the Apostle of God went out into the wilderness [that is, at the beginning of his prophetic career in Mecca] he heard a voice calling out to him, 'O Muhammad!' But when he heard the voice he ran away in fright. Waraqah ibn Nawfal said to him, 'If you hear the call again stand firm and listen to what it says to you, then come and tell me.' When the Prophet went out again, he heard the voice calling, 'O Muhammad!' He answered, 'Here I am.' The voice said, 'Say, "I bear witness that there is no god but God and I bear witness that Muhammad is the Apostle of God."' Then the voice said again 'Say, "All praise be to God, the Lord of all beings . . ."' and so on, until he recited the opening [*surah*] of the Book" (Wahidi, p. 17).

Wahidi relates further on the authority of 'Ali, Ubayy, Ibn 'Abbas, and others of the Prophet's companions that the *Fatihah* was revealed early in Mecca (Wahidi, p. 17; Tabari, I, p. 107; Qurtubi, I, p.115; Zamakhshari, I, p. 23). Later commentators have argued that since the *Fatihah* is the prayer (*salat*), it could not have been revealed in Medina, because that would mean that the Prophet and the early Muslims were for some twelve years without the prayers (Tabari, I, p.107; Qurtubi, I, p. 115). Mujahid alone, in a tradition dealing with the *Fatihah*'s excellences, asserted its Medinan origin (Wahidi, p. 17). Some commentators, wishing to harmonize the two views, have argued that the *Fatihah* was revealed twice, first in Mecca and later in Medina. This, they argued, was due to the fact that the *Fatihah* occupies a prominent place in the five daily prayers. This view, however, has not provided commentators with a satisfactory solution to the problem. Says al-Husayn ibn al-Fadl, "Every learned man has a fault, and the fault of Mujahid was his assertion that *al-Fatihah* was revealed in Medina" (Wahidi, p. 18).

The prominence of the *Fatihah* in the prayers and Muslim piety in general was recognized very early by Muslims, as will be seen below. For this reason, 'Abdallah ibn Mas'ud felt that the *Fatihah* does not belong to any specific place in the Qur'an. Shawkani tells us, on the authority of Ibn Sirin, that Ibn Mas'ud did not include it in his recension. When asked why he did not, he answered, "Were I to write it, I would have to write it at the beginning of everything I write" (Shawkani, I, p. 14). The *Fatihah*, however, was from the beginning accepted by the majority as the opening *surah* of the Book, which is its preeminent title. Further, Shawkani states, "With it the recitation of the Qur'an opens, and the Companions opened with it the canonically accepted recension of the Qur'an [*al-mushaf al-imam*]" (Shawkani, I, p. 14).

The first *surah* of the Qur'an is known by many titles and epithets. Its most widely accepted title is *al-Fatihah* (the opening) because with it the Qur'an opens, whether in recitation or writing. It is also known as *Umm al-Kitab* (Mother of the Book) or *Umm al-Qur'an* (Mother of the Qur'an), because it contains the essence of the Qur'an (Tabari, I, pp. 107ff.). Another of its titles is *al-Sab' al-Mathani'*, meaning the seven twice-repeated verses. Hasan al-Basri was asked concerning the verse, "We have given you [Muhammad] seven of the twice-repeated verses and the great Qur'an" (Q. 15:87). He answered, "It is the opening *surah* of the Book" (Tabari, I, pp. 109–110). It is so called because it consists of seven verses and is repeated at least two times in every prayer (see Wahidi, p. 18). Scholars have differed as to whether the invocation or *basmallah*, "In the name of God, the All-merciful, the Compassionate," is one of the seven verses. (This problem will be discussed below.) Other titles of the *Fatihah* are *al-Kafiyah* or *al-Wafiyah* (the sufficient one); *al-Asas* (the foundation); *al-Shifa'* or *al-Shafiyah* (the healing); *al-Salat* (the prayer); and *al-Hamd* (the *surah* of praise). (Ibn Kathir, I, p. 17; Qurtubi, I, pp. 111–113.)

The Excellences of *Surat al-Fatihah*

Tabarsi relates on the authority of Ubayy, "Anyone who recites the *Fatihah* will be given as much merit as if he had recited two-thirds of the Qur'an and as if he had given alms to every man and woman of faith" (Tabarsi, I, p. 36). When Ubayy recited *al-Fatihah* to the Prophet, the latter exclaimed, "By Him in whose hand is my soul, neither in the Torah, the Psalms [*Zabur*], the Gospel [*Injil*], nor in the Qur'an was the like of it revealed" (Ibn Kathir, I, p. 20).

The significance of the *Fatihah* lies primarily in its prominence in daily worship, for it is repeated seventeen times. In spite of its brevity, it contains the two most important elements of prayer: supplication (*du'a'*) and thanksgiving (*hamd*). It is, moreover, a balanced expression of God's oneness, power, His mercy and of man's privilege as the servant of the one God. Thus God, in a divine saying (*hadith qudsi*) reported by both Shi'i and Sunni commentators, declared, "I have divided the prayer [*salat*] between me and my servant, and my servant shall have what he prays for. For when the servant says, 'All praise be to God, the Lord of all beings,' God says, 'My servant has praised me.' When the servant says, 'The All-merciful, the Compassionate,' God says, 'My servant has magnified me.' When the servant says, 'Master of the day of judgment,' God says, 'My servant has glorified me . . . this is my portion and to him belongs what remains'" (Tabari, I, p. 201; Tabarsi, I, p. 36).

Mujahid said, "Satan was four times frightened: when he was cursed by God, when he was expelled from Paradise, when Muhammad was sent, and when the *Fatihah* was sent down" (Qurtubi, I, p. 109; Shawkani, I, p. 15; Shawkani relates the tradition on the authority of Abu Hurayrah).

Of *Surat al-Fatihah*, the invocation or *basmallah* has from the beginning occupied a special place in Muslim piety. The words *Rahman* and *Rahim* both signify mercy. *Rahman*, however, is the intensive form of the noun. God's mercy as *Rahman* encompasses the entire creation, whereas His mercy as *Rahim* is limited to His faithful servants. It may therefore be said that God is All-merciful (*Rahman*) toward both this world and the world to come and *Rahim* (Compassionate) with regard to this world only. It may also be said "He is *Rahman* of this world and *Rahim* of the next, because His mercy in this world includes the rejecter of faith as well as the faithful and the reprobate as well as the righteous, while in the next it is limited to the faithful" (Nisaburi, I, p. 75).

The Prophet is said to have declared, "God, the Exalted, possesses a hundred mercies; one of these He sent down to the earth and parceled it out among His creatures. Through it they exercise mercy and show compassion to one another. The other ninety-nine He withheld for Himself to exercise over His faithful servants on the day of resurrection" (Nisaburi, I, p. 76).

Nisaburi reports a tradition in which 'Ali asserts that the *basmallah* was first revealed to Adam, who said, "My progeny will be protected against the torments [of Hell] so long as they continue to recite it." Then it was revealed to Abraham, who recited it as he was being hoisted into the fire, but God made the fire "coolness and peace" for him (Q. 21:69). Then it was withdrawn until it was sent down to Solomon; the angels addressed him, saying, "Now, by God, your dominion has become complete!" (see Tabarsi, I, p. 36, and Q. 27:30). Then the Prophet said, "It was again withdrawn until God sent it down to me. My community [*ummah*] shall come on the day of resurrection, repeating, 'In the name of God, the All-merciful, the Compassionate.' When their acts shall be weighed in the balance, their good deeds shall outweigh their evil ones" (Nisaburi, I, p. 79).

The *basmallah* bestows great blessing and is a means of salvation in this world and the next. Nisaburi relates that Moses complained to God of Pharoah's hardheartedness and arrogance. Pharoah, however, had the words of the *basmallah* inscribed above his outer gate. Moses complained, "O God, how often do I call him [to faith in God], but I see no good in him." God answered, "O Moses, perhaps you wish his perdition; you look at his rejection of faith, but I look at what he has written above his gate." Nisaburi concludes, "Whoever writes the *basmallah* over his door will be saved from perdition, even if he be a rejecter of faith [*kafir*]." A Sufi gnostic directed that when he died the *basmallah* was to be written on a piece of parchment and placed in his shroud. When asked why, he answered, "I will say on the day of resurrection, 'My Lord, you sent down a Book and made its heading, "In the Name of God . . ."'; judge me therefore according to the heading of your Book'" (Nisaburi, I, p. 79).

Nisaburi also relates that tradition asserts that all branches of knowledge are contained in the four sacred books: the Torah, Psalms, Gospel, and Qur'an. The knowledge contained in the first three is all contained in the Qur'an. The knowledge of the Qur'an is expressed in the *Fatihah* and that of the *Fatihah* is contained in the *basmallah* (Nisaburi, I, p. 77).

As a source of divine knowledge, the *Fatihah* possesses deep mysteries and healing powers. It is thus used as a formula of healing (*raqyah*). The Prophet told Jabir ibn 'Abdallah al-Ansari, "The *Fatihah* is a source of healing for every ailment except death" (Tabarsi,

I, p. 36). The *Fatihah* (and often only the *basmallah*) has been used to cure illnesses, to dispel fear, and to bless every act of a Muslim. A popular tradition attributes to the Prophet the words: "The curtain between the eyes of the *jinn* and the nakedness of the children of Adam, when they take off their clothes, is their saying, 'In the name of God . . .'" (Nisaburi, I, p. 80).

Finally, in the *basmallah* Muslim piety has seen man's true purpose and destiny. Thus Nisaburi argues that because *Surat al-Tawbah* (Repentance) includes statements on fighting and disassociation (*bara'ah*), it does not begin with the *basmallah*. Moreover, at the slaughter of animals, the invocation, "In the name of God [*bismillah*]" is repeated but the words "*al-Rahman, al-Rahim*" are omitted. The author concludes, "Since God has blessed you in repeating these words seventeen times daily in the obligatory prayers, it means that He did not create you for killing and torment, but rather for mercy and good recompense" (Nisaburi, I, p. 79).

Verses of *Surat al-Fatihah*

(I take refuge in God from the accursed Satan.)
1. In the name of God, the All-merciful, the Compassionate.
2. All praise be to God, the Lord of all beings.
3. The All-merciful, the Compassionate.
4. Master of the day of judgment.
5. You alone do we worship, and You alone do we beseech for help.
6. Guide us on the straight way.
7. The way of those upon whom You have bestowed Your favor, not of those who have incurred Your wrath or those who have gone astray.

Every recitation of the Qur'an must begin with the formula of refuge. The *isti'adhah*, that is, the words *a'udhu billahi min al-shaitani al-rajim*, has been made obligatory through Q. 16:98: "When you recite the Qur'an, take refuge in God from the stoned [*al-rajim*] Satan." Tabari reports that Ibn Mas'ud began his recitation of the Qur'an with the words, "I take refuge in God, the All-hearing, All-knowing, from the stoned Satan" (Q. 7:200), but the Prophet told him, " 'I take refuge in God from the stoned Satan' is what Gabriel

taught me to recite from the Well-Guarded Tablet as inscribed by the Pen" (Qurtubi, I, p. 87; see also Nisaburi, I, p. 115). "I take refuge in God" means taking refuge from the accursed Satan in God alone and in no one of His creatures (Tabari, I, p. 113).

Any rebellious creature, be it human, *jinn*, or animal, is called by the Arabs *shaytan*, which is said to be the noun of the verbal root *shatana* meaning to be removed far away. Thus God removed Satan from all good. The word *rajim* (stoned) means one who is cursed and vilified by word and deed. It also means being stoned with flaming meteorites from heaven (see Q. 67:5; Tabari, I, p. 111; Tabarsi, I, pp. 37ff.).

1. In the name of God, the All-merciful, the Compassionate.

(1) Scholars have disagreed as to whether the *basmallah* is a complete verse at the beginning of every *surah*, part of a verse at the beginning of every *surah*, or part of a verse of the *Fatihah* only. Still others have asserted that it is not a verse of any *surah* and that it is written at the beginning of the *surah* only to separate the end of one from the beginning of another. The reciters of Mecca and Kufa affirmed that it is a verse of the *Fatihah* and also of every *surah* before which it appears. The reciters of Basra, Medina, and Syria, on the other hand, considered the *basmallah* to be a verse of neither the *Fatihah* nor of any other *surah* and claimed that it is written simply to separate the *surahs*, as well as for its blessing. A tradition from Ibn 'Abbas states that the Apostle of God did not know the separation of one *surah* from another until the words, "In the name of God, the All-merciful, the Compassionate," were revealed to him (Shawkani, I, p. 17).

Scholars have also differed as to whether the *basmallah* should be said aloud in prayer. Shawkani relates on the authority of Abu Hurayrah and Ibn 'Abbas traditions affirming that the Prophet did recite the *basmallah* aloud in prayer. Those who say that it should not be recited aloud have based their arguments on a tradition which says, on the authority of 'A'ishah, "The Apostle of God used to begin the prayer with the *takbir* [the words *Allahu akbar*—God is most great] followed by the recitation of *al-hamd* [that is, the *Fatihah* without the *basmallah*]." It is also related that Malik ibn Anas said, "I prayed behind the Prophet of God, Abu Bakr, 'Umar, and 'Uthman, and they all began with *al-hamd*" (Shawkani, I, p. 17; see also Ibn Kathir, I, p. 32; and Zamakhshari, I, pp. 24–25). Shi'i scholars have, on the authority of the imams, emphatically affirmed the *basmallah* to be a verse of the *Fatihah* as well as of every other *surah*. The sixth imam declared the *basmallah* to be the "greatest verse in the Book of God" (Tabarsi, I, p. 38; Tabataba'i, I, pp. 22ff.).

2. All praise be to God, the Lord of all beings.

(2) *Al-hamd* (praise) is thanks to God for all His favors in this world and His reward in the world to come. The Apostle of God said, "When you say, 'All praise be to God, the Lord of all beings,' you will have thanked God and He will increase His favor to you." He also said, "There is nothing more pleasing to God than praise. For this reason, He praised Himself by saying, 'All praise be to God'" (Tabari, I, p. 136). In a divine utterance (*hadith qudsi*) cited by Qurtubi, God says, "Praise by Me of Myself precedes the praise of all My creatures of Me. My praise of Myself from eternity [*azal*] was for no other reason but itself, while the praises of My creatures are blemished with motivations." Qurtubi asserts that God praised Himself in beginningless eternity for the greatness of His blessings. His servants are incapable of offering praises worthy of Him, therefore He praised Himself on their behalf. Thus the Apostle of God said, "I cannot enumerate the praises due to You" (Qurtubi, I, p. 135).

Commentators have differed with regard to the meaning of *'alamin* (lit. worlds). *'Alamin* is the plural of *'alam* (world). It refers to rational beings or to those things which are known. *'Alamin*, as the plural of *'alam*, includes all beings other than God. Qurtubi says that the people of every age are a world (*'alam*), as expressed in, for example, God's saying, "Would you then come unto the males of *al-'alamin!*" (Q. 26:165). Qurtubi further states, on the authority of Ibn 'Abbas, that *al-'alamin* are men and *jinn*, as God says, "That he may be a warner to the *'alamin*" (Q. 25:1). Some have said that *'alamin* refers to rational beings in the four communities of human beings, *jinn*, angels, and devils. Animals cannot be said to constitute an *'alam*. Others have asserted that *'alamin* refers to all beings sustained by God and includes every living creature that moves on the face of the earth. Wahb ibn Munabbih said, "God has created eighteen thousand worlds, and this world is only one of them." The grammarian al-Khalil said, "The world [*'alam*] is that which bears the sign [*'alamah*] indicating that it has a creator and ruler" (Qurtubi, I, pp. 138–139).

Razi explains the term *'alamin* thus: "It has been established through clear evidence that outside this world there is infinite space. It has been likewise proven that God, the Exalted, is capable of actualizing all possibilities. Thus He is able to create a thousand worlds outside of this world, and every one of these worlds would be larger and greater than this world. In every world, moreover, there would exist the same objects as in this world, such as the Throne and Footstool [*kursi*], heavens and earth, and sun and moon. Thus the Lord of the worlds is the Lord of all things; things which can be seen and imagined and things which can neither be seen nor imagined" (Razi, I, pp. 6–7).

3. The All-merciful, the Compassionate.

4. Master of the day of judgment.

(4) *Malik* (lit. owner or master) of the day of judgment and *malik* (king) of the day of judgment are the two readings over which commentators have differed. Those who prefer *malik* have argued, as related on the authority of Ibn 'Abbas by Tabari, that on the day of judgment God will be the master of all things. No one of the masters of this world would be allowed to pass judgment with Him. Those who prefer "king" (*malik*), which is the variant reading, have argued that "dominion belongs to God alone and to no one of His creatures, [as it is said in the Qur'an] 'To whom does all dominion belong today [the day of judgment]—to God, the One, the All-conquering' [Q. 40:16]. Dominion belongs to none but God, and therefore He is also *malik* [master]. It is, however, possible that a master be not at the same time a king, while a king is always a master" (Tabari, I, pp. 148–150; see also Qurtubi, I, p. 140; Zamakhshari, I, pp. 56–59; and Shawkani, I, p. 22). Shawkani, like other Shi'i commentators, prefers *malik* (see Tabarsi, I, p. 52, and Tabataba'i, I, pp. 22–25).

5. You alone do we worship, and You alone do we beseech for help.

6. Guide us on the straight way.

(6) *Ihdina* (guide us) was very early interpreted to mean, according to Tabari reporting on the authority of 'Ali, "set us firmly." The

word *sirat* is said to be derived from the verb *sarata*, meaning "to swallow," as the road "swallows" a person out of sight. In this world it is the way of truth, the religion of Islam. In the world to come, the *sirat* is the bridge stretched over Hell, which all human beings must traverse in order to reach Paradise (see Tabari, I, pp. 166–167; Qurtubi, I, p. 147; Zamakhshari, I, p. 67; and Razi, I, pp. 254–258). The sixth imam, Ja'far al-Sadiq, declared, "It is the distance of a thousand year ascent and descent . . . it is finer than a hair and sharper than a sword. Some shall traverse it with the speed of lightning; others like a galloping mare; others shall walk with faltering steps; still others shall crawl. Some will traverse it suspended and their bodies will be partially consumed by the fire [over which they hang]" (Qummi, I, p.29).

Other commentators explain *sirat* as the Qur'an, as related from the Prophet, on the authority of 'Ali and Ibn Mas'ud. Some have explained it as "the true faith, other than which God will not accept from His servants" (Tabarsi, I, p. 59). Shi'is have long understood the *sirat* to refer to 'Ali, the first imam, or to the Prophet and his descendants, the imams, who "are his true representatives" (Tabarsi, I, p. 59).

> 7. The way of those upon whom You have bestowed Your favor, not of those who have incurred Your wrath or those who have gone astray.

(7) Most commentators have included the Jews among those who have "incurred" divine wrath and the Christians among those who have "gone astray" (Tabari, I, pp. 185–195; Zamakhshari, I, p. 71). Some commentators, however, have questioned this view, because the text makes no specific reference to any religious community, and have chosen instead to retain the general meaning of the text, which refers to two types of people rather than any particular religious community. Nisaburi asserts that "those who have incurred God's wrath are the people of negligence, and those who have gone astray are the people of immoderation" (Nisaburi, I, p. 113; for a comprehensive discussion of different views, see Tabarsi, I, pp. 59–66).

In contrast with Nisaburi's pietistic interpretation, Ibn 'Arabi presents a highly mystical exegesis of *Surat al-Fatihah*, reflecting his own philosophy of the unity of being (*wahdat al-wujud*). Since his frame of reference is so different from all those represented in this work, his commentary on the entire *surah* is presented as a continuous narrative.

Ibn 'Arabi begins by observing that names are signs by which things are known. The names of God are generic images which disappear in their own properties. He assigns them to His attributes signifying His manifestations (*zawahir*) of mercy, power, and the like but also pointing to His absolute unity. God's names are manifestations (*mazahir*) of His attributes or actions by which He is known.

(1) After this general observation, Ibn 'Arabi goes on to consider the three names of God invoked in the *basmallah*. He writes, " *'Allah'* is the name of the divine Essence as it is in Itself absolutely. *'Al-Rahman'* is He Who causes existence and perfection to flow upon all things in accordance with the dictates of [divine] wisdom and according to the capacities of the receivers to bear it in their primary stages. *Al-Rahim* is He Who causes ideal perfection [in the Platonic sense] to flow upon the human species, which is proper to it in its final stages. For this reason it is said [in invoking God], 'O *Rahman* of this world and the next and *Rahim* of the hereafter!' This means, in the perfect human all-encompassing form, general and specific mercy, which is the manifestation of the divine Essence as well as of the Truth of supreme exaltation with all His attributes. It [the name of *Allah*] is the greatest name of God; it is to this name that the Prophet referred when he said, 'I have been given comprehensive speech [*jawami' al-kalim*—the Qur'an, which is of a finite number of words but infinite number of meanings], and I was sent to complete the excellences of morals.' For words are the realities of existents and their concrete substances. That is why Jesus was called 'a Word from God' [see for example Q. 3:45]. The excellence of morals are the states of existents and the special properties which are the sources of their actions and which are all contained in the comprehensive human microcosm. Prophets placed words side by side with the ranks of existence. I found things at the time of Jesus and that of the Prince of the Faithful ['Ali] and some of the Companions which point to this truth."

Ibn 'Arabi then illustrates the point that the Divine Word is the source of all being. He continues, "It is therefore said that all existing things come into being from the letter *ba'* of *bismillah* [in the name of God]. This is because it follows the letter *alif* [that is, in the alphabet], which is deleted [that is, it becomes assimilated in the word *bismillah*], for it is the essence of God. It [the letter *ba'*] refers to the first intellect which is the first to be created by God and addressed by Him: 'I have created nothing which is more beloved to Me and more favored by Me than you. Through you will I give and take away and through you will I reward and punish.' The letters which are pronounced of this phrase [that is, the *basmallah*] are eighteen, but those which are written are nineteen. But if its words are separated and likewise their letters, they become twenty-two letters. The number eighteen is a reference to the eighteen thousand worlds. God has referred to the sources [lit. mothers] of all worlds—the world of power [*jabarut*] and the world of dominion [*malakut*], the Throne [*'arsh*] and Footstool [*kursi*], [see below 2:255], the seven heavens, four elements, and their three offspring [the mineral, plant, and animal kingdoms]. The number nineteen refers to the human world which, even though it is part of the animal kingdom, must be distinguished from it because of its special honor as an independent world. The three hidden *alifs* which complete the number twenty-two refer to the divine realm with regard to the [divine] essence, attributes, and actions." Ibn 'Arabi then argues that just as these letters are hidden, so also is the divine essence hidden in the attributes, the attributes in the actions and the actions in creation. Such truths, he asserts, "are known only to their people."

Ibn 'Arabi then relates these truths to the different types of men and their various capacities. He says, "He to whom attributes manifest themselves with the removal of the veils of created universes trusts [in God]. He to whom the attributes manifest themselves with the removal of the veils of actions submits and is content. But he to whom the essence manifests itself with the removal of the veils of the attributes becomes annihilated in the unity and thus becomes an absolute proclaimer of divine oneness no matter what else he does or recites." Ibn 'Arabi finally argues that in the *basmallah* the unity of actions precedes that of attributes, which precedes that of the essence. That is, in the name *Allah* the unity of essence is manifested. In the name *al-Rahman*, the unity of attributes is manifested, and in the name *al-Rahim*, the unity of actions is manifested. Thus unity is the meaning of the Prophet's statement in his prostration, "I take refuge in Your forgiveness from Your punishment. I take refuge in Your pleasure from Your wrath, and I take refuge from You in You."

(2) Praise, Ibn 'Arabi argues, must be in word, deed, and whatever condition a person may be in. The act of praising is in itself a manifestation of higher perfections. All things praise God: this is

their final end and purpose. "All existents with all their properties and special stations glorify and praise Him as they seek to fulfill their ends and bring forth their perfections from the state of potentiality to that of actuality. God says, 'There is nothing but that it glorifies Him and proclaims His praise' [Q. 17:44]. Their praise of Him is their exalting Him above any association or any attribution to Him of deficiency and powerlessness. This they do by affirming their dependence on Him alone, and thus by affirming His oneness and omnipotence. Their mode of praise is their manifestation of their degrees of perfection and their reflection of the attributes of majesty and beauty [these are the two classes of divine attributes]. God's essence is here affirmed through His initiation of all things into being, His preservation of them, and providential sovereignty over them. This is the meaning of the 'lordship of all beings,' that is, of all created things which are stamped by God's power as things would be stamped by a seal."

(4) Ibn 'Arabi defines God's mastership (*malikiyah*) of the day of judgment as follows: "The meaning of mastership over all things on the day of reckoning is that all things shall return to Him. This is because no one has the power in reality to recompense except the worshiped Lord to whom all dominion shall belong at the time of recompense. This may be seen through the reward of eternal favor, instead of an ephemeral bounty. This comes when the servant frees himself through asceticism from [desire for] favor, and this takes place when divine actions are manifested to him as he wrenches himself away from his own actions. It occurs when he assumes, instead of his own attributes, God's attributes; then he himself sinks into effacement [*mahw*]. It is when he is able to receive [God's] gift of divine [*haqqani*] existence that he himself is annihilated. To Him alone, exalted be He, belongs all praise . . . from eternity to eternity, as befits Him in His essence; for He is the One praising and the One praised, the One worshiping and the One worshiped . . . forever and ever."

(5) As before, Ibn 'Arabi first presents the attributes of divine beauty and majesty as reflected in the sacred word, then relates this to the mystical quest of the friends of God. He writes, "When He manifests Himself through His word to His servants in His attributes they behold Him in His greatness and resplendence, omnipotence and majesty. They address Him in word and deed ascribing worship to Him alone and beseeching Him alone for help. For they see no one other than Him worthy to be worshiped, nor has anyone power

or strength, except in Him. Were they to be in the divine presence [that is, the mystical presence of the servant of God] then all their movements and quietudes would be acts of worship of Him and in Him. They would be constant in their prayers, praying with the tongue of love as they behold His beauty on every countenance and in every mode: 'You alone do we worship and You alone do we beseech for help.'"

(6, 7) Although Ibn 'Arabi agrees in some ways with traditional commentators on these two verses, he goes beyond them. For instance, he accepts the view that those who have incurred God's wrath are the Jews and that those who have gone astray are the Christians, but his interpretation is highly original and interesting.

"'Guide us on the straight way' means 'set us firmly upon right guidance and confirm us with rectitude in the way of unity, which is the way of him upon whom You bestowed the special favor of mercifulness, which is gnosis and love and the guidance of the divine [*haqqani*] essence. [It is the way] of prophets and martyrs, and the righteous and friends [*awliya'*] of God who behold Him as the First and Last, the Outer and the Inner, and therefore disappear in their beholding of the radiance of His eternal countenance from the existence of the perishing shadow." The reference here is to the world of creation, which is no more than a shadowy reflection of the eternal countenance (*wajh*) of God (see Q. 28:88 and 55:27).

"'Not of those who have incurred Your wrath' means those, such as the Jews, who remained simply with appearances, veiling themselves with the favor of mercifulness [*rahmaniyah*], corporeal bliss, and sensory pleasures from the realities of the spirit, the inner bliss of the heart, and intellectual pleasure. This is because their call was to appearances such as gardens, houris, and palaces. [These words are not to be taken literally because *hur* and *qusur* are commonly used in rhyme to indicate wealth and pleasure.] Thus God became wrathful with them. Because wrath demands expulsion and removal, remaining at the level of appearances, which are the veils of darkness, constitutes the greatest distance away [from God].

"'Or those who have gone astray' refers to those, such as the Christians, who remain at the level of inner dimensions which are veils of luminosity, thus veiling themselves with the favor of compassionateness [*rahimiyah*] from the favor of mercifulness. They therefore become oblivious to the manifestation of the truth and go astray from the straight way. They are deprived of beholding the beauty of the Beloved in all things. This is because their call was only to the inner dimensions and to the lights of the realm of holiness. The call of the Muhammadans who profess divine oneness is to both; it is combining love of the beauty of the essence with love of the beauty of the attributes" (Ibn 'Arabi, I, pp. 7–11).

(AMIN)

The word '*amin*' [so be it] is added in prayer. Shi'is, however, repeat instead, "All praise be to God" (see Qurtubi, I, pp. 127–131; and Tabarsi, I, p. 65).

Surat Al-Baqarah (The Cow)

Occasion of Revelation and Titles of *Surat al-Baqarah*

SURAT AL-BAQARAH WAS REVEALED in Medina on different occasions, except verse 281, which was revealed during the Prophet's farewell pilgrimage (Wahidi, p. 19). It is divided into 286 verses, according to the school of Kufah; 287 according to that of Basrah; 285 according to the scholars of Mecca and Medina; and 284 according to the school of Syria. The Kufan numbering, however, is the one most widely accepted and is also related on the authority of 'Ali, the first Shi'i imam (Tabarsi, I, p. 67).

Surat al-Baqarah takes its title from the story of the cow (verses 66–72). Some commentators, however, seem to have objected to the title, as they did to the titles of all the other *surahs* of the Qur'an except that of *Surat al-Fatihah*. It is related on the authority of Anas ibn Malik that the Apostle of God said, "Do not say, '*Surat al-Baqarah*,' nor '*Surat al-'Imran*' [the House of 'Imran], neither '*Surat al-Nisa*' and so forth for the entire Qur'an. Say rather, 'The *surah* in which the cow is mentioned'" (Ibn Kathir, I, p. 63; see also Qurtubi, I, p. 153). Ibn Kathir rejects this tradition on the grounds that the *surah* has always been known by this title. He cites the example of the Prophet, who, seeing his companions slacken during the battle of Hunayn, called out to them, "O people of *Surat al-Baqarah*" to encourage them to carry on the fight. His companions used the same battle cry in later wars to strengthen the resolve of the Muslim fighters (Ibn Kathir, I, pp. 63–64).

Excellences of *Surat al-Baqarah*

It is related on the authority of Ubayy that the Prophet said, "Whosoever recites it, on him are God's prayers and His mercy.

He shall have the merit of one who has kept the siege in the way of God for an entire year without wavering." Then the Apostle of God said, "O Ubayy, command the Muslims to learn *Surat al-Baqarah*, for in learning it is a blessing and in neglecting it is great remorse" (Qurtubi, I, pp. 152–153; see also Tabarsi, I, p. 67).

Sahl ibn Sa'd related that the Apostle of God said, "Of everything there is a pinnacle [*sanam*] and the pinnacle of the Qur'an is *Surat al-Baqarah*. Whoever recites it in his house during the day, Satan would not enter his house for three days, and whoever recites it at night, Satan likewise would not enter his house for three nights." It is related that the Prophet sent an army on a mission and followed them to test their knowledge of the Qur'an. He asked every man in turn, "What do you have [that is, by memory] of the Qur'an?" This he did until he came to the youngest . . . who said, "I have such and such and *Surat al-Baqarah*." The Prophet said, "Set out and let this man be your leader." They said, "O Apostle of God, he is the youngest of us!" The Prophet replied, "But he has *Surat al-Baqarah*" (Ibn Kathir, I, pp. 58–60; Qurtubi, I, pp. 152–153; see also Tabarsi, I, p. 68).

In the name of God, the All-merciful, the Compassionate

1. *alif, lam, mim.*

Much has been said by commentators concerning the meaning and significance of the unconnected letters that appear at the head of twenty-nine of the *surahs* of the Qur'an. Three main approaches to these letters may be distinguished. The first is that they are "of the *mutashabih* (obscure) verses which God alone knows, and of which none should speak. We assent to them and recite them as they were sent down" (Qurtubi, I, p. 154). This tradition was related on the authority of Abu Bakr and 'Ali. According to 'Umar, 'Uthman, and Ibn Mas'ud, "The unconnected letters belong to the hidden [in the Qur'an], which cannot be interpreted" (Qurtubi, I, p. 154).

Those commentators who insisted that the letters should be understood because there could not be anything in the Qur'an without meaning took great pains to explain them. Tabari provides a comprehensive summary of the main views of the great authorities on *tafsir* of the generation of the Companions and their successors. Qatadah, Mujahid, and Ibn Jurayj asserted that *alif lam mim* "is one of the names of the Qur'an." Mujahid is said to have declared that they are simply "openings with which God opens the Qur'an," or simply "letters at the beginning of the *surahs*." 'Abd al-Rahman ibn Zayd ibn Aslam related from his father that *alif lam mim*, as well as other letters, are "a name for the *surah*." Among the many views attributed to Ibn 'Abbas is that the letters are those of the "greatest name of God." They are therefore used in the Qur'an as an oath, "by which God swore, for it is one of His names." It is further related on the authority of Ibn 'Abbas that each of these letters indicates a name or act of God; thus *alif lam mim* means "*ana allahu a'lam*" (I am God, most knowing) (Tabari, I, pp. 205–207.) A somewhat later commentator, al-Rabi' ibn Anas, took an even broader view. "These letters . . . are on the tongues of all men. There is no one of them but that it is a key to one of God's names, nor is there one of these letters but that it is [one of the letters recording] His favors and calamities [toward men] and there is no one of these letters but that it signifies the decreed term and end [*ajal*] of a people" (Tabari, I, p. 208).

Commentators who did not wish to indulge in esoteric exegesis sought to discover at least the function of the letters, if not their actual meaning. In support of the theory that the letters are symbols in the Arabic language which refer to words or sentences, they quote many examples of ancient poetry and unusual figures of speech (Tabari, I, pp. 209–214; Zamakhshari, I, p. 98; and Qurtubi, I, pp. 155–156). The letters were said to serve yet another function: as the Prophet began the recitation of a *surah*, he wanted to shock the Meccan Arabs into listening to the rest of the recitation. They refused to listen to the Qur'an, but when they heard apparently meaningless letters being recited, they listened to what followed out of curiosity (see Qurtubi, I, p. 155). Other commentators asserted that the letters were simply used to distinguish one *surah* from another (Zamakh-shari, I, p. 83).

Razi advanced the following theological explanation: "God knew that a group of this community would assert the eternity of the Qur'an; thus He mentioned these letters to indicate that His words are made up of letters and that therefore the Qur'an could not be eternal" (Razi, II, p. 7). Perhaps the most widely accepted view is that the letters indicate that "the Qur'an, the like of which men are unable to produce, is nonetheless composed of such familiar letters" (Zamakhshari, I, pp. 96–98; and Razi, II, p. 6). Sayyid Qutb, one of the most recent commentators, argues, "These letters are an allusion to the fact that this book is composed of these and similar letters which were familiar to the Arabs to whom the Qur'an was addressed. Yet in spite of this, it is the Book; a miracle the like of which they were unable to compose out of these same letters. For such is the way of God with all His creatures; all that men can produce from the particles of this earthly soil are different shapes and devices. God, the Originator, makes from it life endowed with movement and reason" (Sayyid Qutb, I, p. 38).

These and similar views achieved currency early in the history of *tafsir*. Tabari presents and criticizes most of the major views up to his time; little has been added since Tabari except for a few significant modifications such as the ones cited from Zamakhshari and Sayyid Qutb. Thus it has become the practice of every commentator to review the major opinions and argue in support of one over all the others, or to attempt to reconcile several similar opinions. Tabari, after reviewing a number of interpretations of the meaning and significance of the unconnected letters, concluded: "God . . . made them unconnected letters and did not connect them so as to render them into words like the rest of His speech . . . because He willed that every one of these letters should have more than one meaning." Tabari could therefore reconcile several views in such a broad statement. (Tabari, I, p. 220).

Zamakhshari offers the same objections and argues that the general consensus of scholars is that each group of letters may serve as a name of a *surah*. He further observes that there is a divine wisdom in the fact that there are fourteen unconnected letters, if we discount repetitions, which is half the number of the Arabic letters of the alphabet. "They further include all the kinds of possible sounds from the point of view of speech." In this he sees an aspect of the miraculous character and challenge of the Qur'an (Zamakhshari, I, pp. 100–103).

The third approach to the interpretation of the unconnected letters is that of *ta'wil*, or esoteric exegesis. It belongs to Sufi exegesis, pietistic *tafsir* influenced by Sufi piety, and Shi'i *tafsir*. Nisaburi, in his popular work *Ghara'ib al-Qur'an*, collects several such exegetical interpretations. "Every one of these letters signifies one of God's names or attributes. Thus *alif* means that He is One [*ahad*], Eternal without beginning [*azali*] or end [*abadi*]. The *lam* means that He is most Gracious [*latif*] and the *mim* that He is most Glorious [*majid*] . . . *alif* signifies Allah, *lam* Jibril [Gabriel] and *mim* Muhammad; that is to say, God sent down this Book through the mediation of Gabriel to Muhammad" (Nisaburi, I, p. 135). Nisaburi reports that the Sufis said, "*Alif* is *ana* [I], *lam li* [mine] and *mim, minni* [from me]." They also say, "The *alif* is an allusion to the necessity of following the straight path of the *shari'ah* at the beginning [of the disciples' course of initiation] . . . the *lam* signifies the bowing down which the disciple experiences at the time of *mujahadat* [spiritual struggles, or struggles with the carnal soul]; this is the heeding of the *tariqah* [Sufi path]. . . . The *mim* signifies the servant's becoming in the station [*maqam*] of love like a circle, whose end is its beginning and whose beginning is its end. This can be achieved only through complete annihilation [*fana'*] in God. This is the station of *haqiqah* [absolute reality]" (Nisaburi, I, pp. 136 and 138; see also Razi, II, pp. 7–8) "The letters also mean '*alastu bi rabbikum?*' ['Am I not your Lord?'], [Q. 7:172], and that is the sealing of the Book of Covenant ['*ahd*] on the day of the primordial covenant [*mithaq*]" (Nisaburi, I, p. 137).

Ibn 'Arabi offers yet another Sufi interpretation of the unconnected letters. God, according to Ibn 'Arabi, "has referred in these three letters to the entire existence from the point of view of its totality. Thus *alif* refers to the divine essence which is the First of existence . . . *lam* refers to the active intellect which is called Gabriel. It is the middle point of existence, receiving the emanation of the First, and itself overflowing upon the end of existence. *Mim* refers to Muhammad, who is the end of existence. Through him the circle of existence is completed, where its end is connected to its beginning. Thus he [the Prophet] said, 'Surely, time has turned about back to its original form on the day when God created the heavens and the earth.'" Ibn 'Arabi then argues that *alif*, as the name of the divine essence, is the basis of all letters, so that the *lam* is composed of two *alifs* and the *mim* includes it. Thus "every name is a reference to the essence which includes one or another of the attributes. The *mim* is, however, a reference to the essence with all its attributes; it is as well a reference to the actions which became hidden in it in the Muhammadan image which is the greatest name of God." Hence, according to Ibn 'Arabi, Muhammad and Gabriel, as concrete expressions of the divine essence, each represents one of God's names. "Gabriel is the manifestation of knowledge; he is His name 'the All-knowing [*al-'alim*]; Muhammad is the manifestation of wisdom; he is His name the All-wise [*al-hakim*]."

Ibn 'Arabi concludes his interpretation with a typical Shi'i exegesis of the letters. He writes, "The meaning of the verse '*alif lam mim*' is: this is the Book promised as the all-encompassing form alluded to in the *jafr* and the *jami'ah* which contains everything." The *jafr* is a receptacle or a book which 'Ali is said to have inherited from the Prophet and passed on to his descendants the imams. The *jafr* contains knowledge of what has already passed and what is yet to come until the day of resurrection. The *jami'ah* is a scroll which contains knowledge of lawful and unlawful things. It was dictated by the Prophet to 'Ali, who passed it on to the imams as part of their inheritance of prophetic knowledge. Ibn 'Arabi continues, "It is a promised [book] in that it shall be with the Mahdi [expected messiah] at the end of time. No one shall read it truly as it is except him. The *jafr* is a tablet of the great void [*fada'*], which is the world of intellect. The *jami'ah* is the tablet of destiny, which is the world of the universal soul."

According to one of the earliest Shi'i commentators, 'Ali ibn Ibrahim al-Qummi, the sixth imam Ja'far al-Sadiq when asked concerning the letters *alif lam mim* replied, "*Alif lam mim* is one of the letters of the greatest names of God, which consists of unconnected letters in the Qur'an. It is the letter with which prophets and imams are addressed, and when they pray to God through it, their prayers are answered" (Qummi, I, p. 30). Tabarsi states on the authority of the imams, "The letters are of the *mutashabihat* [obscure utterances of the Qur'an], the knowledge of which God has safeguarded for Himself and the true exegesis of which He alone knows" (Tabarsi, I, p. 68). It is further related on the authority of the eighth imam 'Ali ibn Musa al-Rida that "Ja'far ibn Muhammad al-Sadiq was asked concerning the meaning of God's saying '*alif lam mim*' and he said, '*alif* signifies six of God's attributes!" The first is "the beginning, for He began all of creation, and *alif* is the beginning of all letters." The second is "straightness [or rectitude], for God is just, not a tyrant, and *alif* is straight in itself." The third attribute is "singularity, for God is one and unique and *alif* is singular and alone." That is, in writing, the *alif* stands alone, unconnected. The fourth is "the link of creation to God, yet God is not linked to creation." The fifth is "that all creatures need God for their existence, yet God is self-sufficient and does not need them." Finally, the letter *alif* "is not connected with other letters, yet they are linked to it. It is separate from all other letters" (Tabarsi, I, p. 69). It is related on the authority of Sa'id ibn Jubayr, "The letters are the unconnected names of God; were men able to know their proper composition, they would know the greatest name of God. Thus you say '*alif lam ra*,' '*ha mim*,' and '*nun*,' and these together spell '*al-Rahman*.' It is likewise with the rest of them, except that we are unable to connect them or arrange them properly" (Tabarsi, I, p. 69).

Speculations that the numerical values of the unconnected letters were used to signify the divine decrees concerning the destinies of human beings appear very early in the history of Qur'anic interpretation. Muqatil ibn Sulayman, one of the earliest authorities of this science, is said to have declared, "We have computed the numerical values of the letters which are at the heads of the *surahs*, discounting repetitions, and they came to 744 years, which is the remainder of the history of this community" (Tabarsi, I, pp. 69-70). Ibn Kathir comments on this approach as follows: "As for those who claim that the letters are indications of the knowledge of periods [of history] from which can be deduced the times of events, tribulations, and eschatological happenings, such men have claimed things of which they have no knowledge." Ibn Kathir then relates a "weak" *hadith* which, in his words, "is nonetheless the best proof of the absurdity of this approach. Ibn 'Abbas said, on the authority of Jabir ibn 'Abdallah ibn Ziyad, that Abu Yasir ibn Akhtab with a group of his fellow Jews passed by the Apostle of God as he was reciting the beginning of *Surat al-Baqarah*. . . . [Abu Yasir] went with his brother Hayy ibn Akhtab and Ka'b ibn al-Ashraf to speak to the Apostle about the letters '*alif lam mim*.' They said, 'We adjure you, by God [to tell us]. . . : Is it true that these came to you from heaven?' He answered, 'Yes, thus did they come down.' Then Hayy said, 'It is the truth you tell, for I know the number of years of the duration of this community.' Then he said, 'How can we enter into the religion of a man, the duration of whose community shall be 71 years according to the computation of these letters?' The Apostle of God smiled; then Hayy asked, 'Is there more?' He said, 'Yes, *alif lam mim sad.*' Hayy said, 'That means 161. Is there still more?' He said, 'Yes, *alif lam ra'.*' Hayy said, 'We bear witness that if you really speak the truth, your community will have dominion for no more than 231 years! Is there more still?' 'Yes', said the Prophet, '*alif lam mim ra'.*' Hayy then said, 'We do not know which of your statements we should accept.' Abu Yasir then said, 'As for me, I bear witness that our prophets foretold the dominion of this community but did not say how long it would endure. Thus if Muhammad speaks the truth, I see that all this shall be granted to him by God'" (Ibn Kathir, I, pp. 68-69; see also Nisaburi, I, p. 136; and Shawkani, I, pp. 29-32).

Perhaps the most that can be said with certainty is what Ibn Kathir has argued: "There is no doubt that these letters were not sent down by God in vain. They must therefore have some meaning. If we discover a true *hadith* of the infallible one [the Prophet], we accept it; otherwise we take no stand on this matter." Ibn Kathir argues that in every *surah* that opens with the letters, there follows the mention of the Qur'an and the proclamation of its miraculous character and greatness (Ibn Kathir, I, pp. 67 and 68).

> 2. This is the Book in which there is no doubt, a guidance to the God-fearing.

Most commentators have agreed that *dhalika al-kitab* (that is the Book) means *hadha al-kitab* (this is the Book). Tabari reports the view on the authority of 'Ikrimah, al-Suddi and Ibn 'Abbas that, "*Kitab* may refer to the *surahs* which were sent down before *Surat al-Baqarah* in Mecca. This is as though God said to His Prophet, "O Muhammad, know that the *surahs* of the Book which I have sent to you contain the Book in which there is no doubt" (Tabari, I, pp. 225–226). Some commentators have claimed that the word *kitab* here refers to the Torah and the Gospel and not the Qur'an (see Tabari, I, pp. 227–228).

Commentators have differed concerning the reading of *la rayba fihi* (in which there is no doubt). It is related that Nafi' and 'Asim, two famous scholars of Qur'anic recitation, paused after "there is no doubt." According to this reading, the verse would be as follows: "This is the Book there is no doubt / in it is guidance to the God-fearing" (Zamakhshari, I, pp. 115–116). Zamakhshari, however, with whom most commentators agree, concludes, "Such views must be ignored and instead it must be said that *alif lam mim* is an independent phrase or a group of alphabetical letters. 'This is the Book' is another phrase, 'in which there is no doubt' is a third phrase, and 'guidance to the God-fearing' is a fourth" (Zamakhshari, I, p. 121).

Commentators have disagreed concerning the word *kitab*. Qurtubi cites the following opinions: "It is said that 'this is the Book' means, which I [God] prescribed for humankind, preordaining their happiness or misery and their term of life and sustenance. 'In which there is no doubt' means that there is nothing which can alter it. Others said that 'this is the Book' means that which I [God] have prescribed for myself from eternity: 'My mercy preceded my wrath.'

It has also been said that God promised His Prophet that He would send down to him a book which water could not erase." It is related on the authority of 'Ayyad ibn Himar al-Mujashi'i that the Prophet said, "God looked at the inhabitants of the earth and despised them all, Arabs and non-Arabs, except for small remnants of the People of the Book. God then said to me, 'I have sent you in order that I might try you and try others by means of you. I have sent down to you a book which water cannot wash away, a book which you shall recite in sleep and waking'" (Qurtubi, I, pp. 157–158). Other commentators have said that the word *kitab* here refers either to the Torah and the Gospel in which the Qur'an is explained or to them both, meaning that the Qur'an included both the Torah and the Gospel. Others have considered that the word *kitab* refers to the Preserved Tablet (that is, to the tablets of destiny preserved with God in heaven). Still others said that God had promised the People of the Book that He would send down to Muhammad a book; the verse is then a reference to that promise (Qurtubi, I, p. 158; see also Ibn Kathir, I, pp. 69–70; Shawkani, I, pp. 33–34; and Tabarsi, I, pp. 77–78.

3. Those who have faith in that which is hidden, observe regular worship and give in alms of that which we have bestowed upon them;

4. Those who have faith in that which was sent down to you and that which was sent down before you, and believe with certainty in the last day;

5. These are truly guided by their Lord, they are indeed the prosperous ones.

6. As for those who have rejected faith, it is the same for them whether you warn them or not; they shall not have faith.

7. God has set a seal upon their hearts and their hearing and upon their sight a covering; theirs shall be a great torment.

8. There are among men those who say, "We have faith in God and the last day," yet they are not men of faith.

9. They seek to deceive God and those who have faith; they deceive only themselves and do not perceive.

10. There is a sickness in their hearts, and God has increased their sickness. A painful torment awaits them for all the lies which they have perpetrated.

11. When they are told, "Do not spread corruption in the earth," they say, "Surely we are ones who put things right."

12. They are the corrupters, yet they do not perceive.

13. When they are told, "Have faith as others have faith," they say, "Shall we have faith, as the foolish have faith?" Indeed they are the foolish ones, yet they do not know.

14. When they meet those who have faith, they say, "We too have faith," but when they are alone with their satans, they say, "We are surely with you, we were only mocking."

(14) Tabari relates on the authority of Ibn 'Abbas, "'Their satans' in this verse refers to the Jews who used to incite the Hypocrites to reject the message of Muhammad. According to some of the Companions, 'their satans' were the chiefs of the Hypocrites and their accomplices in wickedness and rejection of faith" (Tabari, I, p. 297; see also Ibn Kathir, I, pp. 89–90).

15. God shall mock at them and increase them in their insolence, so that they wander blindly.

16. They are those who have exchanged guidance for error, yet neither did their bargain profit them, nor were they guided aright.

17. They are like one who kindled a fire so that it illuminated the place around him; then God took away their light and left them in darkness, unable to see.
(See commentary for verse 26, below.)

18. They are deaf, mute, and blind; they will not heed and turn back.

19. Or like a raincloud from heaven with darkness, thunder and lightning; they stop their ears with their fingers for fear of death by lightning. God encompasses the rejecters of faith.

20. The lightning all but snatches away their sight. Whenever it gives them light, they walk therein, but whenever it darkens, they stand still. Had God so willed, He would have taken away their hearing and sight; surely God has power over all things.

21. O humankind, worship your Lord who created you and those before you, that perhaps you may fear God,

22. Who spread the earth for your repose and raised the heaven for shelter, who sent down water from heaven by which He brought forth different kinds of fruits for your sustenance. Do not, therefore, set up equals with God, while you know better.

23. If you are in doubt concerning that which we have sent down to our servant, then produce one *surah* like it and call upon your witnesses other than God, if you are truthful.

24. But if you are unable to do so—and you shall never be able—then heed the fire whose fuel shall be human beings and brimstone, prepared for the rejecters of faith.

(23) This verse is the first to offer the challenge to the Arabs of the Prophet's time to produce the like of the Qur'an. The Qur'an is here presented as a miracle (*mu'jizah*) in proof of the truth of Muhammad's claim to be the Apostle of God. The same challenge is presented in the Qur'an at different points of the Prophet's career (see Q. 10: 37–38; 28:49; 17:88; 11:13). All these verses belong to the Meccan period. Verse 23 is the first to repeat this challenge in Medina.

Tabari argues that verses 23 and 24 are addressed to the associators and Hypocrites of Mecca as well as the rejecters of faith of the people of the two books, that is, Jews and Christians. In this verse, Tabari argues further, God challenges those who contend that Muhammad was the author of the Qur'an to produce a *surah* like it. Commentators have, however, differed as to what the words "like it" refer to. Tabari reports on the authority of Qatadah that "the phrase 'produce one *surah* like it' means a *surah* like this Qur'an." The same view is reported on the authority of Mujahid. Others understood the words "like it" to refer to Muhammad (this reading is possible because of the absence of neuter in Arabic; both Muhammad and the Qur'an are represented by masculine pronouns), that is "produce a *surah* by a man from among you like Muhammad." This opinion is based on the assertion that there is nothing that would rival or match the Qur'an either in form or content, even though Muhammad was, according to tradition, an unlettered man and could not have produced such a literary marvel. Tabari argues at length, however, in favor of the first view because even though the Qur'an is indeed a peerless miracle, it nonetheless is composed of words that resemble the speech of the Arabs here challenged. Otherwise the challenge would be meaningless because it would be directed at a people who could in no way take it up (see Tabari, I, p. 372–376).

The words "and call upon your witnesses other than God, if you are truthful" mean, according to Ibn 'Abbas and many others, "call on your allies for help." Tabari likewise argues in favor of this interpretation (Tabari, I, pp. 376–378). Ibn Kathir gives three possible interpretations of this phrase. The first is the same view as reported by Tabari from Ibn 'Abbas. According to al-Suddi, the phrase means "call on other people as collaborators" that is, "seek the help of your gods in this matter so that they may assist and support you." According to Mujahid, "witnesses" here refers to experts on rhetoric and eloquence to witness and judge. Ibn Kathir argues for the possibility of all three views together (see Ibn Kathir, I, pp. 103–106; see also Qurtubi, I, pp. 231–232).

Zamakhshari adopts a rational approach to this verse. He argues first that the people here challenged were extremely foolish in that they took their idols to be equals with God (see the previous verse) even though they claimed to be people of discernment and eloquence. Zamakhshari continues, "Thus God has contended against them (in the previous verse) with arguments nullifying *shirk* [association of other things with God] and completely destroying it. God then followed this by an argument establishing the prophethood of Muhammad and the miraculous nature of the Qur'an." Zamakhshari then argues that God here mentions *tanzil* rather than *inzal* (sending down all at once) because "what is intended here is sending down in a gradual way [*tanzil*], that is, in separate portions, which is an even greater challenge. For the Arabs said, 'Had this been from God, it would not have been sent down in separate *surahs* and verses following one another . . . and relating to different circumstances.' They argued therefore in this way that the Qur'an resembles the collections of poems which poets compose as they are moved by mood or circumstance. Had the Qur'an been truly from God, they said, He would have sent it down all at once." Zamakhshari replies that God here challenged them to produce at least one portion like the Qur'an, be it large or small, a *surah* or several verses (Zamakhshari, I, pp. 238–239; see also Razi, II, pp. 114–120, in which he argues at great length for the miraculous nature [*i'jaz*] of the Qur'an compared with the poetry of pre-Islamic as well as Islamic poets. See also Nisaburi, I, pp. 201ff; Tabarsi, I, p. 131, agrees with Ibn Kathir; see Shawkani, I, p. 52, for a general discussion without arguing for any view over another).

(24) Commentators have read these two verses together because the second completes the challenge of the first and adds the threat of eternal punishment in the fires of Hell. Ibn Kathir sees in the phrase, "But if you are unable to do so—and you shall never be able," yet another proof of the miracle of the Qur'an: "This is because Muhammad foretold something without fear or hesitation. It is that this Qur'an will never be opposed by anything like it, for ever and ever. This has indeed been the case because it was not opposed from that time to ours. This is impossible for anyone to do; for how could it be when the Qur'an is the word of God who is the Creator of all things" (Ibn Kathir, I, p. 105). This in general is the interpretation which most commentators have adopted. The main question that will concern us in this verse, however, and which the verse has raised for commentators, is: What kind of stones are here intended and what might be their purpose?

Tabari first asks, "Why were stones specifically mentioned together with humans as fuel for the fires of Hell?" He answers, "It has been said that these shall be sulphur stones which become the hottest stones when heated." Tabari then reports from Ibn Mas'ud, "These are stones of sulphur which God created when He created the heavens and the earth and placed them prepared for the rejecters of faith in the heaven of this world." In another tradition also from Ibn Mas'ud and other Companions we are told, "They are stones of black sulphur which shall be added to the torment of the rejecters of faith in the Fire" (Tabari, I, pp. 380–382).

Ibn Kathir first reports traditions which, like those of Tabari, assert that they shall be sulphur stone, but exceedingly foul. He reports this view on the authority of Muhammad al-Baqir, the fifth Shi'i imam, as well. Still another view is that these shall be the stone idols which the rejecters of faith made equals with God. Ibn Kathir cites, in support of this interpretation, the verse, "Surely both you and what you worship instead of God shall be fuel for Hell" (Q. 21:98; Ibn Kathir, I, pp. 106–107).

With regard to sulphur stones, Qurtubi lists five aspects of torture which they would add to that of the fire. These are "the swiftness of burning, filthiness of odor, density of smoke, adhesion to the body, and the intense heat they emit when heated." Qurtubi argues that the text does not imply that only men and stones shall be in the Fire because other verses indicate that *jinn* and satans shall also abide in it. Qurtubi then presents the view which asserts that the stones here referred to mean the idols, as in other commentaries. He, however, shows no preference for any one view (Qurtubi, I, p. 135).

Zamakhshari contends that from the argument of the previous verse it must be assumed that the people knew the truth of Muhammad's claim—hence they deserved the fire because of their perverse stubbornness. (This theory is consonant with the Mu'tazili view that men are responsible for their actions and are rewarded or punished accordingly.) Thus the cautionary phrase, "heed the fire" means "cease your stubbornness." Zamakhshari asserts that the fire here mentioned is distinguished from other fires in that it would not blaze except with human beings and stones as fuel. There are, he speculates, different fires in Hell, each designed especially for its inhabitants (Zamakhshari, I, pp. 151–152; see also Razi, II, pp. 121–122; and Nisaburi, I, pp. 205–209).

Ibn 'Arabi treats these two verses together, as do other commentators. He takes the Qur'an and the Prophet to be manifestations of the supernatural realm of the Divine. As for the challenge establishing the *i'jaz* of the Qur'an, Ibn 'Arabi essentially repeats the ideas of earlier commentators but in a Sufi context. Thus he counsels the stubborn men who reject the prophethood of Muhammad and his divine revelation to admit their impotence and accept faith. Otherwise their stubbornness would surely lead them to the Fire. Ibn 'Arabi defines the Fire as "their being consumed in the raging tumult of their own souls and the burning ashes of their natures which are turned away from the spirit of sanctity and the cool breezes of the [breath] of the All-merciful, of their natures which are deprived of the pleasant coolness of certainty and the safety of the abode of repose. It is their souls which are occupied with familiar sense and corporeal pleasures, their souls which are separated from the divine realm but which are still possessed by longing for it. . . . This is because of the firm establishment of the lower forms in them and their love for earthly bodies, which belong to these forms. It is this love which is the cause of the soul's blazing fires. For this reason God says, 'Its fuel shall be men and stones.' Stones are earthly forms or idols to which they are attached in love. Thus these forms become firmly established in their hearts. Their souls become prisoners of their attachment, as the Apostle of God said, 'Every man shall be brought together [on the day of resurrection] with what he loves. If a man loves a stone, he shall be gathered together with it'" (Ibn 'Arabi, I, p. 30).

25. Give good tidings to those who have faith and perform good deeds, that for them are prepared gardens beneath which rivers flow. Whenever they shall be given a fruit thereof for sustenance, they will exclaim, "We have been given this before!" for they shall be given similar fruits always. There they shall have pure spouses and there shall they dwell eternally.

26. God does not disdain to strike the similitude of a gnat or even of that which is more despicable. As for those who have faith, they know it is the truth from their Lord, but those who have rejected faith say, "What did God intend by such similitude?" He leads many astray thereby and guides many, but He leads none astray save the transgressors.

27. Those who break the covenant of God after being bound by it sever that which God commanded to be joined and spread corruption in the earth: these are truly the losers.

28. How could you not have faith in God, who gave you life after you were dead and who shall cause you to die, then bring you back again to life; then to Him shall you be returned.

29. It is He who created for you all that is in the earth, then turned to heaven and formed it into seven heavens. He is the knower of all things.

(26) Tabari says, "When God struck the two previous similitudes [see verses 17 and 18] the Hypocrites said, 'God is more exalted than to strike such similitudes.' Thus God revealed this verse" (Tabari, I, p. 398). It is also related on the authority of al-Rabi' ibn Anas, "This is a parable which God made of the life of this world, for as the gnat thrives when it is hungry and dies when it becomes fat, so it is with these people for whom this similitude was struck by God in the Qur'an. When they become full of the goods of this world, God's punishment overtakes them" (Tabari, I, pp. 398–399; see also Ibn Kathir, I, pp. 111–112).

(27) "The covenant ['ahd] is either the primordial covenant between God and humanity [mithaq], [Q. 7:172], the measure of the knowledge of God which He has implanted in the minds of human beings as proof against them [if they reject faith in spite of this native knowledge] or the reference may be to the Jews and Christians with whom the Prophet came into contact" (Ibn Kathir, I, pp. 114–115). "That 'which God commanded to be joined' means honoring the obligations of blood relationship or any relationship in general" (Ibn Kathir, I, p. 116).

(28) The issue for commentators in this verse is the two lives and the two deaths which the verse stipulates for humankind. This idea is more clearly enunciated in Q. 40:11. Tabari says, "They were dead in the loins of their fathers, then God created them and granted them life. Then He caused them to die the death from which there is no escape; then will He revive them on the day of resurrection" (Tabari, I, p. 420). Ibn Kathir cites al-Dahhak as relating on the authority of Ibn 'Abbas, in interpretation of Q. 40:11, "You were dust before He created you: this is one death. Then He gave you life by creating you: this is one life. Then will He cause you to die and return to the tomb: this is another death. Then will He raise you up on the day of resurrection: this is another life. Thus there are two lives and two deaths" (Ibn Kathir, I, pp. 116–117).

(29) The manner of God's creating the heavens and the earth has been variously related in the Qur'an (see, for example, Q. 41:9 and 12). I shall return to this question later. The question that concerns us with the verse at hand is God's "rising" (*istiwa*') to the heavens. Tabari states that the word *istawa'* (turned to) means ascended to heaven, in the sense of the ascension of dominion and authority rather than of movement (Tabari, I, p. 430). Qurtubi reports, "Some said, 'We recite it, assent to it, and do not interpret it.' Thus Malik ibn Anas said, 'Ascension [*istiwa*'] is not unknown, but the how of it is beyond comprehension; to assent to it, nevertheless, is obligatory and enquiry into it is an innovation [*bid'ah*].' Others said, 'We recite it and interpret it in accordance with the literal meaning of the words in the Arabic language.' Still others said, 'We recite and interpret it and consider its interpretation in accordance with its literal meaning'" (Qurtubi, I, p. 254). Qurtubi further observes that the word "then" (*thumma*) in the phrase "then turned to heaven" does not signify a time sequence between creation and turning to heaven but only relates what in reality is an instantaneous event based on divine command (Qurtubi, I, p. 254; see also Ibn Kathir, I, pp. 117–120). He concludes that the principle that must be followed in interpreting this phrase and others like it is the non-attribution of movement to God (Qurtubi, I, p. 255).

Zamakhshari clearly declares God to be beyond time and movement. After discussing the linguistic usage of *istiwa'*, he continues, "'Then *istawa'* to heaven' means He turned toward it with His will after creating what is in the earth, without willing to create anything between the two actions." Zamakhshari then argues, "If you say our interpretation of *istawa* is contradicted by the word *thumma* [then], which gives a sense of the lapse of time, I answer that the word 'then' here signifies the difference between the two creations and the excellence of the creating of the heavens over that of the earth, and not a lapse of time" (Zamakhshari, I, p. 271; for a comprehensive discussion of rational views, see Tabarsi, I, pp. 156–158).

30. Remember when your Lord said to the angels, "Behold, I am about to place a vicegerent in the earth," they said, "Would You place therein one who will spread corruption and shed blood, while we proclaim Your praise and sanctify You?" He said, "I know what you do not know."

31. And He taught Adam all the names; then He displayed them before the angels, saying, "Inform me of the names of these if you speak the truth."

32. They answered, "Glory be to You! We have no knowledge, save what You have taught us. Surely You are all-knowing, all-wise."

33. He said, "O Adam, inform them of their names," and when he had informed them of their names, He said, "Did I not tell you that I know what is concealed in the heavens and the earth, and I know what you disclose and what you hide!"

34. And remember when we said to the angels, "Prostrate yourselves before Adam," they all prostrated themselves except Iblis, who refused, was puffed up with pride and was among the rejecters of faith.

35. We said, "O Adam, dwell you and your spouse in the garden. Eat of its fruits abundantly wherever you wish, but do not approach this tree, for then you would be among the wrongdoers."

36. But Satan caused them to slip from the garden and drove them out of the state they were in. Then we said, "Come down [from the garden]; you are enemies one to the other. You shall have a place of repose and comfort in the earth for a time."

37. Then Adam received certain words from his Lord, and He turned toward him, for He is truly relenting, compassionate.

38. We said, "Come down all of you from it [the garden]! Yet guidance from me will surely come to you, and whosoever follows my guidance, no fear will come upon them, nor shall they grieve."

39. Those who have rejected faith and given the lie to our signs: they are the people of the Fire, to dwell therein eternally.

The story of Adam (30–38) is told in earlier *surahs* belonging to the later Meccan period. His creation, the obeisance of the angels to him, his dwelling in the garden and subsequent expulsion are all told in some detail. These verses may be seen as a commentary on an already well-known story, because they raise new issues and because they are placed before other and more explicit verses. These nine verses have raised many questions and controversies: Why did God tell the angels of His plan to establish a representative for Himself on the earth? How did the angels know that Adam's progeny would act wickedly? How could they question the will and wisdom of God? How was this vicegerent of God created and why did he so soon disobey God's command against eating the forbidden fruit? What sort of fruit did the forbidden tree bear? Who was Satan and how was he able to enter the garden in order to lead the innocent Adam and his spouse astray? Adam's stay in Paradise, the creation of a mate for him, and their sin and expulsion are but briefly mentioned in the Qur'an. The Qur'an leaves many other questions unanswered. It does not, for example, mention Eve by name, or the manner in which she was created. For the answers to these and other questions, commentators had to resort to the People of the Book. Shi'i commentators deal with these nine verses in a continuous narrative. For this reason I have not integrated their views in my selection of individual verses but instead present them together after Ibn 'Arabi. Likewise, commentators have not been interested in details but rather in a general appreciation of the story of Adam and its significance for human religious history. Citations from these will conclude this discussion of the Adam narrative.

(30) Tabari relates, "Ibn Ishaq said, 'Behold, I am about to place a vicegerent in the earth' means a dweller and builder who will build up the earth and inhabit it; a representative not of you [the angels]'" (Tabari, I, p. 449). Tabari supports the view that *khalifah* means a substitute and successor (Tabari, I, p. 449). Further, Ibn 'Abbas is reported to have said, "The first to inhabit the earth were the *jinn*, but they spread corruption in it, shed blood, and killed one another. Then God sent against them Iblis [Satan] with a great army of angels. Iblis and his army defeated the *jinn* and drove them into the furthest islands of the sea and the highest peaks of the

mountains. Then God created Adam and made him to dwell in the earth; hence His saying to the angels, 'Behold, I am about to place. . . .'" Al-Rabi' ibn Anas said, "God created the angels on Wednesday, the *jinn* on Thursday, and Adam on Friday. A group of *jinn* rejected faith. The angels used to come down to fight against them; hence the shedding of blood and corruption in the earth came about" (Tabari, I, pp. 450–451).

The following dialogue between God and the angels is reported on the authority of Ibn 'Abbas, Ibn Mas'ud, and others of the Prophet's companions. "God said to the angels, 'Behold, I am about to place a vicegerent in the earth.' They said, 'Our Lord, who shall this vicegerent be?' He answered, 'He shall have progeny who will spread corruption in the earth. They shall envy and kill one another!' " Tabari comments: "Thus the *khalifah* . . . is my vicegerent who shall represent me in judging among my creatures. That representative was Adam and whoever [of his descendants] occupies his place in obedience to God, judging justly among His creatures. As for the shedding of blood and corruption, they were not committed by the representatives of God such as Adam and those who follow his example of obedience and true worship. This is because the angels did not attribute the shedding of blood and corruption to the vicegerent of God Himself, but rather said, 'Would you place therein one who will spread corruption?'" God had informed them of this; hence their question (Tabari, I, pp. 452–453).

Tabari then raises the question, "Did the angels know that which is hidden with God, or did they speak in conjecture [*zann*], which would be against their nature?" In answer, Tabari cites the following explanation on the authority of Ibn 'Abbas: "Iblis was one of a group of angels called *al-hinn*. They were created of fire [*samum*], [Q. 15:27]. Iblis was called al-Harith, and he was one of the guardians of Paradise. The rest of the angels were created of light. . . . The *jinn* were created of smokeless fire . . . and man of potter's clay [Q. 55: 14–15]. The *jinn*, moreover, were the first to inhabit the earth, and they spread corruption in it, shed blood, and killed one another. After Iblis had defeated them in battle he was filled with secret conceit. He said to himself, 'I have done something which no one else is able to do.' God knew that which was in his heart, but the angels who were with him did not. Thus God said to the angels, 'Behold, I am about to place . . .'" (Tabari, I, p. 455). According to this view, God spoke not to all the angels but only to those who were with Iblis. These were, as we have seen, quasi-angels. According to another tradition related on the authority of Ibn 'Abbas, Ibn Mas'ud, and others of the Prophet's companions, "When God had completed the creation of all He wished, He gave Iblis dominion over the heaven of this world. He was one of a multitude of angels called the *jinn*. They were so called because they were among the guardians of Paradise [*jannah*]. Pride then entered his heart and he thought, 'Surely God did not grant me all this except for a virtue which I possess over all the other angels.' God knew that, and therefore said, 'I know what you do not know.' This referred to Iblis and not to Adam" (Tabari, I, pp. 458–459).

It may be argued that the purpose of the entire drama of creation was for God to manifest His knowledge and power and to expose the pride of Iblis. This is clearly shown in the creation of man. According to Tabari, God sent Gabriel, then Michael, to fetch clay, but the earth said, "I take refuge in God from you, if you have come to diminish and deform me." The angels returned empty-handed; then God sent the angel of death, who took dust from all the regions of the earth—hence the variety among the children of Adam. He took the dust up to heaven and soaked it until it became mud, which was left to stink. Thus God says, "from formed mud" (Q. 15:28). Then God said to the angels, "Behold, I am about to create a human being out of clay. When I will have shaped him and breathed into him of my spirit, you shall fall prostrate before him" (Q. 38:71–72). God formed Adam with His own two hands (Q. 38:75) in order that Iblis would not be proud (Tabari, I, p. 459). Tabari continues, "Adam remained on the ground a dry body for forty years. The angels used to pass by him and be frightened when they saw him, but Iblis was more frightened than all of them. He would strike the body and it would make a sound like the ringing of a clay pot. Then Iblis would enter Adam's mouth, come out from his anus, and say to the angels, 'Do not be afraid of this, for your Lord is solid [*samad*] but this body is hollow. If I shall be given authority over him, I will surely destroy him'" (Tabari, I, pp. 459–460).

Tabari relates in an earlier tradition from Ibn 'Abbas, cited above, that "God then breathed into Adam the spirit of life, beginning with the top of his head. As the spirit penetrated his body, bones and flesh grew. When it reached his navel, Adam looked at his body and was pleased with it. He tried to stand up, but could not. When the spirit had completely permeated his body, he sneezed and said, 'All praise be to God, the Lord of all beings.' God answered, 'May God have mercy upon you, O Adam'" (Tabari, I, p. 456). (The purpose of this story is no doubt to explain the widespread tradition in the Muslim world of exchanging these words when someone sneezes.) Tabari relates that "God ordered the angels who were with Iblis, excluding the rest of the angels who were in the heavens, 'Prostrate yourselves before Adam' . . . but He did not command the rest of the angels. They all prostrated themselves save Iblis . . . who refused and was puffed up with pride. He said, 'I will not bow before him since I am better than he, of greater age and of stronger constitution. You created me of fire, but him of clay.' Thus he refused and God made him to despair [ablasahu] of all good." (For the use of this verb in the Qur'an, see Q. 6:24; Tabari, I, p. 456).

Qurtubi, the jurist, explains the term khalifah as referring to Adam, "for he is the vicegerent of God, executing His judgments and commands, because he was the first messenger to earth." In a hadith related on the authority of Abu Dharr, he said, "I asked, 'O Apostle of God, was Adam a prophet sent by God?'" The Prophet answered, "Yes . . . he was an apostle to his children, who were forty, each two being twins, male and female . . . '[for] it is He who created you from one soul, and from it created its mate, and from them scattered many men and women." (Q. 4:1) "God revealed to them the prohibition of eating dead animals, blood, and flesh of swine. He lived 930 years; thus have the people of the Torah reported" (Qurtubi, I, pp. 263–264).

Zamakhshari offers a somewhat different interpretation, which typifies the rationalistic approach. "Would you place therein" is an exclamation of wonderment by the angels regarding the command of God of creating creatures who would not be immune from error, for only angels possess this characteristic. "Their wonderment concerned the fact that God would substitute for the people of obedience people of rebellion, yet He is the Wise Creator who does nothing but the good and wills nothing but the good" (Zamakhshari, I, p. 271).

Ibn Kathir sees in God's declaration to the angels, "Behold, I am about to place a vicegerent in the earth" an indication of the special favor of man with God. "God tells in this verse of His favor toward the children of Adam by mentioning them in the highest company before creating them" (Ibn Kathir, I, p. 120). Ibn Kathir argues that the word khalifah here refers not only to Adam but also to his progeny. This argument is based on the angels' protest, "Would You place therein one who spread corruption and shed blood?" He argues further, "By saying this the angels did not intend to contradict God, nor did they intend to show envy toward the progeny of Adam as some commentators may wrongly assume. God says concerning the angels, 'They do not precede Him in speech' [Q. 21:27]. This means that they are unable to ask Him anything except what He permits them to ask" (Ibn Kathir, I, p. 121; see also p. 122).

Razi, the philosopher-theologian, constructs arguments and counterarguments in a series of questions and answers. He argues, "Either Adam was the vicegerent, and hence corruption would refer to his progeny, or his descendants are the vicegerents. That Adam succeeded the *jinn*, who were before him, is possible and is supported by God's saying, 'We have made you a vicegerent in the earth, so judge aright among men' [Q. 38:26]. The view that his descendants are meant by the verse as vicegerents succeeding one another may also be supported by God's saying, 'For it is He who made you vicegerents of the earth succeeding one another' [Q. 6:165]. Thus His saying, 'Behold, I am about to place a vicegerent on the earth' was either that the angels should ask Him and hear the answer, 'I know what you do not know,' or in order to teach men the virtue of consultation" (Razi, II, pp. 165–166).

Razi then argues at length whether the angels were guilty of questioning God's will, or whether they said what they said through divine inspiration. In a series of answers to several arguments asserting or denying a variety of classical views on the subject, Razi offers several interpretations of the verse. "The purpose of the question was not to doubt God's wisdom, but to marvel at the perfection of His wisdom and its encompassing of all things. They asked simply to have an answer, since they denied the attribution of foolishness to God. The Mu'tazilah, who are the proponents of this view, said, 'This proves that the angels did not allow that evil could come from God.' They attributed corruption and the shedding of blood to the creature, not the Creator." (Razi, II, p. 168). Another possibility advanced by Razi is that the angels could have known that man would be corrupt either through inference (from the case of the *jinn*) or through inspiration. Neither of these would be considered insulting to humankind or an act of rebellion on the part of the angels (Razi, II, p. 169).

Razi also relates on the authority of Ibn Zayd, "When God created Hell, the angels became exceedingly afraid. They said, 'O our Lord, for whom did You create this fire?' God answered, 'For whoever of my creatures rebels against me.' At that time, there were no creatures of God except the angels, and no creatures in the earth. Thus God said, 'Behold, I am about to place a vicegerent in the earth . . .' in order that they would know that corruption would come from humans." The final possibility which Razi considers is that the angels could have known the divine secret through having seen the Well-Guarded Tablet of destiny (Razi, II, p. 170).

Razi's philosophical approach, as well as the interpretive exoteric approach of the commentators so far considered, may be contrasted with the esoteric approach of the Sufis. According to Nisaburi, "God did not say 'I am about to create,' but 'I am about to place [or make]' . . . because vicegerency belongs to the world of *amr* [divine creative command] and not to the world of *khalq* [creation] . . . for man is God's vicegerent over all things: earthly and heavenly, spiritual and corporeal beings. None of these can be vicegerents over him, because none of them possesses all the qualities which he possesses. The world has no other lamp illumined by the fire of the light of God, manifesting the lights of His attributes as His representative, except the lamp of man. This is because he is given the lamp of the innermost faculty [*sirr*] in the glass of the heart, 'the glass being in the niche' of the body. In the glass of the heart is the oil of the spirit; 'its oil would almost shine forth' with the purity of the intellect, 'though no fire touched it' [see Q. 24:35]. The light of the innermost faculty [*sirr*] is lit by the wick of the divine mystery. Thus, when man's lamp is so illumined with the fire of the light of God, he becomes God's vicegerent in His earth, manifesting the lights of His attributes in this world through justice ['*adl*], well-doing [*ihsan*], compassion [*ra'fah*], mercy [*rahmah*], kindliness [*lutf*], and domination [*qahr*]. These attributes, moreover, are manifested in neither animal nor angelic beings" (Nisaburi, I, p. 231).

Ibn 'Arabi carries further the esoteric approach of Nisaburi and uses the verse to expound an impressive cosmological system. He takes the word "Lord" in verse 30 to refer to "the eternal Being [*sarmad*] who is from beginningless eternity [*azal*] to eternity [*abad*]." God's saying the word "said" is communicating the meaning or sense of His will to bring Adam into existence (that is, He does not act or speak). This sense was communicated to the sacred beings who belong to the realm of power (*jabarut*), who are the angels brought near to God. They are also the spirits belonging to the realm of dominion (*malakut*) which are the heavenly souls. "This is because whatever takes place in the actual world has an ideal primordial form in the world of spirit. It is the world of the first world [*al-fada' al-sabiq*]. This ideal form exists also in the realm of the heart [*'alam al-qalb*] which is called the Preserved Tablet. It also exists in the world of the soul which is the tablet of effacement and confirmation, referred to in the revealed Qur'an as the heaven of this world, as God says, 'There is nothing but that We possess its treasures, nor do We send it down except in prescribed measure'" (Q. 15:21).

Ibn 'Arabi then returns to the Quranic text to assert that "God did not say, 'I am about to create' because making is more general than origination [*ibda'*] and bringing into being [*takwin*]. This is because man is composed of the two realms." Ibn 'Arabi then offers the following (with God as the speaker): "Man is My vicegerent forming his character according to My character, and is known by My characteristics. He executes My command and rules over My creatures—managing their affairs, organizing their government, and calling them to obedience to Me."

Ibn 'Arabi accepts the view that the angels protested the creation of man and asserted their superiority over him. But they did so not because they were imperfect beings; rather, "it was their being veiled from the manifestation of the meaning of divinity [*ilahiyah*] and the divine characteristics which are in man. These belong to the societal form of the human community and the structure combining the two worlds and possessing all that is in the two realms [that is, the spiritual and temporal realms]. They knew the crude and beastly actions which denote the spreading of corruption in the earth and shedding of blood, actions which belong to the potentiality of lust and anger. They knew also that these actions are necessary for the attachment of the spirit to the body. They knew further their own freedom from such actions because of the sanctity of their souls. This is because every class of angels can see that which is below . . . but cannot see that which is above it. The angels knew that it was inevitable in the process of the attachment of the luminous spirit of the higher realm to the mundane body that a kind of harmony with the body on the one hand, and the human spirit on the other, must exist. This is the carnal soul which is the abode of every evil and source of every corruption. The angels did not know however that humanity attracts the divine light, for this is a mystery" (Ibn 'Arabi, I, pp. 35–37).

(31–33) The names which God taught Adam have been the subject of much speculation. According to some commentators, God taught Adam the names of things animate and inanimate. Other commentators asserted that God taught Adam the names of the angels, and still others that he taught him the names of all his descendants until the day of resurrection. Tabari, after reviewing various opinions, argues, "The closest of these assertions to the truth and nearest to the literal meaning of the recited text is the assertion of those who say that these were the names of his descendants and those of the angels, but not the names of the rest of the species of creation." This is because, he argues, in the Arabic language the masculine pronominal suffix *hum* indicates human beings and angels, while the feminine endings of *ha* or *hunna* refer to other things (Tabari, I, p. 485; see also pp. 482–486). Disagreeing with this view, Ibn Kathir argues, "This is unnecessary because there is no reason for other things not to be included with them. The reference to rational beings is only on account of their prominence." He argues further that God taught Adam the names of all things and essences. It was, moreover, on the basis of this great favor that God commanded the angels to prostrate themselves before Adam. Thus, according to Ibn Kathir, Adam was taught the names of all things before the angels were commanded to bow down (Ibn Kathir, I, pp. 126–130; see also Zamakhshari, I, pp. 272–273; and Shawkani, I, pp. 64–65).

Nisaburi relates that according to some commentators, languages are necessary (that is, for the life of society) and thus God taught Adam all languages. Mu'tazili thinkers, however, argued, "Languages were invented by human beings; therefore what is intended is that God inspired Adam and created in him the capacity to invent languages. It is also possible that He taught him all the expressions of peoples who were before him. It may also be that He taught him the attributes of things, their descriptions, peculiarities, and religious and worldly uses" (Nisaburi, I, pp. 238–239; for an elaboration of this and other similar views, see Razi, II, pp. 175–208).

Commentators are generally agreed that God displayed before the doubting angels the essences of the things named with the challenge, "Inform me of the names of these if you speak the truth." Tabari paraphrases the divine challenge thus: "Inform me of the names of those which I have displayed before you, O angels who say, 'Would you place therein one other than us who would spread corruption in the earth and shed blood, while we glorify and sanctify you?' Inform me then of the names of these if you are truthful in your claim that if I place my vicegerent on the earth from another creation, his descendants would spread corruption in it and shed blood" (Tabari, I, pp. 490–491). As the angels admit their impotence before the divine majesty, they receive the divine reproach: "Did I not tell you that I know what is concealed in the heavens and the earth, and I know what you disclose and what you hide!" What they disclosed, according to Tabari, was their saying, "Would you place therein," and "what they concealed" refers to the pride and self-conceit which Iblis concealed in his heart (Tabari, I, p. 498; see also Shawkani, I, pp. 64–65).

Ibn 'Arabi interprets God's teaching Adam all the names as "injecting into his heart the characteristics of things by which they are known, including their benefit and harm." "Then He displayed them" means that "He displayed the named things to the angels through their witnessing of the human constitution and their accompanying him in the process of divine revelation." The reason for the divine challenge to the angels, "Inform me of the names of these if you speak the truth," was, according to Ibn 'Arabi, "to revive them with human knowledge, which comes from the communal structure of human society and the specific qualities which human beings possess. Because the knowledge of the angels is below that of Adam, God commanded him to inform them."

Ibn 'Arabi interprets the words of the angels, "Glory be to You! We have no knowledge, save what You have taught us," to mean "their own testimony of their inadequacy with regard to human perfections and their inability to attain to them. The angel's words also signify the exaltation of God over all actions that may contain corruption or imperfection. By these means the angels knew that their own attainment of higher stations comes from the acquisition of knowledge . . . and that God's knowledge is above their knowledge. For He is the All-knowing who does only that which needs to be done. For this reason He said, 'O Adam, inform them,' and not 'O Adam, instruct them.' This is because acquired knowledge necessitating higher attainments belongs especially to the human community." Finally, Ibn 'Arabi sees in God's retort, "Did I not tell you that I know what is concealed in the heavens and the earth, and I know what you disclose and what you hide!" an allusion to the "mystery which is the manifestation of knowledge and love which God deposited in man—a mystery which He had safeguarded in His knowledge [from the angels]." Ibn 'Arabi goes on to assert that God's saying, "I know what you disclose," means, "of your knowledge of man's acts of corruption," and "what you hide" means "your claiming superiority for your essences over him because of their purity and sanctity" (Ibn 'Arabi, I, p. 38).

Verse 34, narrating the prostration of the angels before Adam, will not be discussed at this point. Commentators are interested in this verse for identifying Iblis and his function. Since this point has been discussed in some detail, the significance of the angels' obeisance to Adam will be dealt with in another context (see Q. 15:30 and 38:72 and 73).

(35) Tabari preserves a wealth of *tafsir* tradition going back to the earliest authorities on this science. He relates on the authority of Ibn 'Abbas, Ibn Mas'ud, and others of the Prophet's Companions that "Adam was lonely in Paradise, having no mate to keep him company. He went to sleep and when he awoke he found a woman beside him whom God had created from his rib. He addressed her, saying, 'Who are you?' 'I am a woman,' she replied. 'Why were you created?' Adam asked. 'So that you may have companionship,' she said" (Tabari, I, p. 513). There are traditions going back to the early authorities of *tafsir* such as Ibn 'Abbas asserting that God created Eve from Adam's rib, which he took from his left side. This information they claimed to have transmitted from the People of the Book, and more specifically the Jews. They differed, however, as to whether she was created before or after Adam was made to dwell in Paradise. Tabari also relates, concerning the name of Adam's spouse, "The angels, wishing to test Adam's knowledge, asked, 'What is her name, O Adam?' He answered, 'It is Hawa' [Eve]. They said, 'Why did you call her Hawa?' and he answered, 'Because she was created of a living thing'" (Tabari, I, pp. 513–514).

Commentators have widely differed concerning the tree whose fruit Adam and his wife ate. According to a tradition related on the authority of Ibn 'Abbas, it was an ear of wheat, for whatever rises above the ground on a stock may be called a tree, in contrast to plants that grow close to the ground with no stock, such as grass (see Q. 54:6). According to Wahb ibn Munabbih, "It was wheat, but every grain in Paradise is as big as the kidney of a cow. It was, moreover, softer than butter and sweeter than honey. The people of the Torah say it was wheat" (Tabari, I, p. 518). In yet another tradition related on the authority of Ibn 'Abbas and Ibn Mas'ud, it was the grapevine. Still others claimed that it was the fig tree. Tabari, however (and most major commentators after him agree), observes that "God did not provide for His servants who are addressed by the Qur'an any indication as to which of the trees of Paradise God forbade Adam to approach. It is therefore right to say that God forbade Adam and his wife to eat the fruit of one particular tree of all the trees of Paradise" (Tabari, I, pp. 519–521).

(36) Commentators found great scope for their imagination in the story of Adam's fall. In this as in many other biblical stories Jewish converts such as Wahb ibn Munabbih and their descendants provided the main impetus and framework for such hagiographical tales. Thus Tabari relates on the authority of Ibn Munabbih that the forbidden tree had many branches intertwined with one another. It bore fruit which the angels ate in order that they might live forever. Iblis, who was prevented by the angels guarding Paradise from entering it, hid himself in the mouth of the serpent, which was then a large beast with four legs. He took the fruit of the forbidden tree to Eve and said, "Look at this tree, how fragrant is its odor, delicious its fruit, and beautiful its color!" Thus she ate and gave Adam to eat. "Then they ate from it, and their shame appeared to them" (Q. 20:121). Adam then went into the hollow of a tree to hide from God, who called out to him, "Adam, where are you?" He answered, "Here I am, my Lord." God called out, "Will you not come out?" "I am ashamed before You, O my Lord," replied Adam. Then God said, "Cursed be the earth of which you are made. Its fruits shall turn into thorns." Then He said, "O Eve, it was you who deceived my servant; you shall therefore not bear a child except with pain, and when you are about to deliver that which is in your womb, you shall come near to death each time." To the serpent He said, "You are the one in whose mouth the accursed one entered in order to deceive my servants. Cursed are you, so that your legs shall disappear into your stomach and your food shall be nothing but dust. You shall be an enemy to the children of Adam and you shall bite his heel, but wherever he finds you, he shall crush your head" (Tabari, I, pp. 525–526).

Another tradition related on the authority of Ibn 'Abbas, Ibn Mas'ud, and others of the Prophet's Companions contains even greater embellishments and incorporates relevant Qur'anic verses. Here Iblis is made to talk to Adam from the mouth of the serpent, but Adam does not listen. Then he comes out and says, "Shall I lead you to the tree of life and a dominion which shall never perish?" (Q. 20:120). He swears to them that he is giving them good counsel (see Q. 7:21), yet in reality he only wanted to disclose their shame. Adam did not know that he was naked, but Iblis knew by reading about it in the books of the angels. When Eve ate, no harm came to them; they discovered their nakedness only when Adam ate, and they began to cover themselves with the leaves of the trees of the garden (see Q. 7:22; Tabari, I, p. 527).

Al-Rabi' ibn Anas, on the authority of Abu al-'Aliyah, said, "Satan entered the garden in the form of a large beast with four legs appearing like a camel. He was then cursed, his legs fell off and he was turned into a serpent" (Tabari, I, p. 528). According to another tradition which Tabari relates on the authority of 'Abd al-Rahman ibn Zayd, "Satan whispered to Eve concerning the tree until he brought her to it. Then he made her appear beautiful in the eyes of Adam, who called her to him. She answered, 'No, not until you come here.' When he came, she said, 'No, not until you eat of this tree.' God then cursed Eve, saying, 'I shall make her bleed every month, as she made this tree bleed. I shall make her foolish, whereas I created her wise. I shall make her bear children with hardship, and deliver with hardship, whereas I created her bearing children with ease and delivering with ease'" (Tabari, I, p. 529). Here again, Tabari prefers to stand by the literal sense of the Qur'anic text. Thus he argues on the basis of several verses (see, for example, 7:22 and 27) that Satan has authority to tempt humans in every situation. Yet, in the end, Satan's authority is limited by divine will and decree. It was therefore God and not Satan who expelled Adam and his wife from the garden. Commentators are in general agreement that God expelled Adam and Eve and Iblis at the same time from the garden, because the plural address, "Come down from the garden all of you," is used (see Q. 20:120 and 38:76; Tabari, I, pp. 535–536).

(37) Much disagreement has arisen among commentators regarding the words Adam received from his Lord. The Qur'an provides what may be regarded as an 'Adam prayer,' which most commentators accept as the words: "Our Lord, we have wronged ourselves, and if you do not forgive us and have mercy upon us, we shall surely be among the losers" (Q. 7:23). Some commentators put in the mouth of Adam long and elaborate prayers, and still others make of the words a theological argument between God and man. In one example of an extra-Qur'anic prayer, Adam is made to say, "O God, there is no God but You. Glory be to You and all praise. My Lord, I have wronged myself; forgive me therefore, for You are the best of forgivers" (Tabari, I, p.545). The following dialogue between God and Adam typifies well the theological debate concerning predestination in the early Muslim community: "O Lord, this sin which I have committed, is it something which you decreed for me before you created me, or is it something which I have invented of my

own accord?" God answered, "Rather, it is something which I decreed for you, before I created you." Adam said, "Then as you have decreed it for me, so do now forgive me my sin" (Tabari, I, p. 544).

In contrast with the hagiographical tales presented by other commentators, Ibn 'Arabi concentrates on the inner meanings and significances of the story of Adam and Eve. He identifies Adam's spouse as "the soul who was called Eve because of its attachment to the material body. Adam is the heart which is so called because of its attachment to the body, but without being affected by it. The garden in which Adam and Eve were to dwell is the heaven of the realm of the spirit, which is the garden of sanctity." The words "eat of it freely wherever you wish" mean, according to Ibn 'Arabi, "freely and pleasurably in receiving its meanings, gnoses, and wisdom which are food for the heart and fruits for the spirit." Ibn 'Arabi does not identify the forbidden tree (Ibn 'Arabi I, pp. 39–40).

With regard to the words Adam received from God, Ibn 'Arabi says that these were "lights and states [*ahwal*] or stations [*maqamat*] of the realm of dominion and power and the realm of the subtle [*mujarradah*] spirits. Every subtle being is a divine word because it belongs to the realm of command [*amr*], as Jesus is called 'Word.' It may also be that Adam received from God gnoses, sciences, and truths."

Ibn 'Arabi interprets the words, "and He turned toward him," as follows: "That is, He accepted Adam's turning [*tawbah*] to Him through freeing himself of the garments of material existence and joining himself to the multitudes of lights which belong to the realm of dominion, and through his acquiring the perfections of sanctity and manifestations of true knowledge." Ibn 'Arabi then asserts that God's turning toward Adam means that He caused Adam to turn toward Him. Ibn 'Arabi concludes, "Be my life! This is the accepted *tawbah* [repentance], not the act of turning of which Adam is the author." God's mercy toward Adam is, according to Ibn 'Arabi, that "He shows mercy to His servants even in His wrath. Thus He made His wrath toward Adam the cause of Adam's perfection and return to Him. He made Adam's distance from Him a cause of drawing near to Him" (Ibn 'Arabi, I, pp. 39–41).

The following are some of the earliest Shi'i traditions concerning Adam. It will be seen that they broadly resemble the classical traditions in Sunni *tafsir*. The main distinction of Shi'i tradition from that of Sunni Islam lies in the special exegesis (*ta'wil*) of the sacred text. For Shi'i tradition the primary aim of creation was for God to manifest His prophets and favored friends (*awliya'*), the imams, for whose sake the universe was created.

It is related on the authority of Ja'far al-Sadiq that "Iblis was with the angels in heaven, worshiping God, and the angels thought him to be one of them, but he was not one of them. Thus when God commanded the angels to prostrate themselves before Adam, God revealed the envy which Iblis kept in his heart. By this the angels knew that Iblis was not like them." Al-Sadiq was further asked, "How did the command include Iblis, when it was the angels who were commanded to prostrate themselves before Adam?" He answered, "Iblis was one of them only by association, or loyalty— he was not of the species of the angels. God created a species of creatures before Adam, among whom was Iblis, who rules over the earth. They spread corruption and shed blood, so that God sent the angels to fight against them. They captured Iblis and took him up to heaven. Thus he was with the angels, worshiping God, until God created Adam" (Qummi, I, pp. 35–36).

Qummi relates a tradition attributed to 'Ali, the first imam, in which the angels were filled with wonderment, sorrow, and anger at the state of corruption in which the inhabitants of the earth before Adam lived. They complained to God, begging Him to choose His vicegerent from among them. Then God answered, "I know what you do not know; I wish to create a creature with my own hand and make of his progeny prophets, messengers, faithful servants, and rightly guided imams. These I shall set up as my vicegerents over my creatures in my earth. They shall dissuade them from acts of rebellion, warn them against my punishment, guide them to obedience to me, and lead them to my way. I shall make them my proofs [*hujaj*] over them. I shall obliterate the *nasnas* [evil spirits inhabiting fabulous monkeylike creatures] from my earth and purify it of them. I shall remove the rebellious giants [*maradah*] of the *jinn* from among my chosen creatures and make them inhabit the atmosphere in the furthest corners of the earth. They shall not be neighbors to the progeny of my creature, Adam. I will set a veil between my creatures and the *jinn* so that they will not see the *jinn*, nor will they have any dealings with them. Yet those of my chosen creatures who will rebel against me shall I make to dwell with the rebellious ones and share in their destiny, nor do I care." Then God said, "Behold, I am about to make a human being from formed mud. When I have breathed into him of my spirit, fall prostrate before him" (Q. 38:71 and 72). God then scooped with His right hand of the sweet running waters (for both of His hands are right hands) and shook it in His palm until it congealed. Then He said to it, "From you will I make prophets, messengers, and my faithful servants, the rightly guided imams, those who will call people to Paradise, and their followers until the day of resurrection, nor do I care. Nor will I be questioned about what I do, but they [humankind] will be questioned" (Q. 21:23). God then scooped a handful of the salt waters, which He shook in His palm until it congealed and said to it, "From you will I create the haughty: pharoahs [a term used to designate the arrogant people of the Muslim community], the stiff-necked people, the brothers of satans, those who call men to the fire, and their partisans until the day of resurrection, nor do I care." Then He mixed the two waters in His palm, shook them, and placed them before His throne while they were yet a lump of clay. He then ordered the four angels of the four cardinal directions to trample the lump of clay. They thus polished it, refined it, and made it firm. Finally, they instilled in it the characteristics of love, anger, compassion, and other such qualities and humors. After that, God shaped Adam into a body and left him for forty years on the ground. When Iblis passed by him, he used to say, "No doubt you have been created for some purpose . . . but if God will command me to prostrate myself before this one, I shall surely disobey Him." Then God said to the angels, "Prostrate yourselves before Adam"; they did, but Iblis manifested envy in his heart and refused to prostrate himself. Thus God cursed Iblis and expelled him from Paradise until the day of judgment. Iblis, however, protested, "O Lord, how is it that the just reward of my deeds has been annulled?" God said, "Not so, but ask whatever you wish in this world, and I shall give it to you in reward for your deeds." The first thing he asked for was life until the day of judgment, and God said, "I shall grant you that." Then Iblis said, "Give me authority over the progeny of Adam." God answered, "I have given you authority." Iblis asked further, "Let me be as close to them as the blood which runs in their veins," and God granted him that as well. Then Iblis asked that he be able to see the children of Adam but that they should not be able to see him and that he be able to take any form he might wish before their eyes. After God had granted him all his requests, he said, "My Lord, grant me more!" God answered, "I shall make for you in their breasts a dwelling place." "I am now satisfied," said Iblis. Iblis then vowed to tempt humankind and lead them to perdition, except God's 'pure servants' (see Q. 38:83) over whom God did not grant him authority. Adam, however, protested Satan's power over his progeny, and God said, "Your one evil deed shall be counted as one, but your one good deed shall be counted as ten." "Give me more, O my Lord," said Adam. God answered, "I shall freely accept your repentance until your soul reaches your throat. I shall freely forgive, nor will I care" (Qummi, I, pp. 36–42).

Qummi relates further that "al-Sadiq was asked, 'Was the garden of Adam one of the gardens of the world, or was it one of the gardens of the world to come?' He said, 'It was of the gardens of the world over which the sun and moon rose and set, for had it been of the world to come, Adam would have never been expelled from it, nor would Iblis have been able to enter it. God made Adam to dwell in the garden; he ignorantly ate of his forbidden tree and was expelled from the garden because he was made a creature who exists only through commands and prohibitions, clothing, shelter, and marriage; nor could he discern what was beneficial and what was harmful to him, except through prohibition and prescription.'

"Iblis then came to them and said, 'If you eat from this tree whose fruit God has forbidden you to eat, you shall be two angels and dwell in the garden forever. But if you do not eat, God will eject you from the garden.' He swore to them that he was giving them good counsel. 'Your Lord forbade you this tree so that you would not become two angels, or be among those who have eternal life.' He swore to them, 'I am to you a sincere counselor' [Q. 7:20–21]. Adam accepted Iblis's advice and ate from the tree. Then their nakedness was manifested to them and the garments of Paradise with which God had clothed them fell off their backs. They therefore began to cover themselves with the leaves of the trees of the garden. Their Lord called out to them, 'Have I not forbidden you to come near this tree and told you that Satan is an open enemy to you?' [Q. 7:22]. They said, as God has reported in the Qur'an, 'Our Lord, we have surely wronged ourselves' [Q. 7:23]. Then God ordered them to come down from the garden. Adam came down on al-Safa and Eve on al-Marwah [al-Safa and al-Marwah are two hills in the sacred precinct outside Mecca between which pilgrims run]. [See below, Q. 2:158.] Adam wept over his loss of the garden for forty days. Gabriel then came to him and said, 'O Adam, did not God form you with His own hand, breathe His spirit into you, and make His angels to prostrate themselves before you?' 'Yes,' he answered. 'Did He not command you not to eat of the tree; why did you disobey him?' Adam said, 'O Gabriel, Iblis swore by God that he was a sincere counselor to me. I did not think that God created any creature who would swear falsely by Him.'"

Qummi further relates, on the authority of Ja'far al-Sadiq, that "Adam remained on al-Safa for forty days, prostrate and weeping for Paradise. Gabriel came to him, saying, 'O Adam, why do you weep?' He answered, 'Why should I not weep when God has expelled me from the garden, from His proximity, and made me come down to this world?' Said Gabriel, 'O Adam, turn to Him.' 'How do I turn to him?' Adam asked. God then sent down to him a dome of light containing the sacred House [the Kaaba], and the light of that dome filled the hills around Mecca." Adam was then guided by Gabriel through the various steps of the pilgrimage rite from the first of Dhu al-Qi'dah [the eleventh month of the Muslim calendar] until the end of the pilgrimage on the tenth of Dhu al-Hijjah [the twelfth month]. The rites of the pilgrimage having been completed, Gabriel said to Adam, "Now God has accepted your repentance and your wife has become lawful for you" (Qummi, I, pp. 44–45).

As for the words Adam received from his Lord, it has been related on the authority of the imams that "Adam saw exalted and noble names inscribed on the Throne. He inquired concerning these names and was told that these were names of the noblest of men in the sight of God. The names were those of Muhammad, Fatimah, 'Ali, Hasan, and Husayn. Adam begged his Lord through them to accept his repentance, and thus God exalted his station" (Tabarsi, I, p. 196; see also pp. 193–196).

Modern commentators have in general been sharply critical of traditional interpretations with their hagiographical tales and often fantastic legends. Thus Tabataba'i comments on the vicegerent as follows: "This narrative indicates first that the vicegerency [*khilafah*] here mentioned is the vicegerency of God, and not that of any other species of creatures who were on the earth before humankind but who had perished. . . . This vicegerency is not limited to Adam personally, but rather all his children share in it. Moreover, the teaching of the names means the innate gift of knowledge to man, where its effects appear in him always and gradually and which, when he is guided to the right way, enables him to bring this knowledge out of the realm of potentiality to that of actuality. Many are the texts which support the fact that the vicegerency is meant to include the descendants of Adam [see, for example, Q. 7:69; 10:14 and 27:62]".

Secondly, "God did not exempt His vicegerent on the earth from corruption and the shedding of blood. Rather he disclosed an entirely different matter, which is that there is a responsibility which the angels cannot bear. Yet it was to be borne by this earthly vicegerent who shall transmit God's commands and receive mysteries from Him which are beyond the capacity of the angels to bear. In this there is a definite deterrent from corruption and the shedding of blood.

"The Exalted One first said, 'I know what you do not know,' and then, 'have I not told you that I know the hidden things of the heavens and the earth.' The hidden things signify the names, not Adam's knowledge of them. This is because the angels did not know that there were names which they did not know. The narrative indicates that the angels claimed the vicegerency for themselves and concurred in denying it for Adam. It was necessary for a vicegerent to know those names of which He asked them and of which they had no knowledge, but which Adam knew when God challenged them. By this, Adam's worthiness of the knowledge of the names as well as the unworthiness of the angels of such knowledge was established. God's saying, 'And He taught Adam all the names; then He displayed them before the angels' indicates that these names, or the things of which they were the names, were living and rational beings still veiled by the veil of concealment. Moreover, the knowledge of their names was unlike our knowledge of the names of things; otherwise, the angels would, after Adam had informed them of the names, be possessed of this knowledge and thus become like Adam, his equals. Adam would then have no special favor with God, in that God taught him names which He did not teach the angels. For had He taught them the names, they would be like Adam, or even more exalted than he. There would therefore be nothing in this that would convince them or destroy their argument" (Tabataba'i, I, pp. 115–117).

Tabataba'i argues further, "You have seen that when God said, 'Behold, I am about to place a vicegerent in the earth,' and the angels protested, 'Would you place therein one who will spread corruption and shed blood,' God did not refuse their claim concerning the earthly vicegerent or counter it with anything except 'And He taught Adam all the names.' Had there not been in the teaching of the names something which would answer their protest, their complaint would not have ceased, nor would there have been incontrovertible proof over them. Thus among the things which God taught Adam were those which would benefit the rebellious man when he disobeys and the sinner when he sins. It may therefore be that what Adam received from his Lord was something related to these names. Know further that even though Adam wronged his soul by bringing it to the edge of perdition . . . yet he prepared for himself through his descent to the earth a degree of bliss and a station of perfection which he would not have attained had he not descended, nor would he have attained these without sin. This is because when he was able to discern his state of depravity, humiliation, destitution, and helplessness, he also perceived the reward for all the hardships which he would endure: bliss and repose in the realm of sanctity in the proximity of the Lord of all beings. For God the Exalted has attributes of pardoning and forgiveness, relenting and covering [the defects of His servants], favor and compassion, and a mercy which only sinners may obtain" (Tabataba'i, I, pp. 133–134).

In contrast with Tabataba'i's philosophical approach, Sayyid Qutb remains close to the actual intent of the text. Nonetheless, the two authors reach essentially the same conclusion. Sayyid Qutb asserts first that man, as the vicegerent of God on the earth, was actually created for the earth from the beginning and not for Paradise. Second, he was given a mission or responsibility beyond the imagination of the angels. Third, "Although man sometimes sows corruption in the earth and sheds blood, it is by means of this relative concrete evil that a greater and more inclusive good may be achieved." The names God taught Adam were the symbols of things and persons. This mystery, moreover, was not attained by the angels because it is necessary to the role of man as the vicegerent of God. For this reason, the angels declared their impotence, resorting to the praise of God: "Glory be to You; we have no knowledge save what You have taught us" (Qutb, I, pp. 65–67).

Sayyid Qutb sees in the prostration of the angels before Adam a sign of the honor God accorded "this creature who spreads corruption in the earth and sheds blood, but who, nonetheless, was granted mysteries which elevated him above the angels. He was granted the mystery of knowledge, as he was also granted the mystery of free will capable of choosing the right way. The dual character of his nature, the exercise of his free will in plotting his own course, and his possession of the trust of being guided to God through his own special effort—all these are only some of the mysteries appertaining to his high honor. Thus the angels fell prostrate in obedience to the command of the Exalted Majesty. Here the evil creation appears personified [in Iblis]. It is disobedience to the divine Majesty, it is arrogance in not recognizing excellence where it truly belongs, and it is pride in sin and the closing of Iblis's mind to true understanding. The [Qur'anic] narrative points to the fact that Iblis was not of the species of angels; rather, he was with them. For had he been one of them, he would not have disobeyed. Iblis, according to the text of the Qur'an, was one of the *jinn*, and God created the *jinn* from smokeless fire. This proves conclusively that he was not one of the angels. Thus was the stage of the eternal battle set: the battle between the evil creation in Iblis and the vicegerent of God in the earth. It is the eternal battle in the conscience of man. It is the battle in which the good achieves victory to the extent that man seeks protection in his covenant with his Lord, and evil conquers to the extent that man surrenders to his lust and thus wanders far away from his Lord."

According to Sayyid Qutb, Adam and Eve were allowed to eat of all the fruits of the garden except one tree. "Perhaps it was only a symbol of what is forbidden, which is necessary for human life on earth. For without prohibitions, free will cannot grow, nor would it be possible to distinguish volitional man from the led animal. Free will is the distinguishing mark and those who live without free will belong to the animal world in human form. 'But Satan caused them to slip from the garden'—'caused them to slip' is a pictorial phrase, painting the picture of the motion which it expresses. Thus one can almost see Satan as he pushes them out of the garden, pushing their feet so that they slip and fall. At this point, the temptation is complete and Adam forgot his covenant. Thus the battle began on the stage decreed for it by God between man and Satan and will continue to the end of time. Yet Adam rose up from his low state through that which was inherent in his nature, and the mercy of his Lord came to his aid whenever he turned to it and took refuge in it."

(37) Sayyid Qutb continues, "The last and decisive word of God and His perpetual covenant with Adam and his descendants was accomplished. It is the covenant of vicegerency on this earth and the condition of success or ruin during his sojourn on the earth."

(38) "Thus the eternal battle moved onto its legitimate field, and rages freely without ceasing or respite. Man knew from the dawn of human history the way to achieve victory if he desires it and the way to be vanquished if he desires his own loss. The story of the forbidden tree, the whispering of Satan, tempting them with its fruit,

forgetting the covenant through disobedience, waking after the intoxication, remorse, and the prayer for forgiveness: all this is the perpetual trial of humankind. Thus God's mercy had decreed for this creature that he descend to the place of his vicegerency, having had the experience of this trial which he is to confront always if he is to be ready for the battle, and that it may be for him a lesson and a warning.

"Again we ask, where did all this take place? Where was the garden in which Adam lived for a time? Who were the angels, and who was Iblis? How did God speak to them, and how did they answer him? These matters and others like them in the Qur'an belong to the concealed [*al-ghayb*], which God has safeguarded for Himself. In His wisdom He knew that humankind would gain nothing by such knowledge. For this reason He did not give them the power to discern or comprehend it through the tools which He granted for the purpose of executing their mission of vicegerency in the earth" (Qutb, I, pp. 68–70).

Sayyid Qutb then launches a sharp attack on materialistic ideologies, which he accuses of demeaning man and exalting the machine. Then, turning to a critique of the Christian idea of sin and salvation, he writes, "Both sin and repentance belong to the individual concerned. There is no sin imposed on a human being before his birth, as the Christian church asserts, nor is there divine expiation, which the church claims for Jesus, the son of God, as Christians hold. This expiation [they say], he achieved through his crucifixion in order to save the children of Adam from Adam's sin. No, rather the sin of Adam was his own personal sin. Salvation from it was attained through his turning to God, simply and without difficulty. Likewise, the sin of each of his children is a personal sin, and the way to repentance is open, simply and without difficulty. This Islamic view is clear and consoling. It lays on every man his own burden and inspires every man with determination and activity, continuous attempts at success, and the strength to face despair and hopelessness. 'For He is truly relenting, compassionate'" (Sayyid Qutb, I, pp. 73–74).

40. O Children of Israel! Remember my favor which I have bestowed upon you. Fulfill my covenant that I may fulfill your covenant, and be in awe of me alone.

41. Have faith in that which I have sent down confirming that which is already with you. Do not be the first to reject faith in it. Do not exchange its verses for a meager price, and fear me alone.

42. Do not confound truth with falsehood or hide the truth while you know it.

43. Observe regular worship, give the obligatory alms, and bow down with those who bow down.

44. Would you enjoin righteousness upon others, yet forget yourselves while you recite the scriptures—do you not understand?

45. Seek help in patience and prayer, for surely it is a grave matter, save for those who are humble;

46. Those who reckon that they shall meet their Lord, and that to Him they shall return.

47. O Children of Israel, remember my favor toward you and that I have favored you over all peoples.

48. Fear a day on which no soul shall make satisfaction for another soul, nor will intercession be accepted from it, nor will compensation be required of it, nor will they be rendered support.

49. Remember how we saved you from the people of Pharoah when they inflicted upon you the worst torment: slaying your sons and sparing your females. In that there was a great trial for you from your Lord.

The account of the ancient Hebrews in Egypt and their liberation under the leadership of Moses has occupied a prominent place in the Qur'anic narrative of the history of bygone nations and their prophets. The purpose of these and the following commentaries is to present the understanding of Muslim commentators of such events and what they took as the lessons to be learned from them.

(49) Commentators have generally asserted that Pharoah tormented the Children of Israel by enslaving them. "Some he made to build and others to till and sow the fields. Thus he 'inflicted on them the worst torment'" (Tabari, II, p. 40). Tabari related further on the authority of Ibn 'Abbas that "Pharoah and his ministers discussed the promise which God made to Abraham, His Friend [*khalil*], that there would be among his descendants prophets and kings. They agreed to send men with swords to search in the homes of the Children of Israel and slay every newborn male infant they found; this they did. As they saw the aged among the Children of Israel die a natural death and the young males slain, Pharoah said to them, 'You will soon exterminate the Children of Israel; then you will have to undertake the labor they now perform. Kill therefore the males born in one year and spare those born in the next.' The mother of Moses conceived Aaron during the year in which children were not killed; therefore she delivered him in safety and did not hide him. In the following year she bore Moses" (Tabari, II, p. 42).

Tabari also relates on the authority of Ibn 'Abbas that the priests of Egypt told Pharoah that a child would be born among the Children of Israel who would destroy his dominion. Thus he ordered that all male children be killed and females spared (Tabari, II, p. 43). A story closely paralleling the account in Exodus (I:8–22) is related on the authority of al-Rabi' ibn Anas, who related it on the authority of Abu al-'Aliyah (see Tabari, II, p. 43). In yet another account, we are told that Pharoah dreamed that a fire sparked from Jerusalem and consumed all the houses of the Egyptians. His priests interpreted the dream as pointing to a child of the Israelites who would destroy his reign (Tabari, II, p. 44). "In this is a great trial for you from your Lord" means "in our saving you from the torments which you suffered at the hands of the people of Pharoah, there is a trial for you from your Lord." The word *bala'* (trial) may be used to denote a test of faith either through hardship or relief, as is related on the authority of Ibn 'Abbas, Mujahid, and al-Suddi (Tabari, II, pp. 48–49; see also Ibn Kathir, I, p. 156; Qurtubi, I, pp. 381–385; Zamakhshari, I, p. 279; Razi, III, pp. 66–69; Nisaburi, I, p. 307; Tabarsi, I, pp. 234–235; Tabataba'i, I, p. 188).

Ibn 'Arabi observes, "The exoteric interpretation of this verse is what may be understood from the literal sense, as God reminding them of His favors and stirring in them love for Him." He then interprets the text in accordance with its esoteric meaning. Pharoah is therefore "the carnal soul, enjoining evil, which is veiled by its own ego. It is set in authority over the city of existence. Egypt is the 'city of the body' in which this soul is enshrined. The powers of the soul are imagination [khayal], illusion [wahm], seclusion [takhliyah], anger, and lust." The phrase "your sons" refers to "the spiritual powers which are the sons of the elect of God, the Jacob of the spirit." The torture the Children of Israel endured is, according to Ibn 'Arabi, worldly cares and worries about material things to which men may become slaves. The phrase "slaying your sons" means "your spiritual powers which are the theoretical intellect and the practical intellect, these being the two eyes of the heart. The theoretical intellect is the right and the practical intellect the left eye. Understanding is the ear of the heart, the innermost faculty [sirr] which is the heart of the heart and contemplation [fikr] and remembrance [dhikr]." The word "women" in this verse refers, according to Ibn 'Arabi, to the "natural powers which seek to prevent the other powers from exercising their proper actions. This they do by vanquishing and dominating them and by veiling them from the light of the spirit." The word bala' (trial), if taken positively, means "the great favor of beholding the purity of God's beauty [jamal] and majesty [jalal]." If the word is taken negatively, it means "privation, veiling, and removal" (Ibn 'Arabi, I, pp. 46–47).

50. Then we split the sea for you; we drowned the people of Pharoah while you looked on.

51. Remember when we appointed with Moses forty nights. But you took the calf to yourselves after he had gone from you, and you were wrongdoers.

52. Then we pardoned you, so that you might give thanks.

53. We then gave Moses the scriptures and the criterion, that you might be guided aright.

54. Remember when Moses said to his people, "O my people! Surely you have wronged yourselves by taking to yourselves the calf. Turn therefore to your creator and slay yourselves; that would be better for you with your creator, that He may turn toward you, for He is relenting, compassionate."

55. Then you said, "O Moses, we shall not believe you until we see God openly." Lightning then overtook you while you looked on.

56. Then we raised you up after your death, so that you may give thanks.

57. We then shaded you with a cloud and provided you with manna and quails, [saying,] "Eat of the good things which we have bestowed upon you for sustenance." They did not wrong us, but only wronged themselves.

58. And remember when we said, "Enter this town and eat of its provisions abundantly wherever you wish. Enter the gate prostrate and say 'Forgiveness!' in order that we may forgive you your sins; thus shall we increase those who do good."

59. Then those who had done wrong altered that which was told them with another saying. Thus we sent down on the wrongdoers a plague from heaven in punishment for all their acts of wickedness.

60. Remember when Moses sought water for his people to drink. We said, "Strike the rock with your staff"; then twelve springs of water gushed forth from it. Thus every tribe reckoned their own source of drinking water. "Eat and drink of God's provisions and do no mischief in the earth, nor corruption."

61. And remember when you said, "O Moses, we cannot endure living on only one kind of food; pray your Lord therefore for us that He may cause the earth to bring forth for us of its herbs, cucumbers, garlic, lentils, and onions." He said, "Would you exchange that which is base for that which is good? Go down into Egypt! There you shall have what you ask." Thus were they struck with humiliation and destitution. They incurred God's wrath because they used to reject the signs of God and slay prophets unjustly, and because of their acts of disobedience and transgression.

(50) Tabari relates on the authority of al-Suddi, "When Moses came to the Red Sea he gave it the name 'Abu Khalid.' He hit it with his staff and it split into two huge walls of water. Thus the Children of Israel entered and the sea was split into twelve paths, one for each tribe" (Tabari, II, p. 50). Pharoah, at the head of seventy thousand horsemen, then pursued Moses. It is related on the authority of 'Abdallah ibn Shaddad, "When the Children of Israel entered the sea and no one was left behind, Pharoah raced on his horse until he stood at the edge of the sea, which was still standing as it was parted. The horse was frightened and refused to advance. Gabriel stood before the horse on a mare in heat and the horse ran after her. When the army saw Pharoah entering the sea, they followed him. Gabriel was in front, leading them, and Michael appeared behind the people on a horse, driving them on. When Gabriel had crossed the sea, with no one behind him and Michael stood on the other shore with no one before, the sea closed in on the Egyptians. Then Pharoah, seeing the power of God and His authority and feeling his humiliation and fear, cried out, 'There is no god except Him in whom the Children of Israel have faith, and I am one of the Muslims'" (Q. 10:90; Tabari, II, p. 52). Tabari relates further from al-Suddi, "God commanded Moses to 'set out with my servants by night, for you are pursued' [Q. 44:23]. The Copts [that is, the Egyptians] were afflicted with death so that every firstborn male died. They woke up before sunrise to bury their dead, and thus were distracted from pursuing the Children of Israel until the sun had risen, as God says, 'they pursued them at sunrise'" (Q. 26:60; Tabari, II, p. 55).

Qurtubi reports, "Israel, that is, Jacob, entered Egypt with only forty-six of his children and grandchildren. God, however, multiplied their number and blessed them so that when they departed Egypt and stood at the sea they numbered six hundred thousand fighters besides old men, children, and women." Qurtubi cites a number of hagiographical embellishments to the tale just quoted from Tabari (see Qurtubi, I, pp. 389-390).

Qurtubi observes further that "God recounted the drowning of the people of Pharoah and the salvation of the children of Israel, but did not mention on what day this took place." Qurtubi then relates from Ibn 'Abbas, "When the Apostle of God came to Medina he found the Jews fasting on the day of 'Ashura'." (This is the Day of Atonement, the tenth of Tishri, subsequently observed by Muslims on the tenth day of Muharram, the first month of the Muslim calendar.) The Prophet asked the Jews, "Why are you fasting on this day?" They answered, "This is a great day, the day on which God saved Moses and his people and drowned Pharoah and his people. Moses fasted on this day in thanksgiving to God and we likewise fast on it." The Prophet answered, "We are more worthy of Moses than you are." He therefore fasted that day and ordered the Muslims to do the same (Qurtubi, I, p. 390; see also p. 392).

The sea, according to Ibn 'Arabi, is "the black bitter sea which is the corporeal matter which was split, by your existence as the earth is split for plants. Thus we saved you by freeing you from it. We drowned the people of Pharoah [who represent the psychic powers] in the sea. They adhered to it and perished in its corruption. Of all this you are witnesses" (Ibn 'Arabi, I, p. 47).

(51) The main issue this verse presented for commentators was which "forty nights" were here intended. Tabarsi gives a convenient summary of the various views concerning this matter. First, he says, they "are the ones which God mentioned in *surah* 7: 'We appointed for Moses thirty nights and fulfilled them with yet another ten nights' [Q. 7:142]; they were the months of Dhu al-Qi'dah and ten of Dhu al-Hijjah." 'But you took the calf to yourselves' means you took the calf as a god. 'After he had gone from you' means after the absence of Moses; or after God had promised to give you the Torah; or after the drowning of Pharoah and the signs you witnessed. All these are possible" (Tabarsi, I, pp. 242–243; Ibn Kathir, I, p. 159; Qurtubi, I, p. 395).

There was a strong tendency among classical commentators to view the history of any ancient community, and especially that of the Hebrews, within an Islamic framework. Thus the two months mentioned as being those during which Moses communicated with his Lord are the two sacred months of pilgrimage for Muslims. Moreover, the Children of Israel at the time of Moses and other prophets were, in the view of the commentators, "Muslims," which means in Arabic "submitters" to the one and only God. Their worship of the golden calf, therefore, was a grave sin, the sin of associating other things with God. Hence the details of this great sin occupied commentators from the very beginning, and the result was an impressive body of pious tales and legends.

The Children of Israel were led astray by the Samaritan, so we are told (Q. 20:85, 87, and 95). Thus the first question concerned the identity of this Samaritan. Ibn Ishaq related, "The Samaritan was a man from a city called Bajarma. He was a cow worshiper;

love for which remained in his heart, although he professed Islam with the Children of Israel" (Tabari, II, p. 66). Tabari further relates on the authority of Ibn 'Abbas that this was the Samaritan, "who was hidden in a cave at birth by his mother for fear of being slain. Gabriel used to come and nurse him by placing his fingers in his mouth to suck; in some there was honey, in others milk, and still others ghee for the infant's nourishment. This went on until the boy grew up. Thus he recognized Gabriel when he saw him at the seashore. He took a handful of earth where the angel's horse stood. God inspired the Samaritan with, 'You shall not place the handful of dust on anything and say, "Be such and such" but that it would be according to your words.' When Moses and the Children of Israel crossed the sea and God caused the people of Pharoah to drown, Moses said to his brother Aaron, 'Be my representative among my people, and do well.' Then Moses left for the appointed meeting with his Lord. The Children of Israel had in their possession much gold and jewelery which they had taken from the Egyptians unlawfully; they thus committed an act of transgression. They gathered the jewelery together so that a fire would come down from Heaven to consume it" (Tabari, II, p. 64). Tabari also relates that the Samaritan threw the handful of earth which he held in his hand in with the gold and said, "Be a calf, a living body, lowing." Then he said, "This is your God and the God of Moses," and they worshiped the calf with devotion (Tabari, II, p. 64).

According to al-Suddi, Aaron commanded the people to dig a hole in the earth and bury the gold in it until Moses returned and decided what to do with it. The Samaritan threw in the handful of earth, and God turned the jewelery into a living calf, lowing. The calf came out of the hole after twenty nights, whereupon the Samaritan said, "This is your God and the God of Moses, for he has forgotten" (Q. 20:88), that is, Moses forgot his God, which was the calf, and went to look for it on the mountain (Tabari, II, p. 65).

This story raised two important problems for commentators. The first is that the Samaritan was able not only to lead men astray but could also deceive a prophet (Aaron). In one version of the tale, Aaron commands the people to cleanse themselves of the gold of the Egyptians. For this purpose he kindled a hot fire into which every man threw that which was in his hand. The Samaritan came, saying, "O prophet of God, shall I throw in what is in my hand?" "Yes," answered the prophet, but he did not know that it was earth from the hoofprint of Gabriel's horse. This was, some commentators argue, by God's permission, a trial for the Children of Israel. "Thus when God spoke with Moses, He said, 'What made you depart from your people so quickly, O Moses?' Moses answered, 'These are my people, and they are following close behind me. But I hastened to You, my Lord, so that You may be pleased' [Q. 20:83–85]. God said, 'We have led your people into temptation after you had left them, for the Samaritan led them astray.' Moses said, 'My Lord, do You see the spirit? Who breathed it into the calf?' The Lord said, 'I did.' 'Then, Lord,' said Moses, 'You have led them astray'" (Tabari, II, p. 65). Thus we see that the Samaritan was able to lead the people into the sin of association of other things with God (*shirk*) and to deceive the prophet Aaron only because he was acting as an instrument to execute a preordained divine decree. Indeed, he was from his birth prepared for this task by the angel Gabriel. (For further discussion see Ibn Kathir, I, p. 159, and Qurtubi, I, p. 395.)

The second problem this story raises is a theological one. Tabarsi relates that, according to Hasan al-Basri, "the calf became a living being with flesh and blood." Others, however, objected, saying, "This is not possible, because it would then be a miracle such as only prophets are empowered by God to perform." Those who agreed with Hasan argued that "because the handful of earth bore the trace of the angel, God allowed that when it was thrown at any image, that image became a living thing. Therefore, this was not a miracle, since the Samaritan did what anyone possessing the sacred soil could have done." Those who did not allow that an image could become a living body explained the lowing of the animal by asserting that the Samaritan actually made a calf with holes in it; when the wind passed through the holes, a sound like the lowing of a calf was produced. This view was advanced by the Mu'tazali theologian Abu 'Ali al-Jubba'i (Tabarsi, I, p. 244).

(53) Commentators are generally agreed that by the word *kitab* (scriptures) is meant the Torah and that the *Furqan* (criterion) is that by which truth may be distinguished from falsehood. *Furqan*, then, would here be an attribute of the Torah (see Tabari, II, pp. 70–71; see also Qurtubi, I, p. 39; and Shawkani, I, p. 86). Razi discusses several possible meanings of the word *Furqan*. "The *Furqan* [separator, or that by which things may be distinguished] could be either the Torah as a whole or in part. It may also refer to something other than the Torah, perhaps one of the miracles of Moses, such as his staff, and so forth. It may mean relief and victory, as God said concerning the Apostle, 'and what we sent down to our servant

on the day of the criterion [*Furqan*], the day when the two parties met' [Q. 8:41]. The word *Furqan* may refer to the splitting [*infiraq*] of the sea, or as some have said, to the Qur'an, which was also sent down to Moses." Razi, however, rejects this last view as a false interpretation. He finally concludes, "The *Furqan* is that by which truth may be distinguished from falsehood. Thus it may either be the Torah or something external to it." (Razi, III, p. 77; see also Tabarsi, I, pp. 245–247, and Qutb, I, p. 89.)

(54) Tabari relates on the authority of Ibn 'Abbas that "Moses commanded his people, as the command came from his Lord, saying, 'Slay yourselves.' Thus those who persisted in worshiping the calf sat hiding their faces and those who did not worship the calf rose up, whereupon a thick darkness covered them and they began to kill one another. When the darkness was dispelled, there were seventy thousand dead. Every one who was killed had turned to God and expiated his sin [by being killed] and those who survived likewise had turned to God [by killing the guilty]" (Tabari, II, pp. 73–74; Ibn Kathir, I, pp. 160–161).

Qurtubi cites some Sufi masters who have interpreted the command "slay yourselves" to mean "humble your souls with acts of obedience and restrain them from lusts." Qurtubi, however, rejects this interpretation saying, "It is actual slaying which is here intended." After reviewing various other opinions, Qurtubi adds: "Those who did not worship the calf were punished by slaying themselves . . . because they did not seek to change an evil when their fellows worshiped the calf. Rather, they isolated themselves when their duty was to fight against those who worshiped it. For this is the law of God with His servants; when evil is spread and not checked, the entire community is punished. Qurtubi then cites a prophetic *hadith* which declares, "No people among whom there are those who commit acts of disobedience shall be better or safer [from God's punishment] than the guilty ones. If they do not change, God shall visit them all with punishment" (Qurtubi, I, pp. 401–402).

This view has generally been accepted by commentators even to the present. Sayyid Qutb comments on the verse as follows: "That is to say, let the obedient man among you slay the rebellious one in order that he may purify him as well as himself. It was indeed a harsh obligation that a brother kill his brother, as though killing himself by his own volition." This obligation Sayyid Qutb considers to have been an expiation for both the disobedient and the obedient, but "then the mercy of God came to their rescue after their purification: 'that He may turn toward you, for He is relenting, compassionate'" (Qutb, I, pp. 89–90).

A notable exception to this view is that of Razi, who objects to it on the grounds that "it is not possible that God, the Exalted, command killing. This is because acts of worship [that is, through obedience] are good only because they are of benefit to the person charged [to perform them]. There can be no benefit except in matters of the future. But, since there is no situation of obligation after death, there can be no benefit in killing" (Razi, III, pp. 80–81). Razi therefore concludes that the text should not be explained in accordance with its literal sense. Thus "slay yourselves" may mean "submit to being killed at the hands of others, that is, those who did not defile themselves with idolatry" (Razi, III, pp. 81–82; for a comprehensive discussion, see Tabarsi, I, pp. 251–253).

Qummi offers the following narrative in interpretation of this verse: "When Moses went out for the appointed time and returned to his people who had worshiped the calf, he said, 'O my people, surely you have wronged yourselves by taking to yourselves the calf. Turn therefore to your creator and slay yourselves.' Moses said, 'Go every one of you to the holy city [Jerusalem] with a knife, iron bar, or sword in hand. When I mount the pulpit of the Children of Israel, stand ready with veiled faces so that no one shall recognize his companion, then slay one another.' Thus they gathered together seventy thousand men, all of whom had worshiped the calf, and went up to Jerusalem. When Moses led them in prayer and mounted the pulpit, they began to slay one another. They continued until Gabriel came down and said to Moses, 'Say to them, O Moses, "Cease the killing, for God has turned toward you."' Ten thousand were killed. Then God sent down 'That would be better for you with your creator, that He may turn toward you, for He is relenting, compassionate'" (Qummi, I, p. 47).

(55, 56) These verses have raised two questions for commentators. First, who were those to whom the verses refer? Second, what is meant by "the lightning" (*sa'iqah*). Ibn Kathir relates on the authority of Ibn Ishaq, "When Moses returned and saw what his people were doing he took seventy of the most pious and honorable men and, having all purified themselves, they returned to the mountain to pray for forgiveness. The men said, 'O Moses, pray your Lord that we too may hear the words of our Lord.' Moses then approached the mountain, which was entirely enveloped by a white cloud. He came forward and entered into the cloud and called upon the men to enter as well. Whenever Moses went to speak with God, a radiant light fell upon his forehead, which no one of the Children of Israel was able to gaze upon. He therefore placed a veil between himself and the men who approached, but as soon as they entered into the cloud, they fell upon their faces. They heard God speak with Moses, communicating His commands and prohibitions. When the cloud was lifted from Moses, the men said to him, 'O Moses, we shall not believe you until we see God openly.' Thus they were overtaken by a quake [*rajfah*] and lightning [*sa'iqah*], and they fell dead. Moses then rose up and called upon his Lord, saying, 'O Lord, had you so willed, you would have caused them and myself to perish, even before all this had happened. They have surely acted foolishly, but would you cause all the Children of Israel who were left behind to perish in punishment for what the foolish among us have done?' [cf. Q. 7:155]. God answered his prayers and returned to the men their spirits. Moses then prayed to God to turn toward the Children of Israel and forgive them their worship of the calf, but God said, 'No, not until they slay themselves'" (Ibn Kathir, I, p. 163).

Tabari interprets the word *sa'iqah* as follows. "It is a dreadful portent or event which causes the person experiencing it to die of fear. It may also cause a person to lose his mind or another of his senses. It matters not whether the *sa'iqah* is fire or earthquake. Death does not necessarily follow, as God says of Moses, '*Kharra sa'iqan*' [he fell, stunned], [Q. 7:143]; that is, he swooned" (Tabari, II, p. 83; see also Qurtubi, I, pp. 403–404; Zamakhshari, I, p. 282). Most early traditionists, however, asserted that the men actually died and were later brought back to life. 'Urwah ibn Ruwaym, wishing to retain the literal meaning of the verse, said, "Some of them were killed by the *sa'iqah*, while the others looked on; then they were revived, and the others killed" (Ibn Kathir, I, p. 162). Early Shi'i tradition asserted that the people here mentioned were the seventy companions of Moses who died and were brought back to life as prophets. Qummi sees in the death and revivification of the seventy men who were with Moses a proof "of the return of the imams of the community of Muhammad, for he said, 'Nothing happened to the Children of Israel but that the like of it shall happen to my community'" (Qummi, I, p. 47).

Ibn 'Arabi interprets the refusal of the Children of Israel to believe Moses until they saw God openly as follows: "You said, 'O Moses, we shall not have faith in your guidance [that is, true faith] until we arrive at the station of direct vision [*mushahadah*] with the eyes.

Thus were you overtaken by the *sa'iqah* of death which is annihilation [*fana'*] in the manifestation of the Essence, while you witnessed it. Then we brought you back to true life, to subsistence [*baqa'*] after annihilation, in order that you may give thanks for the grace of the knowledge of divine oneness [*tawhid*] and the attainment [*wusul*] through journeying [*suluk*] in God" (Ibn 'Arabi, I, p. 51).

(57) Commentators have differed over the interpretation of the word *ghamam* (clouds). Tabari relates on the authority of Ibn 'Abbas that "*al-ghamam* was cooler and more wholesome than this cloud [ordinary clouds]. It is the cloud in which God shall come down on the day of resurrection, as He says, 'in canopies of white cloud' [see below, verse 210]. It is also the cloud in which the angels came down on the day of the Battle of Badr. It is the cloud which was with the Children of Israel in the wilderness" (Tabari, II, pp. 90–91; see also Ibn Kathir, I, p. 164; Qurtubi, I, pp. 406–408).

Qummi relates in interpretation of this verse the following tale: "When Moses crossed the sea with the Children of Israel they stopped in a desert place. They complained to Moses, saying, 'You shall cause us to perish by bringing us out of civilization [*'umran*] a desert in which there is neither shade, trees, nor water.' Thus a white cloud used to come over them to shade them from the sun. At night manna came down to them falling on the trees, plants, and rocks. After eating this, later in the night a roasted bird [the quail] alighted on their tables. When they had eaten and were sated it flew away. Moses also had a stone which he placed in the midst of the army and struck with his staff, whereupon twelve springs of water gushed out" (Qummi, I, p. 48).

Shi'i commentators found the second part of the verse problematic: "They did not wrong us, but only wronged themselves." Thus Tabataba'i states that the verse refers to the imams and their enemies. He reports a tradition from the tenth imam, who said, "God is too great and magnanimous to wrong anyone or ascribe wrong to Himself. Rather, God, comingled us with Himself, making a wrong committed against us a wrong committed against Him, and our *walayah* [love for the imams and acceptance of their authority] *walayah* to Him" (Tabataba'i, I, p. 191).

Sayyid Qutb sees all these verses which deal with the ancient history of the Jews as lessons the Qur'an directed at the Jews of Medina at the time of the Prophet. He observes that these events were all related in earlier Meccan *surahs*. The purpose behind their repetition is for the Jews of Medina to imagine the way God dealt with their ancestors through these events and to learn a lesson form them. "It is as though they themselves were witnessing the splitting of the sea and the salvation of the Children of Israel under the leadership of Moses. This vivid picture is one of the most distinct characteristics of this marvelous Qur'an" (Qutb, I, pp. 188–189). Sayyid Qutb further asserts that those who asked to see God openly (verse 55) were the seventy men Moses took up to the mountain. He uses this and other verses to argue that from the beginning, the ancient Israelites, as well as the Jews of the Prophet's society and later, were blinded with the concrete and material world and thus unable to conceive of the deeper spiritual realities and truths. They asked to see God as though He were a concrete object. Sayyid Qutb accepts the dominant view that Moses brought the ancient Hebrews to the holy city of Jerusalem but the people did not wish to fight. Thus they were made to wander in the wilderness for forty years until a new generation of men grew up and conquered the holy city under the leadership of Joshua (Qutb, I, pp. 188–192).

(58) Commentators have disagreed as to the town intended in this verse, as well as the meaning of the word *hittah* (forgiveness). Tabari relates from Qatadah, al-Suddi, and al-Rabi' ibn Anas that the town was the holy city, Jerusalem. 'Abd al-Rahman ibn Zayd said, "It is the town of Jericho, which is near Jerusalem" (Tabari, II, pp. 102–103; see also Ibn Kathir, I, pp. 170–174). Qurtubi reports that some took the town to be Damascus, others Ramlah, still others Palmyra, and some as an unspecified city east of the river Jordan (Qurtubi, I, p. 409).

Commentators have also differed as to whether the verse refers to the Children of Israel during the time of Moses or later under the leadership of Joshua. Ibn Kathir relates the following account: "When they came to the Holy Land with Moses, they were commanded to enter the land which was their inheritance from their father, Israel, and fight against the Amalakites, who were its inhabitants [see Q. 5:21 and 22]. But they were reluctant to do so. God therefore punished them with desert wandering." The author, however, doubts this interpretation because, he observes, the Children of Israel conquered the Holy Land under the leadership of Joshua "on the eve of the Sabbath, and God made the sun stand still for them for a short time until they had achieved their conquest" (Ibn Kathir, I, pp. 170–171).

The gate was, according to most commentators, the gate of Jerusalem. The gate called *hittah* was the eighth gate of Jerusalem, according to Mujahid. It has also been related that it was the gate of the dome in Jerusalem toward which Moses and the Children of Israel used to pray. Other *tafsir* authorities said that it was the gate of the town which the Children of Israel were ordered to enter. Abu 'Ali al-Jubba'i said, "The verse is more likely to support the view of those who say that it was the gate of the dome than that of those who say that it was the gate of the town which they were ordered to enter, because they did not enter any town during the life of Moses" (Tabarsi, I, p. 264; see also Ibn Kathir, I, p. 171). Sayyid Qutb, perhaps more aware of the biblical account, asserts that the verse refers to the time of Joshua (see Q. 5:23). The Children of Israel were, he says, commanded to enter the gate prostrate, "but instead of entering it prostrate, as God had commanded them . . . they entered it in a posture different from that enjoined upon them" (Qutb, I, p. 92).

The word *hittah*, in the view of most commentators, means to take a burden off something, thus meaning in this context, "take off from us the burden of our sins." 'Ikrimah said, "They were enjoined to say, 'There is no god but God,' because it takes away the burden of sin" (Tabari, II, p. 106; see also pp. 105–108). Tabarsi asserts, "Each of these explanations refers to the acts of removing the burden of sin and therefore can rightly serve as an interpretation of the word *hittah*." It is also related that the fifth imam, Muhammad al-Baqir, said, "We [the imams] are the gate of your *hittah* [that is, the source of divine mercy and forgiveness]" (Tabarsi, I, p. 264).

(59) The reference in this verse to those who "altered that which was told them" is to people who changed the meaning of the word *hittah* (see commentary on the previous verse) and entered the gate creeping on their behinds rather than prostrate, as they were commanded. All this they did in mockery of the divine command. Thus God sent upon them punishment from heaven which, according to Ibn Zayd, was the plague, killing twenty-four thousand of them in one hour (see Tabari, II, pp. 112–118; see also Tabarsi, I, pp. 265–266). Qurtubi reports a prophetic *hadith* from Abu Hurayrah in which the Prophet said, "The Children of Israel were told to 'enter the gate prostrate and say '*hittah!*' that God may forgive you your sins,' but they altered what they had been told to do and entered the gate creeping on their behinds and saying, 'A grain [*hintah*] in a hair' [that is, speaking nonsense]" (Qurtubi, I, pp. 410–411; see also p. 420 and Zamakhshari, I, p. 283).

(61) Commentators have differed as to whether the word *misr* refers in this verse to any settled country or specifically to Egypt. Tabari argues at length for both views. He cites in favor of the view that it was Egypt the readings of Ubayy and Ibn Mas'ud, where the word *misr* is read without the indefinite article, as in the reading in use today. Tabari concludes, "There is no indication in the Book of God as to which of these interpretations is the true one, nor is there a *hadith* from the Apostle which would provide the decisive word. . . . We therefore think that Moses asked his Lord to give his people what they asked . . . and God answered his prayers and commanded Moses to dwell in a land which would bring forth the foods they asked for." Tabari prefers the generally accepted reading in opposition to that of Ubayy and Ibn Mas'ud (Tabari, II, pp. 133–135; see also Ibn Kathir, I, pp. 175–178; Qurtubi, I, p. 429). Tabarsi relates on the authority of Hasan al-Basri, al-Rabi', and Qatadah that it was Egypt, "the *misr* of Pharoah," out of which they made the exodus. Abu Muslim said, "God meant the holy city [Jerusalem]"; the same was related on the authority of Ibn Zayd. Al-Suddi, Qatadah, and Mujahid said, "He meant any city [*misr*] of the lands, that is to say, what you ask for can be found in towns and not in desert places" (Tabarsi, I, p. 277; for a contemporary interpretation, see Qutb, I, p. 94).

62. Surely those who have faith, those who are Jews, Christians, and Sabaeans—whosoever has faith in God and the last day and performs good deeds—these will have their reward with their Lord. No fear will come upon them, nor shall they grieve.

63. And remember when we established a covenant with you and raised the mount over you, saying, "Take that which we have given you with power, and remember what it contains, that you may act righteously."

64. Even after that you turned away, and had it not been for God's favor and His mercy toward you, you would have been among the losers.

65. You know well those of you who transgressed on the sabbath; how we said to them, "Be you apes, despised!"

66. Thus we made them an example for those who were
    with them and those who came after; and an admonition
    for the God-fearing.

(62) This verse has raised many questions that have occupied
commentators throughout the history of *tafsir*. The most important
of these is the actual purport of the verse and to whom it refers.
Another question is who were the various groups and especially the
Sabaeans mentioned here? Third, some commentators used this verse
to deduce certain legal principles, which will be touched on briefly
here but more fully in considering *surah* 5, verse 69. Tabari identifies
the groups mentioned in this verse as follows: "Those who have
faith are those who assent to the Book of God. Those who have
turned [*hadu*] to God, are the Jews [*al-yahud*], as He says, 'We have
turned [*hudna*] to you.' [Q. 7:156]. . . . Those who are Christians
[*nasara*] were so called because they inhabited a land called Nasirah
[Nazereth]." Ibn 'Abbas said, "The town of Jesus was called Nasirah
and its people Nasiriyun [Nazerenes], and Jesus was likewise called
the Nazerene." Tabari adds, "It is also possible that they were called
'Nasara' because of the saying of Jesus, 'Who shall be my helpers
[*ansar*] to God?'" (see Q. 61:14 and 3:52; Tabari, II, pp. 143–148).
    The identity of the Sabi'in (Sabaeans) has been the subject of
much controversy among commentators as well as jurists. According
to Tabarsi, "It seems that the meaning of al-Sabi' [singular of Sabi'in]
is one who has left his religion which was promulgated for him in
favor of another. The faith they left was the worship of the one
God, adopting instead the worship and exaltation of the stars. Qatadah said, 'They are a well-known people, having their own unique
religion which includes the worship of the stars. Yet they profess
the existence of the Creator, the last day, and accept some of the
prophets.' Mujahid and Hasan al-Basri said, 'The Sabaeans are between the Jews and the Magians; they have no religion [unique to
themselves].' Al-Suddi said, 'They are a sect of the People of the
Book who recite the Psalms.' Al-Khalil said, 'They are people whose
religion is similar to that of the Christians, except that their *qiblah*
[direction of prayer] is toward the south, when the sun is at its
meridian. They claim to be the followers of the faith of Noah.' Ibn
Zayd said, 'They are the people of one [unspecified] religion, who
inhabit the peninsula of Mosul [in northern Iraq]. They say, 'There
is no god but God,' but do not believe in the Apostle of God. For
this reason, the associators [of Mecca] used to say of the Prophet

and his Companions, 'These are the Sabaeans'" (Tabarsi, I, p. 281). According to some commentators, the Sabaeans worshiped angels and prayed toward the *qiblah*. Tabari relates on the authority of Mujahid, Qatadah, and al-Suddi that Muslims could neither eat the animals slaughtered by Sabaeans nor marry their women. Therefore, they were not regarded as People of the Book. Ziyad ibn Abih (the famous governor of Iraq under Mu'awiyah) wished to exempt the Sabaeans from the poll tax (*jizyah*) because he was told that they prayed the five daily prayers toward the *qiblah*, but he changed his mind when told that they worshiped angels (Tabari, II, pp. 146–147). Tabarsi observes, "All jurists have agreed on allowing the poll tax to be received from them, but for us [that is Shi'i jurists], this is not allowed because they are not a People of the Book" (Tabarsi, I, p. 281).

Commentators have differed concerning the intent of this verse and the reason for its revelation. The verse is one of many general statements in the Qur'an in which faith is raised above any religious or ethnic identity. Commentators have, however, sought to limit its universal application in several ways. Four main approaches may be distinguished. The first was to declare the verse abrogated and hence inapplicable. The second was to limit the application of the verse by assigning the reason for its revelation to a specific group of people. The third approach has been to limit the verse to a strictly legalistic interpretation, and the fourth has been to accept the universality of the verse until the coming of Islam, but thereafter to limit its applicability only to those who hold the faith of Islam.

Tabarsi relates a tradition attributed to Ibn 'Abbas which asserts, "This verse was abrogated by God's saying, 'Whoever seeks a faith other than Islam, it shall not be accepted from him'" (Q. 3:85). Tabarsi, however, rejects this idea because "abrogation cannot apply to a declaration of promise [or threat]. It can be allowed only of legal judgments which may be changed or altered with change in the general interest [*maslahah*] [of people]. It is therefore best to assume that this view cannot be attributed to Ibn 'Abbas" (Tabarsi, I, pp. 282–283; see also Tabari, II, p. 155).

Classical commentators have explained this verse through a pious tale related on the authority of al-Suddi in support of the view that the verse was revealed in reference to Salman the Persian and his companions. Salman, we are told, was originally from Jundishapur, a famous Persian city of learning. He was a close friend of the son of the king of the city. As he and the prince were hunting one day, they came upon a monk who was reading the Gospel and weeping. After the monk recounted to them what was in the Gospel, they became Muslims and followed him. He then said to them, "The meat of animals slaughtered by your people is now unlawful for you to eat." A short time later, the king held a feast and called his son to the banquet, but the son refused to eat. Learning of the influence of the monk on his son, the king ordered the monk out of the city. He then left for a monastery in Mosul and invited the prince and Salman to join him.

After some time, the monk decided to leave the monastery for one less rigorous and asked Salman to choose between staying where he was or leaving with him. Salman chose to remain and continue his harsh discipline of ascetic and spiritual exercises. The new head of the monastery was greatly impressed with Salman's spiritual fervor and decided to take him on pilgrimage to Jerusalem. On the way they came upon a paralytic lying on the side of the road, who cried out as he saw them, "O master of all monks! Have mercy upon me; may God have mercy upon you." The monk, however, did not pay attention to him. During their stay in the holy city, the old monk said to Salman, "Go out and seek knowledge." One day Salman returned to the monk, heavy with grief, and said, "I see that all goodness was the lot of the prophets who were before us, and their followers." The monk answered, "O Salman, do not grieve, for there remains one prophet; there can be no greater act than to follow him. Now is the time when he should appear. I am an old man and I doubt whether I shall live to see him; but you are still a youth; you may therefore live to see him. He shall appear in the land of the Arabs. If you meet him, give assent to him and follow him." The monk informed Salman that the sign of that prophet would be that he would accept a gift but would not accept charity and that he would be sealed with the seal of prophethood between his shoulders. On their way out of the holy city they again saw the crippled man, who repeated his previous call for mercy. This time, the monk raised him up and prayed to God to heal him. The man walked away healthy and sound.

The monk then vanished, and Salman could not find him. Salman finally, and after much chagrin at the loss of his master, was captured by two men of the tribe of Kalb who carried him to Medina. There they sold him to an old woman who employed him as a shepherd. In Medina Salman met the Prophet, whom he recognized by the signs the monk had given him. He told the Prophet about his former companions, who had occupied themselves with prayer and fasting and had had faith in the Prophet, whose appearance they awaited. The Prophet, however, answered, "O Salman, they are of the people of the Fire." This grieved Salman deeply, and thus God sent down this verse concerning his companions, in order that he might be consoled (Tabari, II, pp. 150–154; see also Wahidi, pp. 23–24).

The legalistic approach is best observed in Razi's arguments and counterarguments concerning both the implications of the verse and the people to whom it refers. He begins by attempting to identify the people intended in this verse. "'Those who have faith' before Muhammad were Waraqah ibn Nawfal, al-Qiss ibn Sa'idah [both Christians], Salman, and others like them. Of the Jews, they were the hypocrites who turned away from their hypocrisy and accepted the prophethood of Muhammad." Razi continues, "Then God, exalted be He, declared concerning these four groups that if they had faith in God, they would have their reward in the hereafter. [This He did] in order to make known that even the masters of those who are in error, were they to turn away from their error and accept the true faith, God would accept their faith and acts of obedience. . . . Faith in God includes faith in His messengers and His books as well as the last day. . . . These two demands [that is, faith in God and the last day] include all things relating to religion during the time of obligation [*taklif*] as well as in the hereafter with regard to rewards and punishments" (Razi, III, p. 105).

Sayyid Qutb begins by denying that God's favor toward men, "can be conditioned by any particular ethnic or racial consideration. Rather, it is for the people of faith in every age and everywhere. It is for every one according to the faith by which he lived until the subsequent revelation had come, bringing the faith to which the faithful must turn." This however, Sayyid Qutb asserts, applies only to the time before the apostleship of Muhammad. "Thereafter, the final form of faith has been unalterably determined" (Qutb, I, pp. 95–96). This view may be supported by the following traditions quoted by Tabari. The Prophet is said to have told Salman, in reassuring him concerning the fate of his companions who had faith but had not heard of Islam that, "whoever has died in the faith of Jesus, and died in Islam before he had heard of me, his lot shall be good. But whoever hears of me today and yet does not assent to me, he shall surely perish" (Tabari, I, p. 155).

(63) The reason for God's making a covenant with the Children of Israel, as related by Tabari on the authority of 'Abd al-Rahman

ibn Zayd and Wahb ibn Munabbih, was that, "when Moses returned [from Mount Sinai] with the Tablets, he said, 'These are the Tablets containing the Book of God in which are His commandments which He has enjoined upon you and His prohibitions of things which He has made unlawful for you.' They replied, 'But who would accept it on your word? No, by God, not until we see God openly, not until God appears to us and says, "This is my Book; receive it!" Why does He not speak to us as He spoke to you, O Moses?' Then God's anger was kindled against them and a punishment [from heaven] came upon them; they were stunned and died, all of them. God then revived them and Moses said to them, 'Receive the Book of God!'" They refused his plea three times. Finally God sent His angels and they lifted up the mountain over them, saying, "Do you know this?" They answered, "It is al-Tur [Mount Sinai]." The angel then threatened them, saying "Receive the Book of God, or we shall throw it down upon you." They therefore received the Book of God through a covenant (Tabari, II, p. 156; see also Ibn Kathir, I, pp. 182–183; and Qurtubi, I, pp. 436–437).

Commentators have differed as to what the covenant here refers to. Some said it was "the covenant in accordance with which God created humankind in the state of pure faith [*fitrah*] in His oneness and justice." Others said that God intended by it the covenant which He made with the apostles in His saying, "Remember when God made a covenant with the prophets concerning that which I have given unto you of the Book and wisdom. Then came to you an apostle confirming that which is with you, that you would give assent to him and lend him support" (Q. 3:81). According to other commentators, the covenant here refers to the Children of Israel receiving the Torah from Moses and their refusal to accept it, whereupon the angels threatened them with the mountain, as has already been explained (Tabarsi, I, pp. 284–285; see below Q. 2:171; Qummi, I, p. 49; and Tabataba'i, I, p. 198).

(65–66) The story to which these two verses allude is told in some detail in *surah* 7, verses 163–166. Commentators have generally endeavored first to locate the time and place of the people and second to explain the nature and justification of the punishment they suffered. The people here mentioned lived, according to Ibn 'Abbas, during the time of the prophet David in a town on the sea between Aylah (the modern port city Eilat) and Medina (Razi, III, p. 109). Tabari locates the town between Aylah and Mount Sinai and relates, also on the authority of Ibn 'Abbas, that it was called Midian (Tabari, II, p. 169).

The reason for punishment was the refusal to observe Friday instead of Saturday as a sacred day of prayer. God accepted Saturday as their sabbath but commanded them to desist from all activity on that day. They disobeyed the divine command; hence the punishment. Tabari relates on the authority of Ibn 'Abbas that "God enjoined the observance of Friday upon all prophets, telling them of its great sanctity in the heavens for the angels. . . . Thus Moses commanded his people to observe Friday. They protested, however, saying, 'How could you enjoin Friday upon us and proclaim its sanctity over all other days when Saturday is in reality the best of all days, for God created the heavens and the earth and all provisions in six days, and on the sabbath everything stood still [*sabata*] in obedience to Him.' Thus they chose the sabbath, which was accepted from them by God on condition that they would not engage in any work on it" (Tabari, II, pp. 167–168).

The story as related by Razi is as follows. On the sabbath fish gathered close to the shores of the town. The people dug pools for the fish and filled them from large canals that were also dug for that purpose. They then gathered the fish trapped in the pools on Sunday. This was their act of transgression. They continued in this custom a long time, the sons following in the footsteps of their fathers (Razi, III, pp. 109–110; see also Nisaburi, I, pp. 336–337). It is related on the authority of Hasan al-Basri that the Jews transgressed by fishing on the sabbath even though they were forbidden to do so. Tabarsi reports that Ibn 'Abbas said, "God transformed them into apes in punishment for their disobedience. . . . They lived for three days, neither eating nor drinking nor procreating. Then God sent a strong wind which carried them off and threw them into the sea." Mujahid said, "They were not transformed into apes, but it was a similitude which God made for them [the Jews of Medina]. . . . Their hearts were transformed and were made like the hearts of apes, neither accepting admonition nor fearing threats" (Tabarsi, I, p. 288). Razi speculates, "That they were transformed into apes may mean that their human accidents [*a'rad*] were changed into those of apes, or that their forms were changed, but they retained the mental awareness of their conditions" (Razi, III, pp. 111–112).

This view is not essentially different from that of Mujahid, Ibn 'Arabi, or the modern explanation by Sayyid Qutb. Ibn 'Arabi sees the transformation of a human being into animal form as symbolic.

He sees in the acts of worship a way of purifying the soul and keeping it above the animal level of existence. Ibn 'Arabi interprets the three days of rest (Friday, Saturday, and Sunday) as indicative of spiritual stages and realities characterizing the three religious communities that observe these days.

He asserts that "God prescribed first for the Jews a day of rest in a week because they are the people of the beginning [*mabda'*] and exoteric truth. He then decreed for the Christians a day of rest because they are the people of the *ma'ad* [that is, the return of men to God after death] and esoteric truth. He last prescribed for the Muslims the day of Friday because they belong to the end of time. They are the people of prophethood and the end [*khatimah*]. They are the people of unity combining all [three] even though Saturday is the last day of the week, as it is the seventh day. The realm [*'alam*] to which the Jews were called is the realm of concrete phenomena; it is the last realm. The Christians were called to the realm of the intellect [*'aql*], which is the first realm. Friday, however, is the day of gathering [*jam'*] and sealing [*khatm*]."

Ibn 'Arabi concludes: "Whoever does not heed these situations and acts of vigilance [*muraqabat*], the light of his potentiality would be extinguished. He would be transformed as were the people of the sabbath."

Ibn 'Arabi then interprets allegorically not only the transformation of the people mentioned in these verses but also its cause. He writes, "'They were forbidden fishing' means the attainment of sense pleasures belonging to the carnal soul and possessing them. The canals which they dug in order to trap the fish on the sabbath means that they hoarded on weekdays the water of the ocean of matter and its bodies. Hence all the moments [*awqat*] of their presence before God [*hudur*] were instead spent in quest of sense pleasures. Such things lead to abasement from the higher human realm to the lower animal realm. This is the meaning of God's saying, 'We said to them, "Be apes"' That is: resembling human beings in form but in reality not humans." Ibn 'Arabi, however, adds that actual transformation (*maskh*) is real and cannot be denied either in this world or in the world to come. He adduces Qur'anic verses and *hadith* traditions to support this conclusion. God says, "And He turned some of them into apes and swine." The Apostle of God said, "Some people shall be gathered [on the day of judgment] in such ugly forms that apes and swine would look better" (Ibn 'Arabi, I, pp. 56–57).

Sayyid Qutb interprets the verse as referring to the people's falling into the state of animals, or beasts: "the animal which has no will and the beast which cannot rise above the demands of the stomach. . . . It is not necessary, therefore, for them to have been changed into apes in their bodies; rather it was in their spirits and minds. This is because impressions and inner feelings and thoughts reflect on faces and complexions signs which leave their deep shadow" (Qutb, I, pp. 97–98). Most classical commentators, however, prefer the literal sense of the text over such allegorical interpretations (see Tabari, II, p. 173; and Tabarsi, I, p. 288).

67. And remember when Moses said to his people, "Behold, God commands you to slaughter a cow." They answered, "Do you take us for a mockery?" He said, "I take refuge in God from being among the foolish."

68. They said, "Call upon your Lord, that He may make clear to us what cow it is." He answered, "He says, 'She is neither an old cow nor a young heifer, but of middle age, between the two.' Do therefore as you have been commanded."

69. They said, "Call upon your Lord that He may make clear to us her color." He answered, "He says that it is a cow of intense color, pleasing the beholders."

70. They said, "Call upon your Lord, that He may make clear to us which cow it is, for cows look alike to us; then we shall, if God wills, be guided aright."

71. He answered, "He says, 'She is a cow not yet broken to plow the earth or water the fields, sound and with no blemish in her.'" They said, "Now you have brought us the truth." Thus they slaughtered her, although they almost did not.

72. And remember when you killed a soul and were in dispute concerning it; yet God shall bring to light what you have concealed.

73. Then we said, "Strike the dead man with some of its parts." Thus God revives the dead and shows you His signs, that you may understand.

These seven verses present an account of the cow of the Children of Israel during the time of Moses. It is also the tale that gives the present *surah* its title. The story is told in an unusual way in that it begins in the middle with a dialogue between Moses and his people concerning the details of the cow. Only in the last two verses do we see the reason for choosing and sacrificing the cow.

The Qur'an tells us that Moses transmitted the command of God, saying, "Behold, God commands you to slaughter a cow." Commentators have generally inferred that, "had they slaughtered any cow, it would have been accepted of them. But they made hardships for themselves [that is, by asking for details]; hence God made it even more difficult for them" (Tabari, II, p. 186; Ibn Kathir, I, pp. 188–195).

Classical Sunni and Shi'i commentators recount several variants of a story in which a man killed another and denied his crime. God then revived the dead man, who identified his murderer. Commentators have added yet another moral to this story. Since the cow was finally specified, it was necessary to obtain it at any cost. Therefore, either a widow and her orphaned children, or a pious but poor man, were paid large sums of gold for the cow (see Tabari, II, p. 185; Qurtubi, I, p. 456; Razi, III, p. 114).

The following story, related on the authority of the sixth imam Ja'far al-Sadiq, is typical of the many tales told by classical commentators in explanation of the story of the cow. "A man among the best and most learned of the Children of Israel sought the hand of a woman, who assented. A cousin of that man, who was a corrupt apostate, also sought the woman's hand, and was refused. . . . He envied his good cousin and secretly killed him. He then carried the dead man to Moses and said, 'O Prophet of God, this man is my cousin; he was killed.' Moses asked, 'Who killed him?' The man answered, 'I do not know.' Murder was regarded as a great crime among the Children of Israel; thus Moses was greatly troubled. He therefore gathered all the Children of Israel for consultation. There was a man among them who had a cow and had a righteous son. The son had something to sell, but when some men came to buy, the key to his house was under the pillow of his father, who was asleep. The son did not wish to disturb his father. Thus the men went away without buying the merchandise. When the father woke up he asked him, 'What have you done with your merchandise?' He answered, 'It is still there; I have not sold it because the key was under your head.' . . . The father said, 'I shall give you this cow in compensation for the profit you have lost.' . . . God was pleased with the son's treatment of his father and thus commanded the Children of Israel to slaughter that same cow. When they came to Moses, weeping and wailing . . . he ordered them to sacrifice a cow. They went to buy the cow from the son, but he said, 'I shall not sell it, except for its skinful of gold.' Moses said, 'You must sacrifice this very cow.' Having thus sacrificed the cow, they asked Moses, 'What now would you command us to do, O prophet of God?' God then revealed to him, 'Say to them, "Strike [the dead man] with a part of it, then ask him who killed [him]."' [This they did] and struck the dead man with its tail, saying, 'Who killed you?' He replied, 'So and so, son of so and so, my cousin, who carried me here.' This is in accordance with God's saying, 'Thus God revives the dead'" (Qummi, I, pp. 49–50; see also Tabarsi, I, pp. 300–301).

Ibn 'Arabi does not concern himself with the story of the cow as such. Rather, he sees the cow as "the animal soul." "Slaughtering it means curbing its caprices which are its life and restraining it from exercising its own peculiar actions. It must be slain with the knife of spiritual discipline." As for the qualities of the cow, Ibn 'Arabi interprets the phrase "neither an old cow nor a young heifer" to mean "not old so as to have lost its potential or that its erroneous belief has become so firm that it could no longer adapt." The phrase "nor a young heifer" signifies "the soul in the middle state, neither too old that it can no longer grow, nor too young that its potential is as yet undeveloped and it is unable to endure the severe spiritual discipline required of it." As for its color, Ibn 'Arabi says, "God mentioned its intense color because the body in its original state is black because it lacks luminosity. The vegetable soul has a green color caused by the appearance of luminosity in it. The color of the heart, however, is white because of its freedom from the body and its power of discernment and the perfection of its luminosity." Ibn 'Arabi then presents a hierarchy of colors applying to the soul in its various stages of spiritual development. The phrase "pleasing the beholders" refers to those who are perfect and aware of all potential because of their intense love. It pleases them with its radiance. Ibn 'Arabi interprets the words "not yet broken to plow" to mean "not yet subject to the commands of the *shari'ah*" (Ibn 'Arabi, I, pp. 59–60).

Tabataba'i makes the following observation: "The story of the cow is not mentioned in the Torah that is in the hands of the Jews of today. It would therefore have been more appropriate that [the Jews of the Prophet's time] not be addressed with this story at all or at least only after indicating the alterations [in the Torah] which they made [with regard to this story]. Nonetheless, in one of the laws of the Torah, there is some proof of the actual occurrence of this story." Tabataba'i then quotes at length Deuteronomy 21:1–9, in which the sacrificing of a young heifer is enjoined as a ransom for the blood of an innocent man whose murderer cannot be found (Tabataba'i, I, p. 200). But he modifies this view by observing, "It has been said that the story was intended to show the actual reason for the [biblical] law" (Tabataba'i, I, p. 200).

Sayyid Qutb notes three important aspects of this story. The first was to show the nature of the Children of Israel and their searching for excuses to disobey God's command. The second is to illustrate the power of God to give life. The third is the unusual way in which the story is told, thus clearly illustrating the great artistic qualities of the Qur'an. Sayyid Qutb then elaborates these three points but without resorting to the usual tales of the early commentators (Qutb, I, pp. 102–103).

74. After that your hearts were hardened as stones, or even harder, for out of some stones rivers burst forth, some are split and water flows therefrom, and some stones fall down in awe of God. God is not unaware of what you do.

75. Do you therefore desire that they should have faith in you when a party among them used to hear the word of God, then alter it after they had comprehended it, knowing full well what they had done.

76. And when they meet those who have faith, they say, "We have faith." But when they are alone with one another, they say, "Would you inform them of that which God has revealed to you in order for them to contend therewith against you before your Lord?" Do you therefore not understand?

77. Do they not know that God knows that which they conceal in their hearts and that which they disclose?

78. There are some among them who are unlettered, not knowing the scriptures except as hearsay. They only follow their own conjecture.

79. Woe therefore to those who write the scriptures with their own hands, and then say, "It is a revelation from God" in order to exchange it for a small price. Woe to them for that which their hands have written and woe to them for that which they have gained thereby.

80. They say, "The fire shall not touch us, save for a certain number of days." Say, "Have you received a promise from God of this—for God shall not revoke His promise—or do you utter concerning God that of which you have no knowledge?"

(75) This verse was addressed to the Prophet and the Muslims of Medina. Commentators have differed as to the group of Jews intended in it, the meaning of the words of God which they altered, and the nature and purpose of this alteration. It is related on the authority of al-Rabi' and Ibn Ishaq by Tabari that the people intended were the men who heard the words of God with Moses (Tabari, II, p. 245). When the men returned with Moses, after they were caused to die and then revived, they said to the people, "We heard God say such and such, which, if you are able to do, do so, but if you are not able, there shall be no blame in you" (Zamakhshari, I, p. 291; see also Ibn Kathir, I, p. 201).

Others said, "It was the Torah which they altered, rendering the sanctions in it prohibitions, and the prohibitions sanctions; the truth in it they rendered untrue, and what is false, truth. Thus if a man came to them with a valid accusation, and offered them a bribe, they would bring out the Book of God to judge him thereby. But if a man came to them with a false accusation and offered them a bribe, they would bring out the altered book according to which he would be judged to be truthful. If, however, a man came to them inquiring concerning a matter wherein there was neither truth nor falsehood, nor was a bribe offered, they would enjoin upon him to act truthfully" (Tabari, II, p. 246; see also Tabarsi, I, p. 317).

With regard to what was actually changed or altered, many commentators, and especially those who attributed the alteration to the Torah, said that it was the description in the Torah of the physical features, character, and prophethood of Muhammad which was altered or obscured. Razi, as usual, questions such traditional interpretations and in the end prefers to leave the matter open. He begins by observing, "Alteration [*tahrif*] must refer either to the actual words or to their meaning. . . . Unbroken transmission [*tawatur*], however, prevents alteration of the actual words. Thus if those who altered were the seventy men at the time of Moses, they would have altered nothing relating to Muhammad, but only injunctions and prohibitions. If, on the other hand, they lived at the time of Muhammad, it is more probable that what is intended by altering are things relating to Muhammad. The literal sense of the Qur'an does not indicate what they actually altered" (Razi, III, pp. 134–135). Tabataba'i gives as an example of alteration the story of the cow, which, he claims, the Jews deleted from the Torah (see Tabataba'i, I, p. 213).

Sayyid Qutb assumes that the people here intended were the learned men of the Jewish community of Medina. He does not specify the nature of their alteration of the Torah, but he argues that if they could alter their own scriptures they would do so, and thus would be even more ready to alter by false interpretation the revelation sent down to Muhammad (Qutb, I, p. 109).

(78) The term *ummi* (unlettered) and its plural *ummiyun* have raised a number of questions for commentators. Since the term has been applied to the Prophet, who is characterized as *al-nabi al-ummi* (the unlettered prophet), the meaning and significance of this term for both Muslim and Western scholars have been a matter of controversy. Most commentators have understood the word *ummiyun* to mean those who neither read nor write. Ibn Zayd said, "They are those among the Jews who do not read the scriptures" (Tabari, II, pp. 257–258; see also Ibn Kathir, I, pp. 203–206). The word *ummi* is derived by some commentators from the word *umm* meaning mother, because the mother's attachment to the child prevents her from sending him to the traditional schools (Tabataba'i, I, p. 215). Tabarsi offers a derivation based on linguistic usage: "The word *ummah* means *khilqah* [that is, the original state in which a person was created]. Therefore [a person] is said to be *ummi* because he has remained in his original state [that is, without learning]." Tabarsi states further that Abu 'Ubaydah said, "The *ummiyun* are

the nations [*umam*] to whom no book was sent down . . . but an *ummi* prophet is one who does not write" (Tabarsi, I, p. 322).

Qurtubi cites a *hadith* in which the Prophet says, "We are an unlettered community [*ummah*]: we neither write nor are able to do arithmetic." Qurtubi then presents several views on *ummiyun* and its reference. The first is that they were the Jews who did not accept the Mother (*umm*) of the Book. The second is that they were so called because the Mother of the Book was sent down to them. Third, according to 'Ikrimah and al-Dahhak, the people here intended "were the Christians of the Arabs who did not know the scriptures" (Qurtubi, II, p. 5).

The other issue that concerned commentators in this verse is the meaning and significance of *amani* (hearsay). It is related on the authority of Ibn 'Abbas and Qatadah that the book referred to in this verse is the Torah, which the Jews in the Prophet's time knew only as "memorization and recitation [*amani*] without true understanding and care for what it contains." The word *amani* is derived from the verb *tamanna*, which means to read or recite (see Q. 22:52). *Amani* may also mean "false words which they [the Jews] utter with their tongues, or reports or tales [*ahadith*] which their scholars used to relate to them and which they recited, but did not comprehend." Other commentators have asserted that "*amani* means desires, that is, desiring mercy from God." The word *amani*, according to this interpretation, would be the plural of the word *umniyah*, meaning wish or desire, which is the most commonly accepted meaning of the term *amani* (Tabarsi, I, p. 325; see also Tabari, II, p. 261; Qurtubi, II, p. 6; Zamakhshari, I, p. 291; Nisaburi, I, pp. 349–355).

(80) Wahidi reports from Ibn 'Abbas, "When the Prophet came to Medina the Jews used to say, 'The duration of this world shall be seven thousand years. People will endure the punishment of one day of the days of the hereafter in the Fire for every thousand years of the years of this world. It will be only seven days, after which punishment shall cease.'" Thus God sent down this verse (Wahidi, p. 24).

Tabari asserts that the Jews, confident of their lineage and of their status with God, said to the Prophet, "The fire shall not touch us." He relates on the authority of Ibn 'Abbas that they said, "God will not cause us to remain in the Fire except for the time required for the oath [which he made] to be fulfilled. It shall be only the days during which we worshiped the calf: forty days. Once these days expire, our punishment and the oath will end." Al-Suddi reported another tradition which presents an even clearer assertion by the Jews of their special privilege with God: "God shall consign us to the Fire wherein we shall remain for only forty nights. When the fire will have consumed our sins and purified us, a crier shall cry out, 'Bring out of the Fire every circumcised child of the children of Israel.' For this reason we have been commanded to be circumcised" (Tabari, II, pp. 274–275; see also Ibn Kathir, I, pp. 206–207; Qurtubi, II, p. 10; Zamakhshari, I, p. 292; Tabarsi, I, p. 329).

81. Whosoever commits an evil deed and is encompassed by his transgression, such are the people of the Fire; in it they shall abide forever.

82. But those who have faith and do good works: these are the people of the Garden; in it they shall abide forever.

83. And remember when we took the covenant of the Children of Israel, saying, "Do not worship anyone other than God, do well toward parents, kindred orphans, and the destitute, speak kindly to others, observe regular worship, and give the obligatory alms." Yet you turned away, save a few of you, and behaved heedlessly.

84. And when we took your covenant saying, "You shall not shed your own blood, nor drive one another out of your dwellings."—Then you confirmed the covenant and were witness to it.

85. Yet you are the same people who now kill one another and drive some of you out of their dwellings, conspiring against them in transgression and enmity. But if they come to you captives, you ransom them, though it is unlawful for you to expel them from their homes. Would you then have faith in parts of the scriptures and reject others? The only punishment for those who do so among you is disgrace in this world, and on the day of resurrection they shall be sent to the most grievous torment, for God is not unaware of what you do.

(85) Tabari relates on the authority of Ibn 'Abbas that "God reproached them for this, for He had made unlawful for them in

the Torah the shedding of one another's blood, but ordained in it for them the ransoming of their captives. They were two groups: one of the tribe of Qaynuqa', allied with the Khazraj tribe, and the second the tribes of Nadir and Qurayzah, who were the allies of the tribe of Aws before Islam. Thus when there was a war between the Aws and Khazraj, the people of Qaynuqa' came out in support of the Khazraj, and Nadir and Qurayzah in support of the Aws—each group supporting their allies against their own brothers—until they shed one another's blood; this they did even though they had the Torah in their hands, through which they knew what was ordained for them. When the war was at an end, each of the two groups ransomed its captives in accordance with the law of the Torah." Thus each group ransomed its captives from the allies of its opponents (Tabari, II, pp. 305–306; see also Tabarsi, I, pp. 343–345).

86. These are they who have exchanged the hereafter for the life of this world. Therefore torment shall not be lightened for them, nor will they be helped.

87. We gave Moses the scriptures and made other apostles to succeed him. We also gave Jesus son of Mary clear proofs and fortified him with the Holy Spirit. Whenever an apostle came to you with that which your souls did not desire, you became arrogant. To some you gave the lie, and others you willfully slew.

(87) Commentators are agreed that the spirit here means Gabriel. This view is related on the authority of Qatadah, al-Suddi, Ibn 'Abbas, and Rabi' ibn Anas. Ibn Zayd, however, said, "God fortified Jesus with the Gospel, which is a spirit, as God also called the Qur'an a spirit. Both the Gospel and the Qur'an are the spirit of God, as He says, 'And thus have we sent down to you a spirit of our command'" (Q. 42:52). Ibn 'Abbas said, "The spirit was the name of God through which Jesus was able to revive the dead" (Tabari, II, pp. 320–321). Al-Rabi' ibn Anas said, "It was the spirit which God breathed into him." Tabarsi, however, said, "The best interpretation is to say that it was Gabriel. If it is asked why Jesus was, among all prophets, specially mentioned as being supported by Gabriel, when every prophet was also supported by him, it will be said that he was so mentioned because Gabriel accompanied him from his youth to his manhood. He was with him wherever he went,

so that when the Jews conspired to kill him he did not leave him until he took him up to heaven. Gabriel also appeared to Mary when she conceived Jesus; he announced him to her and breathed the spirit of God into her" (Tabarsi, I, p. 349).

Commentators have differed concerning the meaning of the word *qudus* (holy); according to some it means purity and to others, blessing. Tabarsi relates, on the authority of Hasan al-Basri, al-Rabi' ibn Anas, and 'Abd al-Rahman ibn Zayd that "*al-qudus* is God, the Exalted . . . *al-qudus* and *al-quddus* are the same" (see Q. 54:23; Tabarsi, I, pp. 348–349; see also Tabari, II, pp. 319–323; and Ibn Kathir, I, pp. 214–215.

88. They say, "Our hearts are uncircumcised." Thus God cursed them for their rejection of faith, and they have but little faith.

89. And when, moreover, a book came to them from God confirming that which is with them—and they having before that prayed for victory over those who rejected faith—yet when that which they did recognize had come to them, they rejected it. God's curse be upon the rejecters of faith.

90. Wretched is the price for which they sold their souls, that they have out of envy rejected what God had sent down, for God sends down His favor to whomever He wills of His servants. They incurred wrath upon wrath; the rejecters of faith shall suffer a humiliating torment.

91. If they are told, "Have faith in that which God sent down," they say, "We should rather have faith in that which was sent down to us." Yet they reject that which came after it, even though it is the truth, confirming that which is already with them. Say, "Why did you slay the prophets of God in times past, if you were true men of faith?"

92. Although Moses came to you with manifest signs, yet you worshiped the calf after this and were wrongdoers.

93. And remember when we established a covenant with you
and raised the mount over you, saying, "Receive that
which we have given to you with power, and obey." But
they said, "We hear and we disobey." Thus they were
made to drink the calf into their hearts for their rejection
of faith. Say, "Miserable indeed is that which your faith
enjoins upon you, were you true men of faith."

(93) Commentators have generally interpreted the verse metaphorically to mean, "They were made to drink the love of the calf
so that it penetrated into their hearts" (Ibn Kathir, I, p. 220). A
more literal interpretation, which Ibn Kathir relates on the authority
of al-Suddi and 'Ali, asserts that the children of Israel were made
by Moses actually to drink the calf. "Moses took the calf, ground
it with files and strewed it on the water. Every one of those who
worshiped the calf drank of the water and his face turned yellow,
like gold" (Ibn Kathir, I, pp. 220–221; see also Tabari, II, pp. 357–359;
Shawkani, I, p. 114). Tabarsi offers the following Shi'i interpretation:
"The meaning of God's saying 'they were made to drink' is not that
someone else made them do so; rather, they themselves were the
ones who committed the deed. . . . His saying 'for their rejection
of faith' could not mean that they were made to drink the love of
the calf as punishment for their rejection of faith, because love for
the calf is in itself evil rejection of faith [*kufr*]. God does not cause
kufr in the servant, neither in the sense that He decrees something
then changes His decree [*ibtida'*] nor as a punishment. It rather
means that they rejected faith in God, the Exalted, through their
having drunk the love of the calf" (Tabarsi, I, p. 366). (For a
discussion of the covenant and the raising of the mountain, see Q.
2:63, above.)

94. Say, "If the abode of the last day shall be yours alone to
the exclusion of the rest of humankind, then wish for
death if you are truthful."

95. But they shall never desire it because of that which their
hands have wrought; God is all-knowing of the wrongdoers.

96. You will surely find them the most greedy of men for life,
even more than the associators. Each one of them

wishes that he could live a thousand years; yet were he to live a thousand years, this would not remove him from punishment. God is all-seeing of what they do.

97. Say, "Who is an enemy to Gabriel! For he brought the Qu'ran down upon your heart by God's leave, confirming that which was before it, a guidance and glad tidings to the faithful.

98. Who is an enemy to God, His angels, His apostles and to Gabriel and Michael!" God Himself is the enemy of the rejecters of faith.

(97, 98) These two verses were sent down, as Wahidi relates, on the authority of Ibn 'Abbas, when the Jews of Medina came to the Prophet saying, "We shall ask you concerning certain matters. If you answer us truthfully, we will follow you. Tell us who of the angels comes to you, for there is no prophet but that an angel comes to him from his Lord with the [charge] of apostleship and revelation. Who is your angel?" He answered, "He is Gabriel." They said, "He is the one who comes down with strife and battle; he is our enemy. Had you said 'Michael', the angel who comes down with rain and mercy, we would have followed you" (Wahidi, p. 26). Wahidi further relates on the authority of al-Sha'bi that 'Umar ibn al-Khattab said, "I used to frequent the Jews in their schools when they studied the Torah and marvel at how the Torah concurs with the Qur'an and how the Qur'an concurs with the Torah. They said to me, 'O 'Umar, there is no one dearer to us than you.' 'Why?' I asked. 'Because,' they said, 'you come to us and enjoy our company.' I answered, 'I come to marvel at how the Books of God confirm each other.' . . . As I was with them one day, the Apostle of God passed behind me . . . and entered an alley of Medina. I turned to them saying, 'I adjure you, by God and the Book which was sent down to you, do you know that he is the Apostle of God?' . . . Their rabbi said, 'We do know that he is the Apostle of God.' I said, 'You are most deserving of perdition if you know that he is the Apostle of God and still do not follow him.' They said, 'We have enemies and friends among the angels.'" They then repeated to 'Umar what they had already said to the Prophet (Wahidi, p. 27; see also p. 28 and Tabarsi, I, pp. 375–377).

99. It is we who have sent down to you manifest signs;
none shall reject them save the evildoers.

100. Whenever they make a covenant, does a group of them
reject it? Surely most of them have rejected faith.

101. When an Apostle of God has come to them confirming
that which is with them, a group of those who were
given the scriptures cast the Book of God behind their
backs as though they do not know.

102. And they followed that which the satans have recited
concerning the reign of Solomon. Solomon did not reject
faith; rather the satans rejected faith. They teach people
magic and that which was sent down to the two angels
in Babel, Harut and Marut. Yet these two would not
teach anyone until they had said, ''We are surely a temptation; do not, therefore, reject faith.'' People learn from
them that by which they can cause dissension between a
man and his wife. But they harm no one by means of it
except by God's leave. They learn that which harms them
and does not benefit them. They know well that whoever
deals in it has no portion in the life to come. Miserable is
the price for which they sold their souls, if they but
knew!

(102) This verse has been the subject of much controversy. Commentators have disagreed concerning every phrase and even word
in it (see Tabataba'i, I, p. 234). These many disagreements may,
however, be reduced to two general areas: the first concerning the
actual meaning of some words and their references and the second
concerning the general context of the verse. I shall present some of
the most widely accepted classical interpretations, as well as the
critical views of later commentators.

The verse must be read in relation to the previous one, which
asserts that "a group of those who were given the scriptures cast
the Book of God behind their backs." Tabari asserts that "the Jews
who were in Medina during the time of the Prophet contended with
him through the Torah, but found the Torah to be in full agreement
with the Qur'an, commanding them to follow Muhammad and to
assent to all that the Qur'an enjoins. They instead disputed with

him on the basis of books which people wrote down from the dictation of soothsayers [*kuhhan*] who lived during the time of Solomon" (Tabari, II, p. 405).

Tabari reports that al-Suddi said, "The satans used to ascend to heaven and sit close in order to listen to the conversations of the angels concerning happenings in the earth such as death, rainfall, or divine commands. Satans then came down to the soothsayers and recounted to them what they heard. The soothsayers in turn related it to the people, who found what they were told to be true. As the soothsayers began to trust the satans, the latter began to mix the truth they heard with falsehood, so that they added to every word they related seventy false ones. People wrote down what the soothsayers told them in books. Thus the belief that the *jinn* knew that which is concealed spread among the Children of Israel. God then sent Solomon, who gathered these books in a box which he buried under his throne. No one of the satans was able to approach the throne for fear of being consumed by fire. Solomon also warned the people, saying, 'Anyone I hear saying that the satans know what is concealed, I shall cut off his head.' After Solomon and the pious scholars of his time died, Satan appeared to the Children of Israel in human form and said, 'Shall I lead you to a treasure which you will never be able to consume?' Thus he told them to dig under the throne, where they found the books. Satan then told them that Solomon was able to control men, *jinn*, and birds through this magic. He then flew away and the books were spread among the people. When Muhammad came, they used these books to dispute with him" (Tabari, II, pp. 405–406; see also Wahidi, pp. 29–31).

Tabari reports that Ibn Ishaq related that when Solomon died, the satans wrote different kinds of magic in a book, which they sealed with a seal similar to that of Solomon. On the cover they inscribed, "Here is what Asif ibn Barkhiya the prophet wrote for King Solomon." The book was buried under Solomon's throne until the Jews later discovered it; hence they claimed that Solomon was a magician. Another tradition related on the authority of Ibn Ishaq asserts that God took kingship away from Solomon, at which time groups of men and *jinn* apostatized. When, however, God returned kingship to him, they returned to the true faith. Then he gathered the books of magic and buried them under his throne. Satan later brought them out, and people claimed that these books were sent down by God to Solomon, who concealed them. Thus they followed these books, claiming them to be scriptures (see Tabari, II, pp.

407–408; see also pp. 408–411). According to these interpretations, the verse would read, "And they followed that which the satans have recited [that is, magic] concerning the reign of Solomon. Solomon did not reject faith [by practising magic]; rather the satans rejected faith [in that they taught men magic]" (Tabari, II, pp. 417–418).

Commentators have differed also with regard to the identity of the satans mentioned in this verse. "Some said that they were the satans of the *jinn* . . . and others that they were the satans of humankind who persist in their error. Still others said that they were the satans of both men and *jinn*" (Tabarsi, I, pp. 391–392). "God therefore made clear that what these satans taught men and related to them was in itself an act of *kufr* from which He dissociated Solomon. The Jews attributed magic to Solomon, whom God vindicated in His saying, 'Solomon did not reject faith'" (Tabarsi, I, p. 392).

Commentators have likewise disagreed with regard to the meaning of the phrase, "and that which was sent down to the two angels in Babel, Harut and Marut." Tabari relates on the authority of Ibn 'Abbas, "The word *ma* means 'not' [instead of its alternate meaning, that which]; that is to say, magic was not sent down [*ma unzila*] to the two angels. Thus the exegesis of the verse would be, 'And they followed the magic which the satans recited concerning the reign of Solomon; yet neither did Solomon reject faith, nor did God send down magic to the two angels. Rather, satans rejected faith in that they taught people magic in Babel, that is, Harut and Marut'" (This tradition assumes that Harut and Marut were the people who learned magic from the satans in Babel; thus they were not angels. The two angels are taken to be Gabriel and Michael.) "This is because magicians among the Jews used to claim that God sent down magic to Solomon by the tongues of Gabriel and Michael. Thus God revealed their false claim, for Gabriel and Michael never brought down magic. Harut and Marut were therefore two men who learned magic from satans" (Tabari, II, pp. 419–420). Tabari also cites Qatadah, who said, "'*Ma*' means 'that which', or 'what.' Thus Harut and Marut were two of the angels. They taught men magic, but were charged not to teach anyone until they had said, 'We are surely a temptation; do not, therefore, reject faith.' Magic here is of two kinds: one which the satans taught, and another which was taught by the two angels" (Tabari, II, p. 420).

Most early commentators have agreed, however, that Harut and Marut were two angels. Their story appears very early in the history of *tafsir* on the authority of the first masters of this science among the Companions and their Successors. The story, as related by Tabari on the authority of Ibn Mas'ud and Ibn 'Abbas, is as follows: "When the children of Adam had increased in the earth and committed acts of disobedience, the angels, heavens, earth, and mountains invoked God against them, saying, 'Our Lord, would You not destroy them?' God revealed to the angels, 'Were I to put lust in your hearts and give Satan authority over you, and were you then to descend to earth, you would do the same.' The angels thought in their hearts that if they were sent down, they would not sin. God then revealed to them, 'Choose two of the best angels among you,' and they chose Harut and Marut. They were thus sent down to earth, and Venus was sent down to them in the image of a beautiful Persian woman. They fell into sin [by lusting after her]. They were therefore given the choice between the punishment of this world or that of the world to come, but they chose the punishment of this world" (Tabari, II, pp. 428).

This tradition presents the basic elements of the story accepted by most classical commentators. Some traditions, however, related the story of the two angels to God's saying, "Behold, I am about to place a vicegerent in the earth" (see above, Q. 2:30). According to this view, God sent down Harut and Marut to demonstrate to the protesting angels man's uniqueness as a creature endowed with special faculties which even angels could not possess without also falling into sin and disobedience (see Nisaburi, I, p. 391, who relates the story on the authority of Ibn 'Abbas). Razi, on the other hand, for reasons which are discussed below, asserts that the two angels were sent down at the time of the prophet Enoch (Idris). (Razi, III, p. 220.)

The trend in the development of the story of Harut and Marut appears to have aimed at achieving two main purposes: first, to fill in an already popular outline, and second, to emphasize a particular theological or juristic idea. Tabarsi relates that God sent Harut and Marut down to earth because they were the most critical among the angels of the sinful state of humankind and most persistent in inciting God's anger against them. Thus God said to the angels, "Go down to the earth, for I have put in you faculties of eating and drinking, lust, fear, and hope, as I have put them in the children of Adam. But beware that you do not associate anything with me, kill the soul which God has prohibited to be slain, commit adultery, or drink wine" (Tabarsi, I, p. 395). Ibn Kathir quotes a tradition from the *Musnad* of Ibn Hanbal, which relates on the authority of the Prophet that when Venus appeared to the two angels as a beautiful woman and they wished to lie with her, she said, "No, by God, not until you utter words of association [*shirk*] against God." They answered, "By God, we shall never associate anything with God." She left them and returned later with an infant. When they again asked to lie with her, she exclaimed, "No, by God, not until you kill this infant." Again they refused, but when finally she returned with a cup of wine, they drank. In their drunkenness they committed adultery, killed an innocent soul, and uttered words of association (see Ibn Kathir, I, pp. 241–242; see also Tabarsi, I, pp. 395–396). Ibn Kathir, however, questions the authenticity of this tradition, which he says was transmitted by 'Abdallah ibn 'Umar on the authority of Ka'b al-Ahbar. It is clear that this tradition is meant, among other things, to show the evils of the drinking of wine. The woman is made to reproach the angels after they awaken from their drunkenness, saying, "By God, you left nothing undone which you refused to do before, when you became intoxicated" (Ibn Kathir, I, p. 242).

One final version of this story deserves mention for its interesting theological synthesis. The Qur'an clearly states that man is the vicegerent of God and that righteous men are the friends (*awliya'*) of God. It also asserts that angels never disobey God and that they are free from sin and impurity (see, for instance, Q. 16:50 and 21:27). The tradition we are about to consider preserves the purity of the angels, if not their infallibility (*'ismah*) and clearly demonstrates man's special favor with God.

Ibn Kathir relates on the authority of al-Rabi' ibn Anas and Ibn 'Abbas that God sent down the two angels with commands and prohibitions. There was, however, no apostle between them and God (that is, a man charged to transmit a sacred law [*shari'ah*]). They ruled the earth by day and ascended to heaven by night, dealing justly, until Venus came to them. Then "they uncovered their private parts, but their shameful acts were in their hearts, for they were not like the children of Adam with regard to lust for women and its pleasures. . . . When they tried to ascend that night, it was not permitted them to do so, nor were their wings able to carry them. They therefore begged for help from a righteous man of the children of Adam, saying, 'Pray your Lord on our behalf.' The man answered,

'How could the inhabitants of the earth intercede for the inhabitants of heaven?' They said, 'We heard your Lord speak well of you in heaven.' . . . He prayed for them and his prayers were answered. Thus they were made to choose between the punishment of this world and that of the world to come. . . . It is said that they are chained with heavy iron chains, hanging upside down in the air and flapping their wings . . ." (Ibn Kathir, I, pp. 247–248).

Ibn 'Arabi interprets this verse symbolically. Thus those "who followed that which the satans have recited" could either be the Jews or, as Ibn 'Arabi prefers, the "spiritual powers which follow human satans." These are rebellious and disobedient men. "They also follow the satans of the *jinn*, who are illusions [*awham*], imaginations [*khayalat*], and imagined things which are veiled from the light of the spirit. These satans are disobedient to the intellect [*'aql*] and rebellious against the commands of the heart."

Solomon may be the prophet, but he is also, according to Ibn 'Arabi, the "Solomon of the spirit." Solomon, says Ibn 'Arabi, "'did not reject faith,' [that is] he did not ascribe effect on things to anyone but God. 'The Satans rejected faith,' [that is] they were veiled and did not know that there was no one capable ultimately of affecting things except God."

Ibn 'Arabi identified the two angels, Harut and Marut, as "the theoretical and practical intellects which are inclined toward the soul. They are hung upside down in the well of material nature because they turned toward it attracted by the soul." They are punished in Babel, which is the breast; "they are punished in a narrow space among the humors and smokes of the fires of lust." Ibn 'Arabi interprets "man and his wife" to mean the heart and soul. Magic is the act of veiling oneself or others from the divine light. It is therefore *kufr* (Ibn 'Arabi, I, pp. 73–74).

The story of the angels Harut and Marut has been questioned by many commentators on various grounds. Ibn Kathir observes that the story was told by such Successors of the Companions of the Prophet as Mujahid, al-Suddi, Hasan al-Basri, Qatadah, Abu al-'Aliyah, and others. "It has, moreover, been recounted by a large number of commentators, both ancient and contemporary. The story in all its details goes back to the rabbis of the Children of Israel; there is no sound [*sahih*] *hadith* relating it with an unbroken chain of transmission going back to the truthful and infallible one [Muhammad], who does not speak out of caprice" (see Q. 53:3). Ibn Kathir concludes, "We assent therefore to what is narrated in the

Qur'an as God the Exalted had intended it, for He knows best the truth of all matters" (Ibn Kathir, I, p. 248).

Another important question has been whether the teaching of magic, which the Qur'an declares to be rejection of faith (*kufr*), may be imputed to angels. Tabari answers this question thus: "God sent down all good and all evil, all of which He made clear to His servants through revelation to His messengers. He commanded them to teach His creatures and make known to them what is lawful and what is unlawful for them. Magic is one of the acts of disobedience, such as adultery, stealing, wine drinking, and so forth. There is no transgression in learning magic, as there is no transgression in knowing how to make wine. Rather, transgression is dealing in magic and causing harm by means of it to another" (Tabari, II, pp. 422). He concludes, "It is not therefore reprehensible for God to have taught two angels magic, and made them a temptation for His servants of the children of Adam in order to test through them His servants, whom He forbade to cause discord between a man and his wife" (Tabari, II, p. 426; see also Zamakhshari, I, p. 301, Shawkani, I, pp. 120–121; and Qutb, I, pp. 126–130).

Some commentators rejected the story. Thus Qurtubi says, "Harut and Marut are here substitutes for satans. They were specifically mentioned for their stubborn rebelliousness. All this [that is, traditions concerning them] is weak—and completely wrong. It is also refuted by the principles [*usul*, that is, of theology and jurisprudence] concerning angels, who are the trustees of God over His revelation and His ambassadors to His messengers" (Qurtubi, II, pp. 50–52). Qurtubi presents the view of the famous commentator al-Zajjaj, who said, "The two angels taught men magic in order to warn them against it and not to invite them to practice it. . . . What was sent down to them was only prohibitions, as if to say to people, 'Do not do such and such; do not deceive in this or that way in order that you may be able to cause discord between a man and his wife.'" Al-Suddi said that the two angels used to say to whoever came to them, "We are surely a temptation, so do not reject faith." If the person then refused to be warned, they said to him, "Go to this stone oven and urinate in the ashes in it. As he did so, a pillar of light would go out of him to heaven—that was his faith. Then a pillar of black smoke would come out of the oven and enter his ears—that was his *kufr*." After he had related to them what he had seen, the angels would teach him "that by which they can cause dissension between a man and his wife" (Qurtubi, II, pp. 54–55; see also Razi, III, pp. 217–218).

Razi also rejects the story, which, he asserts, is falsely attributed to Ibn 'Abbas. It is, he says, "totally false and unacceptable, because there is nothing in the Book of God to support it, but much to refute it." He rejects the story on two main grounds. The first is the protection (*'ismah*) of the angels from all acts of disobedience. The second is the falseness of the claim that the angels were made to choose between the punishment of this world and that of the next. It would have, Razi argues, been more appropriate for the angels to be given the choice between turning to God (*tawbah*) and punishment. God has granted this choice to beings who associate others with Him all their lives. How could He then withold His favor from the angels? (Razi, III, pp. 219–220).

Razi, not wishing to commit himself to any specific opinion, speculates about the reasons for which the two angels could have been sent down to earth. "It may have been because magicians multiplied in those days and discovered new and marvelous practices in the art of magic. They claimed prophethood and challenged men with their claims. God then sent these two angels to earth to teach men magical practices in order that they would be able to oppose those who claimed prophethood falsely. It is also possible that the angels came to teach men magic in order to render obligation [*taklif*] more exacting. This is because if a man learns ways enabling him to attain pleasures quickly, but is forbidden to practice these ways, this would create for him extreme hardships. Therefore, he would merit great reward." The descent of the two angels to earth served yet another purpose, according to Razi. He argues that to every prophet God gave some miracles in proof of the truth of his claim. Thus Harut and Marut were sent down at the time of the prophet Idris as his miracle because they could not be sent as messengers to humankind (Q. 6:9; Razi, III, p. 220).

The role of Venus, the goddess of love, suggests a non-Islamic origin for the story. In one version of the story related on the authority of 'Ali and characterized by Ibn Kathir as "extremely strange," the beautiful woman learned from the two angels the word by which they were able to ascend to heaven and descend to earth. She thus uttered the word of ascent, but God caused her to forget the word of descent. He then changed her into a radiant star (Ibn Kathir, I, p. 242). Nisaburi, in his sharp criticisms of the story, offers several arguments for its spuriousness. With regard to Venus, he objects, "It is not acceptable to reason that a lewd woman could ascend to heaven and be made by God a luminous star" (Nisaburi, I, p. 392). It is related that whenever 'Abdallah ibn 'Umar saw Venus in the night, he cursed her, saying, "She is the one who tempted Harut and Marut!" (Tabari, II, p. 431). In another tradition related on the authority of Ibn 'Abbas, which Ibn Kathir accepts as being the closest to the truth, we are told that the two angels judged among men justly for a long period during the time of the prophet Enoch. But "there was in those days a woman whose beauty among women was like the beauty of Venus among the stars." In this tradition it is not Venus but an actual woman who was sent by God to test the two angels (Ibn Kathir, I, p. 245).

Commentators have also differed in their interpretation of the words, "People learn from them that by which they can cause dissension between a man and his wife." Tabarsi relates on the authority of Qatadah, "The magicians incite one of the two spouses against the other, thus causing hatred between them, and that leads to separation" (Tabarsi, I, pp. 398). Nisaburi observes that it may also be that "when a man practices magic, he becomes a rejecter of faith; hence his wife would be legally divorced from him. Separation would then be on the basis of faith or religious allegiance. Magic in itself, however, has no effect" (Nisaburi, I, pp. 391–392; see also Tabarsi, I, p. 398).

Although the story of the two angels has been related on the authority of the Companions of the Prophet, as well as of the Shi'i imams, modern commentators have rejected it as a myth denigrating the angels of God. Tabataba'i says, by way of characterizing this and other such stories in *hadith* and *tafsir* books, "They are not free from interpolations introduced into them by Jewish rabbis. These *hadiths*, moreover, show the subtle intrusion and deep influence of *hadith* transmitters in the earliest period [of Islamic history]. These intruders tampered at will with *hadith* transmission . . . assisted in all this by other people [whom he does not specify]" (Tabataba'i, I, p. 239; see also pp. 233–239). Neither Tabataba'i nor Sayyid Qutb, however, offers an alternative interpretation of the story of the two angels.

103. If they had faith and feared God, the reward they would
     receive from God would be better, if they but knew.

104. O you who have faith, do not say [to the Prophet] "Lend
ear to us" [*ra'ina*]. Rather say "Look upon us" [*unzurna*]
and hearken. Surely the rejecters of faith shall have a
painful torment.

(104) Even though this verse is explained in part by another verse
of the Qur'an (Q. 4:46), commentators have offered different interpretations of it. Thus Tabari relates on the authority of 'Ata' that
ra'ina was "a word which the Helpers [*ansar*] used to say in the
time of Jahiliyah. When Islam came, God forbade them to say it
to the Prophet." Al-Rabi' ibn Anas related on the authority of Abu
al-'Aliyah, "When the associators of the Arabs talked to one another,
a man would say to his friend *'ar'ini'* [turn your ear to me], but
they were forbidden to do so [after Islam]" (Tabari, II, pp. 461–462).
    A tradition related on the authority of Ibn Wahb, who transmitted
it from 'Abd al-Rahman ibn Zayd, cites verse 46 of *surah* 4 as being
the words the Jews uttered. The tradition then explains the word
ra'ina as meaning sinner (*ra'in*); thus God says to the faithful, "Do
not say 'sinner,' as the people say; rather, say *'unzurna'* [look upon
us] and listen." This God said "because they used to look at the
Prophet, speak to him, listen to his words, and ask him questions,
and he used to answer them" (Tabari, II, p. 461). Zamakhshari offers
yet another interpretation: "The Muslims used to say to the Apostle
of God, when he imparted to them new knowledge, *'Ra'ina*, O
Apostle of God,' which means watch over us, wait upon us, and be
patient with us, so that we may understand and keep [what you
teach us]. The Jews, however, had a word in Hebrew or Syriac with
which they used to curse one another; that word was *'ra'inan.'*
Hearing the faithful say, *'ra'ina,'* they took the opportunity to address
the Apostle of God while they actually meant their curse word. Thus
the faithful were forbidden to use it, but were told to use instead
another word with the same meaning, which is *'unzurna'*" (Zamakhshari, I, p. 302).
    Nisaburi reports first that the Jews had an insult with which they
used to address one another. The word was *ra'inan*, or something
similar. The Muslims were therefore enjoined not to use the word.
This view has been doubted by several commentators. Nisaburi
reports further that Qutrub, an early traditionist and grammarian,
said, "Even if this had a good meaning, still the people of the Hijaz
used it in mocking and jesting. God therefore enjoined the Muslims
not to use it." Nisaburi presents yet another interpretation. "The

Jews used to say to the Prophet, '*ra'ina*,' meaning 'you are a shepherd of our flocks'" (Nisaburi, I, p. 397).

Shawkani prefers the view which asserts that the word in Arabic means "watch over us and give us your attention or ear". Because there was a Hebrew word with similar pronunciation, God forbade its use. Shawkani sees in this a general principle of avoiding the use of words that may be misinterpreted or misused (Shawkani, I, p. 124; see also Tabarsi, I, p. 401; and Qutb, I, pp. 134–135).

The word *unzurna* means, in the view of all commentators, "Look upon us," or "Watch over us patiently, that we may understand." Thus Tabari explains the verse as follows: "O you who have faith, do not say to the Prophet 'Lend us your ear [*ra'ina*] and turn it fully toward us so that we may understand you and you may understand what we say'; rather say, 'Attend to us [*unzurna*] and watch over us, so that we may understand what you teach us and make clear to us'" (Tabari, II, p. 469; see also Tabarsi, I, p. 402).

105. Neither those who have rejected faith among the People of the Book, nor the associators desire that any good from your Lord be sent down upon you. Yet God favors with His mercy whomsoever He wills, and God is of infinite bounty.

106. No verse do we abrogate or cause it to be forgotten, but that we bring one better than it or one like it. Do you not know that God is all-powerful?

107. Do you not know that to God belongs dominion of the heavens and the earth, and that you have no one other than God, neither protector nor helper?

108. Would you wish to ask your Apostle as was Moses asked before? Surely he who exchanges rejection of faith for faith has strayed from the straight way.

(106) This is the first verse to deal with the important question of abrogation, a subject which was discussed in the introduction. The two issues that are of concern here are, first, what is abrogation and to what kind of verse does it apply and second, what is meant by the phrase "or cause it to be forgotten"?

Wahidi says that this verse was sent down because the associators said, "Do you not see Muhammad, how he commands his people to do something, then forbids them to do it and commands them to do its opposite? Today he says one thing and tomorrow he changes his mind regarding it. This Qur'an is no more than the words of Muhammad, which he utters from himself. It is composed of words which contradict one another." Thus, says Wahidi, God sent down verse 101 of *al-Nahl* (Q. 16), and this verse (Wahidi, p. 32; see also Zamakhshari, I, p. 303). Tabari interprets abrogation (*naskh*) broadly as "what we [that is, God] abrogate regarding the precept of a verse which we change, or for which we substitute another, so that what is lawful may become unlawful and what is unlawful may become lawful; what is permitted may become prohibited and what is prohibited may become permitted. This, however, can only be done with regard to commands and prohibitions . . . but as for reports or narratives, they can neither be abrogated nor can they abrogate" (Tabari, II, pp. 471–472; see also Shawkani, I, pp. 125–126). Tabarsi relates on the authority of Ibn 'Abbas, "It means that we [God] abolish, whether it be a verse or precept of a verse; or it may mean that we substitute another for it" (Tabarsi, I, p. 407).

Two views have been expressed regarding the words "or cause it to be forgotten" (*aw nunsiha*). The first view is that *aw nunsiha* means *aw natrukha*, that is "or leave it unchanged." This, according to Tabari, means that a precept may stand unchanged while another is substituted for it, either soon after that precept was revealed or later on in Muhammad's prophetic career. In either case, the superseding sanction is better for the faithful in this world or in the world to come. Abrogation of the obligation of spending the night in prayer, for example, relieved the faithful of a physical hardship; conversely, the fast of Ramadan, which abrogated the fast of "a certain number of days" (see below, Q. 2:183–185) assures the faithful of a greater reward in the hereafter (Tabari, II, p. 482; see also Tabataba'i, I, pp. 249–256).

The second view is that the verb *nasiya* here means to forget. Tabarsi presents this opinion from the point of view of Shi'i interpretation. "It is possible that the imams would command people to neglect the abrogated verse which they would then forget as days go by. This would not, however, be possible for the Prophet because that would lead to mistrust. A group of scholars has nonetheless declared it possible for the Prophet as well. They said that it does not lead to mistrust because of its relevance to the general interest [*maslahah*]. It may also be possible for God to cause the faithful to forget it in actuality, even though they may be a large group and although it may be a breach of custom, in which case it would be a miracle of a prophet. People who interpreted the verse to imply forgetting, and who assumed that it was the Prophet who was the one addressed, cited in support of their argument the verse, 'We shall teach you to recite, and you shall not forget save what God wills' [Q. 87:6], that is, what God wills you to forget. Hasan al-Basri, in support of this opinion, said, 'Your Prophet was taught to recite the Qur'an, but then forgot it'" (Tabarsi, I, pp. 407–408).

Ibn 'Arabi takes the principle of abrogation in its widest possible sense. He writes, "Know then that the principles which are established in the Preserved Tablet are either particular or general. Particular principles appertain to particular persons or epochs. When these verses descend upon the heart of the Apostle, those which appertain to specific individuals remain operative so long as they live. Those belonging to specific epochs shall likewise be abolished with the passing of these epochs, be they short, such as those verses belonging to the Qur'an, or long, such as ancient sacred codes of law. This does not contradict their being inscribed in the Preserved Tablet because they are there inscribed only for the time during which they are operative here on earth. General principles, however, continue for all time. Some of these are, for example, the principles behind the faculty of speech in human beings, and the erectness of their stature" (Ibn 'Arabi, I, pp. 75–76).

(108) Wahidi reports on the authority of Ibn 'Abbas that this verse was sent down in answer to 'Abdallah ibn Abi Umayyah and a group of the Quraysh who challenged the Prophet, saying, "O Muhammad, turn al-Safa [one of the two hills of pilgrimage in Mecca] into gold for us; enlarge the land of Mecca and cause rivers to burst forth through it; then would we believe in you" (Wahidi, p. 32). Tabari reports that al-Suddi said, "'Would you wish to ask your Apostle as was Moses asked before' means to show them God openly. Likewise, the Arabs asked the Apostle of God to bring God down to them so that they could see Him openly." Mujahid related, "The men of Quraysh asked Muhammad to turn al-Safa into gold for them. 'Yes,' he said, 'and it shall be for you like the table of the Children of Israel [see Q. 5:112], if you would reject faith.' Thus they refused and turned back" (Tabari, II, p. 490; see also Zamakhshari, I, p. 303; Ibn Kathir, I, pp. 266–267; Nisaburi, I, p. 405; Tabarsi, I, pp. 413–414; and Shawkani, I, pp. 128–129).

109. Many among the People of the Book wish out of the envy in their souls that they could turn you into rejecters of faith after your faith has been established; even after the truth had become manifest to them. Yet pardon and be indulgent toward them until God sends His command, for God is all-powerful.

110. Observe regular worship and give the obligatory alms, for whatever good you advance for your souls, you shall find it with God. God is surely all-seeing of what you do.

111. They say, "None shall enter Paradise save those who are Jews or Christians," for such are their desires. Say, "Produce your proof, if you speak the truth."

112. Not so: rather, whosoever turns his face to God in submission, performing good deeds, he shall have his reward from his Lord. No fear shall come upon them, nor shall they grieve.

113. The Jews say, "The Christians are grounded on nothing," and the Christians say, "The Jews are grounded on nothing", yet both recite the scriptures. Likewise those who do not know say similar things. God shall judge between them on the day of resurrection concerning that wherein they differ.

(113) Commentators have generally agreed that this verse was sent down, as related by Wahidi on the authority of Ibn 'Abbas, in answer to the denials of the Jews and Christians of the validity of each others' faith. "When the Christian people of Najran [see Q. 3:61 and introduction to *surah* 3] came to the Apostle of God, the Jewish rabbis came to them and they disputed with one another before the Apostle of God. Rafi' ibn Huraymilah, a Jewish notable, said to the Christians, 'You have nothing on which to stand,' and rejected Jesus son of Mary and the Gospel. A Christian of the people of Najran replied, 'You have nothing on which to stand'; he then denied the prophethood of Moses and rejected the Torah" (Wahidi, p. 33; Tabari, II, pp. 513–514). Tabari comments on the verse thus: "The Jews said that the Christians are not in the right in their religion and the Christians likewise said that the Jews are not in the right in their

religion. God therefore told the faithful of their claims in order that they might know how each of the two parties rejected the injunctions of its own book which declares the book of the other party to be true, and that it is from God. This is because the Gospel, on whose authenticity and truth the Christians have based their faith, confirms what is in the Torah concerning the prophethood of Moses as well as all the obligations [fara'id] which God laid upon the Children of Israel. Likewise, the Torah, on whose authenticity and truth the Jews have based their faith, confirms the prophethood of Jesus and the obligations and injunctions which he brought from God" (Tabari, II, p. 514).

Commentators have disagreed as to the identity of those "who do not know." Zamakhshari identifies them as "the foolish ones who have no knowledge or scriptures, such as idol worshipers, deniers of divine attributes [mu'attilah], and others like them. They said to the people of every religion. 'You have nothing on which to stand.' This is a great reproach by God to the Christians and Jews because they rank themselves, in spite of their knowledge, with those who have no knowledge" (Zamakhshari, I, pp. 305–306).

Shawkani reports that Ibn Jurayj, a well-known commentator, asked 'Ata', another well-known traditionist, "Who were these who did not know?" He answered, "They were communities of men who existed before the Jews and Christians." Shawkani further reports that al-Suddi said, "These were the Arabs of the Prophet's time because they said: 'Muhammad has nothing on which to stand'" (Shawkani, I, p. 130).

Sayyid Qutb offers a more specific explanation. Those who do not know were, according to him, the unlettered Arabs who had no book. They renounced the religion of both the Jews and Christians because of the similarity of their incredible myths and legends, declaring them to have nothing on which to stand. "The Qur'an, however, records what all these people have said concerning one another after clarifying the claims of the Jews and Christians as to the ownership of Paradise. Then the Qur'an leaves the matter of dissension between them to God" (Qutb, I, p. 140). It may be important that Tabari preferred to take no position on the matter. "It is possible that they were the Arab associators, or another community which existed before the Jews and Christians. No community could be said to have been meant to the exclusion of the other, because there is no evidence in the verse itself for one or the other, nor is there a report from the Apostle of God presenting clear proof and transmitted on the authority of either single truthful transmitters or through the transmission of a large number of authorities" (Tabari, II, p. 517).

Ibn 'Arabi, like other mystics, goes beyond the apparent differences among religious communities springing from theological or legal positions. Thus he writes concerning the charge of religious inauthenticity which each of the two communities leveled at the other, "The Jews said what they said because they were veiled by their religion from their faith; likewise, the Christians said what they said because of their being veiled by the esoteric from the exoteric, as the Jews were veiled from the esoteric by the exoteric. This is also the case with the adherents of different sects in the Muslim community; they all nonetheless 'recite the scriptures' which contain guidance for them that they may remove the veil so as to have the vision of the truth of every religion and denomination. The truth of every religion is not that its people should be blindly bound to the imitation of others in their faith. Otherwise what is the difference between them and those who do not know, who have no scriptures, such as the associators? The people of faith speak like them but these have against them only the proof of the intellect, while the others must contend in addition with the proof of the divine law. God shall judge among them in truth before the day of the great resurrection [*al-qiyamah al-kubra*] and the manifestation of the unity of essence [*al-wahdah al-dhatiyah*] when the Mahdi shall appear at the end of time. There is a *hadith* to the effect that God shall manifest Himself to His servants in the forms of their creeds, and they would recognize Him. Then He would assume another form and they would deny Him. At that time they will all be in error and veiled from the truth, except him whom God wills to be a true believer in divine oneness, and who was not bound by the form of his creed" (Ibn 'Arabi, I, pp. 78–79).

114. Who does greater wrong than he who bars the houses of worship of God, that His name be not remembered therein, and seeks their destruction? Such men should never have entered them except in fear. For them is disgrace in this world, and in the world to come a great torment.

115. To God belongs the east and the west. Wherever you turn, there is the face of God, for God is all-encompassing, all-knowing.

116. They say, "God has taken for Himself a son." Glory be to Him! Rather, to Him belongs all that is in the heavens and the earth; all are subservient to Him.

117. He is the originator of the heavens and the earth; whenever He decrees a thing, He only says to it, "Be!" and it is.

118. Those who do not know say, "If only God would speak to us or a sign come to us!" So said those before them, as these men say. Their hearts are alike; yet we have made manifest the signs to people who believe with certainty.

119. Surely we have sent you with the truth, a bearer of glad tidings and a warner. You shall not be questioned concerning the people of the Fire.

120. The Jews will not be pleased with you, nor will the Christians, until you follow their religion. Say, "Only the guidance of God is true guidance." If you follow their vain desires after the knowledge which has come to you, you shall have against God neither protector nor helper.

121. They to whom we have given the scriptures and who recite it with its true recitation; these have faith in it. Yet whosoever rejects faith in it, these shall be the losers.

122. O Children of Israel! Remember my favor which I have bestowed upon you and that I favored you over the rest of humankind.

123. Fear a day wherein no soul shall make satisfaction for another soul, nor will compensation be accepted from it; intercession shall not avail it, nor shall they be helped.

(114) Commentators have differed as to whether this verse was revealed to speak to a special situation or should be taken in its general sense without any specific reference. Those who wished to relate it to a particular event also disagreed among themselves.

Wahidi first relates, on the authority of al-Suddi and Qatadah, that Bukhtnassar (Nebuchadnezzar?) destroyed Jerusalem with the aid of some of the Byzantine Christians. He reports further on the authority of Ibn 'Abbas, "This verse was sent down concerning the associators of Mecca when they prevented the Muslims from worshiping God in the Kaaba" (perhaps on the day of the famous Treaty of Hudaybiyah) (Wahidi, p. 34.) Nisaburi reports also on the authority of Ibn 'Abbas, "The king of the Christians attacked the holy house [the temple of Jerusalem], which he destroyed and desecrated with dead carcasses. He besieged the inhabitants of Jerusalem, killed them, and took their women and children captive. He also burned the books of the Torah. Jerusalem, moreover, remained in ruins until the Muslims rebuilt it during the time of 'Umar ibn al-Khattab. Thus the verse was sent down concerning the sanctuary of Jerusalem" (Nisaburi, I, p. 417). Commentators have generally confused Nebuchadnezzar with the Roman general Titus, who destroyed the Temple of Jerusalem (see, for instance, Tabari, II, pp. 520–522 and Shawkani, I, pp. 131–132). Zamakhshari attributes the destruction and desecration of the Temple to the Christians, perhaps the Byzantines (*Rum*). (See Zamakhshari, I, p. 306.)

Tabarsi relates on the authority of Ja'far al-Sadiq, "They [the people meant in this verse] were the people of Quraysh when they prevented the Apostle of God from entering Mecca and the Sacred House" (Tabarsi, I, p. 427). Tabarsi defends this view, asserting that the building up of houses of worship means their being used for that purpose by the community; hence their destruction means the prevention of people from worshiping in them. Tabarsi, nonetheless, relates another tradition on the authority of Zayd ibn 'Ali, who related it on the authority of 'Ali ibn Abi Talib that "God intended in this verse the entire earth, for the Prophet said, 'The whole earth was made a place of worship for me, and its soil [a means of] purification' [that is, *tayammun*, ablution with sand]" (see Q. 4:43; Tabarsi, I, pp. 427–428). Qurtubi, likewise, after recounting various traditions, says, "It is whoever prevents people from entering any house of worship until the day of resurrection. This is because the verse is general and because of the plural use of *masjid* [house of worship]: *masajid*. Thus to make it refer either to particular houses of worship or particular persons would be weak, but God knows best" (Qurtubi, II, p. 77). Sayyid Qutb also prefers the general reading of the verse and asserts further that this and the following verses belong together and may have been revealed at the same time. This is because even though people may prevent others from entering the houses of God, "still His face is everywhere" (Qutb, I, pp. 141–142).

Commentators have also differed with regard to the people who had to enter houses of worship in fear. Tabarsi relates on the authority of Ibn 'Abbas, "It means that no Christian enters the Holy City [Jerusalem] but that he would be beaten to exhaustion and punished severely, and so it is to this day." (Ibn 'Abbas does not elaborate on who were the persecuted Christians or their persecutors.) Those who interpreted the verse to refer to the sacred House of Mecca said, "When this verse was sent down, the Prophet sent out a crier to Mecca, declaring, 'Let no associator perform the pilgrimage after this year, nor let any naked man circumambulate the House [Kaaba]'; thus they did not enter it thereafter" (see commentaries on Q. 9, 1–3). Another interpretation offered by Abu 'Ali al-Jubba'i and approved by Abu Ja'far al-Tusi, the Shaykh of the Shi'i community, asserts that "God thus made clear that associators should not enter the Sacred House or any other house of worship; it would be incumbent upon Muslims to evict him from it, unless he enters in order to bring before the judge [holding court in the house of worship] a case against another person. In this circumstance, he would enter in fear of being evicted after his case had been heard. Thus he would not sit in the house of worship in security as would a Muslim" (Tabarsi, I, pp. 428–429).

(115) This is the first verse in this *surah* dealing with the change of the *qiblah* or direction of prayer. Because commentators interpreted it in relationship to later verses that declared the change of the *qiblah* from Jerusalem to Mecca unambiguously, as will be seen below, they differed widely concerning its actual intent. Perhaps the real problem was with integrating this verse into the general development of jurisprudence.

Wahidi reports that commentators differed about the occasion of its revelation. Thus Jabir ibn 'Abdallah al-Ansari related, "The Apostle of God once sent a detachment on a mission, in which I was included. Darkness covered us so that we could not discern the *qiblah*. A group among us said, 'We can discern the *qiblah*; it is in this direction, toward the north.' They prayed and drew lines [in order to verify the next morning the direction toward which they prayed]. Others said, 'No it is in this direction, toward the south,' and they also drew lines. When, however, they woke up in the morning and the sun had risen, the lines appeared not to be in the direction of the *qiblah*. When we returned from our journey, we asked the Prophet about this, but he remained silent. God then sent down this verse."

Wahidi further reports that the Prophet and his Companions once on a journey could not determine the direction of the *qiblah*, so each prayed alone in the direction he chose. In the morning they asked the Prophet concerning the validity of their prayers, and the verse was revealed. Wahidi reports that when Najashi, the king of Ethiopia, died, Gabriel came to the Prophet ordering him and the Muslims to perform the funeral prayer for the king. Some among the Prophet's Companions thought, "How can we pray over a man who died while praying in a direction other than our *qiblah*?" (Najashi is said to have prayed toward Jerusalem.) Thus God sent down "wherever you turn, there is the face of God" (Wahidi, pp. 34–36).

For mystics before and after Ibn 'Arabi the east signifies light or the source of illumination and the west darkness or the veils that separate humankind from the light. He therefore offers the following esoteric interpretation of this verse: "'To God belongs the east' means the realm of light and manifestation [*zuhur*] which is the paradise of the Christians and their *qiblah*, but it is actually the east's inner reality. 'And the west' means the realm of darkness and concealment, which is the paradise of the Jews and their *qiblah*, but actually it is the west's outer reality. 'Wherever you turn' means whether you turn to the direction of the outer or inner dimension, 'there is the face of God.' This means the one essence of God which is manifested in all His attributes."

The verse could also mean, according to Ibn 'Arabi, "To God belongs the illumination or shining forth [*ishraq*] upon men's hearts through His being reflected in them and manifesting Himself to them in the attribute of His beauty in the state of their presence [*shuhud*], and annihilation [*fana'*]. To Him also belongs the westering [*ghurub*], that is, concealing Himself in them by veiling Himself in the forms and essences of their hearts. It is His self-concealment in the attribute of His Majesty in the state of their subsistence [*baqa'*] after annihilation. To whatever direction you turn then there shall be His face. For there is nothing in reality but He alone" (Ibn 'Arabi, I, p. 80).

Tabarsi relates on the authority of Ibn 'Abbas that the Jews of the Prophet's society denied the validity of the change of the *qiblah* from Jerusalem to the Kaaba. God therefore sent down this verse in answer to their denial. Al-Jubba'i said that in this verse, "God made clear that He is not in any direction to the exclusion of another, as the anthropomorphists [*mushabbihah*] assert" (Tabarsi, I, p. 431). Tabarsi also relates that the Muslims were at first free to face any direction they chose, in accordance with this verse. This, however, was later abrogated by the injunction, "turn your face toward the Sacred House of worship" (Q. 2:149 and 150; see below). Qatadah said, "The Prophet chose to face the holy city of Jerusalem, yet he was free to face any direction he wished" (Tabarsi, I, p. 431). Tabarsi also relates on the authority of the Shi'i imams, "The verse was sent down concerning voluntary prayers [*salat al-tatawwu'*] on horseback, which you may perform in whatever direction you face if you are on a journey. But as for the obligatory prayers [*fara'id*], they must be performed in accordance with His saying, "Wherever you may be, turn your faces toward the Kaaba, which means that you should not perform the obligatory prayers except facing the *qiblah*" (Tabarsi, I, p. 431).

Zamakhshari interprets the verse as follows: "'To God belongs the east and the west' means that the lands of the east and the west, and the entire earth belong to God. Wherever, therefore, you turn your face, that is, in whatever place you perform the act of turning your faces [toward the Kaaba] there is the face of God. The face of God here means the direction which he decreed and with which He was pleased. The verse means, therefore, that if you are prevented from performing the prayers in the sacred House [the Kaaba] or in the Holy House [Jerusalem], pray in any spot of the earth you wish, for the entire earth has been made a place of prayer [*masjid*] for you. Therefore turn your faces [toward the Kaaba], wherever you may be, because turning the face [*tawliyah*] is possible everywhere. It is limited neither to any specific house of worship, nor to any place" (Zamakhshari, I, pp. 306–307; see also Qurtubi, II, pp. 79–83; and Ibn Kathir, I, pp. 276–277).

(116, 117) Wahidi reports that these verses were sent down concerning the Christians of Najran, who say that Jesus is the son of God, or concerning both the Christians and the associators among the Arabs of Mecca, who said that the angels were the daughters of God (Wahidi, p. 36). Other commentators include the Jews because they claim 'Uzayr [Ezra] to be the son of God (see Q. 4:30; Wahidi,

p. 36; see also Tabarsi, I, p. 434). It has been related that Talhah ibn 'Ubaydallah asked the Prophet concerning the meaning of the word *subhanahu* (glory be to Him). He answered, "This means the elevation [*tanzih*] of God over all evil, for to Him belongs all that is in the heavens and the earth. This verse is therefore an answer to those who say, 'God has taken for Himself a son'; it is not as they claim, but rather, 'to Him belongs all that is in the heavens and the earth.' A child cannot be the possession of the father, because sonship and possession [that is, as slaves are possessed] are never combined. How could, therefore, the angels who are in heaven and Jesus, who was on earth, be His children?" (Tabarsi, I, p. 434; see also Tabari, II, p. 538; Ibn Kathir, I, p. 280; Qurtubi, II, p. 85; and Zamakhshari, I, p. 307).

Finally the modern commentator, Tabataba'i, offers a different interpretation of these verses, intended to explain why the Jews and Christians made such grievously erring claims regarding 'Uzayr and Jesus. "The People of the Book first said, 'God has taken for Himself a son' only in order to exalt their prophets, as they said, 'We are the children of God, and His beloved' [see Q. 5:18]. Later, however, this idea took on an aspect of seriousness and reality. Thus God refuted their claim with these two verses"(Tabataba'i, I, p. 261).

(119) Wahidi relates on the authority of Ibn 'Abbas, "The Apostle of God said one day, 'Would that I knew what became of my parents!' [that is, in the hereafter, because they died before Islam]; God then sent down this verse" (Wahidi, pp. 36–37). Commentators generally agree that "You shall not be questioned concerning the people of the Fire" means that the Prophet will not be questioned about the fate of those who were destined for the Fire, because his responsibility was only that of a warner. Tabarsi asserts that this verse was revealed to the Prophet as a consolation, that is, that he should not grieve for those who were destined for perdition (Tabarsi, I, p. 445). Tabarsi adopts this view because according to Shi'i tradition the parents of the Prophet were not rejecters of faith, hence they were not destined for the Fire.

(121) Wahidi relates on the authority of Ibn 'Abbas, "This verse was sent down concerning the people of the ship who came [to Medina] with Ja'far ibn Abi Talib from Abyssinia. They were forty men, thirty-two from Abyssinia and eight of the monks of Syria. The monk Bahirah was said to be among them." In another tradition, related on the authority of al-Dahhak, we are told, "The verse was sent down concerning those among the Jews who accepted faith

[such as 'Abdallah ibn Sallam and others]." Still another tradition related on the authority of Qatadah and 'Ikrimah states, "It was sent down concerning the Companions of Muhammad" (Wahidi, p. 37; see also Ibn Kathir, I, pp. 286–287; Qurtubi, II, p. 95; Tabarsi, I, p. 448; and Shawkani, I, pp. 135–136).

Zamakhshari interprets the verse as follows: "'They to whom we have given the scriptures' are the faithful among the People of the Book who recite the scriptures in their true recitation, neither altering them nor changing what they contain of the description of the Apostle of God. Those who have faith in their scriptures are contrasted with 'whosoever rejects faith in it [the scriptures],' that is, the alterers. 'These shall be the losers' because they exchange guidance for error" (Zamakhshari, I, p. 308).

124. Remember when Abraham was tried by his Lord with certain words, which he fulfilled. He said, "I shall make you an imam to humankind." Said he, "And what of my progeny?" He said, "My covenant shall not include the wrongdoers."

125. And remember when we rendered the House a place of resort for humankind and a sanctuary, [saying] "Make of the station of Abraham a place of prayer." We enjoined upon Abraham and Ishmael, "Purify my House for those who shall circumambulate it, those who shall sojourn therein, assiduous in devotion, and those who shall kneel and prostrate themselves in prayer."

126. And remember when Abraham said, "O my Lord, render this a safe town! Bestow upon its inhabitants various fruits of Your bounty, on those among them who have faith in God and the last day." He said, "But as for him who shall reject faith, I shall allow him indulgence for a while, then will I consign him to the torment of the Fire; a miserable destiny shall it be."

127. And remember when Abraham and with him Ishmael raised the foundations of the House [and said], "Our Lord, accept this from us, for You are all-hearing, all-knowing;

128. "Our Lord, make us submitters to You and of our progeny make a community submitting to You. Show us our sacred rites and turn toward us, for You are relenting, compassionate.

129. "Our Lord, send to them an apostle from among them to recite to them Your revelations, teach them the Book and wisdom and purify them, for You are the almighty, the wise."

130. Who shall be averse to the religion of Abraham, save he who is of foolish mind, for we have chosen him in this world, and in the world to come he shall be among the righteous.

131. When his Lord said to him, "Submit!" he said, "I submit to the Lord of all beings."

132. The same did Abraham enjoin upon his sons, and Jacob likewise, saying, "O my sons, God has surely chosen for you this faith; therefore do not die except as Muslims."

133. Were you witnesses when Jacob was at the point of death, when he said to his sons, "Whom will you worship after me?" They said, "We shall worship your God and the God of your fathers, Abraham, Ishmael, and Isaac—one God. To Him we are submitters."

134. These were a people that have passed away. To them belongs that which they gained, and to you belongs that which you have gained; nor will you be questioned concerning that which they had done.

(124) Among ancient prophets, Abraham has occupied a very prominent place in Muslim tradition. Abraham transcends the limits of human personality and becomes an exemplar of the prophets. He progressed from a primal state of innocence (Q. 6:77 and 78) to the state of uncertainty (Q. 2:260), then to faith, and finally to the state of prophethood and spiritual preeminence. He is, according to Muslim tradition, the recipient of the divine covenant of blessing for

humankind and the builder of the first house for the worship of the one God.

Commentators have therefore interpreted the name Ibrahim (Abraham), which they consider to be a Syriac word, to mean in Arabic *ab rahim* (a merciful father). Qurtubi exclaims, "Do you not see that the meaning of Ibrahim is *ab rahim*, because of his mercy toward children? For this reason he and his wife Sarah were made guardians of the children of the people of faith who die young, until the day of resurrection." This concept is supported by a long tradition related on the authority of Samurah ibn Jundub about the Prophet's vision of Paradise, in which he saw Abraham surrounded by little children (Qurtubi, II, p. 96).

Commentators have differed in interpreting the words with which God tried Abraham. Tabari relates that Ibn 'Abbas said, "No one was tried with this religion and truly fulfilled it except Abraham. God tried him with certain words and he fulfilled them. Hence God ordained for him immunity [*bara'ah*] from disobedience in His saying, 'and Abraham, who fulfilled his promise'" (Q. 53:37). Ibn 'Abbas also said, "Islam is thirty branches. No one was tried with this religion and fulfilled it except Abraham. . . . Thus God ordained for him freedom from the Fire" (Tabari, III, p. 8).

In another tradition related by Tabari on the authority of Ibn 'Abbas, we are told, "God tried Abraham with purification: five acts in the head and five in the body. In the head, they were trimming the mustache, rinsing the mouth and nostrils, cleaning the teeth [with the traditional twig, *miswak*], and parting the hair. In the body they were clipping the finger and toenails, shaving the pubic hairs, circumcision, plucking the hairs under the arms, and washing off traces of urine and feces with water" (Tabari, III, p. 8). Still another tradition related on the authority of Ibn 'Abbas asserts that the ten obligations with which God tried Abraham were six in the body (paralleling the ten just cited) and four dealing with the pilgrimage rites. These were circumambulation (*tawaf*) of the Kaaba, running between al-Safa and al-Marwah, stoning the pillars (*jimar*) and rushing out (*ifadah*) from 'Arafat (see below, verse 199; Tabari, III, p. 10).

Still other commentators interpret the words to refer to God's saying to Abraham, "I shall make you an imam to humankind," as well as the verses concerning the pilgrimage rites (verses 125–128). The view that the words with which God tried Abraham were those exchanged in these verses between Abraham and his Lord is related by Tabari on the authority of Mujahid, as well as many other authorities of *tafsir* both among the Companions and their Successors. Many commentators, however, relate on the authority of Ibn 'Abbas that the words were communications dealing only with the pilgrimage (Tabari, III, pp. 10–13). A man asked Hasan al-Basri about the words with which God tried Abraham, and he answered, "God tried him with the star, but He was pleased with him. He tried him with the moon . . . with the sun . . . [see Q. 6:77–78] and with fire [see Q. 21:69], and He was pleased with him. He also tried him with migration [*hijrah*] and circumcision." Another version of the same tradition adds the slaying of his son (Tabari, III, p. 14; see also Ibn Kathir, I, pp. 288–292; and Zamakhshari, I, pp. 308–309).

Tabari prefers not to specify the words with which God tried Abraham. They could be, he argues, in part those asserted by the commentators, or something else. There is no mention of the words in the Qur'an, he notes, nor has there been an accepted *hadith* from the Prophet concerning this matter (Tabari, III, p. 15). Shawkani comments as follows on traditions which assert that the Prophet trimmed his own mustache in emulation of Abraham. "The action of Abraham itself does not necessitate that the trimming of the mustache be part of the words with which he was tried. If, therefore, there is no certainty of the soundness of any such traditions as being *hadiths* of the Prophet, nor has anything come to us which may be taken as proof of what these words actually were, we have no other resort but to say that they were what God mentioned in His Book, saying, 'He said, "I shall make you an imam."' Otherwise we must assume silence and refer knowledge of this matter to God, the Exalted. As for what has been related on the authority of Ibn 'Abbas, others of the Prophet's Companions and those who came after them regarding the identification of the words, they are only the opinions of Companions, which cannot be taken as proof, let alone the opinions of their Successors" (Shawkani, I, pp. 139–140).

Tabari explains the phrase, "I shall make you an imam to humankind" as follows: "I shall make you a leader of those who shall come after you of the people who have faith in me and my messengers; you shall be the first among them. They shall follow the guidance sent to you and follow the way [*sunnah*] which you practice through my command and revelation to you" (Tabari, III, p. 18).

Commentators have also differed concerning the covenant of God which shall not include the wrongdoers. Al-Suddi said that the covenant here means prophethood, that is, "the people of wrongdoing and association of other things with God [*shirk*] shall not be included in the prophetic covenant" (Tabari, III, p. 20). The divine covenant here means, according to Mujahid, the covenant of the *imamah* or spiritual leadership of humanity which God granted to Abraham and the faithful among his descendants (see Tabari, III, pp. 20–24 and especially pp. 20–22; see also Zamakhshari, I, p. 309).

Ibn 'Arabi believes Abraham may be considered as the true archetypal man, the man who had arrived at the end of his spiritual journey to God. In contrast with other commentators, Ibn 'Arabi identifies the "words" with which Abraham was tried by his Lord as "degrees of the spiritual faculties such as: the heart, the innermost faculty [*sirr*], spirit, inner thought [*khafa'*], unity [*wahdah*], states [*ahwal*], and stations [*maqamat*]. These express such states as submission [*taslim*], trust [*tawakkul*], contentment [*rida*], and their sciences." The phrase "which he fulfilled" means "through his journeying [*suluk*] to God and in God until annihilation."

Ibn 'Arabi then sees Abraham's *imamah* as meaning the realization of "subsistence after annihilation and the return to the creation [*khalq*] from the Creator [*haqq*]." He then paraphrases the text as follows: "You [Abraham] shall be their imam, guiding men through their journey on my way. They shall follow you and be guided" (Ibn 'Arabi, I, p. 83).

Qummi relates on the authority of the imams that the trial of Abraham by God was "what He showed him in his dream regarding the slaying of his son, and which Abraham fulfilled. When he had done as God commanded him, God said, 'I shall make you an imam to mankind.' Then Abraham said, 'And what of my progeny?' God answered, 'My covenant shall not include the wrongdoers,' that is, 'There shall not be within my covenant a wrongdoing imam to whom I would send the *hanifiyah*, which is purification consisting of ten things.'" Qummi then enumerates the ten acts listed above (Qummi, I, p. 59).

In another tradition which Tabarsi relates on the authority of al-Mufaddal ibn 'Umar al-Ju'fi, who asked Ja'far al-Sadiq about the words, the latter said, "These were the words which Adam received from his Lord, and He turned toward him. They are what Adam said: 'My Lord, I beg you, for the sake of Muhammad, Fatimah, 'Ali, Hasan, and Husayn to turn toward me,' 'and He turned toward him, for He is truly relenting, compassionate'" (see Q. 2:37). Al-Mufaddal asked further, "O son of the Apostle of God, what does He mean by His saying, 'which he fulfilled?'" He answered, "He enumerated them [the imams] till the one who shall be raised by God [al-Qa'im, that is, the twelfth imam]; twelve imams, nine of whom are of the descendants of Husayn" (Tabarsi, I, p. 454).

Tabarsi pays special attention to the word "imam," which he interprets as including two important principles. The first is that the imam is he whose words and deeds become an example for people to follow. The second is that "he is the one who undertakes the management of the affairs of the community. He administers its political affairs, ensures the execution of its laws, punishes its criminals, assigns government offices, and wages war against its enemies." According to the first principle, "there was no prophet but that he was also an imam." According to the second, "it is not necessary that every prophet be an imam. This is because he may not be charged with punishing criminals, waging wars against enemies, defending the faith, and fighting against the rejecters of faith." Tabarsi then asserts that God made Abraham an imam after he had made him a prophet. Thus the office of the *imamah* is higher than that of prophethood but lower than that of apostleship (Tabarsi, I, p. 456).

Tabataba'i treats the question of the *imamah* in this verse at great length. He observes, "What we find in God's word is that whenever He speaks of the *imamah*, He speaks also of guidance by way of explaining it [see, for example, Q. 21:73 and 32:24]. He therefore identified the *imamah* with guidance and made it subject to His command. He showed that the *imamah* is not merely guidance in general; rather it is guidance which takes place by God's command. In sum, the imam is a guide who guides through a divine celestial [*malakuti*] command. The *imamah*, in accordance with esoteric understanding, is like divine authority [*walayah*] over humankind with regard to their deeds. Its guidance is bringing humanity to the goal by God's command and not simply showing them the way, which is the responsibility of a prophet and apostle as well as of every faithful person who guides to God through wisdom and good counsel.

"The imam must be a man of certainty to whom the celestial realm [*'alam al-malakut*] is unveiled, and whose certitude is attained by certain words from God. The celestial realm is the inner dimension of the two dimensions of this world [that is, the esoteric and exoteric dimensions]. God's saying 'they guide through our command' [Q. 21:73] provides a clear proof of the fact that everything having to do with guidance, that is, of hearts and deeds, both its outer aspect and inner reality, belongs to the imam. Its inner dimension of divine command is always present to him. It is well known that hearts and deeds, like all other things, have two dimensions. To the imam, therefore, are present both the good and evil deeds of human beings, for he is guardian over both the way to happiness and the way to misery. The imam is he who leads humankind to God 'on the day when innermost thoughts shall be uncovered.' [Q. 86:9], just as he leads them to Him in the actual life of this world, as well as its inner dimension. No age or epoch can be without an imam, as seen in God's saying, 'on the day when we shall call every people by their imam' [Q. 17:71]. [For Tabataba'i's interpretation of this verse, see Tabataba'i, XIII, pp. 165–171.]

"The *imamah*, because of its nobility and greatness, cannot be established except in him who is possessed of a felicitous nature in himself. This is because were he one whose nature was subject to wrongdoing and misery, his own felicity could be attained only through his being guided by another. God has said, 'Is not one who guides to the truth more worthy of being followed than he who cannot guide except that he himself be guided?' [Q. 10:35]. This verse compares him who guides to the truth with him who cannot be guided except by means of another. The comparison requires that the guide to the truth be guided by himself, because the one who is guided by another can never be a guide to the truth. From this, two conclusions follow: the first is that the imam must be protected [*ma'sum*] from error and disobedience. Otherwise, he would not be guided in himself [Q. 71:72]. The deeds of the imam, to which he is not guided through the guidance of another but rather through self-guidance—through divine succor and guidance—are all good. The second conclusion is, conversely, that he who is not so protected can never be an imam guiding to the truth. From all this it can be seen that the wrongdoers intended in God's saying, 'My covenant shall not include the wrongdoers,' is anyone who has committed an act of wrongdoing, such as association of other things with God [*shirk*] or disobedience, even if it were during a short time of his life and even though he may later have turned to God and made amends.

"From the preceding argument, these conclusions follow. The first is that the *imamah* is something given by God. The second is that the imam must be protected with a divine protection [*'ismah*]. The third is that the earth and its human inhabitants cannot be without a true imam. The fourth conclusion is that the imam must be strengthened by God. The fifth is that the deeds of creatures are not veiled from the imam's knowledge. The sixth is that the imam must know all the things which human beings need with regard to their lives here on earth and in the hereafter. Finally, there can never be any one among men who excels him in the virtues of the soul" (Tabataba'i, I, pp. 272–275; see also pp. 267–279; and for a critique of the Shi'i concept of the imam, see Razi, IV, pp. 43–47).

(125) Commentators do not agree regarding the actual spot of the *maqam* (place of prayer) of Abraham. They also differ as to whether praying at the *maqam* is an obligation or a voluntary act. Zamakhshari relates that the Prophet took 'Umar by the hand and said, "This is the *maqam* of Ibrahim." 'Umar said, "Should we not regard it as a place of prayer?" The Prophet answered, "I have not been commanded to do so." Before the sun had set that day, this verse was sent down. It is also related on the authority of Jabir ibn 'Abdallah al-Ansari, "The Apostle of God kissed the black stone, then ran three circuits and walked four. When he had finished, he came to the *maqam* of Ibrahim, where he prayed two *rak'ahs* and recited, 'Make of the station of Abraham a place of worship.'" Zamakhshari adds, "The situation of Abraham is the stone bearing the traces of his footprints. The spot where the stone was when Abraham stood on it is the place now called '*maqam* Ibrahim.' According to 'Ata', the station of Abraham is 'Arafah, al-Muzdalifah and the place of the pillars [*jimar*], because he stood in all these spots and prayed. According to Ibrahim al-Nakh'i, the entire *haram* is the station of Abraham" (Zamakhshari, I, p. 310; see also Qurtubi, II, pp. 111–113).

Tabarsi relates that "the House was called *al-bayt al-haram* [the sacred or forbidden house] because the associators were forbidden to enter it. It was also called *al-Ka'bah* ["the cube"] because it is a square structure. It is square because it was modeled on *al-bayt al-ma'mur* ['the populous house' in the fourth heaven, circumambulated by large companies of angels] which is square. The 'populous house' was made square because it was modeled on the Throne, which is also square. The Throne was made square because the words on which Islam is founded are four: glory to God, praise be to God, there is no god but God, and God is most great" (Tabarsi, I, p. 459).

As for the injunction to pray at the station of Abraham, it is related by Tabarsi on the authority of Ja'far al-Sadiq that "God commanded us to pray at the *maqam* after the rite of circumambulation." The same tradition is also related on the authority of several *tafsir* masters and is no doubt based on the Prophet's *sunnah*, as has already been cited. Tabarsi relates that it was asked of one of the imams, "What if a man circumambulates the Kaaba as an obligation [*faridah*], but forgets to offer the two *rak'ahs* at the station of Abraham?" He answered, "He should offer them even after some days, for God, the Exalted, said, 'Make of the station of Abraham a place of worship.'" Tabarsi then asserts, "In the *maqam* there is manifest proof of the prophethood of Abraham. This is because God made the stone under his feet like clay, so that his foot penetrated it; it was one of his miracles. It is related on the authority of the fifth imam, Muhammad al-Baqir, that 'three stones were sent down from Paradise; *maqam* Ibrahim [the stone on which Abraham stood], the stone of the Children of Israel [see Q. 2:60], and the black stone. The black stone, which God put in the charge of Abraham, was then a white stone whiter than white paper, but it became black because of the sins of the children of Adam!" (Tabarsi, I, p. 460). Tabarsi also relates on the authority of 'Abdallah ibn 'Umar, "The Apostle of God said, 'The corner [*rukn*] and station [*maqam*] of Abraham are two sapphires of the sapphires of Paradise, whose light God dimmed. Had their light not been dimmed, it would have illuminated the earth from east to west" (Tabarsi, I, p. 462).

(127) Commentators have disagreed as to whether the foundations of the House were first raised by Abraham and Ishmael or were raised before them. According to some, Adam was the first to build the Sacred House, but it was completely destroyed after him until God ordered Abraham to rebuild it.

Tabari relates on the authority of 'Ata' that Adam complained to God, saying, "O Lord, I no longer hear the voices of the angels [that is, after he was expelled from Paradise]." God answered, "It is because of your sin; still, go down to earth and build a house for me and circumambulate it as you saw angels circumambulating my house which is in heaven" (Tabari, III, pp. 57–58).

Other commentators claim that the foundations meant here are those of a house which God sent down to earth for Adam to circumambulate, but which was taken up to heaven during the flood. God ordered Abraham to raise the foundations of the House in the same spot. In another tradition related on the same authority, we are told that "when God made Adam come down from the Garden [he was so tall that] his feet were on earth and his head touched heaven. He thus could hear the conversations of the denizens of heaven and their prayers. Adam, in his loneliness, found in them pleasant fellowship. The angels, however, were frightened by him and complained to God in their prayers and invocations. God therefore reduced Adam's size, bringing him down close to earth. When Adam could no longer hear the angels, he became lonely and complained to God in his prayers. He was directed to go to Mecca. When he reached Mecca, God sent down one of the sapphires of Paradise onto the present spot of the House. Thus God said, 'And remember when we prepared for Abraham a place for the House'" (see Q. 22:26. Tabari, III, pp. 58-59). Others said, "The spot of the House was a red hill like a dome. For, when God wished to create the earth on the water, he rolled the earth out from under that hill. Thus the House remained until God granted it to Abraham, who built it on its foundations. Its foundations rest on four pillars on the seventh earth." This view is related with minor variations on the authority of Mujahid and many other *tafsir* masters. (Tabari, III, p. 60; see also pp. 60–64).

Zamakhshari relates, "God sent down the House, which was one of the rubies of Paradise having two doors of emerald, one on the east and the other on the west side. God then said to Adam, 'I have sent down for you that which must be circumambulated as my throne is being circumambulated.' Adam then set out on foot to the House from the land of India. Angels met him on the way, saying, 'Blessed be your pilgrimage, O Adam; we too made pilgrimage to this House, two thousand years before you.' Adam thereafter performed forty pilgrimages to Mecca on foot from India. The House remained as it was until God took it up to the fourth heaven during the flood. This was the 'populous house' [*al-bayt al-ma'mur*]. God then ordered Abraham to rebuild it, and Gabriel showed him its location. It is said that he built it of materials taken from five mountains: Mount Sinai, Mount Zaytah [Jerusalem], Mount Lebanon, Mount Ararat, and Mount Hira, from which he took its foundation stone. Gabriel brought him the black stone from heaven" (Zamakhshari, I, p. 311).

Ibn 'Arabi begins his commentary of this verse by recounting the tale of the descent of the Kaaba from heaven. He emphasizes that the Kaaba, before the deluge, had two doors, one facing east, the other west. Ibn 'Arabi then allegorizes this tale as follows:

"The descent of the Kaaba at the time of Adam is an allusion to the appearance of the heart. . . . The fact that it had two doors, eastern and western, is an allusion to the manifestation of the knowledge of origination [*mabda'*] and return [*ma'ad*] to God, as well as the knowledge of the realms of light and darkness. These appeared during the time of Adam; they did not, however, include the science of divine oneness. Adam's journey to it [the Kaaba] from the land of India is a reference to his turning away from the corporeal realm of nature, through origination [*takwin*] and equilibrium [*i'tidal*], to the station of the heart. His meeting with the angels is an allusion to the attachment of the animal and vegetative powers of the body and the appearance in it of their effects prior to those of the heart. This was during the forty years during which his constitution was shaped and his clay set. His setting forth toward the Kaaba is his journey [*suluk*] from the dark realm of the carnal soul to the realm of the heart. His meeting with the angels is his being received by the psychic and corporeal powers and their subordination to him by submitting to the beautiful morals and virtuous qualities. His rising from one station to the next before his arrival at the station of the heart and his circumambulation of the House all refer to his attainment of the heart. His entry into it means his abiding in it.

"The lifting of the House to the fourth heaven during the time of the flood is an allusion to the veiling of the people from the station of the heart by the overpowering caprice of the flood of ignorance at the time of Noah. Its remaining in the fourth heaven, which is the populous house and which is the heart of the world, and its descent once more to earth at the time of Abraham, is an allusion to the guidance of men through him to the station of the heart. Abraham's raising of its foundation stones and making for it only one door is an allusion to his receiving the heart through his journey from his station to that of the spirit, which is the innermost faculty, and the raising of his stations till he attained the station of divine oneness. This is because Abraham was the first to whom the Unity of Essence manifested itself, as he says, 'I turn my face to Him who created the heavens and the earth, a man of pure faith, nor am I one of the associators' [Q. 6: 79]" (Ibn 'Arabi, I, pp. 86–87).

Shi'i tradition very early attempted to fill in details presenting a full account of the events leading to the building of the Kaaba. Thus Qummi writes, "Abraham dwelt in the lands of Syria. When Ishmael was born to him of Hagar, Sarah was exceedingly grieved because he did not beget a child by her. She therefore used to trouble Abraham and cause him much grief on account of Hagar and her son. Abraham complained of this to God, who revealed to him, 'A woman is like a crooked rib. If you let her be, you would enjoy her, but if you attempt to straighten her, she would break.' Then God commanded him to send Ishmael and his mother away. Abraham asked, 'O Lord, where should I send them?' God answered, 'Send them to my sacred house [*haram*], the place of safety [*amn*], to the first spot I created of the earth: to Mecca.'" God then sent down Gabriel to him with Buraq (a celestial horse which, according to Islamic tradition, carried the Prophet Muhammad to heaven on his night journey).

Abraham set out with Hagar and Ishmael, and he never passed a place where there were trees, palm orchards, and other vegetation but that he said, "O Gabriel, come to this place, this place!" Gabriel, however, would answer, "No, keep on going; continue until we reach Mecca." When they came to Mecca, Gabriel left them on the site of the Kaaba. Abraham had, however, promised Sarah that he would not dismount until he had returned to her. When they stopped in that place, there was a tree on which Hagar spread a mantle, under which they shaded themselves.

When Abraham left them in that place and was about to return to Sarah, Hagar exclaimed, "O Abrahm, why do you leave us in such a place, where there is neither companion, water, nor vegetation?" Abraham said, "The God who commanded me to leave you in this place shall be with you." Then he left them and went away. When he reached Kida' (a mountain near Mecca), he looked back at them and exclaimed, "Our Lord, I have settled some of my progeny in an uncultivated valley near your sacred house, in order, Our Lord, that they may observe the prayers. Make therefore the hearts of men to incline toward them; bestow upon them abundant fruits, that they may give thanks" (Q. 14:37). When the sun rose, Ishmael became thirsty and Hagar went to the valley, to the place where the pilgrims run (between the two hills of al-Safa and al-Marwah) and cried out, "Is there any human in the valley?" Then she went up on al-Safa, and a mirage of water appeared to her from the valley. Thus she ran (as pilgrims do), but when she reached the place of running (*mas'a*) the mirage appeared in the direction of al-Safa. This she repeated seven times (but to no avail). On the seventh time, as she stood on al-Marwah, she looked at Ishmael and saw water gushing from under his feet. She hastened down and gathered sand around the running water, which she thus contained. For this reason, the spring was called Zamzam (contained). (Qummi, I, pp. 60–61.)

A tribe called Jurhum dwelt in the area. Noticing the birds and animals coming to the water, the men of the tribe also went to the spot and found Hagar and Ishmael. She told them who she was and that the child was the son of Abraham, the Friend (*Khalil*) of God. Abraham, who came to visit his wife and child several times, allowed the tribe to dwell in the neighborhood. Ishmael grew up and became a shepherd.

"When Ishmael reached manhood, God ordered Abraham to build the House. He asked, 'O my Lord, in which spot?' God answered, 'In the spot where the dome was sent down to Adam, which illuminated the entire sacred area.' The dome remained there until the days of the flood, the days of Noah. When the world was submerged, God took up that dome to heaven, and the whole world was submerged except for the spot of the House. For this reason it was called *al-bayt al-'atiq* [the ransomed House], that is, saved from the flood [Q. 2:126]." (Qummi, I, pp. 61–62.)

God then sent down Gabriel, who plotted for Abraham the place of the House. God also sent the foundation stones (*qawa'id*) from Paradise. Abraham then built the House, and Ishmael brought the Black Stone from the place of Tuwa (near Mecca). Abraham put it in the place where it still stands. He made two doors for the House, one to the east and one to the west, and when the House was finished, Abraham and Ishmael performed the pilgrimage. Gabriel came down to them on the eighth of Dhu al-Hijjah and said to Abraham, "Rise up and quench your thirst with water," for there was no water in 'Arafah and Mina; hence the day is called *yawm al-tarwiyah* (the day of quenching). Gabriel then guided Abraham through the pilgrimage rites as he had done with Adam. Abraham then said, "O my Lord, render this a safe town! Bestow upon its inhabitants various fruits of Your bounty" (Qummi, I, pp. 61–62; see also Tabarsi, I, pp. 469–472).

In another tradition related by Tabarsi on the authority of Ibn 'Abbas and the sixth imam, al-Sadiq, we are told, "When Abraham brought Ishmael and Hagar and left them in Mecca, after a time the tribe of Jurhum came to dwell near the sacred House. Ishmael married one of their women. Abraham asked permission of his wife Sarah to visit Hagar. She consented on condition that he not dismount. Thus Abraham set out; in the meantime, Hagar died. He came to the house of Ishmael and asked his wife, 'Where is your husband?' She answered, 'He is not here; he went out hunting,' for it was the habit of Ishmael to leave the *haram* to hunt by day and return by night. [This is in keeping with the *shari'ah,* which forbids the killing of any living thing within the precinct of the *haram.*] Abraham asked her, 'Can you show hospitality to a guest?' She said, 'I have nothing, and there is no one here.' Then Abraham said to her, 'When your husband returns, convey to him my greetings of peace and say to him that he should change the threshold of his house.' When Ishmael returned, he sensed the fragrance of his father and asked his wife, 'Did anyone come to you?' She said, 'An old man of such and such description came to me.' Ishmael questioned her as to what the old man had told her, and she related it to him. Thus he divorced her and married another. Abraham again, after some time, asked Sarah's permission to visit Ishmael, and she consented on condition that he not dismount. Abraham thus came to the door of Ishmael and asked his wife, 'Where is your husband?' She answered, 'He went out hunting, but will return soon, if God wills. Dismount; may God have mercy upon you.' Abraham asked, 'Can you show hospitality to a guest?' 'Yes,' she said, and brought him milk and meat, which he ate asking God's blessings upon them. Had she brought him bread, wheat, barley, or dates, Mecca would have been the richest land in God's earth in wheat, barley, and dates. Then she said to him, 'Dismount so that I may wash your head,' but he refused to dismount. Thus she brought the *maqam* [stone] and placed it at his right side. He placed his foot on it and his footprint remained in it. She thus washed the right side of his head, then moved the *maqam* to his left side and washed the left side of his head. Abraham's footprints remained in the stone. He then said to her, 'When your husband returns, convey to him my greetings of peace and say to him, "The threshold of your house is now right."' When Ishmael returned and sensed the fragrance of his father, he asked his wife, 'Did anyone come to you?' She answered, 'Yes, an old man with the best countenance of men and sweetest fragrance.' [She then told him what happened and related her conversation with Abraham.] Ishmael then fell on the *maqam*, kissing it and weeping" (Tabarsi, I, pp. 461–462).

(131) Commentators have differed as to when God commanded Abraham to be a Muslim. Tabarsi relates that Hasan al-Basri said, "This was when the sun set [see Q. 6:78] and thus Abraham saw the signs and proofs by which he came to know the oneness of God, and said to his people, 'My people. I am free of what you associate with God. I rather turn my face to Him who created the heavens and the earth.' [Q. 6:78–79]. It was then that he submitted to God.

This proves that Abraham's conversation was before God granted him the gift of prophethood and that God commanded him to become a Muslim by way of inspiration, calling him to Islam. It would not be possible that God communicate with him through revelation before his submission [to God], because he was not then a prophet of God. This is because prophethood is a condition of majesty and exaltation, and that cannot be attained before Islam. The word *aslim* [submit] means 'be straight in Islam and stand firm on the [path] of *tawhid* [divine oneness]'. It has also been said that the meaning of the word *aslim* is 'be sincere in your religion through faith in divine oneness'" (Tabarsi, I, pp. 480–481; see also Ibn Kathir, I, p. 326).

135. They say, "Be Jews or Christians so that you may be guided aright." Say, "Rather, we follow the religion of Abraham, who was a man of pure faith [*hanif*] and was not of the associators."

The term *hanif* has been the subject of much scholarly controversy among Muslim as well as Western scholars. Commentators have disagreed regarding its meaning. Some said, according to Tabari, that *hanif* refers in this verse to one performing the rites of pilgrimage. A man asked Hasan al-Basri about the meaning of *hanifiyah* (adjectival noun of the word *hanif*), and he answered, "'It is the pilgrimage to the House.' Mujahid said, 'The *hanif* is the pilgrim.'" The same opinion is related on the authority of Ibn 'Abbas. 'Abdallah ibn al-Qasim said, "The people of Mudar [the Arabs] used to perform the pilgrimage to the House during the days of Jahiliyah [the days before Islam]; they were then called *hunafa'* [plural of *hanif*]. Thus God sent down the verse, 'Being pure in faith [*hunafa'*] before God, not associating any partners with Him'" (Q. 22:31). Others said that a *hanif* is one who follows the *sunnah* of Abraham. "The religion of Abraham was called *al-hanifiyah* because Abraham was the first imam who established the practice [*sunnah*] of circumcision for men. Thus, whoever circumcises himself, following the example of Abraham, must be considered a follower of the Islam of Abraham, and hence would be a *hanif*." Tabari reports on the authority of al-Suddi that, "the *hanif* is he who is sincere in his faith in God alone." Tabari, however, interprets the word *hanif* as "the religion of Abraham, as well as [the act of] following it. For had it been only pilgrimage to the House, then the people who used to make pilgrimage to it during the days of Jahiliyah would have been *hanifs*. Similarly, were the *hanifiyah* simply circumcision, then the Jews would have been considered *hanifs*, whereas God has excluded them by His saying, 'Abraham was neither a Jew nor a Christian; rather he was a *hanif*, Muslim' [Q. 3:67]. It is therefore correct to say that the *hanifiyah* is neither circumcision alone nor pilgrimage to the House alone, but rather it is following with uprightness the faith of Abraham and accepting him as imam" (Tabari, III, pp. 107–108; see also Qurtubi, II, pp. 139–140; and Shawkani, I, p. 146).

Tabarsi explains the word *hanif* as "one who inclines away from false religions and to the true faith. The *hanif* is therefore one who turns away from one religion to another. Thus the *hanifiyah* [religion of Abraham] is so called because it is a turning away from the Jewish and Christian religions. Al-Zajjaj said that the word *hanif* comes from *hanf*, which is an inclination in the forepart of the foot or inversion of the foot. A person having this distortion of the foot is called *ahnaf*" (Tabarsi, I, pp. 486–487).

136. Say, "We have faith in God and that which was sent down to us, that which was sent down to Abraham, Ishmael, Isaac, Jacob, and the twelve patriarchs, that which was given to Moses and Jesus and all that the prophets were given by their Lord. We make no distinction among them, and to Him we are submitters."

137. Were they to have faith in the like of that in which you have faith, they would have been guided aright. But if they turn back, they shall be clearly in schism. God will suffice for you, for He is all-hearing, all-knowing.

138. The baptism of God [have we received], for who is better than God to baptize? Him alone do we worship.

(138) The word *sibghah* is here used to denote baptism. More generally, however, it means purification or a sign of distinction of one group of people from another. This verse is related by Tabari to the preceding three verses: "The Jews and Christians said to Muhammad and his faithful Companions, 'Be Jews or Christians, so that you may be guided aright' [but God instructed his Prophet to say to them], 'O Jews and Christians, rather follow the religion of Abraham, the *sibghah* of God, which is the best *sibghah*, for it

is the pure faith of Islam. Abandon association of other things with God and straying from the clear proof of His guidance'" (Tabari, III, p. 118).

Wahidi relates on the authority of Ibn 'Abbas, "When a child is born to Christians, after the seventh day they immerse him [*saba-ghuhu*] in a kind of water [which they call the water of baptism] in order to purify him by it. They say that it is a [rite] of purification in place of circumcision. When they have performed this rite they say, 'Now he is a true Christian!'" (Wahidi, p. 38).

Tabarsi relates that Qatadah said, "The Jews give to their children the *sibghah* of Judaism, and the Christians give their children the *sibghah* of Christianity. This means that they inculcate in their children the Jewish or Christian faith. Thus it is related that 'Umar b. al-Khattab made a pact with the tribe of Taghlib that they would not give their children the *sibghah*, that is, not inculcate in them Christianity, but that they would leave them until they grew up to choose for themselves whichever religion they wished through the *sibghah* [here meaning natural inclination] given them by God. It is said also that faith [*din*] is called *sibghah* because it is a visible mark, that is, the traces of purity, worship [*salat*] and other such beautiful characteristics." Tabarsi further relates on the authority of Ja'far al-Sadiq that, "The *sibghah* [sign or mark] of God is Islam." According to Hasan al-Basri, Qatadah and Mujahid, it is the religion of God. According to Ubayy and others, the *sibghah* of God is the *fitrah* (original state of pure faith) in which God created humankind (Tabarsi, I, pp. 492–493).

Qurtubi adds yet another signification of the word *sibghah*: "It is said that *sibghah* is a [ritualistic] bath for one who wishes to enter into Islam, instead of the baptism of the Christians. I say that according to this exegesis [*ta'wil*] the bath is mandatory for a rejecter of faith [*kafir*] as an act of worship. This is because the meaning of the *sibghah* of God is the bath [*ghusl*] of God. This is as if to say, 'Wash yourselves when you enter Islam by performing the *ghusl*, which God has made obligatory for you.' This is in accordance with the unquestionable *sunnah* regarding Qays ibn 'Asim and Thumamah ibn Athal when they entered Islam. It is related on the authority of Abu Hurayrah that Thumamah al-Hanafi was captured. One day the Prophet passed by him and he accepted Islam. He then sent him to the walled date palm orchard of Abu Talhah and ordered him to perform *ghusl*; this he did and performed also two *rak'ahs* of prayer. The Apostle of God then said, 'The Islam of your companion is now good.' It is also related that Qays ibn 'Asim entered into Islam, whereupon the Prophet ordered him to perform *ghusl* with water and *sidr* [the ground leaves of the lotus tree, commonly used in ritualistic washing of the dead]" (Qurtubi, II, pp. 144–145).

139. Say, "Would you dispute with us concerning God, who is our Lord and your Lord? To you belong your deeds and to us our deeds. To Him we turn in sincere devotion."

140. Or would you say that Abraham, Ishmael, Isaac, Jacob, and the twelve patriarchs were Jews or Christians? Say, "Do you know better, or God?" For who does greater wrong than he who withholds testimony which he has received from God? God is not unaware of what you do.

141. Those were a people who have passed away. To them belongs that which they gained and to you belongs that which you gained; nor will you be questioned concerning what they have done.

142. The foolish among the people will say, "What has turned them away from their *qiblah*, toward which they formerly prayed?" Say, "To God belongs the east and the west, and He guides whom He wills to the straight way."

(142) This verse was sent down concerning the change of the *qiblah* (direction of prayer) from the Holy House of Jerusalem to the Kaaba of Mecca (Wahidi, pp. 38–39). Commentators have differed as to when after the Prophet's arrival in Medina the change took place. They also differ as to the reason for the Prophet's facing Jerusalem in the first place (Tabari, III, p. 132).

Tabari relates on the authority of Ibn 'Abbas that when the *qiblah* was changed from Jerusalem to the Kaaba (the change took place seventeen months after the Prophet's arrival in Medina) a group of Jews and their Medinan allies came to the Prophet and said, "O Muhammad, what made you turn away from the *qiblah* which you had previously faced, although you claim to be a follower of the religion of Abraham and his faith? Return to the *qiblah* which you formerly faced; then would we believe you and follow you!" Thus, "They only wanted to tempt him away from his faith. God, however, sent down this verse concerning them" (Tabari, III, pp. 132–133).

In another tradition related by Tabari on the authority of al-Bara' ibn 'Azib, we are told that the Prophet prayed facing Jerusalem for seventeen months, but he wished all the while to turn toward the Kaaba. Al-Bara' said, "As we were praying one day, a man passed by and said, 'Do you know that the Prophet has been turned toward the Kaaba?' We had then prayed two *rak'ahs* in that direction [that is, Jerusalem]; then we prayed two in the other direction [that is, of the Kaaba]" (Tabari, III, p. 133). It is further related on the authority of Ibn al-Musayyab that the Muslims in Medina prayed for sixteen months toward Jerusalem, until two months before Badr (Tabari, III, p. 134). Malik ibn Anas relates, "The Prophet of God prayed toward the Holy House [Jerusalem] for nine or ten months. As one day he was offering the noon prayer in Medina, he prayed two *rak'ahs* toward Jerusalem, then turned his face toward the Kaaba. Thus the foolish said, 'What has turned them away from their *qiblah*, toward which they formerly prayed?'" (Tabari, III, p. 135). Still another tradition related on the authority of Mu'adh ibn Jabal asserts that the Prophet prayed toward Jerusalem for thirteen months after his arrival in Medina (Tabari, III, p. 136).

As for the reason why the Prophet prayed toward Jerusalem before he was turned to the Kaaba, Tabari relates on the authority of 'Ikrimah and Hasan al-Basri, "The first injunction which was abrogated in the Qur'an was that concerning the *qiblah*. This is because the Prophet used to prefer the Rock of the Holy House of Jerusalem, which was the *qiblah* of the Jews. The Prophet faced it for seventeen months in the hope that they would believe in him and follow him. Then God said 'Say, "To God belong the east and the west".'" (Tabari, III, p. 138)

Al-Rabi' ibn Anas related on the authority of Abu al-'Aliyah, "The Prophet of God was given the choice of turning his face in whichever direction he wished. He chose the Holy House of Jerusalem in order that the People of the Book would be conciliated. This was his *qiblah* for sixteen months; all the while, however, he was turning his face toward the heavens until God turned him toward the House [the Kaaba]" (Tabari, III, p. 138). It is related, on the other hand, on the authority of Ibn 'Abbas, "When the Apostle of God migrated to Medina, most of whose inhabitants were Jews, God commanded him to face Jerusalem, and the Jews were glad. The Prophet faced it for some time beyond ten months, but he loved the *qiblah* of Abraham [that is, the Kaaba]. Thus he used to pray to God and gaze into the heavens until God sent down, 'We have seen you turning your face about toward heaven' [Q. 2:144]. The Jews became suspicious and said, 'What has turned them away from their *qiblah*, toward which they formerly prayed?' Thus God sent down, 'Say, "To God belongs the east and the west"'" (Tabari, III, pp. 138–139; see also Qurtubi, II, pp. 150–151).

Qummi asserts that this verse was revealed after verse 144 even though it occurs in the Qur'an before it. "This is because the Jews used to taunt the Apostle of God saying, 'You are one of our followers; you pray toward our *qiblah*.' The Apostle of God was deeply grieved by this. Thus he went out in the night gazing at the horizons of heaven, waiting for God's command concerning this matter. When next day the time of the noon prayer came, he was in the mosque of the tribe of Banu Salim. He led the prayers in two *rak'ahs*. Then Gabriel came down, took him by the shoulders, and turned him toward the Kaaba. After this God sent down, 'We have seen you turning your face about toward heaven' [Q. 2:144]. He prayed the last two *rak'ahs* toward the Kaaba. Therefore the Jews and foolish men said, 'What has turned them away from their *qiblah*, toward which they formerly prayed? The *qiblah* was changed to the Kaaba after the Apostle of God had prayed for thirteen years in Mecca toward Jerusalem. After his migration to Medina he prayed toward Jerusalem for seven months, when God changed the *qiblah* to the House. Then God said, 'Wherever you may be, turn your faces toward it'" (Qummi, I, pp. 62–63; see also Tabarsi, II, pp. 5–7).

Nisaburi comments on the wisdom of changing the *qiblah* as follows: "It is that the servant must turn his face toward the king and serve him. It is also in order that unity and harmony among the people of faith may be established. It is as though the Exalted One says, 'O man of faith! You are my servant, the Kaaba is my house and the prayers are my service. Your heart is my throne and Paradise is my noble abode. Turn your face toward my house and your heart to me, so that I may grant you my noble abode.' The Jews faced the west, which is the direction of the setting of lights. . . . The Christians faced the east, which is the direction of the rising of lights . . . but the people of faith faced the manifestation of lights, which is Mecca. From Mecca is Muhammad, and from him were lights created, and for his sake the circling spheres were set on their course. The west is the *qiblah* of Moses and the East is the *qiblah* of Jesus; between them is the *qiblah* of Abraham and Muhammad, for the best of things is that which is in the middle position. The Throne is the *qiblah* of its bearers, the *kursi* [Footstool] is the *qiblah* of the righteous ones, the populous house [*al-bayt al-ma'mur*] is the *qiblah* of the emissaries [angels] and the Kaaba is the *qiblah* of the people of faith. The truth is the *qiblah* of those who are confused; 'Wherever you turn, there is the face of God'" (Q. 2:115; Nisaburi, III, p. 8).

143. Thus have we made you a community [*ummah*] of the middle path in order that you may be witnesses over humankind and that the Apostle be a witness over you. We appointed the *qiblah* to which you formerly prayed only to make known those who follow the Apostle and those who would turn back on their heels. It [the change of *qiblah*] is indeed a grave matter except for those whom God has guided aright. As for you, God would never count your faith as naught. Truly God is gracious and compassionate toward mankind.

144. We have seen you turning your face about toward heaven. We shall therefore direct you toward a *qiblah* which would please you. Turn your face toward the sacred House of worship; wherever you may be, turn your faces toward it. As for those who were given the scriptures, they know well that it is the truth from their Lord, nor is God unaware of what they do.

145. Even if you were to bring those who were given the scriptures every manifest sign, still they would not follow your *qiblah*, nor will you follow their *qiblah*, nor yet will they follow each other's *qiblah*. If, therefore, you were to follow their desires after the knowledge that has come to you, you would surely be one of the wrongdoers.

146. Those to whom we have given the scriptures recognize it as well as they recognize their own sons. Still a party among them conceal the truth, yet they know it.

147. Truth is from your Lord; do not therefore be one of the doubters.

148. For each there is a direction toward which he turns; vie therefore with one another in the performance of good

works. Wherever you may be, God shall bring you all together [on the day of judgment]. Surely God has power over all things.

149. From whatever place you set out, turn your face toward the sacred House of worship. This is the truth from your Lord, and God is not unaware of what you do.

150. From whatever place you set out, turn your face toward the sacred House of worship, and wherever you may be, turn your faces toward it so that men may not have a contention against you, except those among them who do wrong; do not fear them, rather fear me. Thus will I fulfill my favor toward you so that you may be guided aright.

(143) Three issues in this verse have occupied commentators. The first is the meaning and significance of the word "*wasat*" (middle path). The second is the question of the test of faith implied in the change of *qiblah*. The third issue concerns those who had died before the change of the *qiblah* was instituted. This question may have provided the occasion for the revelation of this verse.

Commentators have differed with regard to the meaning of the word *wasat*. Tabari interprets the word as follows: "I consider the word *wasat* in this context to signify the mean between two extremes. God described the Muslims as being people of the middle path because of their middle position in religion. They are neither people of extremism like the Christians who went to extremes in their monastic practices as well as in what they said concerning Jesus, nor are they people of deficiency like the Jews, who altered the Book of God, killed their prophets, gave the lie to their Lord, and rejected faith in Him. Rather, they are people of the middle path and of equilibrium [*i'tidal*] in their religion. God characterized them as people of the middle path because the things which God loves most are those of the middle position" (Tabari, III, p. 142).

Ibn Kathir links this verse with the one preceding it. He writes, "God the exalted says, 'We have turned you to the *qiblah* of Abraham and have chosen it for you in order that we may make you the best of communities, and that on the day of resurrection you may be witnesses over all communities. They will all confess your excellence over them.' The word *wasat*, therefore, here means the best. It is related on the authority of Abu Sa'id al-Khudri that the Apostle of God said, 'Noah will be summoned on the day of resurrection and asked, "Did you transmit [that is, God's command to his people]?" He will answer, "Yes, I did." Then his people will be summoned and asked, "Did he transmit to you?" They will answer, "No warner came to us, nor was anyone sent to us." Noah will then be asked, "Who shall be your witnesses?" He will say, "Muhammad and his community." . . . You Muslims will be summoned to witness for Noah that he did transmit, and I shall be witness over you'" (Ibn Kathir, I, p. 335).

In another similar tradition also related on the authority of Abu Sa'id al-Khudri, the Prophet tells of how every prophet's community will be asked on the day of resurrection if their prophet conveyed to them God's message; this they would all deny. Each prophet, however, would affirm that he did indeed deliver to his people the message entrusted to him by God. Again he would be challenged, "Who shall be your witnesses?" "Muhammad and his community," he would answer. Then Muhammad and his community would be summoned and asked, "Did this prophet convey to his people [the divine message]?" "Yes," they would say. They would then be asked, "How do you know that he did?" and they would answer, "Our prophet came to us and told us that the apostles of God did convey God's message" (Ibn Kathir, I, p. 335; see also Tabari, III, p. 145; and Zamakhshari, I, p. 317).

Qummi interprets the words *ummatan wasatan* (community of the middle path) to mean "a community of the mean, mediating between the Apostle and humankind." Qummi then asserts that this verse was addressed to the imams, who are the true community of the middle path. This attribution is made in part through a play on words in which the word *ummah* is made to read *a'immah*, (imams) (Qummi, I, p. 63). Tabarsi cites several traditions asserting that the community of the middle path means the imams because, he argues, "If someone were to ask how God could attribute this quality to the entire community when there might be someone in it not possessing it, the answer would be that He intended to refer only to those who have such a quality, since no age could be devoid of a group of people of this quality." Thus it is related that the fifth imam said, "We are the community of the middle path, and we are God's witnesses over His creatures; we are His proofs [*hujaj*] in His earth." It is also related on the authority of Sulaym ibn Qays al-Hilali that 'Ali, the first imam, said, "God intended us by His saying,

'. . . in order that you may be witnesses over humankind,' for the Apostle of God is witness over us and we are God's witnesses over His creatures and His proofs in His earth. We are those of whom God said, 'Thus have we made you a community of the middle path'" (Tabarsi, II, pp. 10–11; see also Tabataba'i, I, pp. 321–323 and 331–332).

Tabari relates on the authority of Ibn 'Abbas that the words, "We appointed the *qiblah* to which you formerly prayed only to make known those who follow the Apostle and those who would turn back on their heels" mean "so that we may distinguish the people of certainty from the people of association [*shirk*] and doubt" (Tabari, III, p. 160).

The word *imanakum* (your faith) here means "your prayers," according to many traditions (see Tabari, III, pp. 167–168). It is also related that the words, "As for you, God would never count your faith as naught," indicated that the verse was revealed concerning those of the Companions of the Prophet who died during the time of the first *qiblah*. Their kinsfolk came to the Prophet to express their concern, saying, "Apostle of God, our brethren died while praying toward the first *qiblah*. Now that God has turned you to the *qiblah* of Abraham, what shall become of our brethren?" (Wahidi, p. 39).

(144) Wahidi reports, "The Prophet told Gabriel 'I wish that God would turn me away from the *qiblah* of the Jews to another,' for he preferred the Kaaba because it was the *qiblah* of Abraham. Gabriel answered, 'I am a servant like you, I have no authority of my own; ask therefore your Lord to turn you from Jerusalem to the *qiblah* of Abraham.' Gabriel then went up to heaven and the Apostle of God gazed long into the heavens hoping that Gabriel would return to him with what he had asked; thus God sent down this verse" (Wahidi, p. 39; see also Tabari, III, pp. 172–173; and Tabarsi, II, pp. 15–16).

Commentators have differed as to the reason why the Prophet preferred the *qiblah* of the Kaaba. According to Tabari, some said, "He disliked the *qiblah* of Jerusalem because the Jews used to say, 'He follows our *qiblah*, yet he opposes us in our religion.'" Others said, "Rather he preferred the Kaaba because it was the *qiblah* of his father Abraham" (Tabari, III, pp. 173–174; see also pp. 175–182; and Zamakhshari, I, p. 319). Qurtubi relates on the authority of Ibn 'Abbas that the Apostle of God said, "The House [Kaaba] is the *qiblah* for the people [surrounding] the place of worship [*masjid*];

the *masjid* is the *qiblah* for the people of the *haram* [the entire site of pilgrimage] and the *haram* is the *qiblah* for the inhabitants of the earth of my community in the east and west" (Qurtubi, II, p. 156).

(146) This verse was sent down, according to Wahidi, concerning the people of faith among the People of the Book, such as 'Abdallah ibn Sallam and his companions who accepted Islam. "They knew the Apostle of God, his characteristics, qualities, and the time of his coming [as foretold] in their scriptures. They recognized him as surely as would one of them have recognized his own son if he saw him playing with the children of the neighborhood" (Wahidi, p. 40).

Tabari relates on the authority of a number of *tafsir* masters that the People of the Book mentioned here were Jewish rabbis and Christian savants. They knew that "the sacred House [Kaaba] is their *qiblah* and the *qiblah* of Abraham and all the prophets before you [Muhammad] as surely as they knew their own sons" (Tabari, III, p. 187).

Commentators assert that the truth (*al-haqq*) here means the *qiblah*. It is the *qiblah*, "which prophets before Muhammad faced. The Jews and Christians, however, concealed this, and some of them [that is, the Christians] faced east and others [the Jews] faced the Holy House of Jerusalem" (Tabari, III, p. 188). According to Mujahid, "They concealed [the prophecies about] Muhammad even though they found it all written in their Torah and Gospel" (Tabari, III, p. 188; see also Ibn Kathir, I, pp. 341–342).

Qurtubi raises the question, "How could they [the Jews and Christians] know it [the change of the *qiblah*] when it is not in their religion nor is it mentioned in their scriptures?" He offers two answers: "Since they know from their scriptures that Muhammad was a prophet, they must also know that he speaks nothing but the truth and enjoins nothing but the truth. They further know from their own religion that abrogation [*naskh*] is permissible, even though some of them may deny it. Thus they know that it is permissible that the *qiblah* [be changed]" (Qurtubi, II, p. 161; see also Tabarsi, II, pp. 21–22).

Sayyid Qutb treats all the verses dealing with the change of the *qiblah* together. He asserts that the Muslims in Mecca faced the Kaaba from the beginning. It was after the Hijrah that they were commanded by God to face the house of Jerusalem, although it was an extra-Qur'anic command. Finally, the last Qur'anic command came in the verse, "Turn your face toward the sacred House of worship; wherever you may be, turn your faces toward it" (Q. 2:144; Qutb, I, p. 172).

As for the wisdom in the change of the *qiblah,* Sayyid Qutb says, "The change of the *qiblah* at first from the Kaaba to al-Masjid al-Aqsa ['the furthest mosque'] was for an educational purpose to which the verse, 'We appointed the *qiblah* to which you formerly prayed' [Q. 2:143] refers. This is because the Arabs used to glorify the Kaaba during the time of Jahiliyah, regarding it as the symbol of their national pride. Since, however, Islam aimed at purifying hearts for God, removing them from attachment to anything other than Him and cleansing them from every bias of kinship tie ['asabiyah] except Islam [which is their direct link to God, free from historical, racial, or earthly blemish], God chose for them the Aqsa mosque for a while in order that He might cleanse their souls from the residues of the Jahiliyah. It was also to show who would follow the Apostle absolutely and without any other consideration and who would turn back on his heels. When the Muslims submitted and faced the *qiblah* toward which the Apostle had turned them, the Jews immediately began to use this issue as an argument against the Muslims. The divine command to face the sacred House was then issued. Still, however, the Prophet directed the heart of Muslims to another reality regarding the Kaaba: the reality of Islam. [He directed them to] the truth that this House was built by Abraham and Ishmael and was intended to be pure for the service of God. It is a heritage for the Muslim community which came into being in answer to the prayer of Abraham, who prayed God to send among his descendants a messenger with the message of Islam, which he and his sons and grandsons followed" (Qutb, I, p. 174).

151. So have we sent to you an apostle from among your-selves to recite to you our revelations, purify you, teach you the Book and wisdom and teach you that which you did not know.

152. Remember me therefore, that I may remember you. Give thanks to me and do not reject faith in me.

153. O you who have faith, seek help in patience and prayer, for God is with those who are patient.

154. Do not say concerning those who are slain in the way of God that they are dead. Rather they are alive, but you do not perceive.

155. We shall surely try you with some measure of fear and hunger and decrease of wealth, lives, and crops. But give glad tidings to those who are patient,

156. Those who, when visited by affliction, say, "Surely to God do we belong and to Him shall we return."

157. Upon these are blessings from their Lord and a mercy, and these are the rightly guided.

(152) The concept of *dhikr* (remembrance) of God has played a crucial role in Muslim piety. *Dhikr* has been especially important for the Sufis and has constituted the most important element of their spiritual exercises and daily worship. Nisaburi, as a representative of popular piety, comments on this verse: "Remember me through obedience to me that I may remember you through my mercy. Remember me in prayer, that I may remember you through answering your prayer. Remember me in this world, that I may remember you in the next. Remember me in places of seclusion [*khalawat*], that I may remember you in open places [*falawat*]. Remember me in times of comfort, that I may remember you in times of affliction. Remember me through spiritual struggle [*mujahadah*], that I may remember you through guidance. Remember me through truthfulness and sincerity, that I may remember you through salvation and increase of special favor. Remember me through servanthood, that I may remember you through Lordship. Remember me through annihilation [*fana'*], that I may remember you through subsistence [*baqa'*]" (Nisaburi, II, p. 30).

(154) It is generally agreed that this verse was revealed concerning the martyrs of Badr, who were eight of the Ansar (helpers) and six of the Muhajirun (immigrants). "People used to say of a man who was killed in the way of God, 'So and so died; he lost the comfort of this world and its pleasures.' Thus God revealed this verse" (Wahidi, pp. 40–41).

158. Surely al-Safa and al-Marwah are two of the signs of God. Therefore whoever goes on pilgrimage to the sacred

House or performs the lesser pilgrimage, in him there is no blame if he runs between them. As for him who voluntarily performs good works, God is surely grateful, allknowing.

Wahidi relates that when asked about al-Safa and al-Marwah, Anas ibn Malik said, "We were of the opinion that they belonged to the Jahiliyah. Thus when Islam came we ceased running between them. God therefore sent down this verse" (Wahidi, p. 44).

Qurtubi, the jurist, relates that 'Urwah ibn al-Zubayr said to 'A'ishah, "I see nothing against anyone who does not run between al-Safa and al-Marwah, nor would I be concerned if I myself did not run between them." She answered, "Ill is that which you speak, O son of my sister! The Apostle of God ran between them and so did the Muslims. It was rather those who sacrificed [that is, the people of Medina before Islam] to Manat, the idol which was in the Mushlal [a mountain facing the sea seven miles away from Medina], who did not run between them. Thus God sent down, 'Therefore whoever goes on pilgrimage to the sacred House or performs the lesser pilgrimage, in him there is no blame if he runs between them.' Had it been as you say, the verse would have read, 'in him there is no blame if he does not run between them'" (Qurtubi, II, p. 178; see also Wahidi, pp. 41–42).

Qurtubi further relates on the authority of Ibn 'Abbas, "In the time of Jahiliyah there were satans spending the night between al-Safa and al-Marwah and there were between them gods [that is, idols]. When Islam came, the Muslims said, 'O Apostle of God, we shall not run between al-Safa and al-Marwah because they are [signs of] *shirk* [association].' Thus the verse was sent down." Al-Sha'bi said, "During the Jahiliyah there was an idol on al-Safa called Isaf and another on al-Marwah called Na'ilah. People used to touch them when they ran [between the two hills]. The Muslims did not wish to run between them on that account; hence God sent down this verse" (Qurtubi, II, p. 179).

Commentators have linked the name al-Safa to the word *safat*, meaning smooth stones, al-Safa being its singular. Similarly, al-Marwah was linked to the word *marw*, meaning small flint pebbles, al-Marwah being also its singular (Tabari, III, pp. 224–225). Qurtubi relates, "The People of the Book have claimed that [a man and a woman] once fornicated in the Kaaba. God therefore turned them into two stones and placed the man on al-Safa and the woman on al-Marwah as an example for others. As time went by, they were worshiped instead of God. But as to the truth of this, God knows best" (Qurtubi, II, p. 180). This tradition is perhaps meant to explain why al-Safa is masculine and al-Marwah feminine. In yet another tradition related by Tabarsi on the authority of Ja'far al-Sadiq and others, we are told, "Adam came down from the garden and stood on al-Safa and Eve on al-Marwah. Hence al-Safa was so called after Adam al-Mustafa [the chosen one] and al-Marwah after the name Mar'ah [woman]" (Tabarsi, II, p. 44).

Early Shi'i tradition gives a somewhat different reason for the revelation of this verse. Qummi reports, "The people of Quraysh placed their idols between al-Safa and al-Marwah. When the Apostle of God [concluded the truce of Hudaybiyah] and the Quraysh prevented him from making pilgrimage to the sacred House, they promised to vacate the Kaaba for him in the following year for three days so he could perform the lesser pilgrimage ['umrah], after which he should depart from Mecca. When the time for the lesser pilgrimage had come, in the seventh year of the Hijrah, he entered Mecca and said to the people of Quraysh, 'Remove your idols from between al-Safa and al-Marwah so that I may perform the Sa'i [that is, running between them].' Thus the Apostle of God performed the Sa'i when the idols were removed. A man of the faithful, one of the Companions of the Apostle of God, had not yet performed the Sa'i. When the Apostle had completed his running, the men of Quraysh put back the idols between al-Safa and al-Marwah. The man therefore came to the Apostle of God and said, 'The people of Quraysh have returned their idols between al-Safa and al-Marwah; therefore I did not run.' God then sent down, 'Surely al-Safa and al-Marwah are two of the signs of God. Therefore whoever goes on pilgrimage to the sacred House or performs the lesser pilgrimage, in him there is no blame if he runs between them.' That is why the idols were still on them" (Qummi, I, pp. 63–64).

Commentators and jurists have differed with regard to the Sa'i between al-Safa and al-Marwah. The view that it is voluntary has been related on the authority of Ibn 'Abbas, Anas ibn Malik and 'Urwah ibn al-Zubayr. Thus Ibn Mas'ud read the verse as "in him there is no blame if he does not run between them." For Abu Hanifah, the Sa'i is obligatory (*wajib*); it is not, however, a fundamental obligation (*rukn*), such as the pilgrimage itself. Anyone not performing the rite must, according to Abu Hanifah, expiate his neglect by an animal sacrifice. According to the school of Malik ibn

Anas, the Sa'i is a *rukn*, being an essential element of the pilgrimage obligation (Zamakhshari, I, pp. 324–325).

Tabarsi argues, "In this verse there is unquestionable proof that the Sa'i is an act of worship. For us [the Shi'ah] it is obligatory both in the *hajj* and *'umrah*. This is because it is said that the *sunnah* [of the Prophet] made Sa'i obligatory, as in the saying of the Apostle of God, 'Sa'i has been ordained for you; therefore perform it.' Apparently, the verse was sent down in answer to the permission given to Muslims before the conquest of Mecca not to perform the Sa'i if they were reluctant on account of the idols" (Tabarsi, II, p. 46; see also Tabataba'i, I, pp. 385–386; and Shawkani, I, pp. 160–161; for a comprehensive discussion see Tabari, III, pp. 224–248).

159. Those who conceal the clear proofs and guidance which we sent down after we had manifested them in the Book to humankind: these shall God curse and they who curse shall curse them,

160. Except those who shall repent and make amends and disclose that which they have concealed; toward them shall I turn, for I am relenting, compassionate.

161. As for those who have rejected faith and died in rejection, upon them is the curse of God, of the angels, and of all humankind.

162. They shall abide in it [Hellfire] forever. Their torment shall not be lightened, nor will respite be given them.

163. Your God is one God; there is no god but He, the All-merciful, the Compassionate.

(159) Commentators have differed as to the identity of the people here mentioned. Zamakhshari asserts that the people meant are the People of the Book and that the Book is the Torah (Zamakhshari, I, pp. 324–325). Wahidi, on the other hand, says that the verse was sent down concerning the learned men of the People of the Book because they concealed the stoning verse (see Lev. 20:10 and Ezek. 16:40; also Q. 5:41–44) and prophecies concerning Muhammad. Those who curse them are the faithful and the angels (Wahidi, p. 42; see also Tabari, III, pp. 257–258).

Tabarsi relates on the authority of Mujahid and 'Ikrimah that those who curse include the beasts of the earth as well. According to Ibn 'Abbas, it is everything except "the two weights [al-thaqalayn] that is, humankind and the *jinn.*" Tabarsi argues, "In this verse there is an indication that concealing the truth, when there is the need to make it known, is one of the gravest sins. It is related that the Prophet said, 'Whoever is asked concerning knowledge which he possesses and conceals it, shall be bridled with a bridle of fire on the day of resurrection'" (Tabarsi, II, p. 48; see also pp. 46–48).

164. Surely in the creation of the heavens and the earth; and the alternation of night and day; and the ship which sails over the sea, laden with goods useful to humankind; and the water which God has sent from heaven to revive with it the earth after its death, and dispersed in it every kind of beast; and the change of the winds; and the clouds made to serve between heaven and earth, are signs for people who understand.

165. Yet there are those among men who take idols as equal to God, loving them with the love due to God alone. But those who have faith are more ardent in their love for God. Would that the wrongdoers perceive when they see their punishment that all power belongs to God and that God is severe in punishment.

166. When those who were followed shall dissociate themselves from those who followed them and see the torment, all recourse being cut off for them;

167. Then the followers will say, "O, if only we could return [to the world] so that we may dissociate ourselves from them as they dissociate themselves from us." Thus shall God show them their deeds as cause of anguish for them, and they will not be released from the Fire.

168. O people, eat only the lawful and good things which are in the earth and do not follow in the steps of Satan, for he is an open enemy to you.

169. He enjoins upon you all manner of evil and abomination and that you should say concerning God what you do not know.

170. When it is said to them, "Follow that which God has sent down," they say, "Rather we follow that which we have found our fathers practicing," even though their fathers comprehended nothing, nor were they guided aright.

171. The similitude of those who have rejected faith is like one who cries out to that which hears nothing but empty calls and shouts. They are deaf, mute, and blind; they do not comprehend.

172. O you who have faith, eat of the good things which we have provided for you and give thanks to God, if you truly worship Him alone.

(171) Two views have been expressed in interpretation of this verse. The first is that the one who cries out is like the shepherd who calls to sheep that hear his voice but do not understand the words. The second is that it is the crying of the people of rejection of faith to their idols, which is like one calling out to something that does not hear (Nisaburi, II, pp. 65–66).

173. He has forbidden you that which dies of itself, blood, the flesh of swine, and any animal over which the name of any other than God has been invoked. But as for him who is forced by necessity, neither transgressing nor lusting, there is no sin in him, for God is forgiving, compassionate.

174. Surely those who conceal any part of the scriptures which God sent down, exchanging it for a small price, shall consume in their bellies nothing but fire. God shall not speak to them on the day of resurrection, nor will he purify them; theirs shall be a painful torment.

175. These are they who have exchanged guidance for error and forgiveness for punishment; but what shall make them endure the Fire!

176. That is because God sent down the scriptures with the truth. Thus those who disagree concerning the scriptures are in great schism.

177. It is not righteousness that you turn your faces toward the east and the west. True righteousness is this: to have faith in God and the last day, the angels, the scriptures, and the prophets; to give of one's wealth, though it may be cherished, to the next of kin and the orphans, the destitute and the wayfarer, to the needy and for the redemption of slaves; to observe regular worship and to give the obligatory alms. Those who fulfill their covenant having bound themselves by it and those who are patient in misfortune and adversity and in times of strife: these are true in their faith; these are the God-fearing.

178. O you who have faith, the law of retaliation has been ordained for you regarding those slain: the free for the free, the slave for the slave, the female for the female. Yet he who is pardoned by his brother should make satisfaction in good faith and pay blood indemnity to him with kindness. This is indulgence and a mercy from your Lord; whosoever transgresses thereafter shall suffer a painful torment.

179. In the law of retaliation there is life for you, O people of intelligence, that you may fear God.

180. It has been ordained for you that any one of you at the point of death, if he leaves any wealth, should bequeath it to parents and next of kin according to what is kind and honorable. This is a duty incumbent upon the God-fearing.

181. But as for him who alters it [the will] after he has heard it, the sin thereof shall be upon those who alter. Surely God is all-hearing, all-knowing.

182. But if anyone fears injustice or sin in a testator, and endeavors to make peace among the legatees, there is no sin in him. Surely God is forgiving, compassionate.

(173) This is the first verse of the Qur'an dealing with dietary laws. These laws are further elaborated in *surahs* 5 and 6, which are of the late Medinan period. We shall therefore return to these laws at greater length when dealing with the appropriate verses of these *surahs* (see Q. 5:3 and 6:145). I depend in this brief discussion on Qurtubi, who was a noted Sunni jurist, and Tabarsi, who was an eminent Shi'i jurist. The latter presents a number of legal views from both Shi'i and Sunni tradition.

Qurtubi defines "that which dies of itself [*maytah*]" as "that which may be slaughtered, but which had expired without being slaughtered." He exempts, however, aquatic animals, in agreement with the Qur'anic precept, "Lawful to you is your catch from the sea" (Q. 5:96), and the Prophet's saying, "Two *maytahs* are lawful for us, fish and locust; and two bloods, the liver and spleen [that is, of legally slaughtered animals]" (Qurtubi, II, p. 217).

Tabarsi presents three opinions in interpretation of the words "neither transgressing nor lusting." The first, as related on the authority of Hasan al-Basri, Qatadah, and Mujahid, is "not seeking pleasure nor enmity in allaying his hunger." According to al-Zajjaj, the phrase means "neither transgressing through indulgence or exaggeration [*ifrat*] nor lusting through negligence [*taqsir*]." The third opinion, related on the authority of the fifth and sixth imams, asserts that the phrase means "neither transgressing against the imams of the Muslims, nor lusting through disobedience but rather following the way of the people of Truth" (Tabarsi, II, p. 83). Qurtubi reports a prophetic *hadith* on the authority of Salman the Persian, which says: "That which God has made lawful in His Book is lawful, and that which He has made unlawful in His Book is unlawful. That about which He said nothing, He has exempted" (Qurtubi, II, p. 221; see also p. 225).

(174) Wahidi relates on the authority of Ibn 'Abbas that this verse was sent down in reference to the chiefs of the Jews of Medina and their rabbis. "They used to receive from men of low character among their people gifts and bribes. They hoped, moreover, that the Prophet to come would be of them. As he was sent among another people, they feared the loss of this source of their livelihood and the end of their authority. Thus they altered the description of Muhammad

[which was contained in their scriptures] and presented it to their people, saying, 'This is the description of the prophet who will come at the end of time; it does not fit this prophet who is in Mecca.' For this reason the people did not follow Muhammad" (Wahidi, p. 44).

(175) The words "*fa ma asbarahum 'ala al-nar*" (what shall make them endure the Fire) may also mean in this context, "How daring are they in the face of the torment of the Fire"; torment (*'adhab*) here being understood (Tabari, III, p. 231; see also p. 235; Qurtubi, II, pp. 236–237; Razi, V, pp. 30–31).

(177) Wahidi relates that Qatadah said, "We have been told that a man asked the Prophet of God about true righteousness, and God sent down this verse. [Qatadah continued] If a man [before religious obligations (*fara'id*) had been instituted] were to bear witness that there is no god but God and that Muhammad is His servant and Apostle and die with that [affirmation], Paradise would be his without any doubt. For this reason God sent down this verse" (Wahidi, p. 44; see also Ibn Kathir, I, pp. 364–366). Tabarsi, however, relates the verse to the change of the *qiblah*. "When the *qiblah* was changed and men delved deep into the question of its abrogation, and it was assumed that the only matter in obeying God worthy of attention was the direction faced in prayer, God sent this verse" (Tabarsi, II, p. 95).

Commentators have differed about the meaning of the words, "though it may be cherished [*'ala hubbihi*, lit. for His/its love]." Ibn Mas'ud said, "It is to give wealth while you are of sound health, desiring life and fearing poverty, yet you do not waiver. Even when your soul has reached your throat you say, 'Such and such [I give] to so and so, and such and such to so and so.'" The other view is to interpret love as referring to the act of giving, so as to say, "He gives of his wealth for the love of giving." Still another view, which is the Shi'i interpretation; understands "love" as referring to God, that is, to give wealth for the love of God (Tabarsi, II, p. 97).

Zamakhshari argues, "God first mentioned the next of kin [*dhawi al-qurba*] because they are more deserving. The Prophet said, 'Your charitable gift to one who is destitute is one act of charity, but to your next of kin, it is two, because it is both an act of charity and an act of good relationship [*silah*]. He also said, 'The best charitable gift is that given to a hostile near relative'" (Zamakhshari, I, p. 330). Zamakhshari continues, "The beggars are those who beg for food. The Apostle of God said, 'The beggar has a right [to food] even if he comes to you on horseback.' The ransoming of slaves here means to aid slaves to buy their freedom. It may also mean buying slaves and setting them free, or ransoming captives" (Zamakhshari, I, pp.330–331).

Commentators and jurists have differed as to whether the acts of giving mentioned in this verse refer to the *zakat* (obligatory religious alms) or are simply acts of charity over and above the *zakat* obligation. Tabarsi argues, "In this verse there is a clear indication of the obligation of giving *zakat*; on this there is no disagreement [among scholars]" (Tabarsi, II, p. 97).

Zamakhshari relates, "Al-Sha'bi said that there is an injunction in this verse to give in charity beyond the *zakat* obligation. It has also been asserted that this verse simply details the different ways in which *zakat* may be distributed. It may also be taken as a series of exhortations to the faithful to give supererogatory charity. A *hadith* says, '*Zakat* has abrogated every other charity.' It has also been asserted that no further gifts are necessary other than those of *zakat*" (Zamakhshari, I, p. 331).

Shi'i commentators have asserted that this verse was revealed with reference to 'Ali, the first imam. "This is because no one in the community denies that he possessed all these qualities. There is therefore no doubt that he was the one intended, for there is no certainty that any other person possessed them as well. For this reason, two well-known commentators and grammarians, al-Zajjaj and al-Farra' said, 'This verse refers specifically to prophets who are protected [*ma'sumun*] from error because no one except a prophet can fully execute the injunctions of this verse with all their attendant obligations'" (Tabarsi, II, p. 98).

(178) It is related by Wahidi that this verse was sent down concerning two feuding Arab tribes. The stronger of the two vowed to kill a free man for a slave, a man for a woman, and two men for only one man of the other tribe. This practice continued until Islam came and the verse was sent down to regulate the practice of retaliation (Wahidi, p. 44; see also Tabarsi, II, pp. 99–100).

Jurists have, however, disagreed concerning the details of this law. Zamakhshari reports, according to 'Umar ibn 'Abd al-'Aziz, Hasan al-Basri, 'Ata, and 'Ikrimah, with whom both Malik and al-Shafi'i agreed, "A free man may not be killed for a slave, nor a male for a female." They regarded the verse as explaining the ordinance (Q. 5:45): "A soul for a soul." On the other hand, according to Sa'id ibn al-Musayyab, al-Sha'bi, al-Nakh'i, Qatadah, and Sufyan al-Thawri, with whom Abu Hanifah agreed, this verse was abrogated by God's saying, "A soul for a soul." Hence the law of retaliation applies equally to the slave and the free man and the male and the female. They base their argument on the Prophet's saying, "The lives [lit. bloods] of all Muslims are equal" (Zamakhshari, I, p. 331).

Some commentators, as Tabarsi reports, have read the word *kutiba* (has been ordained) to mean "it has been prescribed in the Preserved Tablet [*al-lawh al-mahfuz*], which is the Mother of the Book" (Tabarsi, II, p. 100). Retaliation here is said to refer only to intentional murder because "only intentional murder calls for retaliation, and not accidental murder or what may simply resemble intentional murder. If it is asked why God said 'the law of retaliation has been ordained for you regarding those slain,' when their guardians are given the choice between retailiation or pardon upon receiving blood indemnity [*diyah*], and when the one against whom retaliation must be applied has no say in the matter . . . two answers may be given. The first is that retaliation was made an obligation for you if the guardians of the one slain choose retaliation, where the law [of retaliation] may be strictly applied, or left to choice. The second is that it has been made obligatory for you to abide by that which has been ordained as the limit which you shall not exceed. In this case the one who should be authorized to execute retaliation is the imam of the Muslims or anyone empowered [by him] to do so. It shall be incumbent on the murderer to surrender himself [to the imam or his representative]" (Tabarsi, II, p. 100). "As for pardoning ['*afw*], it is to be accompanied with a pledge of blood indemnity by the murderer only in the case of intentional murder. The guardians of the murdered person should not exceed the sum agreed upon and should give the murderer respite until he is able to pay. Thus the words, 'This is indulgence and a mercy from your Lord,' mean that He ordained for you retaliation, blood indemnity, or pardon among which to choose. The people of the Torah were allowed only retaliation or pardon, and the people of the Gospel only pardon or blood indemnity" (Tabarsi, II, pp. 101–102; see also Qurtubi, II, pp. 253–255; Razi, V, pp. 50–60; and Qutb, I, p. 232).

(180) The law of inheritance occupies a prominent place in the Qur'an. Therefore this subject will be treated later. The main issue which this verse has raised for commentators is whether the stipulation to leave a will remains operative or whether it has been abrogated by later verses dealing specifically with inheritance.

The word wealth (*khayran*) here means, according to 'A'ishah and 'Ali, great wealth. It is related that the Prophet said, "God has given every person his right; let there be no will left for an heir." Thus this tradition and the verses concerning inheritance (Q. 4:11 and 12) are said by some commentators to have abrogated this verse (see Zamakhshari, I, pp. 333–334). Others said that the verse was not abrogated, but rather that the heir has the rights of both the will, in accordance with this verse, and inheritance, in accordance with the inheritance verses (Zamkhshari, I, p. 334).

Shi'i jurists, however, have taken the view that the verse is not abrogated because "abrogration of one precept by another requires that the two cannot be simultaneously executed, yet there is no contradiction between this verse and the verses of inheritance. Likewise, those who say that this verse was abrogated by the Prophet's saying, 'Let there be no will for an heir' have strayed from the right path, because a report [*khabar*], even if it is beyond criticism, still remains subject to doubt. It is therefore not possible that the Book of God, which demands certain knowledge, be abrogated by that which is subject to doubt." Tabarsi argues further that even if the *hadith* is sound, "we may interpret it to mean that there shall be no will for an heir exceeding the third [of the portion of the inheritance]." The fifth imam was asked if a will is allowed for an heir; he answered in the affirmative, reciting this verse in support of his opinion. It is also related that 'Ali said, "Whoever does not leave a will at death for those of his near relations who do not otherwise inherit from him ends his deeds with an act of disobedience." It is also related that the Prophet said, "Whoever dies without leaving a will dies the death of Jahiliyah" (Tabarsi, II, pp. 105–106).

183. O you who have faith, fasting is ordained for you as it was ordained for those before you, that you may fear God.

184. [Fast] a certain number of days, but for him among you who may be sick or on a journey, an equal number of other days; and as for those who can afford it, a ransom by feeding a poor man. Yet he who voluntarily does good, it is better for him; that you fast is better for you, if only you knew.

185. Ramadan is the month in which the Qur'an was sent down as a guidance to humankind, manifestations of guidance and the criterion. Therefore whosoever among you witnesses the moon, let him fast [the month], but whosoever is sick or on a journey, an equal number of other days. God desires ease for you, not hardship. Complete therefore the full number of days and proclaim: "God is most great," for He has guided you, that you may give thanks.

186. If my servants ask you concerning me, certainly I am near. I answer the prayers of the suppliant when he calls upon me. Let them therefore answer my call and have faith in me, that they may be rightly guided.

187. It has been made lawful for you on the night of the fast to go into your wives; they are garments for you and you are garments for them. God knows that you were defrauding yourselves, but He has turned toward you and forgiven you. Draw near to them now therefore, and earnestly desire that which God has ordained for you. Eat and drink until you can distinguish the white thread from the black thread of dawn, then complete the fast till night. Do not draw near to your wives while you are in constant prayer in the houses of worship. These are the prescribed bounds of God; do not approach them. Thus God manifests his signs to humankind, that they may fear Him.

These verses are the only ones dealing with fasting. Fasting, however, is one of the five pillars (arkan) of Islam. Thus because fasting is so important and because the Qur'an does not treat it extensively, commentators have occupied themselves with every detail mentioned in these few verses. Fasting, as a public ritual in Islamic society, has evolved into a rich cultural and pietistic phenomenon. The following discussion is concerned with the pietistic and legal aspects of this rite. With regard to the words, "O you who have faith," the sixth imam Ja'far al-Sadiq said, "The pleasure of the [divine] address has abolished the fatigue and hardship which this act of worship entails" (Tabarsi, II, p. 111). The hardship of fasting has been recognized by God Himself as related on the authority of 'Ali, who heard the Prophet say, "God said, 'Fasting is mine and I shall give reward for it.'" The Prophet continued, "To the person who observes the fast belong two joys: one when he breaks the fast, and the other when he meets his Lord. By Him in whose hand is my soul, the bad breath of the mouth of the one who is fasting is sweeter to God than the fragrance of musk" (Nisaburi, II, p. 107).

Ibn Kathir relates on the authority of al-Dahhak ibn Muzahim, "Fasting has continued to be prescribed [for humankind] from the days of Noah until God abrogated it by the fast of the month of Ramadan." Similarly, Hasan al-Basri said, "Yes, by God! Fasting was prescribed for every community which has passed before us, as God has prescribed it for us, a full month" (Ibn Kathir, I, p. 376; see also Razi, II, pp. 75–76).

(184) Commentators have differed as to whether the days mentioned here refer to the month of Ramadan or to some other days of the year. They also differ with regard to the identity of the people for whom the fast of these days was prescribed. Zamakhshari says that according to Mujahid, the communities meant here were the People of the Book. It is related on the authority of 'Ali that fasting was prescribed, "for all prophets and their communities from the time of Adam to that of your own prophet; the first was Adam" (Zamakhshari, I, p. 334). Most early authorities of *tafsir*, however, asserted that the days referred to are those of the month of Ramadan. Tabari relates on the authority of al-Suddi, "As for those who were before us, they were the Christians. The month of Ramadan was prescribed for them, as it was also prescribed for them neither to eat nor drink if they wake up after they had gone to sleep. Nor were they allowed to come into their wives during the entire month of Ramadan. The Christians found the fast of Ramadan hard to endure. Ramadan rotated from winter to summer. As they realized this, they agreed to have the fast between winter and summer. They said, 'We shall add twenty days as expiation for what we have done.' They thus made their fast fifty days. Muslims continued to observe the fast [of Ramadan] in emulation of the Christians until the incidents of Abu Qays ibn Sirmah al-Ansari and 'Umar ibn al-Khattab [see below, commentary on verse 187] when God made lawful for them eating, drinking, and sexual intercourse until the appearance of the [true] dawn" (Tabari, III, p. 411). In another tradition related on the authority of Qatadah we are told, "The fast of Ramadan was prescribed for the people [that is, the Muslims] as it was prescribed for those who were before them. This is because

God prescribed, before the coming down [of the verse concerning] Ramadan, the fast of three days of every month" (Tabari, III, p. 412).

The "certain number of days" whose fast is enjoined in this verse are, according to some commentators, three days of every month and the day of 'Ashura' (the Jewish Day of Atonement on the tenth of Tishri; later the tenth of Muharram, the first month of the Muslim year). Fasting on these days was ordained for the Prophet when he migrated to Medina, but then it was abrogated by the fast of Ramadan (see Zamakhshari, I, p. 334).

Tabari, however, rejects this view on the grounds that there is neither a Qur'anic verse nor a sound prophetic tradition to support it. Thus he asserts, "A certain number of days' are the month of Ramadan" (Tabari, III, p. 417).

Ibn Kathir relates a well-known account of the institution of prayers and fasting attributed to the famous learned companion of the Prophet, Mu'adh ibn Jabal who said, "The prayers were changed three times and the fast three times. As for the changes in fasting, it was that the Apostle of God came from Medina and began to fast three days of every month as well as the day of 'Ashura.' Then God ordained fasting for him by sending down, 'O you who have faith, fasting is ordained for you.' Thus it was that whoever wished to fast did so and whoever wished to feed a poor person instead was absolved from the fast. Then God sent down, 'It is the month of Ramadan in which the Qur'an was sent down,' by which God made its fast obligatory for the person not on a journey and in sound health, thus exempting from it the sick and the traveler. God further affirmed in this [verse] the feeding of a poor person by the aged who are incapable of fasting. These were two changes. People then used to eat, drink, and come into their wives so long as they had not gone to sleep, but after they retired to sleep [and again awoke in the night] they desisted." Mu'adh then related the anecdotes of Abu Qays and 'Umar as occasion for the third change: "It is lawful for you on the night of the fast to go into your wives" (Ibn Kathir, I, p. 377; see also Shawkani, I, p. 181). This view is accepted by most commentators and jurists, with minor differences.

Ibn Kathir summarizes the various views on ransoming or making up the days missed, as follows: "In sum, abrogation is stipulated only in the case of one in sound health and not on a journey. This is based on God's saying, 'Therefore whosoever among you witnesses the moon, let him fast [the month].' The aged one who is near death, however, is allowed not to observe the fast; nor is he obliged to make up by fasting other days. This is because his condition would not change in such a way so as to allow him to make up for the days he missed. But if he does break the fast, he should feed a poor man for every day if he has the means to do so." Jurists have, however, disagreed on this point. Al-Shafi'i said, "He is not obliged to feed [a poor man] because he is incapable of so doing on account of his age. He is not obliged to ransom [his fast] for the same reason that a child is not obliged, for God does not burden a soul beyond its capacity" (Q. 2:286). Most scholars and jurists, however, have concurred with the view of Ibn 'Abbas and others of the Companions, which asserts that an elderly person must ransom his fast. Thus Anas ibn Malik did feed a poor person for one or two years when he grew too old to fast. Other people who may be exempted from the fast include pregnant women or nursing mothers, for fear of their own health or that of the fetus or child (Ibn Kathir, I, pp. 378–379; see also Tabari, III, p. 415).

"Yet he who voluntarily does good" means, in the view of most commentators, feeding two or more poor people or giving more food to one destitute person than the amount required by law. It may also mean fasting and giving ransom, if one is making up for days missed during the month of Ramadan. Fasting, however, is better than both ransoming and the voluntary doing of good (Tabari, III, pp. 417–418; see also Nisaburi, II, p. 106; Shawkani, I, p. 180; and Tabarsi, II, pp. 115–117).

(185) The word "Ramadan" is derived, according to grammarians and commentators, from the verbal root *ramada*, meaning to be exceedingly hot. Thus Qurtubi explains the word as referring to the summer heat in the desert, which causes a person extreme thirst; hence his inside burns (*yarmudu*) from the intense heat. The word *ramda'* is used to designate the intense heat of a summer day. The name Ramadan may have therefore been used before Islam when the month always fell in the summer (Qurtubi, II, p. 290).

Commentators have differed as to the meaning of the words, "in which the Qur'an was sent down." Tabarsi relates on the authority of Ibn 'Abbas, Sa'id ibn Jubayr, Hasan al-Basri, Qatadah, and the sixth imam, that "God sent down the entire Qur'an on the Night of Determination [*laylat al-qadr*; (see Q. 97:1)] to the heaven of this world. Then he sent it down to the Prophet in separate portions [*nujum*] over a period of twenty years." Ibn Ishaq said, "God began to send the Qur'an down on the Night of Determination during the month of Ramadan." Al-Suddi related on the authority of Ibn 'Abbas, "On the Night of Determination were sent down [the portions] needed for that year all at once, then in smaller portions during the months and days, gradually" (Tabarsi, II, p. 121).

Zamakhshari writes that the words, "in which the Qur'an was sent down," may also mean that a Qur'an (that is, a verse) was sent down concerning Ramadan, which is God's saying, "Fasting is ordained for you" (Zamakhshari, I, p. 336). Not only the Qur'an but all the scriptures mentioned in it are said to have been sent down during the month of Ramadan. In a tradition related by Tabarsi on the authority of Abu Dharr al-Ghifari (a well-known companion of the Prophet) and also on the authority of the sixth imam Ja'far al-Sadiq, who transmitted it from his fathers the imams, we are told that the Prophet said, "The scrolls [suhuf] of Abraham were sent down on the third night of Ramadan. The Torah of Moses was sent down on the sixth night of the month of Ramadan. The Gospel of Jesus was sent down on the thirteenth night of the month of Ramadan. The Zabur [Psalms] of David were sent down on the eighteenth night of Ramadan. The Furqan [the Qur'an] was sent down to Muhammad on the twenty-fourth night of Ramadan" (Tabarsi, II, p. 121).

Tabarsi reports on the authority of the fifth imam al-Baqir that the Apostle of God said in a sermon on the last Friday of Sha'ban (the month before Ramadan), "O people, a month is soon to come upon you in which there is a night, 'better than a thousand months' [Q. 97:3]; it is the month of Ramadan. God has made its fast an obligation. He made the standing of one of its nights in voluntary prayers equal to the voluntary prayers of seventy nights in other months. He made one righteous deed voluntarily performed in it equal to the reward for fulfilling one of the obligations [fara'id] of God during another month. Anyone, moreover, who fulfills in this month one of the obligations of God shall be as though he had fulfilled seventy obligations during another month. It is the month of endurance, and the reward for endurance is Paradise. It is the month of equality. It is the month in which God increases His bounty to the faithful. Whoever in this month gives food to a fasting person with which to break his fast, he shall have from God [the reward] for freeing a slave; he shall have forgiveness for all his past sins." Some said to him, "O Apostle of God, not everyone of us is capable of giving food to a fasting person." He said, "God is magnanimous; He shall grant this reward to such among you who can provide no more than a cup of milk, a drink of water, or a few dates with which to break the fast. Whoever during this month lightens the burden of his slave, God shall lighten the burden of His judgment [on the last day]. It is a month whose beginning is a time of mercy, its middle a time of forgiveness, and its end a time when prayers are answered—a time of ransom from the Fire. There are four things you shall not be able to do without during this month. With two of these you please God, and the other two are necessary for you. As for the two with which you please God, they are your witness [*shahadah*] that there is no god but God and that I am the Apostle of God. The two necessary ones are your prayers during this month to God for your needs and for Paradise. In it you must pray God for health and seek refuge in Him from the Fire." The Apostle of God said, "The sleep of him who is fasting is an act of worship, his silence is words of glorification, his prayers are answered, and the reward for his [good] deeds shall be twofold" (Tabarsi, II, pp. 121–122).

"Therefore whosoever among you witnesses the moon, let him fast [the month]" may mean, as related on the authority of the fifth imam by Tabarsi, "Whoever among you is present in his homeland and is not on a journey during the month, let him fast it in its entirety." The fifth imam further said, "Whoever witnesses the month of Ramadan must fast it, but whoever is on a journey, let him break the fast." The words may also mean, "Whoever is under obligation [*mukallaf*], sees the moon, and is not traveling must fast the actual month. This is an abrogation of the choice between fasting and ransom" (Tabarsi, II, p. 123). Most commentators agree, however, that the *sunnah* of the Prophet supports the breaking of the fast when on a journey. Thus Ibn Kathir writes, "It has been confirmed by the *sunnah* of the Apostle of God that when he set out during Ramadan for the Battle of Conquest of Mecca [*ghazwat al-fath*] and had reached al-Kadid [a place near Medina] he broke his fast and ordered the people to do the same." Some among the Companions and Successors argued for the necessity of breaking the fast when on a journey, adducing in support of their argument the words "an equal number of other days." The majority of Muslims have, however, left the matter to the choice of the person involved. During the life of the Prophet, when he and his companions traveled, some observed the fast and others broke it, yet no one blamed the other for his choice. It is related that Abu al-Darda' said, "We set out with the Apostle of God during the month of Ramadan on a very hot day, so that some of us had to cover their heads with their hands because of the severity of the heat. There was no one among us fasting except the Apostle of God and Abdallah ibn Ruwahah." Thus al-Shafi'i asserted on the basis of this incident that fasting during a journey is better because the Prophet had done so. It is, however, related that the Prophet said, when asked concerning fasting on a journey, "Whoever keeps the fast does well, but there is no blame in him who breaks it" (Ibn Kathir, I, p. 382).

Commentators have also differed as to whether making up (*qada'*) the missed days should be done on consecutive days or may be done on different days. Some say it must be made up on consecutive days, as would have been the fast of Ramadan. The majority of jurists, however, left the choice to the individual concerned, asserting that "[fasting on] consecutive days is made obligatory only in order that the fast be observed during the actual month [of Ramadan]. After the end of Ramadan, however, what is required is simply the fasting of the same number of days in which the fast was broken. For this reason God said, 'an equal number of other days.'" Concerning the phrase, "God desires ease for you, not hardship," Ibn Kathir relates that a bedouin heard the Prophet say, "The best observance of your religion [*din*] is that which is accomplished with the most ease"; this he repeated twice (Ibn Kathir, I, p. 383; see also Qurtubi, II, pp. 299–301).

The words, "God is most great," refer to the *takbirs* which are repeated by Muslims as they see the new moon following the month of Ramadan (Qurtubi, II, pp. 306–307; Razi, V, pp. 90–101).

Ibn 'Arabi considers fasting, as stipulated in these verses, to mean not simply abstinence from food but a total fast of body and soul. Fasting is disciplining the soul through devotional exercises on its journey to God.

Ibn 'Arabi interprets the word "Ramadan" to mean "the consuming of the soul in the light of the Truth [God]." The Qur'an here means "the universal and complete knowledge which is called the Qur'anic intellect and which leads to the station of concentration [*jam'*]. It is a guidance for men to unity [*wahdah*] with regard to concentration." The phrase "manifestations of guidance" means "analytical knowledge which is called the distinguishing [*furqani*] intellect." This is to be contrasted with the Qur'anic intellect, which is general and all-inclusive knowledge.

Ibn 'Arabi interprets the injunction, "whosoever among you witnesses the moon, let him fast" to mean "whosoever among you attains to the presence [*shuhud*] of the Essence, let him abstain from any word, deed, or movement in which the Truth is not present." The phrase "but whosoever is sick" means, "whosoever is afflicted with diseases of the heart which are the psychic veils that hinder that Presence." "Or on a journey" means "a distant journey where the traveler has not yet arrived at the Presence of the Essence. In this case he must still traverse more grades of attainment [*maratib*] until he arrives at such a station."

Ibn 'Arabi takes the phrase "God desires ease for you" to mean "through arriving at the station of divine oneness and attaining fortitude in the will of God." The phrase "not hardship" means "in the obligation of performing actions when the soul is weak and incapable of action." "Complete therefore the full number of days" means "realize these degrees, states, and stations which lead [to the truth]." "And proclaim: 'God is most great'" means "Recognize His greatness and exaltation in that He has guided you to the station of *jam'*" (Ibn 'Arabi, I, p. 114).

(186) Tabari related on the authority of Hasan al-Basri that a man asked the Prophet, "Is our Lord near that we can pray to Him in private or is He far that we cannot cry out to Him?" The verse was therefore sent down (Tabari, III, pp. 480–482; Tabarsi, II, p. 225).

This verse has been a great source of devotion and solace to pious Muslims. Ibn 'Arabi considers the verse within the Sufi context of the relationship of man to God and man's quest for Him: "'If my servants' who are journeying toward me 'ask you concerning' knowledge of 'me,' 'certainly I am near' and manifest. 'I answer the prayers of the suppliant when he calls upon me' with the tongue of his state and potential by granting him what his state and potential require. 'Let them therefore answer my call' by purifying their potential with asceticism and acts of worship. For to myself do I call them in order that I may teach them how to journey to me. Let them behold me when they are in the state of purity so that I may manifest myself in the mirrors of their hearts. This, in order that they may be well guided in rectitude and achieve goodness in themselves" (Ibn 'Arabi, I, pp. 114–115).

Modern commentators have dealt with fasting not only as a religious obligation which must be understood and strictly regulated; they have also been interested in its universal significance and spiritual meaning. Tabataba'i was a philosopher, theologian, mystic, and traditionist. All these aspects of his wide erudition are clearly reflected in his work.

He observes at the start of his treatment of the subject that all the verses dealing with fasting were revealed together and there is not among them any abrogating or abrogated verses. He argues further that the Qur'an does not specify which community or people were enjoined to fast before the Muslims. Nonetheless, he says, "Fasting is an act of worship bringing one closer to God and to which man may be guided by his own native intuition." It is, according to this author, one of the activities which man has discovered for himself in his pure state (*fitrah*) of faith.

Tabataba'i argues at great length for the unity of the verses both in narrative and intent. His interpretation is based on *hadiths* of the imams as reported in classical sources. A major reason for his insistence on this point is his argument against the fast of 'Ashura'. Shi'is have always insisted that all traditions exalting this day or giving it any prominence in Muslim piety were fabrications for which the Umayyad caliphs were responsible (Tabataba'i, II, pp. 4–25).

Sayyid Qutb regards the institution of all religious rites in Islam as a gradual process of education and discipline of the nascent community. Fasting was therefore gradually introduced. Sayyid Qutb writes, "In the beginning fasting was a hardship for the Muslims. It was made an obligation in the second year of the Hijrah just before that of *jihad*. Thus God at first allowed those who could not fast, even with difficulty, to break their fast and ransom it with feeding a poor Muslim. Then He made the feeding of the poor a voluntary act of charity, either as ransom or beyond its requirements. God then endeared fasting to them regardless of any hardship they may have to endure saying: 'That you fast is better for you, if only you knew.' This shows us an element of disciplining the human will, the strength to bear hardships, and the preference for the worship of God over comfort. All these are required elements in the Islamic discipline. There are also the health benefits which accrue to the one fasting even when he has to endure great hardships, provided that he is not ill."

Sayyid Qutb then reviews the various opinions regarding the verses dealing with fasting and returns to the original theme of gradual discipline. The final step in this process of disciplining the early Muslims was the institution of the fast of Ramadan. The excellence of this month (which Sayyid Qutb takes as the basis of the institution of fasting) is that "either the beginning of the revelation [of the Qur'an] was in Ramadan, or that most of it was sent down during subsequent Ramadans." He continues, "The Qur'an is the eternal

Book of this community which brought it out from darkness to the light. It gave the community peace instead of fear and strengthened it in the earth. It gave the community the characteristics by which it became a great nation whereas before it was nothing. The least that this community could do in expressing its gratitude for this great favor is to accept to fast during the month in which the Qur'an was sent down" (Qutb, I, pp. 244–245).

(187) Wahidi relates on the authority of Ibn 'Abbas, "It was unlawful for the Muslims [before this verse was revealed] after they had performed the night prayers [during Ramadan] to eat or touch women until the evening of the following day. Some men, however, ate and then went into their wives after the night prayers. They reported that to the Apostle of God; thus God sent down this verse." In another tradition it is related on the authority of al-Bara' ibn 'Azib, "At first, the Muslims used to eat, drink, and go into their wives so long as they had not gone to sleep. Once they slept, they did not do any of these things until the next evening. It happened that Qays ibn Sirmah al-Ansari was fasting, so he came to his wife at the time of breaking the fast, but she had nothing for him to eat. While she went to fetch food for him, he fell asleep. Around noon of the next day he fainted. Likewise, 'Umar ibn al-Khattab came into his wife after she had slept. All this was reported to the Prophet. Thus [this verse] was sent down and the Muslims were pleased with it" (Wahidi, p. 45; see also Tabarsi, II, pp. 129–130; Ibn Kathir, I, p. 388; and Shawkani, I, pp. 183–188).

The words, "and earnestly desire that which God has ordained for you" mean, in the view of Tabari, "seek that which I [God] have prescribed for you in the Preserved Tablet that it may be permitted you. For when a man, through sexual intercourse with a woman, desires a child, it would be what God had prescribed for him in the Preserved Tablet. Similarly, what God has made lawful is that which He has prescribed for a human being in the Preserved Tablet. The nearest interpretation to the actual sense of the verse is therefore the view of those who say that it means to seek what God has prescribed for you of offspring, because it immediately follows His saying, 'Draw near to them now therefore'" (Tabari, III, pp. 508–509).

Tabarsi offers the generally accepted opinion that the words, "until you can distinguish the white thread from the black thread of dawn," mean "until you can distinguish day from night, because the beginning of daybreak is the rise of the second dawn. It is also said that it means the whiteness of dawn from the blackness of night. God likened this to a thread, because the light of day at whose discernment eating becomes unlawful resembles a thread which also shows a similar form of blackness. It is related that 'Adi ibn Hatim said to the Prophet, 'I placed two threads of hair, one white and the other black, before me and looked at them in order that I might distinguish between them.' The Apostle of God laughed so that his teeth were visible and said, 'O Son of Hatim, it is the whiteness of day and blackness of night!'" (Tabarsi, II, pp. 131–132; see also Tabari, III, pp. 509–538, for a comprehensive discussion).

188. Do not consume your wealth among yourselves in vain or offer it in bribes to judges in order that you may devour part of other people's wealth unjustly, knowing full well that you do.

189. They ask you concerning the phases of the moon. Say: "They are times appointed for humankind and for the pilgrimage." It is not righteousness that you enter houses from the back, but righteousness is to fear God. Enter houses therefore from their doors and fear God, that you may prosper.

190. Fight in the way of God those who fight against you, but do not transgress, for God does not love the transgressors.

191. Slay them wherever you find them and turn them out of the places from which they drove you out, for sedition is more grievous than slaying. Do not fight against them near the sacred House of worship until they fight therein against you. But if they fight against you, slay them, for that is the punishment of the rejecters of faith.

192. But if they desist, God is surely forgiving, compassionate.

193. Fight against them therefore until sedition is no more and faith is for God alone. But if they desist then let there be no hostility except against the wrongdoers.

194. A sacred month for a sacred month, and violating sacred ordinances only in retaliation: whosoever transgresses against you, transgress against him as he transgressed against you. And fear God and know that God is with the God-fearing.

195. Spend of your wealth in the way of God and do not cast yourselves with your own hands into destruction. Do good, for God surely loves those who do good.

(189) Wahidi relates that Mu'adh ibn Jabal said, "O Apostle of God, the Jews come to us with many inquiries concerning the phases of the moon." Thus God sent down this verse. Qatadah said, "We have been told that the Prophet of God was asked: Why were the new moons created? God then sent down: 'Say, "They are times appointed for humankind and for the pilgrimage"'" (Wahidi, p. 47; Qurtubi, I, pp. 341–347).

The wisdom in the increase and decrease of the moon is, according to Tabarsi, "in its relationship to the general good (of humankind) with regard to the observances of religious precepts and the general affairs of their life here on earth. For had the crescent been round like the sun, it could not have been used for reckoning. In this there is the clearest proof that fasting cannot be determined through computation, but rather by the crescent. This is because God indicated [in this verse] that the crescent of the new moon is to be used in reckoning time and months" (Tabarsi, II, p. 137; see also Qummi, I, pp. 67–68).

With regard to the interpretation of the words, "It is not righteousness that you enter houses from the back," Wahidi reports that the Ansar (helpers) of Medina as well as other Arab tribes before and after the beginning of Islam, when they observed consecration (*ihram*) for the greater pilgrimage (*hajj*) or lesser pilgrimage ('*umrah*), did not enter any gate of a house or enclosure. This was a religious obligation for the people, so that if a man lived in a house, he would either make a small entrance in the back wall or use a ladder to climb over the outer wall. A tent dweller, on the other hand, entered from the back, avoiding use of the door of his tent. People continued to observe this obligation until they broke their *ihram*. An exception were the Quraysh and some other related tribes who were so enthusiastic in the execution of their religious duties that they were known as *hums* (enthusiasts). They were on this account free from that obligation. One day the Prophet entered a house and a man followed him through the door even though he was in the state of *ihram*. People reproached him for doing so. The Prophet asked him: "Why did you enter through the door while you are in the state of consecration?" He answered, "I saw you enter and I followed you." The Prophet said, "I am *ahmasi* [singular of *hums*]." The man answered, "If you are an *ahmasi*, I am one also. Our faith is one. I accept your guidance, your characteristics, and your religion." Thus God sent down this verse (Wahidi, pp. 48–49; see also Tabari, III, pp. 555–560).

Qummi asserts that this part of the verse was sent down concerning the Prince of the Faithful (this epithet is used only for 'Ali in Shi'i tradition), for the Apostle of God said, "I am the city of knowledge and 'Ali is its gate. Do not therefore enter the city except through its gate" (Qummi, I, p. 68). The fifth imam al-Baqir said, "The people of the family of Muhammad are the doors of God and the means [*wasilah*] of coming to Him. They are those who summon to Paradise; they are the leaders and guides till the day of resurrection" (Tabarsi, II, p. 138; see also Tabataba'i, II, pp. 55–57).

(190) Commentators have differed in interpreting this verse. According to some, as related by Wahidi on the authority of Ibn 'Abbas, this and the following verses dealing with fighting were sent down concerning the truce of Hudaybiyah (March 626). (See commentary on verse 194 below.) "When the Apostle of God and his Companions were prevented from going to the House [that is, on pilgrimage to the Kaaba], he offered the animal sacrifice in Hudaybiyah. The associators then made a truce with him that he go back that year, but return in the next. Then they would vacate Mecca for him for three days so that he might circumambulate the House and do what he willed. At the same time the following year, the Apostle of God and his Companions prepared for the journey to perform the lesser pilgrimage [*'umrat al-qada'*] of the year before. They were afraid, however, that the people of Quraysh would not fulfill their promise but would still prevent them from coming to the sacred House of worship and fight against them in it. The Prophet's Companions did not wish to engage in fighting during the sacred month [the month of Dhu al-Qi'dah]. Thus God sent down, 'Fight in the way of God those who fight against you,' that is, the Quraysh" (Wahidi, pp. 49–50).

According to other commentators, as Tabari relates, this was the first verse that commanded the Muslims to fight against those of the associators who waged war against them, but it was later abrogated by Q. 9:36. Thus it is related on the authority of al-Rabi' ibn Anas, "This was the first verse sent down concerning fighting in Medina. When it was sent down, the Apostle of God used only to fight against those who fought against him and desist from fighting against those who did not, until the verse in *Bara'ah* [Dissociation: 9:36] was sent down." (See also verses 1–5 in the same *surah.*) The same view is related on the authority of 'Abd al-Rahman ibn Zayd (Tabari, III, pp. 561–562).

Ibn Kathir objects to this view "because of God's saying, 'those who fight against you,' which was meant to excite the Muslims against their enemies whose sole purpose was to fight against Islam and its people. Thus the verse means, 'as they fight against you, so do you also fight against them.' This is to say 'let your ambition be directed at fighting against them as theirs is to fight against you. Seek therefore in retaliation to drive them out of the lands from whence they drove you out'" (Ibn Kathir, I, p. 400).

According to still other commentators, the verse was not abrogated. Rather, the injunction against transgression was meant only against killing women and children. This was the view of 'Umar ibn 'Abd al-'Aziz. Ibn 'Abbas commented on this verse as follows: "Do not kill women, children, and old men or anyone who offers you peace and withdraws his sword. If you commit such acts, you have committed transgression." 'Umar ibn 'Abd al-'Aziz included monks as well in his list (Tabari, III, pp. 562–563; see also Ibn Kathir, I, p. 401; and Tabarsi, II, p. 139).

(191) Tabari reports that this verse was sent down concerning a man among the Companions who killed a man of the Meccans during one of the sacred months. Thus God showed in this verse that "sedition in faith [or temptation away from the true faith], which is association [*shirk*], is far graver than the killing of associators during the sacred month, even though this is not lawful" (Tabari, III, p. 565; see also Tabarsi, II, p. 141).

(193) The word *fitnah* (sedition, trial, or temptation) in this verse also means *shirk,* as in verse 191 above (Tabari, III, p. 570; Ibn Kathir, I, pp. 401–403; see also Tabarsi, II, p. 143).

(194) This verse was revealed concerning the truce of Hudaybiyah (March 626/Dhu al-Qi'dah 6 A.H.) and the return of the Prophet and the Muslims during the same month of the following year, at which time they performed the rites of the lesser pilgrimage for three days. Qatadah, on whose authority this interpretation is presented,

said, "The associators, however, arrogantly taunted the Prophet when they turned him back on the day of Hudaybiyah [of the previous year]. God requited him against them by sending down 'a sacred month for a sacred month, and violating sacred ordinances only in retaliation'" (Wahidi, p. 50). The reference here to the sacred month has been interpreted, says Tabarsi, to mean either that "fighting during the sacred month must be requited by fighting in another sacred month" or as meaning "the month of Dhu al-Qi'dah in which you [Muhammad and the Muslims] entered Mecca where you performed your lesser pilgrimage instead of performing it in the sacred month of Dhu al-Qi'dah [of the previous year], during which you were prevented from entering the House" (Tabarsi, II, p. 145).

Tabari explains the name of the month Dhu al-Qi'dah as follows: "God called Dhu al-Qi'dah the sacred month because the Arabs in the time of Jahiliyah forbade fighting and killing in it. They laid down their arms so that no one killed another even if a man met the slayer of his father or son. Thus they called it Dhu al-Qi'dah [the month of sitting down] because in it they sat down, that is, desisted from raids and warfare. God therefore called it by the name with which the Arabs had called it." The word *hurumat* (sacred ordinances), Tabari continues, here refers to the sacred month, the sacred city, and the sacred rite of *ihram* (consecration). (Tabari, III, p. 575.) The sacred months in Islam are four: three consecutive, Dhu al-Qi'dah, Dhu al-Hijjah (the month of pilgrimage), and Muharram (the first month of the year); and the seventh month of the year, Rajab (see Tabarsi, II, p. 145).

(195) Wahidi relates on the authority of al-Sha'bi, "This verse was sent down concerning the *ansar* (helpers) because they witheld alms in the way of God." According to al-Dahhak, they did so because they had a year of food shortage, perhaps because of a drought. It is related on the authority of al-Nu'man ibn Bashir, "When a man committed a sin, he used to say, 'It will never be forgiven me'; thus God sent down this verse" (Wahidi, pp. 50–52).

The words, "and do not cast yourselves with your own hands into destruction" have been interpreted in several ways. Tabarsi relates four of these: the first is "do not destroy yourselves with your own hands by witholding alms in the way of God, that your enemies may not overcome you," which is related on the authority of Ibn 'Abbas and others. The second view, related on the authority of al-Bara' ibn 'Azib, is "do not commit acts of disobedience because of despairing of God's forgiveness." The third interpretation, offered by Sufyan al-Thawri, is that the words mean "do not embark on a war without provocation by the enemy when you are incapable of defending yourselves." The fourth view, from al-Jubba'i, is "do not give alms with such extravagance as may reduce you to destruction." This interpretation is also related on the authority of the sixth imam, al-Sadiq (Tabarsi, II, p. 148).

196. Complete the pilgrimage and the lesser pilgrimage for God. But if you are prevented then send on what you are able as sacrifice and do not shave your heads until the offering has reached its destination. But if there be among you anyone who is sick or suffering a disease of the head, then let him offer a ransom: fasting, almsgiving, or private prayers. When you are safe [from enemies], let him who tarries from the lesser to the greater pilgrimage present what he is able for the sacrifice. Yet he who has not the means, let him fast three days during the pilgrimage and seven when you return: ten complete days. This is incumbent on him whose family is not present in the vicinity of the sacred House of worship. Fear God and know that God is severe in punishment.

197. The pilgrimage is to be performed during well-known months. Let him therefore who intends to fulfill the obligation [beware that] there is to be neither sexual intercourse, wickedness, nor quarrelsome dispute during the pilgrimage. Whatever good you do, God knows it. Take provisions for the journey, but the best provision is piety. Fear me therefore, O people of intelligence.

198. There is no blame in you if you seek the favor of your Lord. When you pour out of 'Arafat remember God near the sacred monument. Remember Him, for He guided you when you were yet among those who had gone astray.

199. Then press on from whence the people proceed and beg forgiveness of God, for God is all-forgiving, compassionate.

200. When you have completed your pilgrimage rites, remember God as you would remember your fathers, but even

with a more fervent remembrance. There are those among men who say, "Our Lord, grant us [wealth] in this world," but these shall have no portion in the world to come.

201. But there are those among men who say, "Our Lord, grant us good in this world and good in the world to come and protect us from the torment of the Fire."

202. These shall have a good portion of that which they have earned, and God is swift in reckoning.

203. Remember God during the specified number of days. But he who hastens in two days, there shall be no transgression in him, and he who tarries there shall be no transgression in him, if he fears God. Fear God, therefore, and know that to Him you shall all be gathered.

(196) Wahidi relates that Ka'b ibn 'Ujrah (a man of the ansar) said, "This verse was sent down concerning me. My head was infested with lice. I mentioned it to the Prophet, who said to me, 'Shave your head and ransom it with the fast of three days, private prayer or sacrifice [*nusk*], or feed six poor people, giving each one a *sa'* [a dry measure of grain or dates]'" (Wahidi, p. 52).

Wahidi further reports on the authority of Ibn 'Abbas that the Apostle of God said, "The fast is three days, the *nusk* is the sacrifice of an ewe, and the gift of alms [*sadaqah*] is the distribution of food among six poor people, to each two measures" (Wahidi, p. 54). Ibn Kathir relates that this verse was revealed in the year of Hudaybiyah (6 A.H.), when "God sent down this verse permitting the Muslims to sacrifice the animals they brought to the pilgrimage . . . and to shave their heads and end their state of consecration [*ihram*]" (Ibn Kathir, I, p. 409).

This and the following seven verses are known as the *hajj* verses. It is not, however, as Sayyid Qutb affirms, absolutely certain when the pilgrimage was actually instituted in Islam. It is known that in the ninth year of the Hijrah the Prophet sent Abu Bakr as the leader of the pilgrimage caravan. The Prophet himself may have wished to perform the pilgrimage on that occasion, but as he did not wish to mingle with the associators who circumambulated the Kaaba naked, he postponed it to the following year, when he performed his last pilgrimage. This view may be supported by the verses in Q. 9:1–3 with which he sent 'Ali to declare to the people that the associators would no longer be allowed to circumambulate the sacred House (Qutb, I, p. 277). Sayyid Qutb thinks it probable that the verses in *Surat al-Hajj* (Q. 22:26–29), which describe the ancient rite as ordained for Abraham, may have served as an injunction for the Muslims to follow the practice (*sunnah*) of their father Abraham, whose faith was the original Islam to which Muhammad came to call the Arabs as well as the rest of humankind. Yet the pilgrimage was not organized as an Islamic communal activity until the Prophet himself led the community to the Kaaba shortly before his death (see Qutb, I, p. 278).

Jurists have differed with regard to the details of the performance of the rites of the lesser pilgrimage (*'umrah*) before commencing the actual pilgrimage. It will not be possible to enter into such details here; the short summary of Sayyid Qutb will serve the purpose of this general work. "If Muslims are not prevented from offering the *'umrah* . . . then as for him who wishes indulgence [that is, releasing himself from *ihram* (consecration) of the *'umrah*] until the greater pilgrimage [*hajj*], let him sacrifice an animal which can be easily spared or obtained. The details of this injunction are that a Muslim may set out for the *'umrah* and begin the new moon in the state of *ihram*. But when he is finished with the *'umrah*, which consists of the rites of circumambulation of the House and running between al-Safa and al-Marwah, he may observe his state of *ihram* and tarry for its proper term. This is provided that it falls during the months of the *hajj*, which are Shawwal, Dhu al-Qi'dah, and Dhu al-Hijjah [the tenth, eleventh, and twelfth months]. This is one way of indulgence [*tamattu'*] from the *'umrah* to the *hajj*. Another way is to combine both *'umrah* and *hajj* in one *ihram*. When the pilgrim has completed the rite of the *'umrah*, he waits for the *hajj* [without breaking his *ihram*] . . . but in either of the two cases, it is incumbent on the person performing the *'umrah* to sacrifice whatever animal he can after the *'umrah*, in order that he may be released from its *ihram*. Then he may indulge himself [that is, resume his normal course of life] between the time he completes his *'umrah* and time he commences his pilgrimage rites" (Qutb, I, p. 281).

"What he is able for the sacrifice," according to Sayyid Qutb, includes animals such as camels, cattle, sheep, or goats. If the pilgrim cannot find an animal to sacrifice, then this should be ransomed by a fast of three days during the pilgrimage and seven afterward, "ten complete days." It is more proper, however, that the pilgrim fast the first three days before standing on the Mount of 'Arafat on the ninth of Dhu al-Hijjah. As for the other seven days, he may fast these when he returns to his country. Because, however, the inhabitants of Mecca have no *'umrah* but only the *hajj*, they have neither indulgence nor release from the *ihram* between the *'umrah* and the *hajj*; hence they are obliged to offer neither sacrifices nor a fast (Qutb, I, p. 281; for the various juristic views on this verse, see Ibn Kathir, I, pp. 407–417, and Qurtubi, II, pp. 365–404; for Shi'i legal views, see Tabarsi, II, pp. 149–155, and Tabataba'i, II, pp. 75–76).

(197) According to all commentators, the months of the *hajj* are Shawwal, Dhu al-Qi'dah, and the first ten days of Dhu al-Hijjah, as has been observed. The emphasis here means that they should not be altered as was done in the days of Jahiliyah (see Tabarsi, II, p. 158).

As for the phrase, "Take provisions for the journey," Wahidi relates on the authority of Ibn 'Abbas, "The people of Yaman used to set out for the *hajj* without carrying provisions for the journey. They said, 'We are those who trust [in God].' When they came to Mecca they had to beg for food; thus God sent down, 'Take provisions for the journey'" (Wahidi, p. 55; see also Tabari, IV, pp. 156–161).

(198) Wahidi reports that a man called Abu Umamah al-Taymi said to 'Abdallah ibn 'Umar, "We are a people of disapprobation for what we do [that is, trading while performing the *hajj*]. There are people who claim that our *hajj* is invalid." He answered, "Do you not raise your voices with the *talbiyah* [the words, 'Here we come in answer to your call, O God,' etc., which the pilgrims repeat on their way to 'Arafat]? Do you not circumambulate [the Kaaba]? Do you not run between al-Safa and al-Marwah, and so on, and so on? A man asked the Prophet what you ask, but he did not know what to say until God sent down, 'There is no blame in you if you seek the favor of your Lord.' He called the man and recited the verse to him . . . saying, 'You are the pilgrims, indeed'" (Wahidi, p. 56).

Commentators have differed as to the derivation of the name 'Arafat. This word comes from the verbal root *'arafa* meaning "to know." Thus it is related by Tabarsi, on the authority of 'Ali and Ibn 'Abbas, that "it was because Abraham recognized it ['*arafaha*] through the description he received of it," and also on the authority of al-Dahhak and al-Suddi that "it was so called because Adam and Eve met in it and knew one another after they had been separated."

Others said, as Tabarsi further reports, "It was so called because of its height, as in the word *'urf* [crest of a rooster]." It has also been said that it was so called because "Gabriel used to show Abraham the rites of pilgrimage and the latter would say, 'I know, I know.' [*'araftu*]'" (Tabarsi, II, p. 160; see also Qurtubi, I, p. 415).

Tabarsi says that the *mash'ar al-haram* (sacred monument) is referred to as *mash'ar* (monument) because it is a monument for the *hajj*, prayer, standing (in prayer), spending the night in it, and invoking God near it, which are all part of the *hajj* ritual. *Al-mash'ar al-haram* was also called *muzdalifah*, because Gabriel said to Abraham on 'Arafat, "Climb down [*izdalif*] to the sacred monument." Mina was so called because Abraham there wished (*tamanna*) that God would grant him a son and a ram which He would command him to sacrifice as a ransom for him (Tabarsi, II, pp. 160–161; for other derivations of these names and the locations of the places to which they refer, see Zamakhshari, I, p. 348).

(196–199) Ibn 'Arabi interprets the pilgrimage ritual not only as the performance of a religious act but also as the inner devotion of a pious person along his journey to God. Thus Mecca is, for Ibn 'Arabi, the breast and the Kaaba is the heart contained in it. The sacred monument (*al-mash'ar al-haram*) is the inner faculty where God must be remembered and in which His beauty may be seen. As for the remembrance of God in this station of the spiritual pilgrimage, Ibn 'Arabi says, "It is the act of witnessing [*mushahadah*]. God first guides you [spiritual pilgrims] to the remembrance [*dhikr*] of the tongue, which is the *dhikr* of the soul. He then guides you to the *dhikr* of the heart, which is the *dhikr* of the actions from which the favors and bounties of God flow. After this He guides you to the *dhikr* of the innermost faculty [*sirr*], which is true vision and revelation of the sciences of the manifestations [*tajalliyat*] of the divine attributes. God then guides you to the *dhikr* of the spirit, which is the witnessing of the manifestations of the attributes and the discernment of the light of the divine essence. He then guides you to the inner *dhikr* [*al-dhikr al-khafi*] which is the witnessing of the beauty of the divine essence where duality is still present [that is, of subject and object]. Finally He guides you to the *dhikr* of the divine essence which is the witnessing of the essence where all other things are abolished."

Ibn 'Arabi, however, does not neglect the legal aspects of the pilgrimage or those pertaining to other acts of worship. Thus he comments on the phrase, "Then press on from whence the people proceed," as follows: "Press on to the actual performance of acts of worship and obedience to God as well as all the other functions of the legal precepts. Do this as all other people do and be one with them. Junayd [a well-known early Sufi master who died in A.D. 910] was once asked 'Where is the end?' He answered, 'It is the return to the beginning'" (Ibn 'Arabi, I, p. 123).

(199) Wahidi relates that the people of Quraysh were called *hums* (enthusiasts in their religion). "Satan came to them . . . and said, 'If you exalt any shrine other than your own, people will treat your shrine with contempt.' For this reason they used not to leave the shrine but rather used to stand in Muzdalifah. When, however, Islam came, God sent down 'Then press on from whence the people proceed,' that is, from 'Arafat" (Wahidi, p. 57).

Tabarsi relates on the authority of Ibn 'Abbas, 'A'ishah, 'Ata', Mujahid, Hasan al-Basri, Qatadah, and the fifth imam al-Baqir that by the word *afidu* (press on) is meant "disperse" (out of 'Arafat). "The people (*nas*)" would then refer to the tribes of the Arabs. Thus the verse was, according to this view, a command to the people of Quraysh and their allies who did not stand with the rest of the people in 'Arafat and disperse with them (Tabarsi, II, p. 163).

(200) Wahidi relates that Mujahid said, "When the people of Jahiliyah used to gather during the time [of pilgrimage], they used to recall with pride the deeds, lives [*ayyam*], and genealogies of their forebears." Thus God sent down, "Remember God as you would remember your fathers, but even with a more fervent remembrance." According to Hasan al-Basri, the Arabs before Islam used to swear by their fathers; hence the verse was revealed (Wahidi, p. 57). A similar view is also related on the authority of the fifth imam (see Tabarsi, II, p. 165).

(201) It is related that the Prophet said, "Whoever is given a thankful heart, a tongue occupied with the mention [of God], and a wife who has faith and who assists him in the affairs of his life in this world as well as the affairs of the life to come, such a man is granted good in this world and good in the world to come and is protected from the torment of the Fire" (Tabarsi, II, p. 167).

(203) Tabarsi relates on the authority of Ibn 'Abbas and a large number of other commentators, including the sixth imam al-Sadiq, that the specified number of days are the days of *tashriq*, which are three days during the pilgrimage following the day of sacrifice. The mention or remembrance of God here enjoined is for the faithful to repeat after each of the five daily prayers during these three days:

"God is most great, God is most great. There is no god but God; God is most great. God is most great and to God belongs all praise. God is most great for that He has guided us. God is most great for that He has granted us sustenance through [the meat] of the dumb beasts" (see Q. 22:28). Shi'is add: "Praise be to God for that He has granted us *walayah* [loyalty or allegiance to the imams]". According to Tabarsi, this invocation must begin after the noon prayer of the day of sacrifice and end after the dawn prayer of the fourth day after the day of sacrifice for those who are in Mina following the pilgrimage ritual. Those who are in other areas must recite the *takbirs* after ten prayers beginning with the noon prayer of the day of sacrifice (see Tabarsi, II, p. 169). Sunni commentators simply enjoin, on the authority of the Prophet, the pronouncement on the same days of *takbirs* after the prayers (see Qurtubi, II, pp. 3–4, and Ibn Kathir, I, pp. 434–435).

The words, "But he who hastens in two days, there shall be no transgression in him, and he who tarries there shall be no transgression in him," refer to the permission to the pilgrims to depart Mina on the second day following the day of sacrifice. It is better, however, that they remain until the third and last of the days of *tashriq*. Those who depart on the second day must do so between mid-afternoon and sunset; otherwise they must remain until the third day (Tabarsi, II, p. 170; see also Qurtubi, II, pp. 4–14; and for a detailed discussion of the rites of pilgrimage in verses 196–203, see Tabataba'i, II, pp. 74–82).

204. Among men there is one whose speech in this world may please you [Muhammad]. He calls upon God to bear witness concerning that which is in his heart, but in reality he is the most contentious of opponents.

205. When he turns away from you he goes about spreading corruption in the earth and seeking to destroy tillage and offspring; yet God loves not corruption.

206. If it is said to him, "Fear God," pride seizes him in his transgression. But Hell shall be his reward: a miserable resting place shall it be.

207. There is yet another who would exchange his life, desiring to attain the pleasure of God; God is gracious toward His servants.

208. O you who have faith, enter into submission all together and do not follow the steps of Satan, for he is to you an open enemy.

209. But if you were to falter after manifest signs have come to you, then know that God is mighty and wise.

(204) Wahidi relates on the authority of al-Suddi that this verse was revealed concerning a man called al-Akhnas ibn Shurayq, who came to the Prophet in Medina pretending to accept Islam. The Prophet was pleased with the man, who said, "By God, I came wishing to accept Islam, and God knows that I tell the truth." When, however, he left the Prophet, he came upon a cultivated field and some beasts belonging to Muslims. He destroyed the crops and injured the animals (Wahidi, p. 58).

Ibn 'Abbas said, "These three verses [204, 205, and 206] were sent down concerning the hypocrite who shows the opposite of what he hides in his heart." Similar views are related on the authority of the sixth imam and Hasan al-Basri (Tabari, IV, pp. 246–251; Ibn Kathir, I, pp. 436–439; and Razi, V, pp. 223–224).

(207) Commentators have differed regarding the person or type of people to whom this verse refers. Tabarsi relates on the authority of Ibn 'Abbas by al-Suddi that it was sent down concerning 'Ali ibn Abi Talib when the Prophet escaped from the associators (the Quraysh of Mecca) to the Cave (al-Ghar, between Mecca and Medina). As the Prophet left by night, 'Ali lay in his bed, thus risking being killed by the men of Quraysh, who came the next morning looking for the Prophet. Tabarsi adds, "When he slept in the Prophet's bed, Gabriel sat at his head and Michael at his feet, while Gabriel repeated, 'Ah! Ah! Who is like you, O son of Abu Talib, in whom God prides Himself before the angels!'" (Tabarsi, II, p. 174).

Wahidi relates on the authority of Sa'id ibn al-Musayyab that the verse was revealed concerning Suhayb ibn Sinan, one of the Quraysh who accepted Islam at an advanced age. Wishing to migrate to join the new Muslim community, he was seized by the Meccans, who forced him to turn over his home and belongings to them before they would allow him to depart. When he finally reached Medina, the Prophet said to him, "Abu Yahya [Suhayb's agnomen] has surely profited by his exchange!" repeating it twice. Others said that outside Medina Suhayb was met by Abu Bakr and 'Umar with a company of other men. Abu Bakr exclaimed upon seeing him, "Your commerce has profited you much, O Abu Yahya!" The latter answered, "May yours never lose! Why is that?" Abu Bakr answered, "God has sent down concerning you such-and-such." Then he recited the verse to him (Wahidi, pp. 58–59).

Hasan al-Basri asserted, according to Wahidi, that the verse was sent down "to refer to any Muslim man who, when meeting a rejecter of faith, would say to him, 'Say, "There is no god but God!" If you utter it you would protect your wealth and your blood!' If he refused to profess it, the Muslim would say, 'By God I shall sell my soul for God. He would then come forth and fight until he is slain'" (Wahidi, p. 59).

It has also been said that the verse was revealed concerning anyone who enjoins good and dissuades from evil. Wahidi relates that 'Umar ibn al-Khattab heard a man reciting this verse and exclaimed, "To God do we belong, this is a man who rose up enjoining the good and dissuading from evil, yet he was slain" (Wahidi, p. 59).

210. Would they [the rejecters of faith] expect that God Himself should come to them in canopies of white cloud with angels? Yet it is a thing decreed, and to God shall all things return.

211. Ask the Children of Israel how many a clear sign we have sent to them! Whosoever alters the grace of God after it has come to him, surely God is severe in punishment.

212. The life of this world has been adorned for those who have rejected faith; they scorn the people of faith. But those who fear God shall be over them on the day of resurrection. God bestows His bounty on whomsoever He wills, without measure.

(210) Commentators have been unanimous in denying motion and corporeality to God. Thus the words, "God Himself should come to them" have been interpreted so as not to impute to God human actions. Zamakhshari says, "The coming of God means the coming of His command and His power . . . or it may be that what is

meant by coming is deleted, being only understood. That would mean that God would bring upon them His power or vengeance, as may be proved by God's saying, 'God is mighty with vengeance'" (Q. 5:93; Zamakhshari, I, p. 353). Tabarsi, expressing the Shi'i theological view of the verse, presents a similar interpretation (Tabarsi, II, pp. 178–179; Tabataba'i, II, pp. 101–110).

Qurtubi, on the other hand, offers a less metaphorical interpretation, which is consonant with the mainstream of Sunni theology. "The meaning of the verse is, 'Would they [the rejecters of faith] wait until God manifests an action through [an act] of His creation by which He would turn upon them with His punishment and execute what He has decreed?' Thus as God created an act which He called descending [nuzul] and ascending or sitting upon the throne [istiwa'], He likewise would create an act which He would call 'coming.' His acts are without instrument or cause." Then, citing a tradition related on the authority of Ibn 'Abbas, Qurtubi continues, "This [verse] belongs to the concealed [ghayb] which cannot be interpreted" (Qurtubi, II, pp. 25–26).

Razi begins by observing, "Wise men have agreed that God is free from such actions as coming and going." This is because, he argues, (1) motion and rest are created acts, and whoever is subject to such actions must also by necessity be created. (2) That which is subject to such actions must be either small in size in order to move in a space larger than itself, or be a large composite being whose full realization means the realization of each of its parts. In this case it must need another being to bestow upon it necessity and existence. (3) Specific actions imply limitation because of the choice of one action over another. (4) If coming and going could be ascribed to an eternal being, then why could not the sun and moon be divinities and why is there a need to posit another being greater than they. Razi claims that some theologians have argued that "there is no defect in the sun and moon that would prevent their being considered two divinities, except that they are bodies subject to motion, and thus presence and absence." For his fifth and sixth arguments, Razi simply cites Qur'anic texts in support of his earlier statements. He then concludes, "God is not a body occupying a specific locus and therefore coming and going cannot be ascribed to Him."

Razi observes further that God's coming "in canopies of white cloud" must have meaning either known only to God, as the pious forebears (al-salaf al-salih) had asserted, or must be interpreted and understood through independent reason. After examining both views at some length, Razi asserts that the verse before it (208) was revealed concerning the Jews. Thus "God's saying, 'Would they [the rejecters of faith]' refers to the Jews. This is as though God says to Muhammad, 'They shall not accept your faith until God shall come to them in canopies of white cloud.' Do you not see that they did the same with Moses when they said, 'We shall not believe you until we see God openly' [Q. 2:55]. If therefore the verse is a report of what the Jews said to the Prophet, it may be taken in its literal sense. The Jews were anthropomorphists, ascribing to God 'coming and going.' They also said that God manifested Himself to Moses on Mount Sinai in canopies of white cloud" (Razi, V, pp. 232–236).

Tabarsi offers a general exegesis of the verse which, I believe, may be accepted by Muslims regardless of their school of thought or sectarian affiliation. "What these people who give the lie to the signs of God expect is the punishment of God, His command and what He has threatened them with for their acts of rebellion, and that it shall come upon them in canopies of white cloud. It may also be said that they expect naught but that the majestic signs of God should come upon them . . . the white clouds [*ghamam*] are mentioned in order that it may be more terrifying, for terrors may be likened to canopies of cloud." All this is to take place on the day of judgment. "Thus the words, 'Yet it is a thing decreed' mean that the matter is finished, that is, the reckoning and the sending of the people of Paradise to Paradise and the people of the Fire to the Fire. It may also mean that punishment has been decreed, that is, the punishment of destruction in this world . . . thus to Him will return the matters of this world and the world to come" (Tabarsi, II, pp. 179–180).

Sayyid Qutb relates this verse to verse 208 above. He does not, however, specify who the people mentioned in this verse are other than to say that they are the waverers who would not "enter into submission all together." Sayyid Qutb then asks rhetorically, "Will they remain in this attitude until God shall come to them in canopies of white cloud and until angels shall also come to them? In other words, would they wait and waver until the promised fearful day shall come upon them; the day on which God is to come in canopies of white cloud." Thus Sayyid Qutb views the verse as a picture of the day of judgment, a threat to those who waver and hesitate in making the awesome decision before the opportunity passes them by (Qutb, I, p. 307).

Tabari cites a tradition related on the authority of Abu Hurayrah, which is, however, generally regarded as weak and theologically suspect. Nonetheless, the tradition is interesting in that it reflects the view of popular piety with regard to the Prophet's intercessory role on the day of judgment and paints a graphic picture of the terrors of that day.

The Apostle of God said, "You shall be all made to stand together on the day of resurrection the duration of seventy years, but you will be neither looked upon nor will you be brought to judgment. You will be so constrained that you shall weep until your tears dry up, then your eyes shall shed blood instead of tears until your blood shall reach your chins or even stop your mouths. Then you shall cry out and say, 'Who shall intercede for us with our Lord, so that He may judge among us!' It shall be said to you, 'Who is more worthy of this than your father Adam, for God Himself kneaded his clay and made him with His own hands; He breathed into him of His spirit and spoke to him face to face.' Adam will be brought and asked to intercede, but he shall refuse. Then every Prophet will be asked, but they shall also refuse. . . . Then they will come to me. I shall proceed until I come to the *Fahs*." Abu Hurayrah asked, "O Apostle of God, what is the *Fahs*?" He answered, "It is the space before the Throne. I shall fall on my face in prostration and thus will I remain until God shall send to me an angel, who will take me by the shoulders and lift me up. God then shall address me, saying, 'O Muhammad!' 'Yes,' I shall answer, but He knows best [that is, what I will say]. He shall ask, 'What is your wish?' I will answer, 'O my Lord, you have promised me intercession; let me therefore intercede with you on behalf of your creatures. Judge O Lord, among them!' He shall say, 'I have accepted your intercession. I shall come to you and judge among you.'"

The Apostle of God said, "Then will I depart and stand with the people. As we so stand, we shall hear a loud noise from heaven, which will frighten us. The inhabitants of the heaven of this world will come down, being twice the number of the inhabitants of the earth, *jinn* and humans. When they come close to the earth, it shall shine with their light; then they shall take their places. We shall ask, 'Is our Lord among you?' 'No,' they will say, 'but He is coming.' . . . [The inhabitants of every heaven shall come down, their multitudes being twice those of the ones before.] Then the All-powerful shall come in canopies of white cloud with the angels, praising God in unison, saying, 'Exalted be the Lord of sovereignty and dominion.

Exalted be the Lord of the Throne, the Lord of all power. Exalted be He, the Everliving, who shall never die. Exalted be He who shall cause all creatures to die, but He shall never die. Praised, praised, and holy, holy is He, the Lord most high; exalted be He, the Lord of sovereignty and majesty; exalted be He for ever and ever.'

"He, the Blessed and Exalted One shall descend; eight angels shall bear His Throne on that day. Now, however, there are only four, their feet resting on the lowest [seventh] earth, their necks reaching heaven and the Throne upon their shoulders. God shall then place His Throne wherever He wills on the earth. A crier shall then cry out, and all creatures shall hear him: 'O people of the *jinn* and humankind! I have listened to you since the day I created you, hearing your words and seeing your deeds. Listen now to me, for it is your books and deeds which we shall recite before you. Let him who finds good thank God, and he who finds otherwise blame no one but himself.' Thus God shall judge among all His creatures: *jinn*, humans, and beasts. Then requital will be given to the hornless against the horned beast" (this is perhaps to demonstrate the exactitude of the divine judgment, or perhaps that the weak shall be vindicated against the strong). (Tabari, III, pp. 266–268; see also Ibn Kathir, I, pp. 440–441.)

213. Humankind were all one community. Then God sent prophets as bearers of good tidings, and warners. He sent down with them the Book with the truth in order that it may judge among them concerning that in which they differ. But none differ concerning it, save those who were given the scriptures after manifest signs had come to them, being envious of one another. God guides aright by His permission those who have faith to the truth, concerning which they differed. God guides whom He wills to the straight way.

This verse has raised a number of questions for commentators. Some of these that will be treated here are: What is the meaning of the word "community" (*ummah*)? When were all people one community and when did they begin to differ? Who were the prophets sent by God and who or what is to judge among men regarding their differences?

According to some, the people of that community were those who lived between Adam and Noah. Tabari relates on the authority of

Ibn 'Abbas, "Between Adam and Noah there were ten generations. They all followed the true law, but thereafter they differed. Hence God sent prophets, 'as bearers of good tidings, and warners.'" Qatadah said, "They were all guided aright, but then disagreed. Thus God sent prophets 'as bearers of good tidings, and warners'; the first prophet who was sent was Noah" (Tabari, IV, pp. 275-276). Tabari explains the word *ummah* as meaning religion; thus 'one *ummah*' here means followers of one religion (Tabari, IV, p. 276).

Other commentators interpreted the word *nas* (humankind) to refer to Adam alone and the word *ummah* to mean obedience to God, professing His oneness and fulfilling His commands. They base their interpretation on the verse, "Surely Abraham was an *ummah*, obedient to God and of pure faith" (Q. 16:120). The first exponent of this view was perhaps Mujahid. Still another view resembling the one just discussed asserts that the word *ummah* here means, as related on the authority of Abu al-'Aliyah and Ubayy, "They [humankind] were all one *ummah*, followers of one faith, when they were displayed before Adam [that is, when God taught him the names; see Q. 2:31-33]. God then created them with the faith of Islam and made them profess their servanthood to Him. Then they were one community, Muslims, all of them. But they disagreed after Adam" (Tabari, IV, pp. 277-278). Tabari agrees with the view that *ummah* here means religion or faith, the true faith of Adam. Since there is no indication in the Qur'an or prophetic *hadith* as to the time when humankind were all one community of faith and, consequently, the time when they first fell into discord, he leaves the matter open (Tabari, IV, pp. 278-280).

Qurtubi asserts that God sent prophets, "whose number was one hundred and twenty-four thousand. Three hundred and thirteen of them were apostles. Those mentioned in the Qur'an by name are eighteen. It is also said that the first apostle was Idris [Enoch]" (Qurtubi, III, pp. 31-32; see also Ibn Kathir, I, pp. 443-444; Zamakhshari, I, p. 355; Razi, VI, pp. 11-17; and Nisaburi, II, pp. 212-215).

Tabarsi asserts on the authority of the fifth imam, "They [humankind] were one community before Noah. They were in the *fitrah* [the state of pure faith created in them by God], neither rightly guided, nor gone astray; God then sent prophets." Tabarsi comments on the tradition as follows: "This means that they were worshipers of God in accordance with their native reason, not guided by any prophetic teaching or sacred law [*shari'ah*]. Then God sent prophets with sacred laws, because He knew that in them would be their welfare" (Tabarsi, II, p. 186).

Tabari says that after dissension appeared among men, God sent to those who obeyed Him prophets who were bearers of good tidings of the rewards awaiting them in the hereafter and bearers to those who disobeyed God of warnings of the punishment awaiting them on the day of judgment (Tabari, IV, p. 280).

The book which God sent with the prophets was, in the view of Tabari, the Torah. The Torah, not the prophets, was to judge among humankind. "This is because whoever among prophets and apostles passed any judgment did so in accordance with the injunctions of the book which God had sent down. Thus the book with its injunctions and proofs of the validity of the judgment was itself the actual judge among people, even though the one who passed judgment over them may have been another [that is, a prophet]." Hence the people who disagreed were, in the view of most classical commentators, the Jews, and they disagreed concerning the Torah (Tabari, IV, pp. 280–281; Shawkani, I, pp. 213–214).

The two modern commentators used in this work treat this verse differently. Tabataba'i discusses the verse at great length. He begins by examining it in relationship to other verses expressing the same idea (see, for instance, Q. 42:14 and 10:19). He finally argues that the people (*al-nas*) here intended were humankind before scriptures were sent down and religious laws instituted. Thus there were two disagreements, the first before prophets came with scriptures, and the second afterward. The first was a natural disagreement, natural in the building of human society. The second was based on knowledge and was the result of envy among men after the truth became known to them. The prophets here mean warners, such as Moses and Muhammad. The book here means the divine word which was transmitted by the prophets. More specifically, the author considers the book mentioned in this verse to have been that of Noah, that is, it was Noah's message to his people before the flood. The verse may also be taken, Tabataba'i argues, to refer to the five prophets of power (*ulu al-'azm*): Noah, Abraham, Moses, Jesus, and Muhammad (Tabataba'i, II, pp. 121–149).

Sayyid Qutb takes the verse somewhat literally. He says that perhaps it was the first human family, Adam and Eve and their immediate children, who were all one community. Disagreement was, according to Sayyid Qutb, both necessary and good. Disagreement was the result of the growth of this first family, as humankind began to scatter into different parts of the globe and evolve different cultures and civilizations. God willed, however, that these differences in natural gifts, needs, and abilities should all be harmonized within a broad framework capable of absorbing them all. Thus God sent prophets and "sent down with them the Book with the truth." This true book is, in the view of our author, "one book in its essence brought by all the apostles. It is one book in its origin, one religion in its general characteristics. It is one Lord and one God to be worshiped alone. He is the one and only legislator for humanity. Thereafter details may differ according to the different needs of different nations and generations." The last system which Islam brought is, according to Sayyid Qutb, that which God chose for humanity to follow (Qutb, I, pp. 321–324).

214. Do you reckon that you will enter Paradise when as yet you have not endured the like of that which those before you endured? They were afflicted with misfortune and adversity, and were made to tremble, until the Apostle and those with him cried out, "When shall the help of God come?" Is not the help of God at hand!

215. They ask you what they should give in alms. Say, "Whatever good you give, let it be given to parents, next of kin, orphans, the destitute, and the wayfarer;" whatever good you do, God knows it.

216. Fighting is ordained for you, though it be hateful to you. Yet you may hate a thing which is good for you, or love a thing which is evil for you. God knows all things, but you do not know.

217. They ask you concerning the sacred month, "Should there be fighting in it?" Say, "Fighting in it is a grave matter, but obstructing the way of God, rejecting faith in Him, and hindering people from the sacred House of worship and turning its people out of it is more grievous in the sight of God, for sedition is more grievous than slaying. They shall continue to wage war against you until they turn you away from your faith, if they are able. But whosoever among you shall turn away from his faith and die a rejecter, these are they whose works in this world

and in the world to come shall come to naught. These
are the people of the Fire; in it they shall abide forever.

218. Surely those who have faith and have migrated and struggled in the way of God hope for the mercy of God, and
God is all-forgiving, compassionate.

219. They ask you concerning wine and gambling. Say, "There
is a great iniquity in them, but also some benefit for humankind. But their iniquity is greater than their benefit."
They ask you what they should give in alms. Say, "What
you can spare." Thus God manifests His signs to you,
that you may reflect—

220. In this world and the world to come. They also ask you
concerning orphans. Say, "It is best that you improve
their lot; if you mingle your affairs with theirs, they are
your brothers." God knows him who deals corruptly and
him who acts righteously. Had God willed, He would have
caused you distress. Surely God is mighty and wise.

221. Do not marry female associators until they have faith, for
a Muslim woman, though she may be a slave, is better
than an associator, though she may please you. Do not
marry male associators until they have faith, for a man of
faith, though he may be a slave, is better than an associator, though he may please you. Those invite you to
the Fire, but God invites you to Paradise and to forgiveness by His leave. He manifests His signs to humankind,
that they may remember.

222. They ask you also concerning women during menstruation. Say, "It is a pollution." Therefore separate yourselves from women during menstruation and do not approach them until they have cleansed themselves. When
they are clean, go into them as God has commanded
you. Surely God loves those who turn to Him and those
who cleanse themselves.

223. Your wives are a tillage for you; go therefore into your
tillage as you wish. Perform good deeds here for the

good of your souls [in the hereafter]. Fear God and know that you shall meet Him; give good tidings to the people of faith.

224. Do not make God an easy object of your oaths. Rather, act righteously, fear God, and make peace among men. God is all-hearing, all-knowing.

225. God will not reproach you for the use of vain words in your oaths, but He will reproach you for that which your hearts have earned. God is all-forgiving, clement.

(214) Wahidi relates on the authority of Qatadah and al-Suddi, "This verse was sent down during the Battle of the Trench [al-Khandaq] (5/627) when the Muslims endured hardships: heat, fear, cold, scarcity of provisions and all manners of hurt, as God the Exalted said, 'Hearts reached throats'" (Q. 33:10).

According to 'Ata', Wahidi continues, the verse was revealed when the Prophet and the Companions migrated to Medina. "They suffered much hardship because they left Mecca without provisions, leaving their wealth and homes in the hands of the associators, for they preferred the pleasure of God and His Apostle. The Jews also showed hostility toward the Apostle of God and some of the rich concealed hypocrisy in their hearts." Thus God sent down this verse to reassure them and gladden their hearts (Wahidi, p. 60; see also Tabari, IV, p. 289).

It is also related that the verse was sent down during the Battle of Uhud (3/625), when 'Abdallah ibn Ubayy said to the Companions of the Prophet, "How long will you kill yourselves? Were Muhammad a prophet, no one would have prevailed over him!" (Tabarsi, II, p. 190).

Commentators have, as we have seen, interpreted this verse within the historical context of the early community's life. Ibn 'Arabi, in contrast, lifts the verse out of its historical context and interprets the hardships mentioned in it as mystical states of veiling and separation. Likewise relief is the removal of the veil and union between the lover and the beloved, that is, the human soul and God.

Ibn 'Arabi begins his interpretation of the verse as follows, "'Do you reckon that you will enter [the] Paradise' of the manifestation [*tajalli*] of beauty, 'when as yet you have not endured' the state of those who were before you! 'They were afflicted with [the] misfortune' of abandonment and deprivation and of poverty [*faqr*] and privation [*iftiqar*], with the adversity of spiritual struggle [*mujahadah*], spiritual exercise [*riyadah*], and the humbling of the soul through devotion. [The terms *faqr*, *iftiqar*, and so on are mystical terms describing the states of the disciple.] They 'were made to tremble' to the core of their souls with longing and love in order that they might bring forth their potential into actuality."

Ibn 'Arabi interprets the phrase, "until the Apostle and those with him cried out, 'When shall the help of God come?'" as "until you become exasperated with the long period of the veil and the intolerable hardship of separation." Ibn 'Arabi then returns to the narrative style: "When they can no longer endure being prevented from witnessing beauty and tasting the sweetness of union [*wisal*], then will they seek the help of God through His manifestation [*tajalli*] to vanquish the attributes of their souls. When they show patience and endurance of what the Beloved does to them—trying them with abandoment and giving them to drink the bitter cup of separation in order that their love may reach greater intensity—and when their endurance shall reach its limits and their strength is exhausted, then they shall be answered, 'Is not the help of God at hand!' The veil shall then be raised and the traces of beauty shall appear" (Ibn 'Arabi, I, p. 130).

(215) Wahidi relates on the authority of Ibn 'Abbas that this verse was revealed concerning a man called 'Amr ibn al-Jamuh, who was an old man with great wealth. He asked the Prophet, "O Apostle of God, what should we do with alms, and to whom should we give charity?" In another tradition, related on the authority of 'Ata', we are told that this verse was sent down concerning a man who came to the Prophet saying, "I have only one *dinar*." He replied, "Spend it on yourself." The man continued, "I have two *dinars*." The Prophet answered, "Spend them in alms on your family." The man said further, "I have three." The Prophet said, "Spend them in alms on your servant." The man said, "I have four." The Prophet advised, "Spend them in alms on your parents." "I have five," the man went on. The Prophet said, "Spend them in alms on your next of kin." The man finally said, "I have six." The Prophet replied, "Spend them in the way of God, for that is the best way" (Wahidi, p. 60).

(217, 218) Commentators have generally agreed that verses 217 and 218 were revealed concerning the raid of Nakhlah, a palm grove between Mecca and Medina. The incident took place in the second year of the Hijrah (A.D. 624), two months before the Battle of Badr. It is related on the authority of 'Urwah ibn al-Zubayr, "The Apostle of God sent a detachment of Muslims under the leadership of 'Abdallah ibn Jahsh al-Asdi [a paternal cousin of the Prophet]. They came to Nakhlah, where they found a caravan belonging to the Quraysh under the leadership of 'Amr ibn al-Hadrami. It was the last day of the sacred month of Rajab, but the Muslims disputed this fact. One of them said, 'We are sure that this day is of the sacred month, and therefore we do not agree that you should violate its sanctity simply because you have agreed on an act of covetousness.' Nonetheless, those who sought the wealth of this world prevailed, and thus they killed Ibn al-Hadrami and took his caravan as booty. Ibn al-Hadrami was the first to be slain [in fighting] between the Muslims and the associators. When news of this reached the Quraysh in Mecca, a group of them came to the Prophet and said, 'Do you sanction fighting during a sacred month?' Thus God sent down, 'They ask you concerning the sacred month'" (Wahidi, p. 61).

It is related on the authority of al-Zuhri, "When the people of that detachment had been released of their sorrow by God [by the revealing of verse 218], they desired God's reward. They thus said, 'O Prophet of God, should we be satisfied with this as a raid without receiving for it the reward of those who fight in the way of God?' God thus sent down, 'Surely those who have faith and have migrated and struggled . . .'" (Wahidi, p. 62; see also pp. 62–64 and Qummi, I, pp. 71–72).

Tabarsi relates the same tradition and adds, concerning the sacred month, "The month of Rajab was so called because of its sanctity and because fighting was prohibited in it. For this reason it was known during the time of Jahiliyah as the month of removing the sharp points from spears and the blades from swords. It was also called the deaf [month] because during it no clatter of arms was heard. Men therefore did not fear one another and highways were safe until the month ended" (Tabarsi, II, p. 198).

According to Tabarsi, "The words, 'For sedition is more grievous than slaying' refer to sedition or temptation in faith, that is, rejection of faith is more grave than killing in the sacred month." Tabarsi relates from Qatadah and others, "The prohibition of fighting during a sacred month and in the sacred House was abrogated by God's saying, 'Fight against them therefore until sedition is no more' [Q. 2:193], and His saying, 'And kill the associators wherever you find them' [Q. 9:5]. 'Ata,' on the other hand, said, 'Fighting is still prohibited.'" Tabarsi asserts that for Shi'i jurists it is still prohibited but only against those who accept the sanctity of the sacred months and thus do not initiate hostilities in them. "It is likewise prohibited in the *haram*, for God allowed it only for the Prophet during the year of conquest [of Mecca]. It is related that the Prophet said, 'God has made it permissible for me in this hour, but will not permit it to anyone after me till the day of resurrection.' However, as for those who do not accept the sanctity of these months, it is allowed to fight against them at any time. This is because in their case prohibition is abrogated" (Tabarsi, II, p. 198).

(219) Wahidi relates that this verse was sent down when 'Umar ibn al-Khattab, Mu'adh ibn Jabal and a group of the Ansar came to the Prophet, saying, "Give us an opinion concerning wine and gambling, for they are a means of losing the mind and plundering wealth" (Wahidi, pp. 64–65).

Tabari relates as reason for the revelation of this verse a tradition on the authority of 'Abdallah ibn 'Umar, who said, "God sent down concerning wine three verses; the first was, 'They ask you concerning wine and gambling.' The people said, 'O Apostle of God, we benefit from it and drink it as God has said in His Book.' Then was sent down, 'O you who have faith, do not approach prayers while you are drunk' [Q. 4:43]. The people said, 'O Apostle of God, we shall not drink it at the time of prayer.' Then was sent, 'Surely wine, gambling [by shuffling arrows], stone idols, and divining arrows are an abomination of the work of Satan; therefore avoid it' [Q. 5:90]. The Apostle of God then said, 'Wine is forbidden'" (Tabari, IV, p. 329; see also p. 330; Nisaburi, II, pp. 231–236 and Shawkani, I, pp. 219–221).

Zamakhshari, after relating the same tradition, cites for each of the verses an occasion of revelation. Thus after the verse in question was revealed, people prayed together and their intoxicated leader recited, "Say, O rejecters of faith, I worship what you worship," instead of, "I shall not worship what you worship" (Q. 111:1–2). Hence the verse forbidding wine-drinking at the time of prayer was revealed.

On another occasion, a few men, among whom were Sa'd ibn Abi Waqqas, a Companion of the Prophet, began to boast of their ancestries; having become drunk, Sa'd recited a poem disparaging the Ansar. A man of the Ansar struck him in anger with a camel quirt and wounded him; then God revealed verse 90 of *surah* 5, forbidding wine.

Zamakhshari reports that 'Ali said, "Were a drop [of wine] to fall in a well over which a minaret were to be erected, I would not raise the call to prayer on it; were it to fall in a sea which then dries up and were grass to grow in it, I would not graze [animals] on it" (Zamakhshari, I, p. 359).

Zamakhshari defines alcohol (*khamr*) as "grape juice after it has been boiled and left to ferment, forming a thick foamy top . . . and similarly, water in which raisins or dates are soaked without being cooked before. If, however, they have been cooked until two-thirds of the liquid evaporates and thus becomes thick, it becomes pure, free from the portion of Satan. It is then lawful to drink, but not to the point of intoxication. According to Abu Hanifah, it is lawful to drink it unless it is intended for intoxication and ecstasy. But according to most other jurists, this is unlawful, just as wine, as well as any drink which may cause intoxication" (Zamakhshari, I, p. 359; see also Qurtubi, III, pp. 51–52).

(220) Wahidi reports on the authority of Sa'id ibn Jubayr and Ibn 'Abbas, "When God sent down, 'Do not approach the wealth of an orphan except in a good way . . .' [Q. 6:152], and, 'Those who consume the wealth of orphans wrongfully . . .' [Q. 4:10], everyone who had an orphan in his home separated his food and drink from that of the orphan. Whatever remained of the orphan's food was kept for him to eat later or left to rot. People found that to be a hardship; thus they complained to the Apostle of God, and God sent down, 'They also ask you concerning orphans'" (Wahidi, p. 65; for a similar tradition see Qummi, I, p. 72).

(221) Wahidi reports on the authority of Muqatil ibn Hayyan, a well-known traditionist, that this verse was sent down concerning a man of the Immigrants called Marsad al-Ghanawi, who asked the Prophet permission to marry a Meccan woman whom he knew before he accepted Islam. He said, "O Prophet of God, she pleases me!" Thus God sent down this verse.

Wahidi relates another tradition from Ibn 'Abbas, who said that this verse was sent down concerning one of the Companions, 'Abdallah ibn Ruwahah. He had a black female slave whom he slapped in a moment of anger. He then feared the punishment of God for his deed so he came to the Prophet to confess. The Prophet asked, "What is she, O 'Abdallah?" The man answered, "O Apostle of God, she fasts, prays, and performs well her ablutions. She bears witness that there is no god but God and that you are His Apostle." The Prophet remarked, "She is a woman of faith!" 'Abdallah then exclaimed, "By Him who sent you as a Prophet with the truth, I shall free her and marry her!" Some among the Muslims who preferred to marry the women of the associators on account of the nobility of their lineage criticized Ibn Ruwahah for marrying a slave girl. Thus God sent down this verse (Wahidi, pp. 66–67).

Qummi asserts that the injunction, "Do not marry female associators until they have faith" was abrogated by the words, "And the chaste women of those who were given the scriptures before you" (Q. 5:5; Qummi, I, pp. 72–73).

Tabarsi reviews the different juristic views regarding whether or not this verse was abrogated and concludes, "There are those who say that the verse was not abrogated and must be read literally, as forbidding marriage with every female rejecter of faith, be she of the People of the Book, or an associator. This is the view of Ibn 'Umar and some Zaydi jurists, and it is the legal position of our school" (Tabarsi, II, pp. 209–210).

(222) Wahidi reports on the authority of Anas ibn Malik that the Jews of Medina isolated the women in menstruation so that they would not eat or drink with them. The Prophet was asked concerning this custom, and God sent down the verse. Wahidi also relates that the Arabs did the same thing during the Jahiliyah in emulation of the Zoroastrians. Abu al-Dahdah, one of the Companions, asked the Prophet, "What shall we do with women during their menses?" Thus God sent down this verse (Wahidi, pp. 67–68; see also Tabarsi, II, p. 212).

226. Those who forswear their wives must abstain for four months. But if they retract, God is all-forgiving, compassionate;

227. But if they resolve on divorce, God is surely all-hearing, all-knowing.

228. As for divorced women, they should keep themselves apart three menstrual cycles. It is unlawful for them to conceal that which God created in their wombs if they truly have faith in God and the last day. Their husbands have the right to take them back at such time, if they desire reconciliation. Women have rights over men as men have over them in kindness, and men are set a degree over them. God is mighty and wise.

229. Divorce is allowed twice; thereafter retention in honor or release in kindness. It is not lawful for you to take anything of that which you have given them [in dower] unless both fear that they cannot fulfill the ordinances of God. If, therefore, you fear that they cannot fulfill the ordinances of God, there is no blame in both of them if she ransoms herself. These are the bounds of God; do not transgress them, for whosoever transgresses the bounds of God are the wrongdoers.

230. If he divorces her [a third time] she will become unlawful for him until she marries another man but if the other man divorces her, there is no blame in them if they return to each other—but only if they think that they will be able to fulfill the ordinances of God. These are the ordinances of God; he manifests them to people who know.

231. If you divorce women, and they have fulfilled their prescribed term, either retain them with kindness or dismiss them in kindness. Do not retain them by coercion so that you transgress, for whosoever does so wrongs only himself. Do not take the signs of God for a mockery; rather remember God's favor toward you and what He has sent down to you of the Book and wisdom, admonishing you thereby. Fear God and know that God knows all things.

232. If you divorce women, and they have fulfilled their prescribed term, do not hinder them from marrying their husbands, if they agree among themselves in an honorable manner. In this there is admonition to those among you who have faith in God and the last day. This is more righteous for you, and more pure; God knows and you do not know.

233. Mothers should nurse their children for two full years, for those who wish the period of nursing to be completed. It is the duty of fathers to provide for and clothe mothers during that period in a fitting manner. No soul is to be charged beyond its capacity. No mother shall be made to suffer harm on account of her child or a father on account of his child. The duties incumbent upon the heir are

the same as those of the father. If they wish to wean their child by mutual consent and consultation, there is no blame in them. If you wish to give your children out to nurse, there is no blame in you, if you pay her in full what you offer her, with kindness. Fear God, and know that God is all-seeing of that which you do.

234. Those among you who die, leaving wives behind, they shall keep themselves apart for four months and ten days. But when they have fulfilled their term, there shall be no blame in you for that which they do with themselves, if they act honorably. God is aware of what you do.

235. There shall be no blame in you whether you make public your overtures of marriage to women or conceal them in your hearts [during the period of abstinence]. God knows that you shall remember them, but do not promise them marriage in secret, except that you use honorable words. Do not resolve on marriage until the prescribed term is fulfilled; God knows that which is in your hearts. Beware, therefore, and know that God is all-forgiving, clement.

236. There shall be no blame in you if you divorce women so long as you have not touched them or settled a dower for them. Provide for them, the man of means according to his ability and the man in straits according to his ability, an honorable portion. This is a duty incumbent upon those who do good.

237. But if you divorce them before you have touched them, and had settled a dower for them, the dower shall be half of what you had settled, unless they voluntarily remit it or he in whose hands is the arrangement of marriage remits it. To remit is nearer to righteousness; do not forget liberality among you. God is surely all-seeing of what you do.

These verses deal with family relations. The subjects of divorce, marriage dowry, final and retractable divorce, and the period of abstinence between the dissolution of one marriage and contracting another all belong strictly to jurisprudence. I shall therefore deal only with those aspects that pertain to *tafsir* proper, presenting the occasion of revelation of a verse and elucidating its meaning when this is not clear from reading the text.

(226) Wahidi reports that Ibn 'Abbas said, "The period of desertion of the wife in the Jahiliyah was a year, two years, or even longer. God therefore fixed this period at four months. Anyone falling short of this period, his forswearing of his wife would not be considered valid" (Wahidi, pp. 72–73; see also Qurtubi, II, pp. 102–125).

Qummi defines forswearing, as related on the authority of the sixth imam, as "when a man swears not to have intercourse with his wife. If she shows patience [until he retracts] she has the right to do so. If, on the other hand, she accuses him before the imam, the latter shall give him respite for four months. Thereafter the man should be told either to take back his wife or divorce her. Otherwise, the imam would say to him, 'I shall imprison you until you make your decision.'" Qummi reports further that 'Ali built a reed enclosure in which he imprisoned a man who had waited four months. He said to him, "Either you return to her, divorce her, or I shall burn this enclosure over you" (Qummi, I, pp. 73–74).

(229) Wahidi relates on the authority of Hisham ibn 'Urwah that he heard his father, 'Urwah ibn Zubayr, say, "In the time of Jahiliyah in early Islam, a man could divorce his wife and remarry her before her term was ended, even if he were to divorce her a thousand times. Thus a man divorced his wife until she was about to finish her term, and remarried her and then divorced her again, saying, 'By God, I will never bring you under my roof, nor will you ever be free!' God then sent down, 'Divorce is allowed twice'" (Wahidi, p. 73). In another tradition related on the authority of the same man, we are told that a woman came to 'A'ishah, complaining that her husband kept divorcing and remarrying her. 'A'ishah told the Prophet, and God revealed this verse (Wahidi, p. 73; see also Tabarsi, II, pp. 232–233; and Qurtubi, III, p. 126).

Verse 229 is known as the verse of *khul'* (annulment of marriage, or divorce of the wife for a ransom or compensation to be paid to the husband). (See Qummi, I, pp. 75–76.) The third divorce is explained in the next verse. It is related that the Prophet was asked, "'Divorce is allowed twice,' but where is the third?" He said, "Thereafter retention in honor or release in kindness" (Tabarsi, II, p. 233).

Tabarsi says that the words, "unless both fear that they cannot fulfill the ordinances of God," were sent down concerning a man called Qays ibn Thabit ibn Shammas and his wife Jamilah, daughter of 'Abdallah ibn Ubayy. The man loved his wife, but she despised him. The Prophet said to her, "Would you return to him his garden?" "Yes," she answered, "and I would give him even more." "No," the Prophet said, "only his garden." Thus she returned his garden to him and the Prophet said, "O Thabit! Take back from her what you gave her and let her go." This he did and thus it was the first *khul'* in Islam (Tabarsi, II, p. 233; Shawkani, I, pp. 238–242).

(232) Wahidi relates on the authority of Hasan al-Basri that Ma'qil ibn Yassar had a sister who married a man of the Muslims. After some time, the man divorced her, but when her term was fulfilled, he came with the other suitors seeking her hand from her brother. Ma'qil refused, saying, "I gladly gave her to you, but you divorced her. No, by God, she will never return to you henceforth." The wife, however, also wished to return to her husband. Hasan said, "God knew the need of a man for his wife and her need for her husband. Thus He sent down a *qur'an* concerning it [that is, a verse], 'If you divorce women. . . .'" It is also related on the authority of al-Suddi that the verse was revealed concerning Jabir ibn 'Abdallah al-Ansari, who had a female first cousin whose husband divorced her; after the woman had fulfilled her term, the man wished to take her back. Jabir, however, refused, and thus God sent down this verse (Wahidi, pp. 75–76; see also Ibn Kathir, I, pp. 499–501; Qurtubi, II, pp. 157–159; Shawkani, I, p. 244).

After relating both traditions, Tabarsi comments, "Both views are unacceptable according to our rite [*madhhab*] because for us neither a brother nor a cousin has the right of guardianship over a woman. Hence their refusal is ineffective. It is therefore best that the verse be generally explained as referring to divorced spouses, in accordance with its literal sense. God's saying, 'Do not hinder them,' means, 'do not take them back just before they have fulfilled their prescribed term in order that you may harm them or because you desire to have them back.' It is also possible that the word *'adl* [hindrance] here signifies coercion and prevention from marrying, without any reference to guardianship" (Tabarsi, II, p. 240).

238. Strictly observe the appointed prayers and the middle prayer, and stay the night constant in prayer before God.

239. If you fear danger, pray on foot or mounted, but when
you are safe, remember God, for He has taught you that
which you did not know.

(238) Commentators have differed as to which of the five daily
prayers is meant here. Tabarsi relates on the authority of Zayd ibn
Thabit, 'Abdallah ibn 'Umar, Abu Sa'id al-Khudri, Usama ibn Zayd,
and 'A'ishah that it is the noon prayer. This view is also attributed
to the fifth and sixth imams. Among jurists, Abu Hanifah and his
followers have also adopted this view. According to some of the
Zaydi jurists, it is the Friday prayer as well as the noon prayer of
the other days of the week. This view is supported by a prophetic
hadith related on the authority of 'Ali, "God has in the heaven of
this world a circle within which the sun reaches the meridian. When
the sun has reached its meridian, everything begins to sing the praises
of our Lord. Thus God commanded that people observe prayer in
this hour, for it is the hour in which the gates of heaven are opened
and are not closed again until the noon prayers are offered. It is an
hour in which prayers are answered" (Tabarsi, II, pp. 261–262; see
also Qurtubi, II, pp. 209–222).

Others said that it is the midafternoon prayer. This is the view
of most commentators and jurists, including 'Ali, Ibn Mas'ud, Qatadah, and others. This opinion is also said to be accepted by Abu
Hanifah. The argument that it is the midafternoon prayer which is
intended in this verse is based on the fact that it is actually the
middle (wusta) prayer between the day and evening prayers (see
Tabari, V, pp. 167–169; Ibn Kathir, I, pp. 514–523; Zamakhshari,
I, p. 376; and Tabarsi, II, p. 262).

Other commentators argue, as Tabarsi reports, that it is the maghrib
(sunset) prayer because it is midway in length among the prayers.
This prayer is composed of three rak'ahs, while that of the morning
is composed of two and the other three prayers of four each. It is
related on the authority of 'A'ishah that the Prophet said, "The most
excellent among the prayers with God is the maghrib prayer. God
exempted from it neither the person who is on a journey nor one
who is at home. [When on a journey all prayers are attenuated to
two rak'ahs except the sunset prayer, which remains three.] With it
God opened the night prayers, and with it He closed those of the
day. Thus whoever performs the maghrib prayer and two rak'ahs
after it, a palace will be built for him in Paradise. But as for him

who performs four *rak'ahs*, God will forgive him the sins of twenty or forty years" (Tabarsi, II, p. 262).

Similar arguments have been made for the night (*'isha'*) and morning prayers. It has also been argued that it is one of the five daily prayers which God did not specify. Thus Razi argues, "It is proven that God did not identify the middle [*wusta*] prayer. The wisdom in this is that since God especially emphasized it, even though He did not make clear which of the five daily prayers it is, it is possible for a man to assume that every prayer he performs is the middle prayer. This would provide the incentive to observe all of them with diligence. For this reason God concealed the Night of Determination [*laylat al-qadr*] in Ramadan, the hour in which prayers are answered in Friday, and His greatest name in all His names. Muhammad ibn Sirin [one of the early Successors and an early mystic and traditionist] related that a man asked Zayd ibn Thabit about the middle prayer; he answered, 'Observe all the prayers, then you would observe it as well'" (Razi, VI, pp. 156–158; see also Nisaburi, II, pp. 294–297).

The most widely accepted view, however, as has been observed, is that it is the midafternoon prayer. It is related on the authority of many traditionists that 'Ali said, "We used to think that it was the dawn prayer until I heard the Apostle of God say on the day of the parties [*yawm al-ahzab* (Dhu al-Qi'dah, 5 A.H./April A.D. 627)], 'They kept us from performing the middle prayer, [which is] the midafternoon prayer; may God fill their graves and stomachs with fire!'" A similar tradition is related on the authority of Ibn Mas'ud (Shawkani, I, p. 256; see also Qutb, I, p. 377).

240. Those among you who die, leaving wives behind, shall bequeath to their wives provisions for one year without turning them out of their houses. But if they leave voluntarily, there shall be no blame in you for that which they do with themselves if they act honorably, for God is mighty and wise.

241. Divorced women shall be entitled to maintenance with kindness. This is a duty incumbent upon the God-fearing.

242. Thus God manifests His signs to you, that you may understand.

243. Have you [Muhammad] not considered those who went forth from their dwellings in thousands in fear of death? God said to them, "Die," then he restored them to life. God is surely gracious toward humankind, but most people do not give thanks.

244. Fight in the way of God and know that God is all-hearing, all-knowing.

245. Who shall lend to God a loan for good reward? Surely God will multiply it for him manifold, for God withholds and extends [His hand].

(243–244) Classical commentators often referred any verse that hints at an event in bygone ages to the ancient history of the Children of Israel. Thus, in interpretation of this verse, both Sunni and Shi'i commentators relate a number of hagiographical tales, most with confused biblical motifs. One of the earliest and simplest of these is the following tale related without any authority by 'Ali ibn Ibrahim al-Qummi.

"One of the towns in Syria was afflicted by the plague. Thus many of the inhabitants left the town . . . fleeing the plague. They reached a desert where they all died in one night. They remained there [unburied] until passersby had to push their bones with their feet off the road. Then God revived them and returned them to their homes, where they lived a long time. Finally, they died and were buried" (Qummi, I, pp. 80–81).

Tabari relates on the authority of Ibn 'Abbas, "They were four thousand people who left their town fleeing the plague. They said, 'Let us go to a land which is free from death.' As they reached a place, God said to them, 'Die!' After a time, a prophet passed by their corpses. He prayed to his Lord to bring them back to life and God did so. The prophet then recited, 'God is surely gracious toward humankind, but most people do not give thanks'" (Tabari, V, pp. 267–268).

In another version of the same tale, Tabari tells us on the authority of Ibn 'Abbas that the Prophet prayed to God to revive the people in order that they might worship Him. In still another version related on the authority of Wahb ibn Munabbih, an attempt is made to provide a more cogent reason for the people's death and their revivification. "Some people of the Children of Israel were afflicted with hardship and tribulation for some time. They complained of what they suffered, saying, 'Would that we die and be free from that which has befallen us!' God then revealed to Hazqil [a prophet], 'Your people have cried out complaining of their trials, wishing to die and rest. What kind of rest will they have after death? Do they think that I am unable to bring them back to life after death? Go, therefore, to such-and-such a graveyard, in which there are four thousand dead.' These were the people of whom God said, 'Have you [Muhammad] not considered those who went forth from their dwellings in thousands in fear of death?' [God continued] 'Stand near them and call out . . . O bones! God commands you to gather together!' The bones of every person came together. Hazqil called out again, 'O bones, God commands you to be clothed with flesh!' Then Hazqil called out a third time: 'O spirits, God commands you to return to your bodies!' They thus rose up by God's leave, and cried out with one voice, 'God is most great!'" (Tabari, V, p. 268).

The prophet Hazqil in this and other tales may perhaps be the prophet Ezekiel (see Ezek. 37:1–15). Tabarsi, however, relates an account in which Hazqil is identified as "the third of the successors among the Children of Israel after Moses; for the one who was to rule over the Children of Israel after Moses was Yusha', [Joshua] son of Nun, then Kalib ibn Yufanna, then Hazqil. He was known as the son of the old woman because his mother was an old woman. She prayed God to grant her a child after she had grown old and barren. Then God gave her Hazqil." Hazqil, according to this story, may refer to Samuel. Hasan al-Basri said, "He was Dhu al-Kifl [the man who cared for or protected]. [See Q. 21:95]. Hazqil was called Dhu al-Kifl because he protected seventy prophets and saved them from death. He said to them, 'Escape! For it is better that I be slain than all of you be slain.' The Jews came, inquiring about the seventy prophets, but Hazqil said, 'They departed, and I do not know where they are.' God, however, protected Dhu al-Kifl from them" (Tabarsi, II, p. 269). Dhu al-Kifl in this story may refer to the prophet Elijah and the prophets of Baal (see 1 Kings 18:17–36).

The Jewish origin of these tales is obvious. In an interesting anecdote concerning 'Umar ibn al-Khattab, we see reflected not only the biblical and hagiographical background of these stories but also the Jewish eschatological framework. It is related that as 'Umar was once praying, two Jewish men were sitting behind him, watching to see how he spread out his shoulders in prostration. When 'Umar finished his prayers, he asked them why they were pointing to him.

They answered, "We find it written in our book [Daniel?] 'an iron horn shall be given, what Hazqil who revived the dead by God's leave was given.'" 'Umar said, "We do not find Hazqil in our book [the Qur'an], nor one who revives the dead by God's leave, except Jesus." They said, "Do you not find in the Book of God, 'and other apostles whom we have not recounted to you . . . ?'" (Q. 4:164). "Yes!" 'Umar answered. They said, "As for reviving the dead, we shall tell you concerning that. It happened that the Children of Israel were once afflicted with a plague. A group of them left their homes so that when they had gone no more than the distance of a mile, God caused them to die. Men erected a wall around them, so that when their bones rotted, God sent Hazqil, who stood over them and said what God willed him to say. God then revived them for him and sent down, 'Have you [Muhammad] not considered those who went forth from their dwelling in thousands in fear of death?'" (Tabari, V, pp. 268–269).

The most developed version of this story locates the town and provides a reason for the people's death consonant with the predominant theological view of classical Islam. In the following tradition, related by Tabari on the authority of al-Suddi, we are told, "There was a city called Dawardan near Wasit [in present-day Iraq] which was afflicted with the plague. Most of its inhabitants fled into the countryside. Those who remained in the city died, but those who ran away escaped death. . . . When the plague ended, they returned to the city." The few who remained in the city and who were not killed by the plague said, "Our friends were more decisive than we! Had we done as they did, we would have been saved. If the plague comes again, we shall go out with them." The plague did come in the following year, and they fled. They were about thirty thousands. When they came to a fragrant valley, an angel called out to them from the bottom of the valley and another from its top, saying, "Die!" They died instantly. When their bodies had decomposed, a prophet called Hazqil passed by them. He stood over them contemplating and twisting his jaws and fingers in amazement. God revealed to him, "O Hazqil, do you wish that I show you how I revive them?" He said, "Yes." It was then said to him, "Call out!" He called, "O bones, God commands you to come together!" They began to fly one to the other until they began to form skeletons. God revealed to him again, "Call out!" He called, "O bones, God commands you to be clothed with flesh," and thus they were clothed with flesh and blood and with the clothes in which they died. It was said again to him, "Call out!" He cried, "O bones, God commands you to rise up!" and they did (Tabari, V, p. 270).

With regard to the reason for the people's death, Ibn Kathir comments, "In this story there is a lesson, and a proof of the fact that no precaution will save one from a [divine] decree, and that there is no refuge from God except in Him. These people fled their homes in search of long life, but they were dealt with contrary to their aim" (Ibn Kathir, I, p. 530). Ibn Kathir then relates a *hadith* of the Prophet on the authority of Abd al-Rahman ibn 'Awf, who said, "I heard the Apostle of God say, 'If the plague is in a land in which you happen to be, do not run away from it, and if you hear of it in a land, do not go thither'" (Ibn Kathir, I, p. 530).

Commentators have also explained the death of the people as due to their refusal to fight in the way of God. Ibn Kathir relates on the authority of Ibn 'Abbas, "A king of the Children of Israel commanded his soldiers to fight, but they were afraid. They said to their king, 'The land we are to go to has the plague. We shall therefore not go there until the plague is no more.' Thus God caused them all to die." They were revived after eight days, but the odor of death remained with them and with their children, supposedly until the time of Ibn 'Abbas. Commentators have based this view on the fact that the verse immediately following this one commands people to fight in the way of God. Again Ibn Kathir comments in linking the two verses, "As precaution does not save from preordination, likewise running away from fighting [in the way of God] does not hasten the end [of a man's life] nor does it prolong it. Rather, the predetermined end and allotted sustenance are preordained and strictly allotted; they can neither be increased nor decreased" (Ibn Kathir, I, p. 530; see also Razi, VI, pp. 173–174; Tabari, V, pp. 274–276; Qurtubi, II, pp. 230–236; and Shawkani, I, pp. 261–263).

Sayyid Qutb here prefers "not to be lost in the desert of exegetical interpretations concerning who left their homes in the thousands in fear of death, who they were, in what land they were and in what time they left their homes. Had God wished to tell us who they were, He would have done so. . . . Rather, this is an exhortation through parable; what is intended is its moral significance and not events, places, and times. What is here intended is to give a true concept of death and life, their external causes and inner reality, and to indicate that matters concerning them must be referred to the Omniscient Power and that we should be content with the divine decree concerning them. This is because whatever is decreed will take place, and life and death are in the end in the hands of God. The verse is meant to say that precaution against death yields nothing and that fear and anxiety do not prolong life, extend a term [*ajal*], or prevent what is decreed. God alone is the giver and taker of life; but in either case He grants favor, whether He gives or takes back. The great divine wisdom is behind both giving and taking back. Human welfare, moreover, is achieved in both, and the favor of God is equally manifest to human beings in taking and granting" (Qutb, I, p. 387).

Tabataba'i prefers to read the verse without such heuristic interpretation. The verse, he asserts, must refer to a story or event which, among other things, is intended to show an account of the miracles wrought by God at the hands of the prophets (see Tabataba'i, II, pp. 279–283).

246. Have you [Muhammad] not considered the assembly of the Children of Israel after Moses when they said to a prophet of theirs, "Set over us a king so that we may fight in the way of God." He said, "What if fighting were prescribed for you and yet you would not fight?" They said, "Why should we not fight in the way of God, seeing that we have been driven out of our homes with our children?" Yet when fighting was prescribed for them, they turned back, save a few of them. God is all-knowing of the wrongdoers.

247. Their prophet then said to them, "Behold, God has set Talut [Saul] a king over you." They said, "Why should he reign over us, seeing that we are more worthy of the kingdom than he, nor was he given abundant wealth." He said, "God has chosen him over you and has increased him in knowledge and stature." God grants dominion to whomsoever He wills and God is all-encompassing, all-knowing.

248. Their prophet said to them, "The sign of his kingdom shall be that the Ark shall come to you. In it is tranquility [*sakinah*] from your Lord and the remains of what the house of Moses and Aaron left behind, the angels bearing

it. In this there is a sign for you, if you are truly men of faith.

249. When Talut departed with the soldiers, he said, "Surely God shall try you by a river. Whosoever drinks from it will not be of my followers. But he who does not taste of it will be of my followers, except those who scoop a draught with their hands." They drank from it, save a few of them. When he and those who had faith crossed the river together, they said, "We have no strength today against Jalut [Goliath] and his army." But those who thought that they would be meeting God said, "How often has a small army defeated a large one, by God's leave, for God is with those who are steadfast!"

250. When they went forth to meet Jalut and his army in battle, they said, "Our Lord, bestow upon us endurance and make firm our foothold and grant us victory over the rejecters of faith."

251. Thus they routed them by God's leave and David slew Jalut. God granted David dominion and wisdom and taught him what He willed. Had God not repelled some people by others, the earth would have been corrupted, but God is beneficent toward His creatures.

(246–247) Commentators have differed regarding the identity of the prophet mentioned here. Tabari relates on the authority of Wahb ibn Munabbih and Ibn Ishaq that he was Shamu'il (Samuel). According to al-Suddi, the prophet's name was Sham'un (Simon) because his mother prayed God to give her a boy. When her prayers were answered, she call the boy Sham'un, meaning, "God has heard my prayer" (Tabari, V, p. 291). Others asserted that the prophet was Joshua, son of Nun. This view is related on the authority of Qatadah, who appears to have based it on a literal reading of the phrase "after Moses": "Their prophet who was 'after Moses' was Joshua, son of Nun" (Tabari, V, p. 292).

Commentators have also differed regarding the reason why the Children of Israel ask their prophet to raise up a king for them. In a long tradition related on the authority of Wahb ibn Munabbih, we have a confused account of biblical history leading to the supposed event in question. According to this account, Hazqil (Ezekiel?) succeeded Kalib ibn Yufanna. After his death the Children of Israel forgot their covenant with God and set up idols which they worshiped instead of Him. God then sent the prophet Ilyas (Elijah). Prophets used to be sent to remind the Children of Israel of their scriptures and to renew the covenant they had with God. Thus the prophet Elijah was sent to guide King Ahab, who at first followed the prophet's guidance. Later, however, Ahab disregarded the prophet's counsel and acted wickedly; he rejected the covenant and worshiped idols. After Elijah, Ilyasa' (Elisha) likewise attempted to turn the Children of Israel and their kings away from their idolatry, but to no avail.

"After Elisha, corruption spread and sins multiplied among the Children of Israel. They possessed the Ark [of the covenant], which was handed down from one chief to another. No enemy came to them but that God defeated that enemy, so long as the Children of Israel fought behind the Ark. Then a king ruled over them, called 'Ila [Eli]. Under him God protected Mount Ilia [Jerusalem] so that no foe came against them. The Mount was so blessed that a man could gather some soil on a rock and sow grains in it. God then would cause the grain to bear such abundant fruit that it would suffice the man and his family the whole year. A man would have an olive tree out of which he and his family would eat and press enough oil for the year. Yet as they committed grave acts and forgot God's covenant with them, an enemy advanced against them. . . . This time the Ark was captured and they were defeated. When King 'Ila was told, his neck was broken and he died in grief.

"There was among them a prophet sent by God, but they did not listen to him or obey him in anything. This prophet was called Shamu'il [Samuel], of whom God made mention to His prophet Muhammad, saying, 'Have you [Muhammad] not considered the assembly of the Children of Israel after Moses when they said to a prophet of theirs. . . .' Thus they asked Samuel, their prophet, to raise up for them a king to lead them in battle against the enemies, in order that they might regain their homes and protect their wives and children" (Tabari, V, pp. 294–296).

In another tradition related by Tabari from al-Suddi, the story of the birth and childhood of Samuel resembles the biblical account. "The Children of Israel used to fight against the Amalakites, who defeated them under the leadership of their king Goliath. The Amalakites subjected them to the poll tax [jizyah] and took away their Torah. At that time the line of prophets had become extinct except for a woman who was with child. They took her and imprisoned her for fear that she would give birth to a girl and claim instead to have delivered a boy. As she saw the anxiety of the Children of Israel concerning her offspring, she began to pray fervently that God grant her a boy. She gave birth to a boy whom she called Shamu'il [Samuel]. When the child grew up, she sent him to the Temple of Jerusalem to learn the Torah with one of the learned men of the Children of Israel, who then adopted him. When the boy reached the age for God to appoint him as prophet, Gabriel came to him as he slept by the side of the old man. . . . He called him with the voice of the old man, 'O Shamu'il!' The boy jumped up, frightened, and said to the old man, 'Father, have you called me?' The old man did not wish to frighten the boy, so he told him to go back to sleep. . . . [This happened again, but on the third time] Gabriel appeared to him and said, 'Go to your people and convey to them the message of your Lord, for God has sent you as a prophet to them.' When he went to them, they did not believe him. They said, 'You have claimed prophethood too soon, but it has not come to you as yet.' They further said, 'If you tell the truth, then raise up a king over us that we may fight in the way of God under him as a sign of your prophethood.' He answered, 'What if fighting were prescribed for you and yet you would not fight?'" (Tabari, V, pp. 297–298).

The story of Samuel in most of its details and different versions goes back to Wahb ibn Munabbih. Tabari attempts to present a coherent account by stringing together different versions of the story (see Tabari, V, pp. 298–317). He relates, paralleling the biblical account, the divine curse on the children of the old priest Eli, who falls off his chair, dead, (instead of taking the news calmly, as in 1 Sam. 3:18), as soon as he hears the divine verdict delivered by the young prophet.

Talut (Saul) was, according to Tabari, a water-bearer. Samuel chose him by having all the men of the Children of Israel measured by his staff, with the stipulation that the man whose height corresponded exactly to the length of the staff would be king over them. Thus Saul was chosen, yet the Children of Israel rejected him because he was not of the royal lineage, nor was he a man of wealth. Samuel answered, "God has chosen him over you and has increased him in knowledge and stature" (Tabari, V, p. 309; see also pp. 306–308).

(248) The tradition just cited then goes on to relate the story of the Ark. "Thus those who captured the Ark took it and placed it in the temples of their idols. They placed it under an idol which

they worshiped, but in the morning they found the idol lying under it. The next day they again placed the idol on it and nailed its feet to the Ark, but in the morning they found the arms and legs of the idol broken and it was lying under the ark. Some said, 'You know that nothing can stand before the God of the Children of Israel. Take the Ark out, therefore, of the temple of your gods.' They took the Ark and placed it in a quarter of their town. But the people of that quarter woke up in the morning with severe pain in their necks. . . . A maid of the Children of Israel whom they had taken captive said to them, 'You shall suffer as long as this Ark is in your midst. Take it away therefore from your town.' 'You lie!' they answered. She said, 'The sign of the truth of what I say is that you bring two cows with young calves on whose necks no yoke has been placed. Yoke the cows to a chariot and place the Ark over it. Conceal the calves and let the cows loose; the cows will carry the Ark and come directly to their calves.' This they did, and when the cows left the town and came to the borders of the land of the Children of Israel, they broke their yokes and ran to their calves. They left the Ark, however, in a ruin filled with the grain harvest of the Children of Israel. The Children of Israel ran to the Ark, but everyone who approached it fell dead. The prophet Samuel said to them, 'Stay away; let only him who finds sufficient strength in himself come near it.' No one dared to touch the Ark except two men who were allowed to do so. They carried it to the house of their mother, who was a widow. There it remained until Saul became king. He took the Ark and with the help of Samuel gained victory over the enemies of the Children of Israel" (Tabari, V, pp. 319–320). According to Qatadah and al-Rabi' ibn Anas, the Ark was entrusted to Joshua by Moses, after whose death it remained in the wilderness until angels brought it and placed it in the house of Saul as a sign of his kingship (Tabari, V, p. 324).

Commentators have also differed with regard to the *sakinah* (tranquility) which was in the Ark. Tabari relates on the authority of 'Ali that the *sakinah* was a fragrant wind having a face like a human face. According to Mujahid, it had a head like that of a cat and two wings. According to a tradition related on the authority of Wahb ibn Munabbih, the *sakinah* was the head of a dead cat; "they were certain of victory when it mewed like a cat." It is related on the authority of al-Suddi and Ibn 'Abbas that the *sakinah* "was a basin of gold from Paradise in which the hearts of prophets were washed." In another tradition we are told that a man asked Wahb ibn Munabbih about the *sakinah*. He said, "It was a spirit from God endowed with speech. Whenever the Children of Israel disagreed concerning a matter, it spoke and made clear to them what they wished." 'Ata' was asked about God's saying, "In it is *sakinah* from your Lord" He answered, "As for the *sakinah*, it was those signs which they recognized and at which their hearts grew calm." According to al-Rabi' ibn Anas, the *sakinah* here means mercy. Qatadah said that it was reverence. Tabari prefers the view of 'Ata'. (Tabari, V, pp. 325–329; see also Qurtubi, III, p. 247).

Commentators have differed as to the "remains" which the Ark contained. 'Ikrimah related on the authority of Ibn 'Abbas that they were the staff of Moses and the pieces of the tablets on which Moses wrote the Torah on Mount Sinai. According to Sufyan al-Thawri, the Ark contained the sandals of Moses, the turban and staff of Aaron, and the jar in which they stored manna. Such opinions have been related on the authority of most early *tafsir* masters, including the fifth and sixth Shi'i imams (see Tabari, V, pp. 331–334; and Tabarsi, II, p. 283).

Qummi relates, "It was the Ark which God sent down to Moses and in which his mother placed him and put him on the water [of the Nile]. The Children of Israel therefore reverenced the Ark and sought blessings from it. When Moses was about to die, he put the tablets in it and whatever signs of prophethood were in his possession and entrusted it to Joshua, his vicegerent [*wasi*]. Thus the Ark remained with the Children of Israel until they treated it with such disrespect that their children used to play with it in the streets. . . . God therefore took it up from them. When God sent Saul to lead them in battle, He returned the Ark to them" (Qummi, I, pp. 81–82).

Qummi relates further, on the authority of the eighth imam 'Ali al-Rida, "The *sakinah* was a wind from Paradise having a face like a human face. When the Ark was placed before the Muslims [that is, the faithful of the Children of Israel] and the rejecters of faith, it advanced so that no man returned until he had either been slain or had achieved victory. Whoever returned otherwise was considered to be a rejecter of faith and thus executed by the imam" (Qummi, I, p. 82).

(249) Ibn Kathir relates on the authority of al-Suddi that Saul went out to meet Goliath with an army of eighty thousand men. The river with which God tried the men was, according to Ibn 'Abbas, the river Jordan. It is also related that Ibn 'Abbas said, "Whoever scooped of the river with his hand, his thirst was quenched,

but whoever drank directly, his thirst was not quenched." According to al-Suddi, only four thousand men did not drink and thus remained with Saul. Al-Bara' ibn 'Azib said, "The followers of Muhammad who took part in the Battle of Badr were three hundred and some men, the number of the men of Talut who crossed the river with him. No one crossed it with him except he who had faith" (Ibn Kathir, I, pp. 536–537). Qummi relates on the authority of Ja'far al-Sadiq, "Those few who did not drink or scoop water in their hands were three hundred and thirteen men" (Qummi, I, p. 83).

Tabataba'i comments on the verse as follows, "The Children of Israel all asked that a king be set over them; they would then bind themselves with a covenant. The narrative necessitates the existence of three groups: those who were not of his followers, those who were, and those who scooped water with their hands. Thus those who remained with him after crossing the river were two groups: his followers, and those who did not secede. It is therefore possible that they all differed as to their endurance, fear, and trust in God. A careful reading of the verse then suggests that those who said, 'We have no strength today against Jalut [Goliath] and his army' were the scooopers and those who answered them were the men who did not taste of the river at all" (Tabataba'i, II, pp. 291–293).

Tabataba'i alone notes the disagreement of the Qur'anic narrative with the biblical account. The Bible (Judg. 7:5–7) tells us that Gideon, in one of his battles with the Canaanites, chose only men who did not take the time to stop and drink, but only to scoop some water with their hands in haste. Tabataba'i, in a general discussion of the Qur'an's treatment of history observes, "It thus becomes apparent that the noble Qur'an should not be judged by historical narratives if they disagree with it. This is because the Qur'an is divine revelation, free from error and falsehood, while any contradiction from history cannot be absolutely immune from falsehood. Most of the Qur'anic narratives, such as this story . . . contradict what is narrated in the books of the two testaments. There is, however, no problem, because the two testaments are no more than history books.' . . . The writer of this story . . . is unknown. Be that as it may, we should not be concerned with narratives in the Qur'an which contradict history books, and particularly the two testaments, because the Qur'an is the word of truth from the Truth [God] glorified be His name! The Qur'an is not a history book, nor is it concerned in its narratives with elucidating history in the way a history book intends. It is rather divine speech implanted in a revelatory mode through which

God guides those who seek His pleasure to the ways of peace. For this reason, you do not see it narrating a story from beginning to end, or giving the background of its events. It rather takes from a story different points which must be contemplated and carefully considered for the wisdom, lesson, or the like, which it contains" (Tabataba'i, II, pp. 307–308).

(250, 251) These verses recount briefly the stories of Saul and of David and Goliath. Classical commentators related a number of tales intended to provide an explanatory narrative of these verses. Among modern commentators Tabataba'i notes the discrepancy between the Qur'anic and biblical accounts. We shall present the various interpretations which commentators have offered in order to illustrate the great interest which Muslims have shown in biblical history. Here also Jewish tradition has played a major role in the growth of classical *tafsir*.

(251) Tabari relates on the authority of Wahb ibn Munabbih, "When Saul came out to face Goliath, the latter said, 'Send one of you to meet me in single combat. If he kills me you shall have my dominion, but if I kill him, I shall have your dominion.' David was brought to Saul, who promised him that if he were to kill Goliath, he would give him his daughter in marriage and authority over his wealth. Saul put armor on David, but David refused to fight against Goliath with arms. . . . He rather went to meet him with a sling and a sack filled with stones. As he faced Goliath, the latter said, 'You come to fight with me?' 'Yes,' said David. Goliath then said, 'You have come as though to meet a dog with a sling and stones! I shall tear your flesh today and feed it to birds and beasts.' David said, 'You, the enemy of God, are worse than a dog!' Then David took a stone and slung it at him; it hit him between the eyes and penetrated into his brain. Goliath fell dead and his army was put to flight. David cut off his head . . . which he brought to Saul. He said, 'Give me what you have promised!' Saul, however, regretted his promise to him. He therefore said, 'The daughters of kings must have a large dowry. You are a brave and daring man; bring therefore as her dowry three hundred foreskins of our enemies.' Saul hoped that David would be killed in this quest. David, however, raided and captured three hundred men; he circumcised them and brought their foreskins to Saul [cf. 1 Sam. 18:25–27]. But Saul again wished to revoke his promise; he therefore sought to kill David. David fled from him to the mountains, but Saul besieged him. One night, both Saul and his guards fell into a deep sleep. David came down upon

them and took the pitcher from which Saul used to drink and with which he used to perform his ablutions. He also cut off some hairs from Saul's beard and the hem of his garment. Returning to his place, David then called out to Saul, "You see how you and your guards fell asleep! Had I wished to kill you last night, I would have been able to do so." Wahb was asked, "Was Saul a prophet who received revelation from God?" He answered, "No revelation came to him; rather, he had a prophet called Samuel who received revelation" (Tabari, V, pp. 355–357).

According to Shi'i tradition, a prophet or imam inheriting the position of another prophet must be able to use the armor of that prophet as one of the signs of his election. Thus Qummi relates on the authority of al-Sadiq, "God revealed to the prophet of the Children of Israel that 'the armor of Moses will fit the one who will kill Goliath. He is a man of the tribe of Levi, son of Jacob, whose name is David, son of Asa [Jesse].' Asa was a shepherd who had ten sons, the youngest of whom was David. Thus when Saul was appointed king over the Children of Israel and gathered men for battle with Goliath, he sent to Asa, saying, 'Bring your sons.' When they came, he called them one after another to try on the armor of Moses. Some found it too long, others too short. He then asked Asa if he had left any one of his sons behind. David was called, and he came with a sling. On his way three stones called out to him, 'O David take us!' He picked them up and put them in his sack. David was a strong man with a powerful body; he was exceedingly brave. When he came to Saul, he put on the armor of Moses and it fit him" (Qummi, I, p. 82).

As a prophet, David must also manifest a miracle; hence the three stones calling out to him and his use of them in killing the powerful foe Goliath. Qummi thus continues, "David came and faced Goliath, who was on his elephant. He had a crown on his head and a dazzling sapphire on his forehead. He was flanked by his soldiers. David took one of the three stones and slung it into the right wing of Goliath's army. As it fell in their midst, they all took to flight. He took another stone and slung it into the left wing. The man likewise ran away as the stone fell into their midst. He then slung the third stone at Goliath. It hit him in the forehead, driving the sapphire into his brain. Thus he fell dead instantly" (Qummi, I, p. 82).

Early *tafsir* masters differed regarding the things which God taught David. Thus by "wisdom" is meant, according to most commentators, the prophethood which David inherited from Samuel. God also taught him the making of garments, as the Qur'an says, "We taught him the making of garments for you which would protect you while you fight in battle" (Q. 21:80). (Tabari, V, p. 371.) Others said, "Wisdom means that God taught him matters of religion and whatever He willed of worldly matters such as the making of armor, for iron used to become in his hands as malleable as wax. Still others said that God taught him the Psalms and the art of judging among men; He also taught him the language of birds and ants. It is also said that this refers to his beautiful voice and music" (Tabarsi, II, pp. 291–292).

The phrase, "Had God not repelled some people by others, the earth would have been corrupted," was given an esoteric interpretation by some early authorities of *tafsir*. Ibn Kathir relates on the authority of Jabir ibn 'Abdallah al-Ansari that the Apostle of God said, "Surely God renders righteous through the righteousness of a Muslim his offspring and the offspring of his offspring and the people of his house and those of other homes around him. They shall all remain under the protection of God as long as he is among them." A similar tradition is also related on the authority of Ibn 'Umar. It is related on the authority of Thawban, one of the Companions, that the Apostle of God said, "Seven men shall remain among you; through them you shall be granted victory, you shall receive rain from heaven, and shall be granted sustenance until the decree of God comes." In another tradition related on the authority of Qatadah, the Prophet is said to have declared, "The substitutes or successors [*abdal*] in my community are thirty. Through them you are given sustenance, through them you receive rain, and through them you are granted victory" (Ibn Kathir, I, p. 538).

In Shi'i tradition this phrase is given an expiatory interpretation. Qummi relates on the authority of the sixth imam that "God protects those of our community [Shi'ah] who do not observe regular prayers through those who pray. Were they all to concur on abandoning prayers, they would perish. God likewise protects those of our community who neglect the obligatory alms [*zakat*] through those who do. Were they all to concur on abandoning *zakat*, they would perish. God also protects those of our community who neglect the pilgrimage through those who perform it. Were they all to agree on abandoning the pilgrimage, they would perish" (Qummi, I, pp. 83–84).

252. These are the revelations of God; we recite them to you with truth, for you [Muhammad] are surely one of the messengers.

253. These are the Apostles; we have favored some of them over others. Among them was one who spoke to God directly; others He raised to high stations. To Jesus son of Mary we gave clear manifestations and fortified him with the Holy Spirit. Had God so willed, those who came after them would not have fought among themselves after manifest signs had come to them, but they disagreed; some of them had faith and others were rejecters. Had God willed, they would not have fought, but God does whatever He wills.

254. O you who have faith, give in alms of that which we have bestowed upon you before a day comes on which there will be neither barter nor friendship nor intercession. The rejecters of faith are truly wrongdoers.

(253) Shi'i tradition has used the last part of this verse, "Had God so willed, those who came after them would not have fought among themselves" to justify the Battle of the Camel (36/656), which 'Ali fought against some of the Companions of the Prophet. Qummi relates that a man came to 'Ali on the Day of the Camel asking, "On what grounds do you fight against the Companions of the Prophet of God and those who bear witness that there is no god but God and that Muhammad is the Apostle of God?" 'Ali answered, "A verse in the Book of God has made fighting against them lawful for me." He then recited the verse in question. The man exclaimed, "By God! These men have indeed rejected faith" (Qummi, I, p. 84; see also Tabarsi, II, p. 295; and Tabataba'i, II, pp. 309–327).

255. God! There is no god but He, the Everliving, the Eternal Sovereign. Neither slumber nor sleep seizes Him. To Him belongs all that is in the heavens and in the earth. Who is there that shall intercede with Him, save by His leave? He knows all that is present with them and that which is to come upon them, but they comprehend nothing of His knowledge save what He wills. His Throne encompasses the heavens and the earth, and the preservation of them

does not burden Him. He is the Most High, the Most
Great.

256. There is no compulsion in religion. Rectitude has become
distinguished from manifest deceit. Thus he who rejects
faith in idols and has faith in God shall take hold of the
firm handle which shall never be broken, for God is all-
hearing, all-knowing.

257. God is the protector of those who have faith. He shall
lead them out of darkness into light. But as for those
who have rejected faith, their masters are idols; they shall
lead them out of the light into darkness. These are the
people of the Fire; in it they shall abide forever.

(255) This verse, known as the Throne Verse (*Ayat al-Kursi*), is
regarded by Muslims as one of the most excellent verses of the
Qur'an. It has therefore played a very important role in Muslim
piety. Moreover, because of its imagery, the verse has been the
subject of a great deal of theological and exegetical controversy. It
has as well evoked much mystical thought and feeling through the
lyrical beauty of its language. These qualities have no doubt given
it the prominent place it occupies in the intellectual and pietistic
life of Musim society.

Qurtubi relates that the Throne Verse was revealed at night and
that the Prophet immediately sent for Zayd ibn Thabit to write it
down. He relates further on the authority of Muhammad ibn al-
Hanafiyah, "When the Throne Verse was revealed, every idol and
king in the world fell prostrate and the crowns of kings fell off their
heads. Satans fled, colliding with one another in confusion until they
came to Iblis [their chief]. . . . He sent them to find out what
happened, and when they came to Medina they were told that the
Throne Verse had been sent down" (Qurtubi, II, p. 268).

There are many traditions related from the Prophet which proclaim
the excellences of this verse. Qurtubi relates that the Prophet asked
Ubayy one day, "O Abu al-Mundhir! Do you know which of the
verses of the Book of God in your possession is the greatest?" Ubayy
said, "God and His Apostle know best." The Prophet repeated the
question, and Ubayy answered, "God! There is no god but He, the
Everliving, the Eternal Sovereign." The Prophet struck Ubayy in the
chest and exclaimed, "You possess true knowledge . . . by Him in

whose Hand is my soul, this verse has a tongue and two lips with which it sanctifies the King at the foot of the Throne" (Qurtubi, II, p. 268).

Tabarsi relates on the authority of 'Abdallah ibn 'Umar that the Prophet said, "Whoever recites the Throne Verse after a prescribed prayer, the Lord of Majesty Himself shall receive his soul at death. He would be as though he had fought with the Prophet of God until he was martyred." In a similar tradition related on the authority of 'Ali, he said, "I heard your Prophet on this pulpit say, 'Whoever recites the Throne Verse after every prescribed prayer, nothing will stand between him and Paradise except death. No one observes its recitation but a righteous or worshipful person. Whoever recites it when retiring to sleep, God would grant him safety; He would also grant it to his neighbor and his neighbor's neighbor.'" 'Ali also said, "I heard the Apostle of God say, 'O 'Ali! The master of humankind is Adam, the master of the Arabs is Muhammad, nor is there pride in this. The master of the Persians is Salman, the master of the Rum [Byzantines] is Suhayb [a Christian convert among the Companions of the Prophet], and the master of Abyssinia is Bilal. The master of the mountains is al-Tur [Mt. Sinai] and the master of trees is al-Sidr [the lote tree]. The master[s] of the months are the sacred months and the master of the days is Friday. The master of all speech is the Qur'an, the master of the Qur'an is *Surat al-Baqarah*, and the master of *al-Baqarah* is the Throne Verse. O 'Ali, it consists of fifty words, every word containing fifty blessings'" (Tabarsi, II, p. 299).

Anas ibn Malik related that the Prophet said, "God revealed to Moses, 'Whoever continues to recite the Throne Verse after every prayer, on him will I bestow more than that granted to those who are ever thankful. His reward shall be as great as that of prophets and that granted the righteous for their good deeds. I shall spread over him my right hand in mercy. Nothing would hinder him from entering Paradise, except the coming of the angel of death to him.' Moses said, 'My Lord, how can anyone hear this and not continue to observe it?' God said, 'I grant this to no one except a prophet, a righteous person, a man I love, or a man I wish to be slain in my way'" (Qurtubi, II, p. 270). Qurtubi relates that the Throne Verse is called in the Torah the Friend [*waliyah*] of God. Its reciter in the celestial and terrestrial domains is called *'aziz* [meaning one who is dear, mighty or noble]" (Qurtubi, II, p. 269).

Like the *Fatihah*, and especially the *basmallah*, the Throne Verse is said to possess powers of protection for human beings against evil or malevolent spirits. It is related that 'Umar ibn al-Khattab one day wrestled with a creature of the *jinn*, whom he vanquished. The *jinni* said, "Let me go and I will teach you that which would protect you from us." Having been released, he continued, "You may be protected from us by the Throne Verse" (Qurtubi, II, p. 269).

Commentators have differed with regard to the meaning of the word *kursi*. (I have rendered this word 'throne' in accordance with the dominant view of commentators, as well as the accepted usage of Western scholarship) In some traditions, the *kursi* is depicted as an actual object containing the heavens and the earth and as independent of the Throne (*'arsh*). In other traditions, it is identified with it. Tabari reports a number of traditions from the Companions dealing with the identity and location of the *kursi*. He relates on the authority of Abu Musa al-Ash'ari, "The *kursi* is the place of the two feet [footstool of God]. It has a squeaking sound like that of a new saddle." According to al-Suddi and al-Dahhak, "The heavens and the earth are inside the *kursi* and the *kursi* is before the Throne. It is His footstool." Al-Rabi' reported that the Companions of the Prophet said to him when this verse was revealed, "O Apostle of God, if this *kursi* encompasses the heavens and the earth, how big then is the Throne?" Ibn Zayd reported that the Apostle of God said, "The seven heavens are contained in the *kursi* just as seven coins placed in a shield." Abu Dharr said, "I heard the Apostle of God say, 'The *kursi* is in the Throne; it is no more than an iron ring placed in a large empty space in the earth'" (Tabari, V, p. 398).

According to al-Dahhak and Hasan al-Basri, the *kursi* is the Throne. It is related that a woman came to the Prophet and asked that he pray God to make her enter Paradise. In the course of his supplications, the Prophet said, "Surely His *kursi* encompasses the heavens and the earth. He sits upon it, and not even the span of four fingers of it remains unoccupied. . . . It has a squeaking sound like that of a new saddle when ridden by a heavy person" (Tabari, V, p. 400).

Sa'id ibn Jubayr related on the authority of Ibn 'Abbas that the *kursi* here means God's knowledge. Tabari accepts this view and comments, "This may be proved by His saying, 'And the preservation of them does not burden Him,' which means that He is not burdened by the preservation of that which His knowledge encompasses, which is all that is in the heavens and the earth. God also said of His angels that they say in their prayers, 'Our Lord, You encompass all things in mercy and knowledge'" (Q. 40:7). (Tabari, V, p. 401.)

Shi'i tradition reflects similar popular ideas regarding the *kursi*. Tabarsi relates that the fifth imam was asked whether the *kursi* or the heavens and the earth are larger. He answered, "No, it is the *kursi* which contains the heavens and the earth, and everything which God created is contained in the *kursi*." 'Ali, the first imam, was asked about the meaning of the phrase, "His throne encompasses the heavens and the earth." He said, "The heavens and earth and all the creatures therein are contained in the *kursi*. Four angels bear it by God's leave. The first angel has a human image; it is the noblest image before God. He invokes God continuously and intercedes for human beings, praying for their sustenance. The second angel is in the image of a bull who invokes God continuously, interceding for all domestic animals and praying for their sustenance. The third angel is in the image of an eagle which is the lord of all birds. He invokes God and intercedes for all birds and prays for their sustenance. The fourth is in the image of a lion which is the king of beasts. In his devotion to God he intercedes and prays for the sustenance of all wild beasts. The most beautiful of all these was the image of the bull; it was of the best stature. When, however, the people of the Children of Israel took the calf for a god which they worshiped with devotion instead of God, the angel . . . bowed his head in shame before God because man had worshiped something resembling him. He feared lest he be afflicted with punishment." Tabarsi further reports that the fifth imam said, "Whoever recites the Verse of the Throne once, God shall spare him a thousand afflictions in this world and a thousand in the world to come; the lightest of those [afflictions] in this world is poverty, and in the next the punishment of the grave" (Tabarsi, II, p. 300).

Ibn 'Arabi declares the Throne Verse to be the greatest in the Qur'an because of its profundity. He agrees with those commentators who interpret the word *kursi* to mean knowledge. He goes further, however, and asserts, "The *kursi* is the locus of knowledge as the heart is the locus of knowledge. Abu Yazid al-Bistami said, 'Were the world and all that is in it to fall a thousand thousand times into a corner of the heart of the gnostic ['arif] he would not feel it because of the spaciousness of his heart.' For this reason Hasan al-Basri said, 'The [concept] *kursi* of His throne is taken from the Prophet's saying, "The heart of the man of faith is of the throne of God."' The word *kursi* denotes a small footstool which cannot be separated from the seat of the Throne. It is like the heart both as imagined and portrayed in its greatness and magnitude. But as for the greatest and most glorious Throne, it is the first spirit and its image. Their ideal form is present in the eighth and greatest sphere, which encompasses the seven heavens and all that is in them."

Ibn 'Arabi interprets the phrase, "the preservation of them does not burden Him," to mean "their preservation does not burden Him because they have no existence without Him so that their preservation may be a burden on Him. Rather the realm of the ideal form is His inner dimension and the realm of forms is His outer dimension. They have no existence except in Him. Nor are they other than He. He is the Most High, higher than whom is nothing—He is above everything. He dominates everything within the great annihilation. His greatness is beyond imagination, and the greatness of anything that can be imagined is no more than a drop of His greatness. Absolute greatness belongs to Him alone and to no one else" (Ibn 'Arabi, I, p. 143).

Zamakhshari declares with regard to the *kursi*, "It is no more than an image expressing God's greatness. In reality, there is neither *kursi*, an act of sitting, nor one who sits" (Zamakhshari, I, p. 385). Zamakhshari sees the entire verse as an affirmation of God's oneness. He thus argues, "The *surah* of Sincere Faith [*al-Ikhlas*] is declared to be excellent because of what it contains concerning God's unity, His exaltation and glorification and His great attributes. For there is no one more worthy of mention than the Lord of Majesty. Thus whatever may be said in remembrance of Him is greater than all remembrances. This means that the highest and noblest of all branches is the knowledge of the people of justice and divine unity [the Mu'tazilah]. Let not the multiplicity of their foes tempt you away from it" (Zamakhshari, I, p. 387).

Other commentators have been critical of anthropomorphic interpretations of the verse under discussion. Razi, after reviewing various interpretations, cites the famous exegete al-Qaffal with approval, "The words, 'His Throne encompasses the heavens and the earth,' are meant to describe God's greatness and exaltation through images. This means that God addressed His creatures in ways familiar to them through their own kings in order that He might make know His essence and attributes to them. He therefore made the Kaaba a house for Himself, and people circumambulate it as they do the houses of their kings. It is also said that the Black Stone is the right hand of God on this earth; thus He made it an object of reverent kissing, as men would kiss the hands of their kings. Hence by analogy He declared a throne for Himself through His saying, 'The All-merciful sat upon the Throne' [Q. 20:5]. . . . Likewise, He declared a *kursi* for Himself in His saying, 'His throne encompasses the heavens and the earth'" (Razi, VII, pp. 2-14; see also Nisaburi, III, p. 18; and Ibn Kathir, I, pp. 541-551).

Sayyid Qutb agrees with Razi and Zamakhshari in taking the phrase, "His throne encompasses the heavens and the earth," metaphorically. He writes, "Expression by means of concrete imagery is used here in place of absolute freedom from anthropomorphism, in the usual manner of Qur'anic expression through images. This is because the picture here employed gives the reality, which is metaphorically presented to the heart with power, depth, and firmness. Thus the word *kursi* is normally used to refer to dominion. Therefore, 'His throne encompasses the heavens and the earth' means that His authority encompasses them. This is reality from the intellectual point of view, but the picture which is impressed on the mind through the use of concrete imagery is stronger and firmer. Likewise, the expression, 'And the preservation of them does not burden Him,' is a metaphor for absolute power. It is presented, however, as concrete imagery; the imagery of the total absence of effort and fatigue. This is because the trend in the Qur'anic expression is toward painting a picture of the actual meaning to the mind so as to be more immediate, deeper, and more powerfully felt. There is therefore no need for all the debate that has raged around such expressions in the Qur'an, if we understand the way in which the Qur'an uses symbols and metaphors, and if we do not borrow the foreign and strange philosophical ideas which have distorted for us much of the simplicity and clarity of the Qur'an. It is well that I note here the fact that I have not come across any sound *hadith* concerning the *kursi* and Throne which would explain and determine what is actually intended in the Qur'an by such words. For this reason I prefer not to enter into greater detail than is here given" (Qutb, I, pp. 323-324).

(256) Commentators have differed with regard to the occasion of the revelation of this verse. Wahidi relates on the authority of Sa'id ibn Jubayr, who related it on the authority of Ibn 'Abbas, "When the children of a woman of the Ansar all died in infancy, she vowed that if a child were to live, she would bring it up as a Jew. Thus when the Jewish tribe of al-Nadir was evicted from Medina [4/625], there were among them sons of the Ansar. The Ansar said, 'O Apostle of God, what will become of our children!' Thus God sent

down this verse." Sa'id ibn Jubayr said, "Therefore whoever wished to join them did so, and whoever wished to enter Islam did so likewise." According to Mujahid, this verse was sent down concerning a man who had a black male servant called Subayh. The man wished to compel him to enter Islam. Al-Suddi said that the verse was sent down concerning a man of the Ansar known as Abu-al-Husayn, who had two sons. One day merchants from Syria came to Medina to sell oil. The sons of Abu al-Husayn came to the merchants, who converted them to Christianity. They then went to Syria with the merchants. When Abu al-Husayn knew this, he came to the Prophet and asked, "Shall I pursue them?" God then sent down, "There is no compulsion in religion." The Apostle of God said, "May God banish them! They are the first two who rejected faith." Mujahid said, "This was before the Apostle of God was commanded to fight against the People of the Book. God's saying, 'There is no compulsion in religion' was abrogated and he was commanded to fight against the People of the Book in *Surat Bara'ah*" (Q. 9:29).(Wahidi, pp. 77–78.)

Wahidi relates further that Masruq said, "A man of the Ansar had two sons, who became Christians before God sent the Prophet. The two sons came to Medina in a group of Christians carrying edible goods. Their father attached himself to them, saying, 'I shall not leave you until you become Muslims,' but they refused. They came to the Apostle of God accusing their father. The man said, 'O Apostle of God! Should a part of me enter the Fire while I look on?' Thus God sent down, 'There is no compulsion in religion'" (Wahidi, pp. 78–79; see also Tabari, V, pp. 407–408; and Qurtubi, II, p. 280). Ibn Kathir reports the same tradition concerning the occasion of the revelation of this verse but adds that its injunction of legal application is general. He thus disagrees with the view of relating the verse to any particular persons or group of people (Ibn Kathir, I, pp. 551–552).

According to other traditions, the verse was revealed in reference to the People of the Book, who should not be compelled to enter Islam so long as they pay the *jizyah* (poll tax). The verse is, therefore, not abrogated. Tabari relates on the authority of Qatadah, "Arab society was compelled to enter Islam because they were an unlettered community [*ummah ummiyah*], having no book which they knew. Thus nothing other than Islam was accepted from them. The People of the Book are not to be compelled to enter Islam if they submit to paying the *jizyah* or *kharaj* [land tax]." The same view is related on the authority of al-Dahhak, Mujahid, and Ibn 'Abbas (Tabari, V, pp. 413–414). Tabari agrees with this view and asserts that the verse applies to the people of the two Books (Jews and Christians) and the Zoroastrians (Majus).

Qurtubi relates that Ibn Zayd ibn Aslam related on the authority of his father that he heard 'Umar ibn al-Khattab say to an old woman, "Become a Muslim, old woman, so that you may be safe [that is, from the Fire], for God sent Muhammad with the truth." She answered, "I am an old woman and death is near at hand." 'Umar said, "O God, bear witness!" and recited, "There is no compulsion in religion." Qurtubi relates yet another view which asserts, "It was in reference to captives who, if they are of the People of the Book, are not to be compelled if they are adults; but if they are Zoroastrians or idolators, be they old or young, they shall be forced to accept Islam. This is because their master could not benefit from them if they were idolators." Qurtubi adds, "Do you not see that animals slaughtered by them would be unlawful to eat and their women could not be married [to Muslims]? They practise the eating of carrion and other such unclean things. Thus their master would find them unclean and therefore it would be difficult to benefit from them as his slaves. Hence it becomes lawful for him to compel them" (Qurtubi, II, p. 280; see also Shawkani, I, p. 275).

Razi cites with some approval the view of al-Qaffal and Abu Muslim, which, he observes, is worthy of Mu'tazili fundamentals (usul) of jurisprudence. He comments, "This means that God did not rest the matter of faith on compulsion and coercion, but rather based it on free will and the ability to choose." He then argues, "This is what is intended here when God made clear the proofs of divine oneness [tawhid]. He said that there is no longer any excuse for a rejecter of faith to persist in his rejection. That he should be forced to accept faith is not lawful in this world, which is a world of trial. For in coercion and compulsion in the matter of faith is the annulment of the meaning of trial and test. This may be supported by God's saying, 'Rectitude has become distinguished from manifest deceit,' meaning proofs have become manifest and elucidations clearly proclaimed. There is nothing left but the way of coercion, submission, and compulsion. This, however, is not lawful because it contradicts the precepts of obligation [taklif]" (Razi, VII, p. 15; see also Zamakhshari, I, p. 387).

Sayyid Qutb argues that Islam, first in contrast with the Roman persecutions of Christians and second with the Christian empire under Constantine, asserts that there is to be no compulsion in the matter of faith. In this principle Sayyid Qutb sees "the manifestation of God's favor toward man. [In it lies] his dignity and respect for his free will, his thinking, and sentiments. The decision is left to him with regard to the matter of guidance and error in belief. He is responsible for the consequences of his deeds. This is the highest degree of human freedom. Freedom of belief is one of the primary rights of man; thus whoever deprives a human being of his freedom of belief, deprives him essentially of his humanity. Freedom of belief includes the freedom to propagate one's faith. It includes also security against harm and sedition; otherwise it is freedom in name only, having no meaning in real life.

"Islam is itself the highest expression of life and being, and is without doubt the best system for human society. It is the system which asserts that 'there is no compulsion in religion.' It is the system which declares to its adherents, before any others, that they are forbidden to coerce men into accepting this faith. The expression is here couched in the form of absolute negation, 'No compulsion in religion.' The narrative does no more than touch human conscience in a way that quickens it and fires it with longing for guidance. It guides it to the way, elucidating the truth of faith which God declares to be clear, as He says, 'Rectitude has become distinguished from manifest deceit.' Faith is the guidance which man must strive for and preserve. Rejection of faith [*kufr*] is the error from which man must flee and by which he must avoid being marked" (Qutb, I, pp. 425–426).

Commentators have differed regarding the meaning of the word *taghut* (idols). This word is usually coupled with the word *al-jibt*. Tabari interprets the word *taghut* to mean satans, idols, or soothsayers (*kuhhan*) to whom satans come and reveal lies and wickedness. Tabari takes the word in its general sense to mean all of these and anything else that may be worshiped instead of God (Tabari, V, pp. 416–419). Ibn Kathir reports on the authority of 'Umar ibn al-Khattab that *al-jibt* is sorcery and *taghut* is Satan (Ibn Kathir, I, p. 553). Zamakhshari explains *taghut* as either Satan or idols (Zamakhshari, I, p. 387). Shawkani, citing al-Jawhari, a well-known lexicographer, says that "*taghut* is the soothsayer, Satan, or every leader into error." Shawkani adds idols as well (Shawkani, I, pp. 275–276). Tabarsi relates on the authority of the sixth imam that *taghut* is Satan. He concludes, "It is intended that anyone who rejects faith by opposing God's command" is *taghut* (Tabarsi, II, p. 307).

Another word whose meaning commentators have argued is the word '*urwah* (handle). Tabari reports that according to Mujahid, '*urwah* here means *iman* (faith). According to al-Suddi, it is Islam. Finally, Sa'id ibn Jubayr and al-Dahhak interpreted the word more specifically to mean the *shahadah* (witness) that there is no god but God. Tabari includes all these views in his explanation. "The phrase, 'Thus he who rejects faith in idols and has faith in God' means that he holds, through obedience to God, to that which protects him so that he never fears being abandoned by God. When he needs Him on the day of resurrection with its terrors, his submission [*islam*] to Him is like holding onto the strongest of handles which fear can never break" (Tabari, V, pp. 421–422).

258. Have you [Muhammad] considered him who disputed with Abraham concerning his Lord, after God had given him the kingdom, when he said, "My Lord is He who brings to life and causes to die." He said, "I give life and I cause to die!" He [Abraham] said, "God causes the sun to rise from the east, so cause it to rise from the west!" whereupon he who had rejected faith was confounded. God guides not the wrongdoers.

259. Or the case of the man who passed by a town which had been destroyed to it foundations. He said, "How shall God bring this town back to life after its death?" God caused him to die for one hundred years, then raised him up, then said to him, "How long have you remained here?" He said, "A day or part of a day." He said, "Not so! Look at your food and drink, how they have not aged, and look at your donkey! We shall surely make you a sign for humankind. Look at these bones, how we set them up, then clothed them with flesh." When all this was made clear to him, he said, "Now I know that God has power over all things."

260. And remember when Abraham said, "My Lord, show me how You raised the dead." He said, "Do you not have faith?" He said, "Yes, but only that my heart may rest at ease." He said, "Take four birds, cut them into pieces and place a part of each on a different mountain. Then

call them to you; they shall come to you in haste." Know
therefore that God is mighty and wise.

(258) The man who disputed with Abraham was, according to
most commentators, Nimrud (Nimrod), son of Kanʿan. It is related
on the authority of Qatadah, al-Rabiʿ ibn Anas, and others, "The
man who disputed with Abraham concerning his Lord was a king
called Nimrod. He was the first to act arrogantly in the earth and
was moreover the one who built the Tower of Babel" (Tabari, V,
p. 430).

The story of Abraham and Nimrod has been related on the
authority of many *tafsir* masters. Tabari relates on the authority of
Zayd ibn Aslam, "The first tyrant to act arrogantly in the earth was
Nimrod. People used to go to him to obtain food. When they came
to him he asked, 'Who is your Lord?' They answered, 'You are!'
But when Abraham came, Nimrod asked him, 'Who is your Lord?'
Abraham answered, 'He who gives life and causes to die.' Nimrod
retorted, 'I give life and cause to die!' Abraham said, 'God causes
the sun to rise from the east, so cause it to rise from the west!'
Nimrod thus sent Abraham away without food. On his way to his
family, Abraham passed by some red sand. He said to himself, 'Let
me take some of this and bring it to my family, so that they would
be happy at least when I come to them.' Having reached home, he
put down his belongings and fell asleep. His wife meanwhile opened
the sack and found the best food ever seen by anyone. She prepared
a meal for him of that food and brought it before him. When he
had left his family, they had no food to eat. Thus he asked, 'Where
is this from?' His wife answered, 'This is the food you brought.'
Abraham knew that God had bestowed sustenance upon him, and
he thanked God.

"God then sent down to the tyrant an angel, saying, 'Have faith
in me and I will keep you over your kingdom.' Nimrod answered,
'Is there any lord besides me?' The angel returned a second and a
third time to him, but still he refused. Then the angel said, 'Gather
your armies together within three days.' When the tyrant had gathered
his armies, God commanded the angel to release against them a
pestilence of flies. There were so many flies that when the sun rose,
they could not see it. God sent the flies against them so that they
ate their flesh and drank their blood, leaving nothing but bones.
The king, however, was spared. Then God sent against him one fly
which entered into his nostril. He remained thus [the fly eating his

brain] for four hundred years, and the people used to beat his head with hammers trying to kill the fly or drive it out. The most compassionate man toward him was one who clasped his hands together and hit him over the head with them. He practised tyranny for four hundred years, so God punished him for the duration of his reign, after which he died. He was the one who built a tower reaching heaven, but God destroyed this edifice from its foundations. He was the one concerning whom God said, 'and God struck at the edifice from its foundations'" (Q. 16:26). (Tabari, V, pp. 433–434.)

Qummi provides another context for the verse under discussion. "It was that when Nimrod threw Abraham into the fire which God made into coolness and peace for him [see Q. 21:69], Nimrod said, 'O Abraham, who is your Lord?' He answered, 'My Lord is He who brings to life and causes to die.' Then Nimrod said, 'I give life and I cause to die!' Abraham asked him how he could give life and cause to die, and Nimrod answered, 'Bring me two people condemned to death. I shall reprieve one and kill the other; thus would I have given life and caused to die.' Abraham said, 'If you tell the truth, then bring back to life the one you have killed! . . . No matter; my Lord causes the sun to rise from the east, so cause it to rise from the west!' Thus it was that God said, 'Whereupon he who had rejected faith was confounded,' that is, had no argument, because he knew that the sun was more ancient than he" (Qummi, I, p. 86; Tabarsi, II, pp. 312–314; and Tabataba'i, II, pp. 348–368).

Commentators have raised the question as to how God could put in authority over His servants one who is a rejecter of faith and a tyrant. According to Zamakhshari, the kingdom may mean here either that God gave Nimrod wealth and power but no authority over Abraham, or that He gave him the kingdom in order to try other people by him. Nimrod acted arrogantly instead of thanking God for His bounties, hence he is called, in this verse, a rejecter of faith. Zamakhshari explains the king's power to give life and cause to die as do Qummi and most other classical commentators. Zamakhshari speculates further that Abraham may have had this confrontation at the time when he broke the idols (see Q. 21:58). It was then that Nimrod imprisoned Abraham for a time, then brought him out to throw him into the fire. Nimrod said, "Who is your lord to whom you call men?" Abraham answered, "My Lord is He who brings to life and causes to die" (Zamakhshari, I, pp. 388–389).

Razi sees in this verse a proof of God's existence. He therefore rejects the story of the two convicts and presents instead Abraham as a philosopher who vanquished his opponents by means of rational arguments (see Razi, VII, pp. 23-26; and Nisaburi, III, pp. 27-29). Shawkani repeats Zamakhshari's arguments, then reports the accounts of this story as found in earlier commentaries and *hadith* collections (Shawkani, I, pp. 276-278).

Sufi piety has seen in the story of Abraham and the tyrannical monarch an entirely different meaning from that presented by other commentators. Nisaburi relates all the traditions discussed here in interpreting this verse. In his *ta'wil* section he attempts to see Abraham and Nimrod as archetypal men or representatives of different human faculties. Of Nimrod he writes, "When God gave Nimrod dominion, such as He had given to no one before him, Nimrod claimed Lordship which no one before him had claimed. The reason for this is that man has an innate drive for the better. Because of his subtle essence he is perpetually moving toward perfection, not ceasing for one moment except when an obstacle stands in his way. Yet man was created 'wrongdoing and foolish' [Q. 33:72]. When he is left to depend on himself, he inclines toward the material world in accordance with his natural instincts. He was made of dust; therefore his natural inclination is toward the lower world. In this state he sees perfection in accumulating wealth and achieving prestige. Were he to possess all things in the lower world and vanquish all the kings of the earth, still he would wish to strive against the King of kings and the Compellor of compellors. He would say, 'I give life and I cause to die.' This happens when he becomes ignorant of true perfection, when his essence becomes corrupt and his potential misguided. If, however, his essence were to be reformed through the discipline of the Prophet or one who takes his place, that is, the *shaykh*, he would then exclaim, 'There is no one in existence save God.'" Nisaburi then says, addressing the disciple, "Know then that there is no god but God and beg forgiveness for your sins. This means to become annihilated entirely to your existence and beg forgiveness for the sin of reckoning any existence besides His existence. Strive to understand well, but if you are not one who strives well, know that such a one must hammer the brain of the Nimrod of the soul with the hammer of 'There is no god but God' until he accepts faith in God and rejects faith in the idols [*taghut*] of his own existence and that of any existence other than God." (Nisaburi, III, p. 36).

(259) This verse has aroused a great deal of interest among commentators. Some of the questions it raised are: Who was the man

who passed by the ruined city? What city was it? What did the man have with him for food and drink? Was his donkey caused to die and brought back to life? Commentators recounted many tales in their attempt to answer such questions. The purpose of the following discussion is to present examples of such hagiographical stories without distinguishing between Sunni and Shi'i versions, since they both belong to the development of popular Muslim piety.

Commentators have taken this and the previous verse as examples of God's power and sovereignty. The ancient prophet was asked to consider first the man who disputed with Abraham, and his end, and also the case of a man who passed by a town which he found in ruins (see Ibn Kathir, I, p. 558; and Zamakhshari, I, p. 389). Commentators, however, differed as to who the man who passed by the ruined town was. It is related on the authority of 'Ali that he was 'Uzayr (Ezra). (See Ibn Kathir, I, p. 558.) The same view is related by Tabari on the authority of Qatadah, al-Rabi' ibn Anas, al-Suddi, Ibn 'Abbas, and other early masters. According to others, the man was Jeremiah, son of Halqiyah. Tabari relates on the authority of 'Abd al-Samad ibn Ma'qil that he heard Wahb ibn Munabbih say, "When Jerusalem was destroyed and the books [of the Torah] were burned, Jeremiah stood near a mountain and exclaimed, 'How shall God bring this town to life after its death?' According to Ibn Ishaq, Jeremiah was al-Khidr [the mysterious Green Prophet] . . . as Wahb claimed to have heard from the children of Israel" (Tabari, V, p. 439; see also pp. 439–442).

Commentators have also differed as to the town here intended. It is related on the authority of Wahb and Qatadah that it was Jerusalem. Qatadah said, "We were told that it was Jerusalem, over which 'Uzayr stood after it was destroyed by Bukhtnassar [Nebuchadnezzar?] the Babylonian." The same view is related on the authority of 'Ikrimah, al-Dahhak, and al-Rabi' ibn Anas (Tabari, V, pp. 442–443).

Others identify the town here mentioned with that mentioned in verse 243 above. The story of the people who ran away from the plague, as related above, is here also told on the authority of Ibn Zayd (Tabari, V, p. 444). Tabari asserts first that there is no way of knowing who that person was, or by which town he passed. Nor would the knowledge of such facts add to the purpose of the narrative, which is to demonstrate to the people of Quraysh and others who did not believe in the resurrection of the dead God's power of giving life and causing death. Tabari nonetheless relates a number of tales in interpretation of the verse (see Tabari, V, pp. 447–484).

The following story related by Qummi on the authority of the fifth imam is a typical example of the hagiographical tales found in many *tafsir* works. "The Children of Israel committed all manner of rebellion and disobeyed the command of their Lord. God therefore wished to set over them one who would humiliate and massacre them. He thus revealed to Jeremiah, 'O Jeremiah! A town which I chose over all other towns and planted in it the best of trees, has instead sprouted locust trees.' Jeremiah related this to the best among the learned of the Children of Israel, but they said to him, 'Return to your Lord, and ask that He tell us the meaning of this parable.' Jeremiah fasted for thirty days; then God revealed to him, 'O Jeremiah! As for the town, it is Jerusalem. As for what sprouted up in it, these are the Children of Israel, whom I made to dwell in it. They acted rebelliously, altering my faith and rendering my grace rejection of faith. By myself I swear, I shall try them with such trials that a man of intelligence would become distraught. I shall set in power over them one of my servants of the most evil lineage and most foul food and drink. He shall rule over them with tyranny, killing their fighting men and taking their women captive. He shall destroy their homes in which they commit sin and throw their stone with which they pride themselves over men [see above, verse 60] into dung mounds for a hundred years.'

"Jeremiah related all this to the notables of the Children of Israel, who said, 'Return to your Lord and ask Him what is the fault of the destitute, the poor, and the weak!' Jeremiah fasted seven days . . . but nothing was revealed to him. Again he fasted, but nothing was revealed to him. The third time, however, God revealed to him, 'O Jeremiah, either desist [that is, from fasting and praying for revelation] or I shall turn your face into your back.' Then was revealed to Jeremiah, 'It is because you saw evil but did not shun it.' Jeremiah said, 'My Lord, tell me who it is [that is, the tyrannical conquerer] so that I may seek security from him for myself and my household.'" God then told Jeremiah where to find Bukhtnassar. He was then a youth, a child of adultery and afflicted with disease. He found him at an inn in ruins, lying on a pile of rubbish. His mother prostituted herself for morsels of dry bread which she brought to him in a bowl and milked a sow over them in order that the sick youth could eat them. Jeremiah recognized the youth and cared for him until he recovered. Then he said to the boy, "I am Jeremiah, the prophet of the Children of Israel. God told me that He would give you authority over them. You shall kill their men and you shall do with them such-and-such. . . . Write a document of security for me and my household." This he did.

Bukhtnassar finally conquered the Holy City and spared Jeremiah in accordance with their agreement. In the middle of the city, he found a sandhill in the middle of which hot blood rose up continuously. He was told, "This is the blood of a prophet of God whom the king of the Children of Israel killed. His blood boils continuously, no matter how we cover it with sand." Bukhtnassar said, "I shall continue to kill the Children of Israel until this blood calms down." The blood was that of Yahya (John the Baptist), son of Zechariah. He lived during the reign of a tyrannical king of the Children of Israel, who committed adultery with the women of the people. John the Baptist reproached the king for his evil deeds. One of the women with whom the king fornicated requested that John be killed. His head was thus brought to her on a tray, but it continued to reproach the king. The blood bubbled up and onto the ground and continued to do so for a hundred years until the conquest of Bukhtnassar.

Bukhtnassar continued to kill the Children of Israel, men, women, children, and even beasts, but the blood continued to boil. Finally he found an old woman; as soon as he killed her, the blood calmed down. The tradition then recounts the story of Daniel and the fall of Nebuchadnezzar (see Dan. 1–4).

After all this Jeremiah went out on the donkey and saw birds and beasts eating the corpses of those killed by Bukhtnassar. He stood and reflected for a while, then said, "How shall God bring this town back to life after its death?" God caused him to die where he stood, as He says, "Or the case of the man who passed by a town which had been destroyed to its foundations" (Qummi, I, pp. 89–91; for another version of this story, see Nisaburi, II, pp. 29–33).

It is related that the food which was with the prophet was green figs and his drink a pitcher of wine or water (see Qurtubi, II, p. 289). The prophet saw that his food and drink were still as fresh as they were a hundred years before. Yet his donkey had decomposed into a skeleton of dry bones. Commentators have differed as to the bones which were raised before the prophet's eyes. According to al-Suddi and others, they were the bones of his donkey. Thus the verse would read, "look at the bones of your donkey." According to al-Dahhak, Qatadah and al-Rabi‘, they were his own bones. These commentators asserted that God first revived his eyes, which were like the whites of an egg. Thus he witnessed how his own bones and those of his donkey were clothed with flesh and how he and it rose to their feet. When he returned to his land, he found his grandchildren old men and women, whereas when he had left their fathers were young men (Tabarsi, II, p. 319).

Tabarsi also relates that when 'Uzayr, who was the prophet in question, returned to his land, he found that Bukhtnassar had burned the books of the Torah. But he dictated it all from memory. "A man of the Children of Israel said, 'I was told by my father that he heard from his father that Ezra had previously buried the Torah in a vineyard.' He said to the people, 'If you show me the vineyard of my grandfather, I will be able to bring out the Torah for you.' They led him to it and when he unearthed the Torah, they compared it with his version, and the text did not differ even one letter from his [Ezra's] dictation. They thus said, 'God did not deposit the Torah in the heart of anyone, except that he be His son.' They therefore claimed that 'Uzayr was the son of God'" (see Q. 9:30) (Tabarsi, II, p. 320).

In contrast with the tales commentators wove around this verse, Nisaburi, after quoting a number of them, presents an esoteric exegesis of the verse. He begins by arguing that this verse and the ones before and after it are meant to confound the philosophers who deny the resurrection of the body. This they do on the grounds that when the soul leaves the body, having gained in knowledge and discipline, it would not return to such a prison after its freedom. Nisaburi then interprets 'Uzayr and his donkey as the spiritual and corporeal aspects of the human individual.

"God caused 'Uzayr and his donkey to die for a hundred years, then revived them both in order that it may be known that as God revived the 'Uzayr of the spirit, so did he also revive the donkey of the body. Furthermore, as the 'Uzayr of the spirit may be in the presence of the King of Majesty, so also the donkey of the body may be in gardens beneath which rivers flow. The 'Uzayr of the spirit shall have a drink of the cups of the manifestation [*tajalli*] of the attributes of majesty and beauty, as supported by 'Their Lord shall give them to drink a pure drink' [Q. 86:21], and the Prophet's saying, 'I spend the night with my Lord and He gives me to eat and drink.' The donkey of the body shall have in store a green pasture in the gardens and sweet springs of water from which to drink, 'all that souls desire, all that delights the eyes'" (Q. 43:71).

Nisaburi concludes with a lyric, "We drank, and spilled on the earth its portion; For the earth shall have its share in the cup of those who are magnanimous" (Nisaburi, III, p. 37).

(260) Muslim tradition holds prophets to be protected (*ma'sumun*, pl. of *ma'sum*) by God from error and unbelief. The problem that occupied commentators in this verse is Abraham's request that God show him how He revives the dead and God's challenge, "Do you not have faith?" Why, then, did Abraham ask that question; was it an expression of doubt or a request that God demonstrate His power in granting His friend Abraham a miracle as proof against Nimrod? Wahidi relates a number of traditions illustrating possible answers. He relates on the authority of Qatadah that Abraham saw a dead animal being devoured by the beasts of the land and the fish of the sea. According to Ibn Jurayj, it was the carcass of a donkey by the seashore, or, according to 'Ata', by the shores of the sea of Tiberius. "Thus when the tide came in, the fish of the sea came and ate of it; hence some of it fell into the sea. When the tide went out, beasts came and ate of it; hence some of it fell on dry land and became dust. When the beasts left, birds came and ate of it; hence some of it was carried away and scattered by the wind. When Abraham saw this, he marveled and said, 'O Lord, I know that You shall gather this beast together, but show me how You shall bring it back to life.'" According to Ibn Zayd, it was a whale which Abraham saw being devoured by beasts and fish. Satan came to him saying, "How can God gather together all these parts from the stomachs of these?" Thus Abraham said, "My Lord, show me how You raised the dead." God said, "Do you not have faith?" Abraham answered, "Yes, but only that my heart may rest at ease, after the departure of the whisperings of Satan from it." Wahidi further relates on the authority of Ibn 'Abbas, Sa'id ibn Jubayr, and al-Suddi, "When God made Abraham His Friend [*Khalil*], the angel of death asked permission of his Lord to carry the good news to Abraham. . . . He said to him, 'I come to bring you glad tidings; God has made you His Friend!' Abraham thanked God and said, 'What shall be the sign of this?' The angel answered, 'It shall be that God will answer your prayers and raise the dead by your supplication.' Thus Abraham prayed, 'My Lord, show me how you raise the dead.' God answered, 'Do you not have faith?' Abraham said, 'Yes, but only that my heart may rest at ease in the knowledge that You shall answer me when

I pray to You and grant me what I ask for, and that You have taken me as a Friend'" (Wahidi, pp. 79–81; see also Tabarsi, II, pp. 324–325).

Tabari relates, in addition to the traditions just cited, a statement of Ibn Ishaq that illustrates well the second possibility. Abraham asked to see how God revives the dead "not because of any doubt he had in God and His power, but he wished to know" how God revived the dead. "His heart inclined toward this knowledge, thus he said, 'Yes, but only that my heart may rest at ease.'" (Tabari, V, p. 487). Tabari reports several traditions that interpret Abraham's request as a sign from God that He indeed had taken Abraham for a Friend (*Khalil*). Abraham's wish to see how God revives the dead was prompted by his meeting with the angel of death, as has already been cited. The possibility of doubt nonetheless continued to play an important part in the interpretation of this verse. Thus Ibn 'Abbas is said to have exclaimed, "There is no other verse in the Qur'an more puzzling to me than this one." Abu Hurayrah is said to have reported that the Prophet said, "We are more worthy of doubt than Abraham, for he said, 'My Lord, show me how You raised the dead.'" Tabari prefers this interpretation but argues that doubt was caused by the whisperings of Satan in Abraham's heart (Tabari, V, pp. 489–493; see also Ibn Kathir, I, p. 559).

Later commentators have generally argued against ascribing doubt to Abraham, because doubt is an act of *kufr*, and prophets are protected from both great and small sins. Qurtubi presents the following typical argument. Abraham's request was not an expression of doubt of God's power, but rather it was for the purpose of seeing the actual process of reviving the dead. "Abraham wished to rise from the knowledge of certainty [*'ilm al-yaqin*] to the reality of certainty [*'ayn al-yaqin*]" (Qurtubi, II, p. 299; see also pp. 296–302; Zamakhshari, I, pp. 391–392; Razi, VII, pp. 40–43; Nisaburi, III, pp. 33–35; and Shawkani, I, pp. 281–283).

Commentators have generally asserted that the four birds which God commanded Abraham to cut to pieces were the peacock, the raven, the cock, and the eagle. Nisaburi takes these birds to represent human attributes veiling the lover (the human soul) from the Beloved (God). The Beloved thus addresses His lover, "Take four birds," which means "You are veiled by your self from me. You are veiled by the veil of your attributes from my attributes and by the veil of your essence you are separated from my essence. The more you die to your attributes, the more you shall live in my attributes. For if you become annihilated to your essence you shall have the subsistence of my essence."

Nisaburi then interprets the four birds as the four human qualities which are generated from the four elements of which the human clay was molded. Each element coupled with its mate gives birth to two attributes. From earth and its mate, which is water, come avarice and miserliness, which are mates, always found together. From fire and its mate air come anger and lust. To each of these two attributes belongs a mate with which it dwells. The mate of avarice is envy and the mate of miserliness is rancor. The mate of anger is arrogance. Lust has no special mate; rather it is like a lover among the attributes; each one is attached to it. These four attributes and their three mates are the seven gates to the seven circles of Hell. Hell has seven gates; to every gate belong its special people. Everyone shall enter it in accordance with the attributes most dominant in him. God therefore asked His Friend (*Khalil*) to slay these attributes which are the four birds—the peacock of miserliness, the raven of avarice, the cock of lust, and the eagle of anger. When the Friend slew these birds with the knife of truthfulness and attributes born of them ceased in him, there remained for him no gate by which he could enter the Fire. Hence when he was thrown into it: "Fire became for him coolness and peace" (Q. 21:69).

Nisaburi then explains how these attributes die, each being related to a human faculty symbolized by the four mountains on which Abraham placed the birds. This is the condition of the elect of humanity. Above these there are the elect of the elect, such as Abraham and Muhammad. After they have killed these attributes, God manifests Himself to them in the attribute of Lifegiver (*muhyi*). "God would then revive these annihilated attributes with His attributes of life–giving power. The servant would, in this condition, live in God's life, revived in His attributes, as He said, 'The servant continues to draw near to me through supererogatory prayers [*nawafil*] until I love him. When I love him I shall be his hearing, sight, tongue, and hand. In me he shall hear; in me he shall see; in me he shall speak; and in me he shall grasp'" (Nisaburi, III, pp. 39–40).

261. The similitude of those who spend their wealth in the way of God is like a grain of wheat which sprouts seven ears, in every ear a hundred grains. Thus God bestows

manifold measure on whomsoever He wills, and God is all-encompassing, all-knowing.

262. Those who spend their wealth in the way of God and do not follow what they spend with reproach or hurt shall have their reward from their Lord. No fear will come upon them, nor shall they grieve.

263. A kind word with pardon is better than alms followed by hurt, and God is all-sufficient, clement.

264. O you who have faith, do not annul your alms by re-proach and hurt, like a man who spends his wealth for appearances before men but does not have faith in God and the last day. His similitude is like a hard rock covered with earth; heavy rain, when it falls, leaves it hard. They have no power over that which they earn, for God does not guide aright people who reject faith.

265. But the similitude of those who spend their wealth, desir-ing to please God, and for the affirmation of this in their souls, is like a garden on a hill on which heavy rain falls; it brings forth its fruits twofold. Even if heavy rain does not fall, then dew; and God is all-seeing of that which you do.

266. Would any of you desire to have a garden of palm trees and grapevines beneath which rivers flow and wherein he would have all kinds of fruits? Yet old age strikes him while his children are still weak. Then a whirlwind with fire in it would strike it, and it is consumed. Thus God manifests His signs to you, that you may reflect.

267. O you who have faith, give in alms of the good things which you have gained and of that which we have brought forth of the earth for you. Do not choose the bad part of it to give out in alms, such as you yourselves would accept only by overlooking its defects. Know that God is all-sufficient, worthy of all praise.

268. Satan promises you poverty and enjoins upon abomination, but God promises you forgiveness and bounty from Him, for God is all-encompassing, all-knowing.

269. He grants wisdom to whomsoever He wills, and he who has been given wisdom has received abundant good. Yet none reflect save those who have intelligence.

270. Whatever alms you give or vow you make, God knows it. The wrongdoers shall have no helpers.

271. If you give alms in public, for others to see, it is well; but if you conceal your alms, and give them to the poor, it shall be better for you. Then will He expiate you some of your evil deeds, for God is aware of what you do.

272. It is not incumbent upon you to guide them; rather God guides aright whom He wills. Whatever of good you spend in alms shall be for your souls and you should not spend except in desire of the face of God. Whatever of good you give in alms shall be repaid you, and you shall not be wronged—

273. It being for the poor who have been restrained in the way of God, unable to journey in the earth: those whom the ignorant think to be rich on account of their modesty. You shall know them by their marks: they do not beg men with importunity. Whatever of good you give in alms, God knows it.

274. Those who give of their wealth in alms night and day, secretly and in public, shall have their reward with their Lord. No fear will come upon them, nor shall they grieve.

(262) Wahidi reports that this verse was sent down concerning 'Abd al-Rahman ibn 'Awf and 'Uthman ibn 'Affan, two close but controversial Companions of the Prophet. 'Abd al-Rahman is said to have brought to the Prophet four thousand dirhams, saying, "I had eight thousand dirhams, four thousand I have kept for me and my family and four I wish to lend to my Lord" (see above, verse 245). The Prophet answered, "May God bless for you both what

you withheld and what you gave." As for 'Uthman, he contributed a thousand camels loaded with goods for the Battle of Tabuk (9/630). Wahidi reports that Abu Sa'id al-Khudri, a famous Companion and traditionist, said, "I saw the Apostle of God lifting his hands to heaven and praying for 'Uthman, saying, 'O Lord, I am well-pleased with 'Uthman ibn 'Affan; may you also be pleased with him!' He continued to pray till dawn" (Wahidi, p. 81).

(267) Wahidi relates on the authority of Ja'far al-Sadiq that he heard his father say on the authority of Jabir ibn 'Abdallah al-Ansari, "The Prophet commanded that the obligatory alms [*zakat*] of *al-Fitr* [breaking the fast of Ramadan] be given as a *sa'* [a weight measure] of dates. Men brought bad dates; thus a *qur'an* was sent down" (that is, the verse just cited). According to al-Bara' ibn 'Azib, the verse was revealed concerning some people of the Ansar who used to bring in alms their bad dates (Wahidi, pp. 81–82).

Tabari reports several traditions in which the command to give alms is taken generally to mean wealth gained by trade and crops of dates, wheat, and so forth. According to 'Ali, "It means grain and dates and everything subject to *zakat* [obligatory alms]" (Tabari, V, p. 556; see also pp. 555–570). Commentators have generally accepted this interpretation, with minor differences (see Ibn Kathir, I, pp. 567–570); Qurtubi, III, pp. 320–328; and Shawkani, I, pp. 288–291).

Tabarsi relates on the authority of the sixth imam that some people who still kept the wealth of usury, which they had accumulated during the time of Jahiliyah, used to give it out in alms. Thus God forbade them to do so in this verse and commanded that alms be given of good and lawfully earned wealth (Tabarsi, II, p. 342).

(271) It is related on the authority of al-Kalbi that the people asked the Prophet, "O Apostle of God, is the free will gift [*sadaqah*] better in private or openly?" God then sent down this verse (Wahidi, p. 82).

Tabari adds, "We were told that a free-will gift extinguishes sins as water extinguishes fire." Early *tafsir* masters generally concurred with the view expressed in the following tradition, which Tabari reports from Ibn 'Abbas. "God made the voluntary free-will gift in private seventy times more excellent than a voluntary gift publicly given." In contrast, obligatory alms, such as *zakat*, are more excellent when offered publicly, it is said, by twenty-five times. This includes all obligations such as acts of worship as well as supererogatory prayers (*nawafil*). (Tabari, V, p. 582; see also pp. 580–584.)

Zamakhshari comments on the reason for disclosing obligatory alms and concealing voluntary charity as follows, "Making obligations [fara'id] public is better in order that no one should be accused of not fulfilling them. But if the one receiving zakat is known to be of straitened means it is better to conceal the gift" (Zamakhshari, I, p. 397; see also Razi, VII, p. 77).

Razi cites a prophetic hadith asserting, "Seven people will God protect under His shadow on the day of resurrection when there shall be no other shadow; one of these is he who gives a free-will gift not letting his left hand know what his right hand has given." The Prophet also said, "A free-will gift in private shall extinguish the wrath of the Lord" (Razi, VII, p. 78; see also Ibn Kathir, I, p. 573, where this tradition is quoted in full).

(272) Wahidi relates on the authority of Sa'id ibn Jubayr that the Apostle of God said, "Do not give alms except to those of your religion." But when God sent down, "It is not incumbent upon you to guide them," the Apostle of God said, "Give alms to the people of other faiths" (Wahidi, p. 83; see also Tabarsi, II, p. 351).

Tabari relates on the authority of Sa'id ibn Jubayr, "The Muslims used to give alms to the poor of the people of dhimmah [Jews and Christians], but when the number of the poor among Muslims multiplied, the Apostle of God said, 'Do not give alms except to people of your religion.' God then sent down this verse allowing alms to those who do not profess the faith of Islam" (Tabari, V, p. 589). Commentators have generally agreed that this verse refers to almsgiving by Muslims to people of other faiths. The Arabs of Mecca were considered neither as having faith nor as People of the Book; still they were included in the list of those to whom alms could be given. Qurtubi discusses the legal aspects of this verse at some length (Qurtubi, III, pp. 337–338).

(274) It is related on the authority of Abu Umamah and Abu al-Darda' that the Apostle of God said, "This verse was sent down . . . concerning owners of horses." He continued, "Satans can never cause a man who keeps an old horse in his house to become forgetful." It is also related on the authority of Asma', daughter of Yazid, that the Apostle of God said, "Whoever keeps a horse in the way of God [that is, ready for war] and spends on it only to please God, for its hunger and satiation thereof, its thirst and the quenching thereof; its urine and feces will be in his balance on the day of resurrection" (Wahidi, pp. 84–85).

According to another view, this verse was sent down concerning 'Ali. Wahidi relates on the authority of Ibn 'Abbas, "This verse was sent down concerning 'Ali ibn Abi Talib. He had four dirhams which he gave in alms: one in the night, one in the day, one in secret, and the last openly." It is related on the authority of al-Kalbi that when 'Ali gave in alms the only four dirhams he had, the Apostle of God asked him, "What made you do so?" He answered, "I did this in order that God fulfill His promise to me." The Prophet said, "It shall be yours!" Thus God sent down this verse. This view is related on the authority of a number of the Companions of the Prophet (Wahidi, p. 86).

Tabari adds a third view. He relates on the authority of Ibn 'Abbas that this and the three preceding verses "were applied before the verse in *Bara'ah* [Q. 9:60]. When the verse in *Bara'ah* was sent down detailing almsgiving, it was applied [and these verses were abrogated]" (Tabari, V, p. 602; see also Ibn Kathir, I, p. 578).

Zamakhshari says that the verse was sent down concerning Abu Bakr when he gave forty thousand dinars in alms, ten thousand at night, ten in the day, ten in secret, and ten in public (Zamakhshari, I, p. 398). Razi adds still another view concerning the occasion of the revelation of this verse and says it is the best interpretation: "The verse is general, including all those who give alms, at all times and in all situations. Whenever the need of a needy person is brought before them, they fulfill it quickly, not limiting their action to any time or condition" (Razi, VII, p. 89; see also Nisaburi, III, pp. 66–69).

275. Those who consume usury shall not rise except as he rises whom Satan had wrestled down by his touch. This is because they say, "Trade is like usury." But God made trade lawful and usury unlawful. Whosoever receives an admonition from his Lord and desists, his past gains shall be his; his affair belongs to God. But whosoever reverts, such shall be the people of the Fire; in it they shall abide forever.

276. God effaces usury, and alms He increases, for God loves not any transgressing rejecter of faith.

277. Surely those who have faith and perform good deeds, observe regular worship, and give obligatory alms shall

have their reward with their Lord. No fear will come upon them, nor shall they grieve.

278. O you who have faith, fear God and remit whatever remains of usury, if you are truly men of faith.

279. But if you do not [remit], then be warned of war against you by God and His Apostle. If you turn back, you shall have the principal; you shall not wrong others, nor will you be wronged.

280. If there be among you anyone in straitened circumstances, let him have respite until times are easier. But if you remit his debt in alms, it shall be better for you, if you but knew.

281. Fear a day wherein you shall be returned to God, when every soul shall be paid in full what it has earned, and they shall not be wronged.

These six verses are known as the usury verses (*ayat al-riba*). They were among the last verses of the Qur'an to be revealed, as related on the authority of Ibn 'Abbas (Ibn Kathir, I, p. 582). The word *riba* comes from the verbal root meaning "to grow" or "increase." Nisaburi distinguishes two kinds of *riba*. The first is called *riba al-nasi'ah* (delayed payment) and was used in the Jahiliyah, where the creditor lends the money on the understanding that the debtor pays a fixed sum every month. If, when the loan becomes due, the debtor cannot pay, the term is prolonged and the interest increased. The second is usury in kind (*riba al-fadl*) in which a measure of wheat, for example, is sold for two measures at the time of harvest. It is related that Ibn 'Abbas declared only the first kind to be unlawful but that later he revoked this opinion and declared both to be forbidden (Nisaburi, III, pp. 71–72). Ibn Kathir observes that the problem of understanding usury and what may lead to it has been one of the most difficult problems for jurists. He cites a statement of 'Umar ibn al-Khattab, who said, "There are three things concerning which I wish the Apostle of God had left us a clear injunction to follow." Among these were the problems of usury (Ibn Kathir, I, p. 581).

(275) Tabari reports on the authority of Mujahid, "'Those who consume usury' refers to the day of resurrection where this shall be their punishment for taking usury in this world." The touch of Satan in this verse means, according to Tabari, madness (Tabari, VI, p. 8; see also pp. 8–12). This interpretation is accepted by all commentators, as well as lexicographers.

(278, 279) Commentators have differed as to the people intended in these verses. Wahidi reports that according to Ibn 'Abbas, they were sent down concerning two tribes in Mecca, Banu 'Umayr of the Thaqif and Banu al-Mughirah of the tribe of Makhzum. Banu al-Mughirah paid usury to Banu 'Umayr before the conquest of Mecca. Thus when Mecca was conquered, two people came to the governor of the city to judge among them. Banu al-Mughirah said, "Why have we remained the most miserable of men through usury? It has been forbidden for all the people except us." Banu 'Umayr argued that it was agreed that they retain their interest. The governor wrote to the Prophet concerning this problem and thus God sent down these verses.

According to 'Ata' and 'Ikrimah, the verses were sent down concerning al-'Abbas ibn 'Abd al-Muttalib, the uncle of the Prophet, and 'Uthman ibn 'Affan, the third caliph. "It was that they lent someone dates. When the time came for the man to pay them back, he said, 'I shall not have enough to feed my children if you take all your share. Would you therefore accept half now and postpone the other half, which I shall double for you?' They agreed, but when the time came and they asked for the interest, the Prophet forbade them to do so. They obeyed and received only the capital" (Wahidi, p. 87). Tabari reports that 'Ali said concerning these two verses, "He who persists in taking usury, it shall be incumbent upon the imam of the Muslims to try and persuade him to repent. If, however, he does not desist, the imam should behead him" (Tabari, VI, p. 25; see also Razi, VII, pp. 103–113; Shawkani, I, pp. 297–298; and Tabarsi, II, pp. 364–365; for Shi'i traditions concerning the verses dealing with usury, see Qummi, I, pp. 94–95).

Sayyid Qutb comments on usury and especially with reference to verse 276 as follows: "God speaks the truth, for we see no society practicing usury but that it loses comfort, blessing, happiness, and contentment. One may see affluence on the surface, production, and many resources, yet blessing is not in the magnitude of resources, it is rather in the wholesome quiet and secure enjoyment of these resources. One can observe the frustration, unhappiness, and fear which exist in the rich nations. We have pointed to the psychological disturbance which wealth magnifies rather than being able to cure. From these nations, unrest, fear, and trouble flow on to the world at large where humanity lives in continuous fear of conflagration." Sayyid Qutb then contrasts this situation with the society organized on the principle of sharing with contentment and almsgiving God's bounties and His favors (Qutb, I, pp. 481–482).

(281) This verse is said to have been the last verse of the Qur'an to have been revealed. It is related that Gabriel said to the Prophet when the verse was sent down, "Put it at the head of the two hundred and eighties of *Surat al-Baqarah*" (Tabari, VI, pp. 39–41; see also Qurtubi, III, p. 375; and Nisaburi, II, p. 83). Shawkani relates that the Prophet lived twenty-one days after this verse was revealed, or nine nights according to Ibn Jurayj. According to Sa'id ibn Jubayr and Muqatil, he lived only seven nights. He died on Monday, the second of Rabi' al-Awwal (the third month of the Muslim calendar), at sunrise. According to Shi'i tradition, he died on the second to the last night of Safar (the second month) of 11 A.H. (see Tabarsi, II, p. 370).

282. O you who have faith, if you contract any debt one with another for a specific period of time, write it down. Let a scribe record your transaction in accordance with justice. Let no scribe refuse to record as God has taught him. Rather, let him record and let him who owes the debt dictate. Let him fear God, his Lord, and not diminish anything [of what the man says]. Yet if he who owes the debt be foolish or weak, or unable himself to dictate, then let two of your men act as witnesses, but if two men are not available, one man and two women such as you would approve of as witnesses, so that if one of the two women forgets the other would remind her. Let not witnesses refuse when they are called upon, nor should you disdain to record [a debt], be it large or small, until it is paid. This is more just in the sight of God, more reliable in testimony, and easier, that you may not doubt. Yet if it is an instant barter which you transact among yourselves, there shall be no blame in you if you do not record it. Call witnesses when you buy and sell among yourselves and let no harm be done to scribe or witness. If you do that, it shall be an act of wickedness on your

part. Fear God that He may instruct you, for God knows all things.

283. If you are on a journey and cannot find a scribe, then let pledges be taken. If you trust one another, let the man who is trusted return that which is entrusted to him and let him fear God, his Lord. Do not conceal your testimony, for he who conceals it surely has a transgressing heart. God is all-knowing of what you do.

284. To God belongs all that is in the heavens and the earth. Whether you disclose or conceal that which is in your hearts, God shall call you to account for it. He shall forgive whomsoever He wills and punish whomsoever He wills, for God has power over all things.

285. The Apostle has faith in that which has been sent down to him from his Lord and also the faithful have faith, every one of them, in God, His angels, His scriptures, and His apostles—we make no distinction among His apostles. They say, "We hear, and we obey; grant us Your forgiveness, O Lord, for to You shall be our destination."

286. God shall not charge a soul except to its capacity; to it belongs whatever it has earned and against it whatever it has acquired. Our Lord, do not reproach us if we forget or err. O our Lord, do not lay upon us a burden such as You have laid upon those who were before us. Our Lord, do not burden us with that which we have no strength to bear. Pardon us, forgive us, and have mercy upon us. You are our Master; help us therefore against the people who reject faith.

(284, 285) Wahidi reports on the authority of Abu Hurayrah that, "When God sent down to His Apostle 'Whether you disclose or conceal that which is in your hearts, God shall call you to account for it,' the Companions of the Apostle of God were troubled. They came to him saying, 'We were charged with duties we could bear: prayers, fasting, struggle in the way of God, and almsgiving. Now God has sent down to you a verse which we cannot bear.' The Apostle of God said, 'Would you then wish to say what the people of the two Books said before you? They said, "We hear but we disobey!" Rather say, "We hear and we obey; grant us Your forgiveness, O Lord, for to You shall be our destination.'" When the people recited this verse their tongues expressed their humility. Thus God sent immediately after it the verse, 'The Apostle has faith. . . .' God abrogated the verse by sending down 'God shall not charge a soul except to its capacity.'"

Wahidi reports further that when verse 284 was sent down, Abu Bakr, 'Umar, Mu'adh ibn Jabal, and 'Abd al-Rahman ibn 'Awf, with a group of the Ansar, came to the Prophet; they fell on their knees saying, "O Apostle of God! By God, there was not a verse sent down more disturbing to us than this one. Every one of us thinks things to himself which he would not wish to have in his heart even if he were to have the world and all that is in it. We shall surely be brought to account for what we think privately; by God we shall perish!" The Prophet answered, "Thus was it sent down!" They said, "We shall perish for we have been charged with things we cannot bear." The rest of this tradition is like the previous one except that after the next verse was revealed the Prophet said, "God shall overlook for my community what they think privately to themselves so long as they do not act in accordance with it or speak about it" (Wahidi, pp. 88–89).

Tabari relates this verse to the two previous verses dealing with the rule of bearing and according testimony. He writes, "God means to say, 'Do not hide your testimony, O witnesses. For whoever hides it his heart shall incline to lewdness. His hiding of his testimony shall not be hidden from me because I am the knower of all things. In my hand is the affair of all things in the heavens and the earth. I know the hidden as well as the disclosed; fear therefore my punishment for hiding your testimony.'" Tabari then discusses two views concerning this verse. The first is that it was abrogated by the next verse, as we have already observed, and the second is that it was not abrogated. Tabari accepts the second view and argues that God will indeed bring everyone to account for his thoughts and deeds, but He shall forgive the man of faith and punish the rejecter of faith (Tabari, VI, pp. 101–119). Other commentators have generally reported what has already been cited from Wahidi and Tabari, without any significant variation (see Ibn Kathir, I, p. 605; Zamakhshari, I, pp. 406–407; Razi, VII, pp. 133–136; and Shawkani, I, pp. 305–306).

(285, 286) Reference has already been made to the great excellences of *Surat al-Baqarah*, and especially those of the Throne Verse. Commentators and traditionists have likewise regarded the two concluding verses (*khawatim*) of this *surah* as having special blessing or grace (*barakah*) of their own. This discussion concludes by citing several *hadiths* extolling the excellences of these verses. It is related on the authority of Abu Dharr and al-Dahhak that these two verses were given to the Prophet as a special favor for which he prayed God (Shawkani, I, p. 309).

Regarding the great blessing (*barakah*) which these verses possess, it is related on the authority of Ibn Mas'ud that the Prophet said, "Whoever recites the last two verses of *Surat al-Baqarah* at night, they shall suffice him." Al-Nu'man ibn Bashir related that the Prophet said, "God inscribed a book two thousand years before He created the heavens and the earth, of which He sent down two verses with which He concluded *Surat al-Baqarah*. Satan will never approach any house in which they are recited for three nights." Hudhayfah related that the Prophet said, "I was given the last two verses of *Surat al-Baqarah* from a treasure under the Throne. They were not given to any prophet before me." It is related on the authority of Ibn Mas'ud "When the Apostle of God was transported by night [Q. 17:1] and reached the lote tree of the outer boundary [*sidrat al-muntaha*], [Q. 53:13–16], he was granted three favors: the five daily prayers, the concluding verses of *Surat al-Baqarah*, and forgiveness for his community, except those who associate other things with God." The Prophet said, as related on the authority of Abu Dharr, "God concluded *Surat al-Baqarah* with two verses which He gave to me from His special treasure, which was under the Throne. Learn them and teach them to your women and children, for they are a prayer [*salat*], a *qur'an*, and a supplication [*du'a*]." It is related on the authority of Abu Hurayrah that the Apostle of God said, "There are two [verses] which are in themselves a *qur'an*, they are a source of healing and they are two of the things which God loves; the two last verses of *Surat al-Baqarah*." On the authority of Ibn Mas'ud it is related that the Apostle of God said, "God sent down two verses from the treasures of Paradise. The All-merciful inscribed them with His own hand two thousand years before He created the world. Whoever recites them after the night prayer will be absolved from standing the whole night in prayer" (Shawkani, I, pp. 309–310).

These two verses have been associated with *Surat al-Fatihah*, in whose great merit, excellence, and blessing they share. It is related on the authority of Ibn 'Abbas, "While the Prophet was with Gabriel one day, they heard a sound above them. Gabriel looked up and exclaimed, 'This is a gate of heaven which has just been opened; it was never open before.' An angel came down through it to the Prophet and said, 'I bring you good tidings of two lights which you have been granted and which were granted to no prophet before you: the opening Surah [al-Fatihah] of the Book and the concluding verses of Surat al-Baqarah. You shall never recite a letter of them but that the prayer expressed therein shall be granted you.'" Thus we are told that Gabriel taught the Prophet the end of Surat al-Baqarah, which is the word "amen" (amin). (Shawkani, I, p. 310; see also Tabari, VI, pp. 129-146; Ibn Kathir, I, pp. 605-607; and Qurtubi, III, pp. 425-428; and for a theological discussion, see Zamakhshari, I, pp. 407-409, and Razi, VII, pp. 148-162.)

Arabic Sources Consulted

'Abd al-Baqi, Muhammad Fu'ad. *al-Mu'jam al-Mufahras li-Alfaz al-Qur'an al-Karim*. Beirut: Dar Ihya' al-Turath al-'Arabi, n.d.

al-'Ayyashi, Abu al-Nasr Muhammad ibn Mas'ud ibn 'Ayyash al-Sulami al-Samarqandi. *Tafsir al-'Ayyashi*. Edited by Hashim al-Rasuli al-Mahallati. 2 vols. Qumm: Chapkhanah-i 'Ilmiyah, n.d.

al-Dawudi, Shams al-Din Muhammad ibn 'Ali b. Ahmad. *Tabaqat al-Mufassirin*. Edited by 'Ali Muhammad 'Umar. 2 vols. Cairo: Dar al-Kutub, 1392/1972.

al-Dhahabi, Abu 'Abdallah Shams al-Din. *Tadhkirat al-Huffaz*. 4 vols. Hyderabad: Da'irat al-Ma'arif al-'Uthmaniyah, 1375–1377/1955–1958.

Ibn 'Arabi, Muhyi al-Din. *Tafsir al-Qur'an al-Karim*. Edited by Mustafa Ghalib. 2 vols. Beirut: Dar al-Andalus, 1399/1978.

Ibn Kathir al-Qurayshi al-Dimashqi, 'Imad al-Din Abi al-Fida' Isma'il. *Tafsir al-Qur'an al-'Azim*. 7 vols. Beirut: Dar al-Fikr, 1389/1970.

———. *Fada'il al-Qur'an* (appended to volume VII of his *Tafsir*).

Ibn Sa'd. *al-Tabaqat al-Kubra*. 8 vols. Beirut: Dar Sadir, 1376–1380/1957–1960.

Ibn Taymiyah, Taqi al-Din Abu al-'Abbas Ahmad ibn 'Abd al-Halim. *Muqaddimah fi Usul al-Tafsir*. Edited by 'Adnan Zarzur. Kuwait: Dar al-Qur'an al-Karim, 1391/1971.

al-Isfahani, al-Raghib. *Mu'jam Mufradat Alfaz al-Qur'an*. Edited by Nadim Mar'ashli. Beirut: Dar al-Kitab al-'Arabi, 1392/1972.

Majlisi, Muhammad Baqir. *Bihar al-Anwar*. 110 vols. Teheran: al-Maktabah al-Islamiyah, 1387–1392/1956–1972. (Vols. XCII and XCIII are used in this work.)

Makhluf, Hasanayn Muhammad. *Kalimat al-Qur'an, Tafsir wa Bayan*. Cairo: Mustafa al-Babi al-Halabi, 1390/1970.

al-Nisaburi, Nizam al-Din al-Hasan ibn Muhammad ibn al-Husayn al-Qummi. *Ghara'ib al-Qur'an wa Ragha'ib al-Furqan.* Edited by Ibrahim 'Atwah 'Awad. 5 vols. Cairo: Mustafa al-Babi al-Halabi, 1381–1384/1962–1964.

al-Qummi, Abu al-Hasan 'Ali ibn Ibrahim. *Tafsir al-Qummi.* Edited by al-Sayyid Tayyib al-Musawi al-Jaza'iri. 2 vols. Najaf: Matba'at al-Najaf, 1386/1967.

al-Qurtubi, Abu 'Abdallah Muhammad ibn Ahmad al-Ansari. *al-Jami' li-Ahkam al-Qur'an.* 18 vols. Cairo: Dar al-Katib al-'Arabi, 1387/1967.

Qutb, Sayyid. *Fi Zilal al-Qur'an.* 7th edition. 8 vols. Beirut: Dar Ihya' al-Turath al-'Arabi, 1391/1971.

al-Razi, Fakhr al-Din. *al-Tafsir al-Kabir.* 32 vols. Cairo: al-Matba'ah al-Bahiyah, n.d.

al-Shawkani, Muhammad ibn 'Ali ibn Muhammad. *Fath al-Qadir al-Jami' bayn Fannay al-Riwayah wa al-Dirayah fi 'Ilm al-Tafsir.* 3rd edition. 5 vols. Beirut: Dar al-Fikr, 1393/1973

al-Suyuti, Jalal al-Din. *al-Itqan fi 'Ulum al-Qur'an.* 2 vols. Beirut: Dar al-Fikr, n.d.

al-Tabari, Abu Ja'far Muhammad ibn Jarir. *Jami' al-Bayan 'an Ta'wil Ay al-Qur'an.* Edited by Mahmud Muhammad and Ahmad Muhammad Shakir. 16 vols. (incomplete). Cairo: Dar al-Ma'arif, 1332/1954.

al-Tabarsi, Abu 'Ali al-Fadl ibn al-Hasan. *Majma' al-Bayan fi Tafsir al-Qur'an.* 12 vols. Beirut: Dar Maktabat al-Hayat, 1380/1961.

al-Tabataba'i, Sayyid Muhammad Husayn. *al-Mizan fi Tafsir al-Qur'an.* 20 vols. Beirut: Mu'assasat al-A'lami lil-Matbu'at, 1393–1394/1973–1974.

———. al-Qur'an fi al-Islam. 1st edition. Trans. into Arabic by Sayyid Ahmad al-Husayni. Beirut: Dar al-Zahra 1393/1973.

al-Wahidi, Abu al-Hasan. *Asbab Nuzul al-Qur'an.* Cairo: Dar al-Kitab al-Jadid, 1389/1969.

al-Zamakhshari, al-Khawarizmi, Abu al-Qasim Jar Allah Mahmud ibn 'Umar. *al-Kashshaf 'an Haqa'iq al-Tanzil wa 'Uyun al-Aqawil fi Wujuh al-Ta'wil.* 4 vols. Cairo: Mustafa al-Babi al-Halabi, 1385/1966.

al-Zarkashi, Badr al-Din Muhammad ibn 'Abdallah. *al-Burhan fi 'Ulum al-Qur'an.* Edited by Muhammad Abu al-Fadl Ibrahim. 4 vols. Beirut: Dar al-Ma'rifah, 1391/1972.

Bibliography of Major Works on the Qur'an in Western Languages

Baljon, J.M.S. *Modern Muslim Koran Interpretation (1880–1960)*. Leiden: E. J. Brill, 1968.

Birkeland, Harris. *The Lord Guideth: Studies on Primitive Islam*. Oslo: Almqvist and Wiksells, 1956.

———. *Old Muslim Opposition against Interpretation of the Koran*. Oslo: Almqvist and Wiksells, 1956.

Blachère, Régis. *Introduction au Coran*. Paris: G.-P. Maisonneuve, 1959.

Böwering, Gerhard. *The Mystical Vision of Existence in Classical Islam: The Qur'anic Hermeneutics of the Sufi Sahl At-Tustari (d. 238/896)*. Berlin: Walter de Gruyter, 1980.

Burton, John. *The Collection of the Qur'an*. Cambridge: Cambridge University Press, 1977.

Cragg, Kenneth. *The Event of the Qur'an: Islam in Its Scripture*. London: George Allen & Unwin Ltd., 1971.

———. *The Mind of the Qur'an: Chapters in Reflection*. London: George Allen & Unwin Ltd., 1973.

Gätje, Helmut. *The Qur'an and Its Exegesis*. Translated and edited by Alford T. Welch. London: Routledge & Kegan Paul, 1976.

Goldziher, Ignaz. *Die Richtungen der Islamischen Koranauslegung*. Leiden: E. J. Brill, 1952.

Hirschfeld, Hartwig. *New Researches into the Composition and Exegesis of the Qoran*. London: Royal Asiatic Society, 1902.

Izutsu, Toshihiko. *God and Man in the Qur'an. Semantics of the Koranic Weltanshauung*. Tokyo: Keio Institute of Cultural and Linguistic Studies, 1964.

————. *Ethico-Religious Concepts in the Qur'an.* Montreal: McGill University Press, 1966.

Jansen, J.J.G. *The Interpretation of the Koran in Modern Egypt.* Leiden: E. J. Brill, 1974.

Jefferey, Arthur. *Foreign Vocabulary of the Qur'an.* Baroda: Oriental Institute, 1938.

————. *Materials for the History of the Text of the Qur'an.* Leiden: E. J. Brill, 1937.

————. *The Qur'an as Scripture.* New York: Russel F. Moore, 1952.

Jomier, Jacques. *Les grandes thèmes du Coran.* Paris: Centurion, 1978.

Masson, Denise. *Le Coran et la révelation judeo-chrétienne: Études comparées.* Paris: Adrien-Maisonneuve, 1958. Librairie d'Amérique et d'Orient

Nöldeke, Theodor. *Geschichte des Qorans.* Leipzig: Dieterich'sche Verlagsbuchhandlung, 1909.

Nwyia, Paul. *Exègèse coranique et langage mystique: Nouvel essai sur le lexique technique des mystiques musulmans.* Beirut: Imprimerie Catholique, 1970.

Paret, Rudi, *Der Koran: Kommentar und Konkordanz.* Stuttgart: 1971.

Rahman, Fazlur. *Major Themes of the Qur'an.* Chicago: Bibliotheca Islamica, 1980.

Seale, Morris. *Qur'an and Bible: Studies in Interpretation and Dialogue.* London: Croom Helm, 1978.

Smith, Jane I. *An Historical and Semantic Study of the Term "Islam" as Seen in a Sequence of Qur'an Commentaries.* Missoula: Scholars Press, 1975.

Wansbrough, John. *Quranic Studies: Sources and Methods of Scriptural Interpretation.* Oxford: Oxford University Press, 1977.

Watt, Montgomery. *Bell's Introduction to the Qur'an.* Edinburgh: Edinburgh University Press, 1970.

Index

DATE DUE

NOV 3 0 1986		
NOV 2 1 1987		
DEC 0 4 1987		
FEB 1 9 1990		
Mar 6		
MAR 2 1 1990		
APR 0 4 1990		
NOV 2 5 1990		
DEC 1 0 1990		
Jan. 9, 91		
1/21/91		
DEC 0 3 2001		
5/14/03		

GAYLORD | | PRINTED IN U.S.A.